CONTROL AND DYNAMIC SYSTEMS

*Advances in Theory
and Applications*

Volume 29

CONTRIBUTORS TO THIS VOLUME

W. L. DE KONING
JOSEPH C. DUNN
R. J. EVANS
CHAO-YIN HSIAO
YUJIRO INOUYE
STEPHEN A. JACKLIN
MAGDI S. MAHMOUD
HAGOP PANOSSIAN
Y. C. SOH
P. VAN DOOREN
M. H. VERHAEGEN
XIE XIANYA
C. ZHANG

CONTROL AND DYNAMIC SYSTEMS

ADVANCES IN THEORY AND APPLICATIONS

Edited by
C. T. LEONDES

School of Engineering
University of California, Los Angeles
Los Angeles, California

VOLUME 29: ADVANCES IN ALGORITHMS AND COMPUTATIONAL TECHNIQUES IN DYNAMIC SYSTEMS CONTROL
Part 2 of 3

ACADEMIC PRESS, INC.
Harcourt Brace Jovanovich, Publishers
San Diego   New York   Berkeley   Boston
London   Sydney   Tokyo   Toronto

ACADEMIC PRESS, INC.
San Diego, California 92101

United Kingdom Edition published by
ACADEMIC PRESS LIMITED
24-28 Oval Road, London NW1 7DX

LIBRARY OF CONGRESS CATALOG CARD NUMBER: 64-8027

ISBN   0-12-012729-6   (alk. paper)

PRINTED IN THE UNITED STATES OF AMERICA
88 89 90 91   9 8 7 6 5 4 3 2 1

CONTENTS

New Insights in the Numerical Reliability Properties
of Existing Kalman Filter Implementations

M. H. Verhaegen and P. Van Dooren

Algorithms for System Fault Detection
through Modeling and Estimation Techniques

Hagop Panossian

Arranging Computer Architectures to Create Higher
Performance Controllers

Stephen A. Jacklin

Computational Techniques in Angle-Only Tracking Filtering

Chao-Yin Hsiao

Gradient Projection Methods for Systems Optimization Problems

Joseph C. Dunn

Algorithms for Decentralized Hierarchical Systems with Application to Stream Water Quality

Magdi S. Mahmoud

CONTRIBUTORS

Numbers in parentheses indicate the pages on which the authors' contributions begin.

W. L. de Koning (197), *Department of Applied Mathematics, Delft University of Technology, 2628 BL Delft, The Netherlands*

Joseph C. Dunn (135), *Mathematics Department, North Carolina State University, Raleigh, North Carolina 27695*

R. J. Evans (251), *Department of Electrical and Computer Engineering, The University of New Castle, New South Wales 2308, Australia*

Chao-Yin Hsiao (101), *Mechanical Engineering Department, Feng Chia University, Seatwan, Taichung, Taiwan*

Yujiro Inouye (209), *Department of Control Engineering, Faculty of Engineering Science, Osaka University, Toyonaka, Osaka 560, Japan*

Stephen A. Jacklin (67), *NASA Ames Research Center, Moffett Field, California 94035*

Magdi S. Mahmoud (283), *Electronics and Communication Engineering Department, Cairo University, Giza, Egypt*

Hagop Panossian (47), *Rockwell International, Rocketdyne Division, Canoga Park, California 91303*

Y. C. Soh (251), *Department of Electrical and Computer Engineering, The University of New Castle, New South Wales 2308, Australia*

P. Van Dooren (1), *Philips Research Laboratory, B-1170 Brussels, Belgium*

M. H. Verhaegen (1), *NASA Ames Research Center, Moffett Field, California 94035*

Xie Xianya (251), *Department of Electrical and Computer Engineering, The University of New Castle, New South Wales 2308, Australia*

C. Zhang (251), *Department of Electrical and Computer Engineering, The University of New Castle, New South Wales 2308, Australia*

PREFACE

Developments in algorithms and computational techniques for control and dynamic systems have matured to such an extent over the last 25–30 years that it is now quite appropriate to devote a volume of *Control and Dynamic Systems* to this subject. However, the proliferation of significant published material and new research in this field has been so great that adequate coverage could not be encompassed in one volume; thus, this volume is the second of a trilogy to be devoted to this subject.

The first contribution in this volume, "New Insights in the Numerical Reliability Properties of Existing Kalman Filter Implementations," by M. H. Verhaegen and P. Van Dooren, presents a comprehensive analysis of some of the pitfalls or computational problems which arose in the applications of Kalman Filters. These were due, for example, to the lack of reliability of the numerical algorithm or to inaccurate modeling of the system under consideration. This contribution compares the performance of a number of different Kalman Filter implementations through simulation studies and other means and presents a number of useful guidelines and conclusions. This unique contribution will be a valuable reference source for many practitioners. In the following contribution, "Algorithms for System Fault Detection through Modeling and Estimation Techniques" by H. Panossian, a comprehensive presentation of system fault detection techniques, is given, and these are analyzed as to their comparative merits. Because of the major significance of this area of system fault detection, this contribution should prove to be quite valuable to practitioners on the international scene. The next contribution, "Arranging Computer Architectures to Create Higher Performance Controllers," by S. A. Jacklin, deals with the often crucial issue of the demands to achieve higher performance controllers for computer-based control systems. The approach used in this contribution is a rather comprehensive examination of computer architecture alternatives. Dramatic differences in system performance are presented as a result of different control computer architectural approaches. This unique contribution is also certain to be a valuable reference source for practitioners. In the following contribution, "Computational Techniques In Angle-Only Tracking Filtering," by C. Hsiao, a major issue which is fundamental to many control systems is treated in a uniquely comprehensive manner. In one way or another all control systems require sensor systems, and these can be of widely differing classes. One of these classes of sensors is passive sensor systems, such as infrared sensor systems, which provide angle-only information in tracking objects. This contribution is perhaps the best single contribution to have appeared to date that comprehensively analyzes and summarizes the many significant issues in angle-only trackers.

The fifth contribution to this volume, "Gradient Projection Methods for Systems Optimization Problems," by J. C. Dunn, deals with a comprehensive treatment of what now appears to be the most effective of the various classes of algorithms for the nonlinear optimal control problem. Dunn has for many years been one of the most significant contributors to developments in this significant area, and so his contribution constitutes a most welcome addition to this volume. The following contribution, "Optimal Control, Estimation, and Compensation of Linear Discrete-Time Systems with Stochastic Parameters," by W. L. de Koning, deals with these issues in the event that system parameters are stochastic in nature. Most of the literature deals with systems whose parameters are set or known time variable. DeKoning presents key results for the development of robust control systems with stochastic parameters, and so it is an important addition to this volume. In the following contribution "An Algorithm for the Approximation of Multivariable Linear Systems," by Y. Inouye, a crucial issue is treated, namely, effective simplification or approximation of increasingly complex systems. Powerful new results and techniques are presented and examined thoroughly in computer studies and simulations. The next contribution, "Algorithms for Discrete-Time Adaptive Control of Rapidly Time-Varying Systems," by R. Evans, X. Xie, C. Zhang, and Y. Soh, examines the significant issue of developing real-time knowledge of system parameters, an issue which is, of course, absolutely essential for adaptive control algorithms. Powerful new techniques for this significant issue, including offset ramp modeling, forgetting factors, and covariance resetting are verified as to their viability through extensive simulation studies presented in this contribution. The final contribution to this volume, "Algorithms for Decentralized Hierarchial Systems with Application to Stream-Water Quality," by M. S. Mahmoud, presents major results for the implementation of feedback controls for interconnected systems which are often widely distributed in space. Because of the continually increasing importance of these major issues this is a most fitting contribution with which to conclude this volume.

This volume is particularly appropriate volume with which to continue this unique trilogy. The authors of this volume are all to be commended for their superb contributions to this volume, which will most certainly be a significant reference source for practitioners on the international scene for many years to come.

NEW INSIGHTS IN THE NUMERICAL RELIABILITY PROPERTIES OF EXISTING KALMAN FILTER IMPLEMENTATIONS

M. H. VERHAEGEN*

NASA Ames Research Center
Moffett Field, California 94035

P. VAN DOOREN

Philips Research Laboratory
Av. E. Van Becelaere 2
B-1170 Brussels, Belgium

I. INTRODUCTION

Since the appearance of Kalman's 1960 paper [1], the so-called Kalman filter (KF) has been applied successfully to many practical problems, especially in aeronautical and aerospace applications. As applications became more numerous, some pitfalls of the KF were discovered, such as the problem of *divergence* due to the *lack of reliability of the numerical algorithm* or to *inaccurate modeling* of the system under consideration [2].

This divergence phenomenon is associated with the use of the so-called conventional KF (CKF). During the past two decades, a large number of "stabilized" implementations have been proposed [3, 4], among which the square-root filters have become accepted to guarantee numerical reliability of the KF computations [5–7]. Of course, we could be satisfied by this "square-root filter use" behavior. However, for a number of people dealing with KF design problems a number of questions remain unresolved:

---

*Associate of the United States National Research Council.

1

(1) For which experimental conditions is the CKF guaranteed to converge, using a specific code implementing it?

(2) Do the stabilized KF implementations guarantee convergence of the filter computations for all experimental conditions?

(3) For which experimental conditions do square-root filters *not improve* the filter computations compared to the CKF?

(4) Having elected to use a square-root filter implementation, which particular implementation do you choose for the filter application at hand?

(5) Do all square-root filters guarantee numerical reliability for all possible experimental circumstances? And, when they fail, what are these circumstances?

This list, which is probably incomplete, clearly demonstrates the vast amount of unresolved questions related to the choice of a KF.

In order to answer these questions, it is still a common practice to perform simulation experiments, and this is often a very cumbersome task. Although the current availability of "user friendly" systems and control design packages alleviates this burden somewhat, the result is very restrictive. Namely that some of the above questions might be answered, but then only for the application considered and for the experimental circumstances evaluated.

A better approach to finding general answers to these questions is to perform a theoretical error analysis. In the literature, different attempts have been undertaken to perform such studies. The reader is referred to [2] for an overview and synthesis of these attempts. From the fact that articles still appear with extensive simulation studies to address some of the above questions [3], we may conclude that these attempts so far have been unsuccessful.

In this article another attempt is undertaken to fill some of the holes in understanding the reliability of KF implementations. The performed error analysis study has resulted in some new and/or better insights in answering the above questions. Here we investigate four "basic" KF implementations: the conventional Kalman filter, the square-root covariance filter (SRCF), the Chandrasekhar square-root filter (CSRF), and the square-root information filter (SRIF). (The implementations chosen come from [8]; these differ substantially from the forms described in [7] with the same names!) This certainly does not cover all possible implementations encountered in practice, but insights gained for these general cases are very useful in judging variants, such as the efficient KF algorithms based on the sequential processing technique [7] or the "condensed form" versions [9, 10]. After a brief description of the above filters in Section II, we perform in Section III a detailed first-order perturbation study of the error propagation due to roundoff for the above four KF implementations. Furthermore, it is demonstrated that this analysis can also be applied to describe the propagation of errors due to modeling errors and errors which result from "discretizing" a continuous linear time system. This is discussed, respectively, in Sections IV and V. In Section VI a realistic simulation study is performed in order to *validate* the results of the theoretical analysis of Sections III, IV, and V. Section VII then outlines a comparison between the different filter implementations using the results of the theoretical error analysis and the simulation study.

Some concluding remarks are presented in Section VIII, and we end with a summary of error analysis results about some basic problems in linear algebra in Appendix A and a brief review of the operation of the so-called "skew" Householder transformation in Appendix B.

II. NOTATION AND PRELIMINARIES

In this section we introduce our notation and list the different Kalman filter types that are discussed in the article. We consider the discrete time-varying linear system

$$x_{k+1} = A_k x_k + B_k w_k + D_k u_k \tag{1}$$

and the linear observation process

$$y_k = C_k x_k + v_k, \tag{2}$$

where x_k, u_k, and y_k are, respectively, the state vector to be estimated ($\in R^n$), the deterministic input vector ($\in R^r$), and the measurement vector ($\in R^p$), where w_k and v_k are the process noise ($\in R^m$) and the measurement noise ($\in R^p$) of the system, and, finally, where A_k,[1] B_k, C_k, and D_k are *known* matrices of appropriate dimensions. The process noise and measurement noise sequences are assumed zero mean and uncorrelated:

$$E\{w_k\} = 0, \ E\{v_k\} = 0, \ E\{w_k c_j'\} = 0 \tag{3}$$

with *known* covariances:

$$E\{w_j w_k'\} = Q_k \delta_{jk}, \ E\{v_j v_k'\} = R_k \delta_{jk} \tag{4}$$

where $E\{\cdot\}$ denotes the mathematical expectation and Q_k and R_k are *positive definite* matrices.

The assumption that Q_k is nonsingular does not restrict the generality of the system description, since for the case of singular Q_k the linearly dependent components in w_k can always be removed first [8]. On the other hand, the regularity of R_k rules out the possibility of including perfect measurements not corrupted by noise. In the particular case of perfect measurements, special adaptations are required for some of the KF implementations, such as the use of the Moore–Penrose inverse for the CKF [8]. Such special implementations are not considered here except for a few comments in the concluding remarks.

---

[1]With nonsingularity required for the SRIF.

The SRF algorithms uses the Choleski factors of the covariance matrices or their inverse in order to solve the optimal filtering problem. Since the process noise covariance Q_k and the measurement noise covariance matrix R_k are assumed to be positive definite, the following Choleski factorizations[2] exist:

$$Q_k = Q_k^{1/2}\left[Q_k^{1/2}\right]', \quad R_k = R_k^{1/2}\left[R_k^{1/2}\right]', \tag{5}$$

where the factors $Q_k^{1/2}$ and $R_k^{1/2}$ may be chosen *upper* or *lower* triangular.

The problem is now to compute the *minimum variance estimate* of the stochastic variable x_k, provided y_1 up to y_j have been measured:

$$\hat{x}_{k|j} = \hat{x}_{k|y_1,\dots,y_j}. \tag{6}$$

When $j = k$ this estimate is called the *filtered estimate* and for $j = k - 1$ it is referred to as the one-step predicted or abbreviated as the *predicted estimate*. The above problem is restricted here to these two types of estimates except for a few comments in the concluding remarks. Kalman filtering is a recursive method used to solve this problem. This is done by computing the variances $P_{k|k}$ and/or $P_{k|k-1}$ and the estimates $\hat{x}_{k|k}$ and/or $\hat{x}_{k|k-1}$ from their previous values, for $k = 1, 2, \dots$. Thereby one assumes $P_{0|-1}$ (i.e., the covariance matrix of the initial state x_0) and $\hat{x}_{0|-1}$ (i.e., the mean of the initial state x_0) to be *given*.

A.   THE CONVENTIONAL KALMAN FILTER

The above recursive solution can be computed by the CKF equations, summarized in the following "covariance form" [8]:

$$R_k^e = R_k + C_k P_{k|k-1} C_k' \tag{7}$$

$$K_k = A_k P_{k|k-1} C_k'\left[R_k^e\right]^{-1} \tag{8}$$

$$P_{k+1|k} = A_k\left[I - P_{k|k-1} C_k'\left[R_k^e\right]^{-1} C_k\right]P_{k|k-1} A_k' + B_k Q_k B_k' \tag{9}$$

---

[2]Notice that historically $Q_k^{1/2}$ and $R_k^{1/2}$ have erroneously been called "square roots" instead of "Choleski factors." However, we will maintain the adjective "square root" as far as the names of the filters are concerned because of the familiarity that they have acquired.

$$\hat{x}_{k+1|k} = A_k \hat{x}_{k|k-1} - K_k \left[C_k \hat{x}_{k|k-1} - y_k \right] + D_k u_k. \tag{10}$$

This set of equations has been implemented in various forms (see [8]). In the error analysis, the "costly" implementation that does not exploit the symmetry of the matrices in (7)–(10) is initially denoted as the CKF for reasons that are explained there.

B.   THE SQUARE-ROOT COVARIANCE FILTER

Square-root covariance filters propagate the Choleski factors of the error covariance matrix $P_{k|k-1}$:

$$P_{k|k-1} = S_k \cdot S_k', \tag{11}$$

where S_k is chosen to be lower triangular. The computational method is summarized by the following scheme [8]:

$$\begin{pmatrix} R_k^{1/2} & C_k S_k & 0 \\ 0 & A_k S_k & B_k Q_k^{1/2} \end{pmatrix} \cdot U_1 = \begin{pmatrix} R_k^{e1/2} & 0 & 0 \\ G_k & S_{k+1} & 0 \end{pmatrix} \tag{12}$$

$$\hat{x}_{k+1|k} = A_k \hat{x}_{k|k-1} - G_k R_k^{e-1/2} (C_k \hat{x}_{k|k-1} - y_k) + D_k u_k, \tag{13}$$

where the first term on the left-hand side of (12) is prearray, the term on the right-hand side is postarray, and U_1 is an orthogonal transformation that triangularizes the prearray. Such a triangularization can, e.g., be obtained using Householder transformations [11]. This recursion is now initiated with $\hat{x}_{0|-1}$ and the Choleski factor S_0 of $P_{0|-1}$ as defined in (11).

C.   THE CHANDRASEKHAR SQUARE-ROOT FILTER

If the system model (1) and (2) is *time-invariant*, the SRCF described in Section IIB may be simplified to the Chandrasekhar square-root filter, described in [12, 13]. Here one formulates recursions for the *increment* of the covariance matrix, defined as

$$\text{inc } P_k = P_{k+1|k} - P_{k|k-1}. \tag{14}$$

In general this matrix can be factored as

$$\text{inc } P_k = L_k \cdot \begin{pmatrix} I_{n_1} & 0 \\ 0 & -I_{n_2} \end{pmatrix} \cdot L_k' \tag{15}$$

where the rank of inc P_k is $n_1 + n_2$ and Σ, the second term on the right-hand side, is called its signature matrix. The CSRF propagates recursions for L_k and $\hat{x}_{k+1|k}$ using [13]:

$$\begin{pmatrix} R_{k-1}^{e1/2} & CL_{k-1} \\ G_{k-1} & AL_{k-1} \end{pmatrix} \cdot U_2 = \begin{pmatrix} R_k^{e1/2} & 0 \\ G_k & L_k \end{pmatrix} \tag{16}$$

$$\hat{x}_{k+1|k} = A\hat{x}_{k|k-1} - G_k R_k^{e-1/2}(C\hat{x}_{k|k-1} - y_k) + Du_k \tag{17}$$

where the first term on the left-hand side of (16) is prearray and the term on the right-hand side is postarray, and with $L_0 \Sigma L_0' = P_{1|0} - P_{0|-1}$. Here U_2 is a Σ_p unitary transformation, i.e., $U_2 \Sigma_p U_2' = \Sigma_p$ with

$$\Sigma_p = \begin{pmatrix} I_p & 0 \\ 0 & \Sigma \end{pmatrix}. \tag{18}$$

Such transformations are easily constructed using "skew Householder" transformations (using an indefinite Σ_p norm) and require as many operations as the classical Householder transformations; see, e.g., [13] or Appendix B. (Later it is noted that numerically they are not always well-behaved.)

D.   THE SQUARE-ROOT INFORMATION FILTER

The information filter accentuates the recursive least-squares nature of Kalman filtering [7, 8]. The SRIF propagates the Choleski factor of $P_{k|k}^{-1}$ using the Choleski factor of the inverses of the process and measurement noise covariances matrices:

$$P_{k|k}^{-1} = T_k' \cdot T_k \tag{19}$$

$$Q_k^{-1} = \left[Q_k^{-1/2}\right]' \cdot Q_k^{-1/2} \tag{20}$$

$$R_k^{-1} = \left[R_k^{-1/2}\right]' \cdot R_k^{-1/2}, \tag{21}$$

where the second factors on the right-hand sides are chosen upper triangular. We now present the Dyer and McReynolds formulation of the SRIF (except for the fact that the time and measurement updates are combined here as in [8]), which differs from the one presented by Bierman (see [7] for details). One recursion of the SRIF algorithm is given by [8]:

$$U_3 \cdot \begin{pmatrix} Q_k^{-1/2} & 0 & 0 \\ T_k A_k^{-1} B_k & T_k A_k^{-1} & T_k \hat{x}_{k|k} \\ 0 & R_{k+1}^{-1/2} C_{k+1} & R_{k+1}^{-1/2} y_{k+1} \end{pmatrix} \tag{22}$$

$$= \begin{pmatrix} Q_{k+1}^{e-1/2} & * & * \\ 0 & T_{k+1} & \hat{\xi}_{k+1|k+1} \\ 0 & 0 & r_{k+1} \end{pmatrix}$$

where the second term on the left-hand side is prearray and that on the right-hand side is postarray, and the filtered state estimate is computed by

$$\hat{x}_{k+1|k+1} = T_{k+1}^{-1} \hat{\xi}_{k+1|k+1} + D_k u_k. \tag{23}$$

III. ERROR ANALYSIS OF THE PROPAGATION OF ROUNDOFF ERRORS

In this section we analyze the effect of rounding errors on Kalman filtering in the four different implementations described in Section II. The analysis is split in three parts: (1) What bounds can be obtained for the errors performed in step k; (2) how do errors performed in step k propagate in subsequent steps; and (3) how do errors performed in different steps interact and accumulate. Although this appears to be the logical order in which one should treat the problem of error buildup in a KF, we first look at the second aspect, which is also the only one that has been studied in the literature so far]2]. Therefore, we first need the following lemma.

Lemma 1. Let A be a square nonsingular matrix with smallest singular value σ_{min} and let E be a perturbation of the order of $\delta = \|E\|_2 \ll \sigma_{min}(A)$ with $\|\cdot\|_2$ denoting the 2-norm. Then

$$(A + E)^{-1} = A^{-1} + \Delta_1 = A^{-1} - A^{-1}EA^{-1} + \Delta_2, \tag{24}$$

where

$$\|\Delta_1\|_2 \le \delta/\sigma_{min}(\sigma_{min} - \delta_- = O(\delta) \tag{25}$$

$$\|\Delta_2\|_2 \le \delta^2/\sigma_{min}^2(\sigma_{min} - \delta) = O(\delta^2) \tag{26}$$

Notice that when A and E are symmetric, these first- and second-order approximations (25) and (26) are also symmetric.

Proof. The proof can be obtained by straightforward application of the matrix inversion lemma stated, e.g., in [14].

A.   PROPAGATION OF ERRORS UNDER INFINITE ARITHMETIC

We now consider the propagation of errors from step k to step k + 1 when no additional errors are performed during that update. We denote the quantities in computer with an overbar, i.e., $\overline{P}_{k|k-1}$, $\overline{x}_{k|k-1}$, $\overline{G}_k$. $\overline{S}_k$, $\overline{T}_k$, $\overline{R}_k^{e1/2}$, or $\overline{L}_k$, depending on the algorithm.

For the CKF, let $\delta P_{k|k-1}$ and $\delta x_{k|k-1}$ be the accumulated errors in step k, then:

$$\overline{P}_{k|k-1} = P_{k|k-1} + \delta P_{k|k-1}, \qquad \overline{\hat{x}}_{k|k-1} = \hat{x}_{k|k-1} + \delta \hat{x}_{k|k-1} \tag{27}$$

By using Lemma 1 for the inverse of $\overline{R}_k^e = R_k^e + C_k \delta P_{k|k-1} C_k'$, we find

$$[\overline{R}_k^e]^{-1} = [R_k^e]^{-1} - [R_k^e]^{-1}C_k \delta P_{k|k-1} C_k'[R_k^e]^{-1} + O(\delta)^2. \tag{28}$$

From this one then derives

$$\bar{K}_k = A_k \bar{P}_{k|k-1} C'_k \bar{R}_k^{e-1}$$

$$\delta K_k = A_k \; \delta P_{k|k-1} \quad C'_k R_k^{e-1}$$

$$\quad - A_k P_{k|k-1} C'_k R_k^{e-1} C_k \quad \delta P_{k|k-1} \quad C'_k R_k^{e-1} + O(\delta^2) \tag{29}$$

$$= F_k \; \delta P_{k|k-1} \quad C'_k R_k^{e-1} + O(\delta^2),$$

where

$$F_k = A_k (I - P_{k|k-1} C'_k R_k^{e-1} C_k) = A_k - K_k C_k \tag{30}$$

and [assuming $\overline{P}_{k|k-1}$ is not necessarily symmetric, which would, e.g., occur when applying (9) bluntly]:

$$\bar{P}_{k+1|k} = A_k (\bar{P}_{k-1|k} - \bar{P}'_{k|k-1} C'_k \bar{R}_k^{e-1} C_k \bar{P}_{k-1|k}) A'_k + B_k Q_k B'_k$$

$$\delta P_{k+1|k} = A_k (\delta P_{k|k-1} - \delta P'_{k|k-1} \quad C'_k R_k^{e-1} C_k P_{k|k-1}$$

$$\quad - P_{k|k-1} C'_k R_k^{e-1} C_k \quad \delta P_{k|k-1}$$

$$\quad + P_{k|k-1} C'_k R_k^{e-1} C_k \quad \delta P_{k|k-1} \quad C'_k R_k^{e-1} C_k P_{k|k-1}) A'_k$$

$$\quad + O(\delta^2) \tag{31}$$

$$= (A_k - K_k C_k) \quad \delta P_{k|k-1} (A'_k - C'_k K'_k)$$

$$\quad + A_k (\delta P_{k|k-1} - \delta P'_{k|k-1}) C'_k K'_k + O(\delta^2)$$

$$= F_k \quad \delta P_{k|k-1} \quad F'_k + A_k (\delta P_{k|k-1} - \delta P'_{k|k-1}) A'_k$$

$$\quad - A_k (\delta P_{k|k-1} - \delta P'_{k|k-1}) F'_k + O(\delta^2).$$

For the estimate $\hat{x}_{k+1|k}$ we have:

$$\bar{\hat{x}}_{k+1|k} = \bar{F}_k \bar{\hat{x}}_{k-1|k} + \bar{K}_k y_k + D_k u_k$$

$$\delta \hat{x}_{k+1|k} = F_k \quad \delta \hat{x}_{k-k|1} + \delta F_k \hat{x}_{k-k|1} + \delta K_x y_k + O(\delta^2) \tag{32}$$

$$= F_k \quad \delta\hat{x}_{k|k-1} + \delta K_k (y_k - C\hat{x}_{k|k-1}) + O(\delta^2)$$

$$= F_k \left[\delta\hat{x}_{k|k-1} + \delta P_{k|k-1} \quad C_k' R_k^{e-1} (y_k - C_k \hat{x}_{k|k-1}) \right]$$

$$+ O(\delta^2).$$

When, on the other hand, $\delta P_{k|k}$ and $\hat{x}_{k|k}$ are given, one derives analogously

$$\delta P_{k+1|k+1} = \tilde{F}_k \quad \delta P_{k|k} \tilde{F}_k' + A_k (\delta P_{k|k} - \delta P_{k|k}') A_k' \tag{33}$$

$$- A_k (\delta P_{k|k} - \delta P_{k|k}') \tilde{F}_k' + O(\delta^2)$$

$$\delta\hat{x}_{k+1|k+1} = \tilde{F}_k [\delta\hat{x}_{k|k} + \delta P_{k|k} \quad A_k' C_{k+1}' R_{k+1}^{e-1} \tag{34}$$

$$\times (y_{k+1} - C_{k+1} A_k \hat{x}_{k|k})] + O(\delta^2),$$

where $\tilde{F}_k = (I - P_{k+1|k} C_{k+1}' R_{k+1}^{e-1} C_{k+1}) A_k$ has the same spectrum as F_{k+1} in the time-invariant case, since $F_{k+1} A_k = A_{k+1} \tilde{F}_k$ [14].

We thus find that when $\delta P_{k|k-1}$ or $\delta P_{k|k}$ is symmetric, only the first term in (31) or (33) remains.

When this condition is imposed, these two mathematical models then demonstrate the *inherent numerical stability* of many Kalman filter implementations. The conditions for this very attractive robustness property are summarized in the following lemma, which is taken from the work of B. D. O. Anderson and J. B. Moore [15]. Before stating this lemma, let us first define exponential stability of a discrete, linear, and time-variant system.

Definition 1 [16]. The discrete, linear, and time-variant system

$$x_{k+1} = F_k x_k + G_k u_k$$

is *exponentially stable* over the time interval $[k_0, k]$ if and only if

$$\left\| \prod_{i=k_0}^{k} F_i \right\|_2 \le M \gamma^k$$

for $M > 0$ and $0 < \gamma_k < 1$.

Lemma 2. When the covariance matrices Q_k, R_k in (4) are *bounded* and *positive definite*, the system matrices $\{A_k, B_k, C_k\}$ in (1) and (2) *bounded*, the pair $[A_k, C_k]$ *detectable*, and the pair $[A_k, B_k]$ *stabilizable*, then the Kalman filter is *exponentially stable*.

Proof. For the proof of Lemma 2 and a definition of detectability and stabilizability for time-varying systems, we refer to [15].

Corollary 1. Let $\|F_i\|_2$ be denoted by γ_i, with $0 < \gamma_i < 1$; then we can bound the errors $\delta P_{k|k-1}$ or $\delta P_{k|k}$ as follows (as long as they remain *symmetric*):

$$\left\|\delta P_{k+1|k}\right\|_2 \leq \gamma_k^2 \left\|\delta P_{k|k-1}\right\|_2 \tag{35}$$

$$\left\|\delta P_{k+1|k+1}\right\|_2 \leq \tilde{\gamma}_k^2 \left\|\delta P_{k|k}\right\|_2 . \tag{36}$$

Here $\tilde{\gamma}_k$ represents $\|\tilde{F}_k\|$. The "stringent" condition $0 < \gamma_i < 1$ might not be satisfied at every single time instant. However, when the requirements stipulated in Lemma 2 are met, some γ_i might be larger than 1 while the exponential stability of F_k or $\tilde{F}_k$ over the time interval $[k_0, k]$ guarantees that the errors $\delta P_{k|k-1}$ or $\delta P_{k|k}$ are bounded on this time interval. Then (35) and (36) can be recast in:

$$\left\|\delta P_{k+1|k}\right\|_2 \leq \gamma_k^2 \left\|\delta P_{k_0|k_0-1}\right\|_2$$

and

$$\left\|\delta P_{k+1|k+1}\right\|_2 \leq \tilde{\gamma}_k^2 \left\|\delta P_{k_0|k_0}\right\|_2$$

respectively, with the γ_k and $\tilde{\gamma}_k$ taken from Definition 1.

Corollary 2. For the time-invariant case we can improve on the result of Corollary 1. For this case, the system matrices F_k and $\tilde{F}_k$ tend to the constant matrices F_∞ and $\tilde{F}_\infty$, respectively, with (equal) spectral radius $\rho_\infty < 1$, so that the sequences $\{\gamma_i\}$ and $\{\tilde{\gamma}_i\}$ in (35) and (36) can be replaced by that single spectral radius ρ_∞. Hence, we can approximate the error propagation of (31) or (33) as:

$$\left\|\delta P_{k+1|k}\right\| \approx \rho_\infty^2 \left\|\delta P_{k|k-1}\right\| \tag{37}$$

$$\left\| \delta P_{k+1|k+1} \right\| \approx \rho_\infty^2 \left\| \delta P_{k|k} \right\| \tag{38}$$

for sufficiently large k and for some appropriate matrix norm [17].

The property (35)–(38) has already been observed (see, e.g., [2]), but for symmetric $\delta P_{k|k-1}$. However, if symmetry is removed, divergence may occur when A_k (i.e., the original plant) is unstable. Indeed, from (31) and (33) we see that when A_k is unstable the larger part of the error is skew symmetric:

$$\delta P_{k+k|k} \approx A_k \cdot \left(\delta P_{k|k-1} - \delta P'_{k|k-1} \right) \cdot A'_k \tag{39}$$

$$\delta P_{k+1|k+1} \approx A_k \cdot (\delta P_{k|k} - \delta P'_{k|k}) \cdot A'_k \tag{40}$$

and the lack of symmetry *diverges* as k increases. This phenomenon is well known in the extensive literature about Kalman filtering, and experimental experience has led to a number of different "remedies" to overcome it. The above first-order perturbation analysis in fact explains why they work:

(1) A first method to avoid divergence due to the loss of symmetry when A_k is unstable is to *symmetrize* $\overline{P}_{k|k-1}$ or $\overline{P}_{k|k}$ at each recursion of the CKF by averaging it with its transpose. This makes the errors on P symmetric, and hence the largest terms in (31) and (33) disappear!

(2) A second method to make the errors on P symmetric simply computes only the *upper* (or lower) *triangular* part of these matrices, which turns out to be cheaper than the remedy outlined in the first part of this list.

(3) A third technique to avoid the loss of symmetry is the so-called (Joseph's) stabilized KF [3]. In this implementation, the set of equations for updating P are rearranged as follows:

$$P_{k+1|k} = F_k P_{k|k-1} F'_k + K_k R_k K'_k + B_k Q_k B'_k. \tag{41}$$

A similar first-order perturbation study, as for the CKF above, teaches that *no symmetrization* is required in order to avoid divergence since here the error propagation model becomes:

$$\delta P_{k+1|k} = F_k \, \delta P_{k|k-1} \, F'_k + O(\delta^2). \tag{42}$$

and there are no further terms related to the loss of symmetry.

Since for the moment we assume that *no additional errors* are performed in the recursions, one *inherently* computes the same equations for the SRCF as for the CKF. Therefore, starting with errors δS_k and $\delta \hat{x}_{k|k-1}$, (29), (31), (32), (35), and (37) still hold, whereby now

$$\delta P_{k+1|k} = S_k \cdot \delta S'_k + \delta S_k \cdot S'_k + \delta S_k \cdot \delta S'_k \tag{43}$$

is clearly symmetric by construction. According to (31) this now ensures the convergence to zero of $\delta P_{k|k-1}$ and hence of δS_k, δK_k, and $\delta \hat{x}_{k|k-1}$ if γ_k is sufficiently bounded in the time-varying case; see Corollary 1.

For the SRIF we start with errors δT_k and $\delta \hat{x}_{k|k}$ and use the identity

$$\delta P^{-1}_{k|k} = T'_k \cdot \delta T_k + \delta T'_k \cdot T_k + \delta T'_k \cdot \delta T_k \tag{44}$$

$$\delta x_{k|k} = (T_k + \delta T_k)^{-1} \delta \hat{\xi}_{k|k} \tag{45}$$

to relate this problem to the CKF as well. Here one apparently does *not* compute $\hat{x}_{k+1|k+1}$ from $\hat{x}_{k|k}$, and therefore one would expect *no propagation* of errors between them. Yet, such a propagation is *present* via (45) with the errors on $\delta \hat{\xi}_{k+1|k+1}$ and $\delta \hat{\xi}_{k|k}$, which *do* propagate from one step to another. This in fact is reflected in the recurrence (34) derived earlier. Since the SRIF update is *inherently equivalent* to an update of $P_{k|k}$ and $\hat{x}_{k|k}$ as in the CKF, (33) and (36) still hold, where now the symmetry of $\delta P_{k|k}$ is ensured because of (44). From this it follows that $\delta P_{k|k}$ and $\delta \hat{x}_{k|k}$, and therefore also δT_k and $\delta \hat{\xi}_{k|k}$, converge to zero as k increases, provided $\tilde{\gamma}_k$ is sufficiently bounded in the time-varying case.

Finally, for the CSRF we start with errors δL_{k-1}, δG_{k-1}, $\delta R_{k-1}^{e1/2}$, and $\delta \hat{x}_{k|k-1}$. Because of these errors, (16) is perturbed *exactly* as follows:

$$\begin{pmatrix} R_{k-1}^{e1/2} + \delta R_{k-1}^{e1/2} & C(L_{k-1} + \delta L_{k-1}) \\ G_{k-1} + \delta G_{k-1} & A(L_{k-1} + \delta L_{k-1}) \end{pmatrix} \cdot U_2$$
$$= \begin{pmatrix} R_k^{e1/2} + \delta R_k^{e1/2} & 0 \\ G_k + \delta G_k & L_k + \delta L_k \end{pmatrix} \tag{46}$$

where $\overline{U}_2$ is also Σ_p-unitary. When $\lambda = \|C \cdot L_{K-1}\| \ll \|R_{k-1}^{e1/2}\|$ (which is satisfied when k is sufficiently large), Lemma A.3 yields, after some manipulations:

$$\begin{pmatrix} \delta R_{k-1}^{e1/2} & C \, \delta L_{k-1} \\ \delta G_{k-1} & A \, \delta L_{k-1} \end{pmatrix} \cdot U_2 = \begin{pmatrix} \delta R_k^{e1/2} & 0 \\ \delta G_k & \delta L_k \end{pmatrix} + O(\delta \cdot \lambda) \tag{47}$$

Now the (1,1) and (1,2) blocks of U_2' are easily checked to be given by $R_k^{e-1/2}$. $R_{k-1}^{e1/2}$ and $R_k^{e-1/2} \cdot C \cdot L_{k-1} \cdot \Sigma$, respectively. From this, one then derives that for k sufficiently large

$$
\begin{aligned}
\delta R_k^{e1/2} &= \delta R_{k-1}^{e1/2} \cdot \left[R_k^{e-1/2} \cdot R_k^{e1/2} \right]' + C \cdot \delta L_{k-1} \\
&\quad \cdot \left[R_k^{e-1/2} \cdot C \cdot L_{k-1} \cdot \Sigma \right] + O(\delta \cdot \lambda) \\
&= \delta R_{k-1}^{e1/2} \cdot \left[R_k^{e-1/2} \cdot R_{k-1}^{e1/2} \right]' + O(\delta \cdot \lambda)
\end{aligned}
\tag{48}
$$

$$
\begin{aligned}
\delta G_k &= \delta G_{k-1} \cdot \left[R_k^{e-1/2} \cdot R_{k-1}^{e1/2} \right]' + A \cdot \delta L_{k-1} \\
&\quad \cdot \left[R_k^{e-1/2} \cdot C \cdot L_{k-1} \cdot \Sigma \right] + O(\delta \cdot \lambda) \\
&= \delta G_{k-1} \cdot \left[R_k^{e-1/2} \cdot R_{k-1}^{e1/2} \right]' + O(\delta \cdot \lambda)
\end{aligned}
\tag{49},
$$

Thus, here again the errors $\delta R_{k-1}^{e1/2}$ and δG_{k-1} are multiplied by the matrix $[R_k^{e-1/2} \cdot R_{k-1}^{e1/2}]'$ at each step. When Σ is the identity matrix (i.e., when inc P_k is non-negative), this is a contraction since $R_k^e = R_{k-1}^e + C \cdot L_{k-1}' \cdot L_{k-1}' \cdot C'$. From this, we then derive similar formulas for the propagation of δK_k and $\delta \hat{x}_{k+1|k}$. Using Lemma 1 for the perturbation of the inverse in $K_k = G_k \cdot R_k^{e-1/2}$, we find:

$$
\begin{aligned}
\delta K_k &= \delta G_k \cdot R_k^{e-1/2} - G_k \cdot R_k^{e-1/2} \cdot \delta R_k^{e1/2} \cdot R_k^{e-1/2} + O(\delta^2) \\
&= \delta G_k \cdot R_k^{e-1/2} - K_k \cdot \delta R_k^{e1/2} \cdot R_k^{e-1/2} + O(\delta^2).
\end{aligned}
\tag{50}
$$

Using (49) and (50) and the fact that for large k, $K_k = K_{k-1} + O(\lambda)$, we then obtain

$$
\begin{aligned}
\delta K_k &= \delta G_{k-1} \cdot \left[R_k^{e-1/2} \cdot R_{k-1}^{e1/2} \right]' \cdot R_k^{e-1/2} \\
&\quad - K_{k-1} \cdot \delta R_{k-1}^{e1/2} \cdot \left[R_k^{e-1/2} \cdot R_{k-1}^{e1/2} \right]' \cdot R_k^{e-1/2} + O(\delta \cdot \lambda) \\
&= \delta G_{k-1} \cdot R_{k-1}^{e-1/2} \cdot \left[R_{k-1}^e \cdot R_k^{e-1} \right]' \\
&\quad - K_{k-1} \cdot \delta R_{k-1}^{e1/2} \cdot R_{k-1}^{e-1/2} \cdot \left[R_{k-1}^e \cdot R_k^{e-1} \right]' + O(\delta \cdot \lambda),
\end{aligned}
\tag{51}
$$

which because of (50) decremented by 1 becomes:

$$\delta K_k = \delta K_{k-1} \cdot \left[R^e_{k-1} \cdot R^{e-1}_k \right]' + O(\delta \cdot \lambda) \tag{52}$$

Using (17) we then also obtain from this:

$$\delta \hat{x}_{k+1|k} = F_k \cdot \delta \hat{x}_{k+1|k} + \delta K_k \cdot (y_k - C \cdot x_{k|k-1}) + O(\delta^2). \tag{53}$$

For the same reason as above, the matrix $[R_{k-1}{}^e \cdot R_k{}^{e-1}]$ is a contraction when $\Sigma = I$, which guarantees the convergence to zero of δK_k and $\delta \hat{x}_{k+1|k}$. Notice, however, that here the contraction becomes closer to the identity matrix as k increases, which suggests that the inherent decaying of errors performed in previous steps will be less apparent for this filter. Besides that, nothing is claimed about δL_k or $\delta P_{k+1|k}$, but apparently these are less important for this implementation of the KF since they do not directly affect the precision of the estimate $\hat{x}_{k+1|k}$. Moreover, when Σ is not the identity matrix, the above matrix has norm larger than 1 and divergence may be expected. This has also been observed experimentally, as shown in Section VI.

B.   THE NUMERICAL ERRORS PERFORMED IN ONE SINGLE STEP

We now turn to the numerical errors performed in one single step k. Bounds for these errors are derived in the following theorem.

Theorem 1. Denoting the *norms* of the absolute errors due to roundoff during the construction of $P_{k+1|k}$, K_k, $\hat{x}_{k+1|k}$, S_k, T_k, $P_{k+1|k+1}{}^{-1}$, and $\hat{x}_{k|k}$ by Δ_p, Δ_k, Δ_x, Δ_s, Δ_t, $\Delta_{p\ inv}$, and Δ_x, respectively, we obtain the following upper bounds (where all norms are 2-norms):

(1) CKF

$$\Delta_p \leq \varepsilon_1 \cdot \sigma_1^2/\sigma_p^2 \cdot \left\| P_{k+1|k} \right\|$$

$$\Delta_k \leq \varepsilon_2 \cdot \sigma_1^2/\sigma_p^2 \cdot \left\| K_k \right\|$$

$$\Delta_{\hat{x}} \leq \varepsilon_3 \cdot \left(\left\| F_k \right\| \cdot \left\| \hat{x}_{k|k-1} \right\| + \left\| K_k \right\| \cdot \left\| y_k \right\| + \left\| D_k \right\| \cdot \left\| u_k \right\| \right)$$
$$+ \Delta_k \cdot \left(\left\| C_k \right\| \cdot \left\| \hat{x}_{k|k-1} \right\| + \left\| y_k \right\| \right)$$

(2) SRCF

$$\Delta_s \le \varepsilon_4 \cdot (1 + \sigma_1/\sigma_p) \cdot \left\|S_{k+1}\right\|/\cos\varphi_1$$

$$\Delta_p \le \varepsilon_5 \cdot (1 + \sigma_1/\sigma_p) \cdot \left\|P_{k+1|k}\right\|/\cos\varphi_1$$

$$\Delta_k \le \varepsilon_6/\sigma_p \cdot (\sigma_1/\sigma_p \cdot \left\|S_{k+1}\right\| + \sigma_1 \cdot \left\|G_k\right\| + \left\|S_{k+1}\right\|/\cos\varphi_1$$

$$\Delta_x \le \varepsilon_7 \cdot \left(\left\|F_k\right\| \cdot \left\|\hat{x}_{k|k-1}\right\| + \left\|K_k\right\| \cdot \left\|y_k\right\| + \left\|D_k\right\| \cdot \left\|u_k\right\|\right)$$
$$+ \Delta_k \cdot \left(\left\|C_k\right\| \cdot \left\|\hat{x}_{k|k-1}\right\| + \left\|y_k\right\|\right)$$

(3) CSRF

$$\Delta_k \le \varepsilon_8 \cdot \kappa(U_2)/\sigma_p \cdot (\sigma_1/\sigma_p \cdot \left\|L_k\right\| + \sigma_1\left\|G_k\right\| + \left\|L_k\right\|/\cos\varphi_2)$$

$$\Delta_x \le \varepsilon_9 \cdot \left(\left\|F_k\right\| \cdot \left\|\hat{x}_{k|k-1}\right\| + \left\|K_k\right\| \cdot \left\|y_k\right\| + \left\|D\right\| \cdot \left\|u_k\right\|\right)$$
$$\Delta_k \cdot \left(\left\|C\right\| \cdot \left\|\hat{x}_{k|k-1}\right\| + \left\|y_k\right\|\right)$$

(4) SRIF

$$\Delta_t \le \varepsilon_{10} \cdot \{\kappa\left(A_k\right) + \kappa\left(R_k^{1/2}\right) + \tau_1/\tau_m \cdot [\kappa\left(Q_k^{1/2}\right)$$
$$+ \kappa\left(A_k\right)]\} \cdot \left\|T_{k+1}\right\|/\cos\varphi_3$$

$$\Delta_{p\,inv} \le \varepsilon_{11} \cdot \left\{\kappa(A_k) + \kappa\left(R_k^{1/2}\right) + \tau_1/\tau_m \cdot \left[\kappa\left(Q_k^{1/2}\right)\right.\right.$$

$$\left.\left. + \kappa(A_k)\right]\right\} \cdot \left\|P_{k+1|k+1}^{-1}\right\|/\cos\varphi_3$$

$$\Delta_p \le \Delta_{p\,inv} \cdot \left\|P_{k+1|k+1}\right\|^2$$

$$\Delta_x \le \varepsilon_{12} \cdot \left\|D_k\right\| \cdot \left\|u_k\right\|$$

$$+ \Delta_t \cdot \left[\kappa^2(T_{k+1}) \cdot \|r_{k+1}\| + \kappa(T_{k+1}) \cdot \|\hat{x}_{k+1|k+1}\| \right.$$

$$\left. + \|r_{k+1}\|/\cos \varphi_4 \right],$$

where σ_i and τ_i are the i-th singular value of $R_k{}^e{}^{1/2}$ and $Q_{k+1}{}^e{}^{-1/2}$, respectively, ϵ_i are constants close to the machine precision ϵ and $\cos \varphi_i$ are defined as follows:

$$\cos \varphi_1 = \left\| S_{k+1} \right\| / \left\| \begin{bmatrix} G_k{}^{-1} S_{k+1} \end{bmatrix} \right\|$$

$$\cos \varphi = \left\| L_k \right\| / \left\| \begin{bmatrix} G_k{}^{-1} L_k \end{bmatrix} \right\|$$

$$\cos \varphi = \left\| T_{k+1} \right\| / \left\| \begin{pmatrix} T_k A_k^{-1} \\ R_{k+1}^{-1/2} C_{k+1} \end{pmatrix} \right\|$$

$$\cos \varphi_4 = \left\| r_{k+1} \right\| / \left\| \begin{pmatrix} \hat{\xi}_{k+1|k-1} \\ r_{k+1} \end{pmatrix} \right\|$$

and are usually close to 1.

Proof.

(1) CKF. Using Lemma A.1, the errors performed when constructing the matrix $R_k{}^e$ can be bounded by $\epsilon_r \cdot \|R_k{}^e\|$ and those for its inverse by $\epsilon_r \cdot \kappa(R_k{}^e) \cdot \|R_k{}^e\|$. By again applying Lemma A.1 several times one finally obtains all bounds for Δ_p, Δ_k, and Δ_x, as given above.

(2) SRCF. The bounds for Δ_k and Δ_s follow directly from Lemma A.2 since K_k and S_{k+1} are the least-squares solution and the residual, respectively, of the problem [A | B], where A' and B' are the top and bottom block rows of the prearray (12). The matrix A_1 of Lemma A.2 here is the matrix $R_k{}^e{}^{1/2}$. The bound for Δ_p then follows directly from the bound for Δ_s using (43) and the fact that $\|S_{k+1}\|^2 = \|P_{k+1|k}\|$. Finally, the bound from Δ_x is obtained from the one for Δ_k and from using Lemma A.1 several times.

(3) CSRF. For the case $\Sigma = I$, one obtains the bound for Δ_k as for the SRCF, from the observation that K_k is the least-squares solution of the problem [A | B], where A' and B' are the top and bottom block rows of the prearray (16). The matrix A_1 of Lemma A.2 here is also the matrix $R_k{}^e{}^{1/2}$. When $\Sigma \neq I$, this bound is multiplied by $\kappa(U_2)$ from the following observation. We can use Lemma A.1 to bound the errors in constructing the prearray (which we call M_k) by $\epsilon_m \cdot \|M_k\|$, and those in constructing the postarray (which we call N_k) by

$$\varepsilon_m \cdot \left\|U_2\right\| \cdot \left\|M_k\right\| = \varepsilon_m \cdot \left\|U_2\right\| \cdot \left\|N_k \cdot U_2^{-1}\right\| \leq \varepsilon_m \cdot \kappa(U_2) \cdot \left\|N_k\right\|$$

In terms of N_k we are now again in a problem of classical least squares, and errors in M_k and N_k are related by a factor $\kappa(U_2)$, whence the bound for Δ_k for general Σ. The bound for Δ_x is then obtained by repeatedly using Lemma A.1 as for the SRCF.

(4) SRIF. As above, T_{k+1} is the residual of a least-squares problem, where A and B are the first and second block columns of the prearray (22). The relative backward errors (δ_a and δ_b in Appendix A) in these matrices A and B are, according to Lemma A.1, bounded by $\kappa(R_k^{1/2}) + \kappa(A_k)$ and $\kappa(Q_k^{1/2}) + \kappa(A_k)$, respectively. Using this and Lemma A.2, we then obtain the bound for Δ_t. The bound for $\Delta_{p\,inv}$ is then obtained from that for Δ_t using (44) and the fact that $\|T_{k+1}\|^2 = \|P_{k+1|k+1}^{-1}\|$. The bound for Δ_p is then in its turn obtained from that for Δ_p using Lemma 1. Finally, $\hat{x}_{k+1|k+1}$ is the least-squares solution of the bottom 2×2 block in the postarray, which on itself is a residue (much as T_{k+1}) and is therefore only known with Δ_t precision. Using Lemma A.2 we thereby obtain the bounds for Δ_x.

Here again we should point out that all bounds hold for several norms when appropriately adapting the constants ϵ_i (see Appendix A).

These bounds are crude simplifications of the complicated process of rounding errors in linear algebra, but are often a good indication of what can go wrong in these problems (see, e.g., [18, 19]). This will be investigated more precisely in the experimental analysis of Section VI. It is interesting to note that the bounds derived in Theorem 1 disprove in a certain sense a result that has been used to claim the numerical supremacy of the SRFs, namely that the sensitivity of $P_{k+1|k}$, K_k, and $\hat{x}_{k+1|k}$ (which according to Theorem 1 depends mainly on the singular values of R_k^e) as computed by the SRFs is the square root of that of the same quantities computed via the CKF (see, e.g., [6], end of Section III). As far as the error analysis is concerned, this can only be claimed for $P_{k+1|k}$ and *not* for K_k or $\hat{x}_{k+1|k}$, as follows from a quick comparison of the CKF and the SRFs in Theorem 1. Therefore, we conclude that for situations that allow the application of the CKF, the SRFs *do not necessarily improve* the calculation of the Kalman gain or filtered estimates, although such a behavior is often observed. Counterexamples are given in Section VI.

Note also that when $\kappa(R_k^e) = 1$ all quantities are computed with roughly the same accuracy in the CKF and the SRCF. This particular situation arises, e.g., when appropriately scaling the output measurements (this is also a known technique [3] to improve the performance of the CKF) or when using the "sequential processing" technique [7] described in the Introduction. This is also investigated in Section VI.

Corollary 3. The above theorem also gives bounds on the errors due to model deviations δA_k, δB_k, δC_k, δD_k, δQ_k, and δR_k, assuming that the latter are sufficiently small, as follows. Let η be the relative size of these errors, i.e., $\|\delta M\| \leq \eta\|M\|$ for M equal to each of the above model matrices, then the above bounds hold when replacing the ϵ_i by numbers η_i, which are now all of order η.

Proof. The model errors can indeed be interpreted as backward errors on the matrices A_k, etc., but then on a machine of precision η. The same analysis then holds, but with ϵ replaced by η.

This corollary indicates that the effect of the modeling errors on the numerical errors performed in one single recursion can be treated as roundoff errors. However, the propagation of these types of errors is different. This will be addressed more concretely in Section IV. Furthermore, note that other modeling errors, such as bias errors on the input signals, discretization errors, etc., do not fall under this category, and a separate analysis or treatment is required for each of them; see, e.g., [7, 9]. This will be discussed in some detail in Section V for discretization errors.

C. ACCUMULATION AND INTERACTION OF THE ROUNDOFF ERRORS

The above theorem is now used together with the analysis of the *propagation* of errors through the recursion of the KF, given in Section III,A, to yield bounds on the *total* error of the different filters at a given step k, which we denote by the prefix δ_{tot} instead of δ.

In order to model this total error at time instant $k + 1$, we simply made the *assumption* that it consists of the propagation of the error at time instant k without introducing new errors *plus* the errors made in the single recursion step from $k + 1$ to k.

In this part we first turn to the (symmetrized) CKF. For the total error $\delta_{tot} P_{k+1|k}$, we then have, according to (29), (31), (33), (35), and Theorem 1 (for any *consistent* norm [20]):

$$\left\| \delta_{tot} P_{k+1|k} \right\| \le \gamma_k^2 \cdot \left\| \delta_{tot} P_{k-1|k} \right\| + \overline{\Delta}_p \tag{54}$$

$$\left\| \delta_{tot} K_k \right\| \le c_1 \cdot \gamma_k^2 \cdot \left\| \delta_{tot} P_{k|k-1} \right\| + \overline{\Delta}_k \tag{55}$$

$$\left\| \delta_{tot} \hat{x}_{k+1|k} \right\| \le \gamma_k^2 \cdot \left(\left\| \delta_{tot} \hat{x}_{k-1|k} \right\| + c_2 \cdot \left\| \delta_{tot} P_{k|k-1} \right\| \right) + \overline{\Delta}_x. \tag{56}$$

Here the overbar on the Δ indicates that these are not the exact bounds of Theorem 1 (which are derived under the assumption that the computations up to step k are exact), but analogous bounds derived for the perturbed results stored in the computer at step k. Under the assumption that at step k the accumulated errors are still of the order of the local errors performed in one step (i.e., those estimated in Theorem 1), one easily finds that the Δ and $\overline{\Delta}$ quantities are $O(\delta^2)$ close to each other. It is thus reasonable to assume that they are equal to each other. Denoting by Δ_{tot} the norm of the corresponding matrix δ_{tot} then finally yields:

$$
\begin{pmatrix} \Delta_{tot}P_{k+1|k} \\ \Delta_{tot}K_k \\ \Delta_{tot}\hat{x}_{k+1|k} \end{pmatrix} \leq \gamma_k \cdot \begin{pmatrix} \gamma_k & 0 & 0 \\ c_1 & 0 & 0 \\ c_2 & 0 & 1 \end{pmatrix} \cdot \begin{pmatrix} \Delta_{tot}P_{k|k-1} \\ \Delta_{tot}K_{k-1} \\ \Delta_{tot}\hat{x}_{k|k-1} \end{pmatrix} + \begin{pmatrix} \Delta_p \\ \Delta_k \\ \Delta_x \end{pmatrix}, \quad (57)
$$

where the inequality is meant elementwise. From this one then easily sees that the total errors will remain bounded and of the order of the local errors due to Corollary 1. This is also confirmed by the experimental results of the next part. For a time-invariant system, γ_k can be replaced by ρ_k — if the norm is chosen appropriately as discussed in (37) — which then eventually becomes smaller than 1.

Using the above inequality recursively from 0 to ∞, one finally obtains

$$
\begin{pmatrix} \Delta_{tot}P_\infty \\ \Delta_{tot}K_\infty \\ \Delta_{tot}\hat{x}_\infty \end{pmatrix} \leq \begin{pmatrix} 1/(1-\hat{\gamma}^2) & 0 & 0 \\ c_1\hat{\gamma}/(1-\hat{\gamma}^2) & 1 & 0 \\ c_2\hat{\gamma}/\left[(1-\hat{\gamma}^2)(1-\hat{\gamma})\right] & 0 & 1/(1-\hat{\gamma}) \end{pmatrix}
$$

$$
\cdot \begin{pmatrix} \Delta_p \\ \Delta_k \\ \Delta_x \end{pmatrix}
$$

(58)

if $\hat{\gamma} < 1$, where γ is the largest of the γ_ks when all the γ_ks are smaller than 1, otherwise $\hat{\gamma}$ becomes the γ_k representing the exponential stability of F_k as defined in Corollary 1. When γ_k tends to a fixed value γ_∞, it is easily shown that $\hat{\gamma}$ can be replaced by γ_∞ in (58), since the contributing terms to the summation are those with growing index k. For a *time-invariant* system, finally, this can then be replaced by ρ_∞, as was remarked in Corollary 2.

For the SRCF, one uses the relation to the CKF (as far as the propagation of errors from one step to another is concerned) to derive (58) in an analogous fashion, but now with Δ_p, Δ_k, and Δ_x appropriately adapted for the SRCF as in Theorem 1. For the SRIF one also obtains analogously the top and bottom inequalities of (57) for Δ_p and Δ_x adapted for the SRIF as in Theorem 1 and where now $\hat{\gamma}$ is the largest of the $\tilde{\gamma}_k$s. Upon convergence the same remarks hold as above for replacing $\hat{\gamma}$ by $\hat{\gamma}_\infty$ and ρ_∞. Finally, for the CSRF, we can only derive from (52) and (53) a recursion of the type:

$$
\begin{pmatrix} \Delta_{tot}K_k \\ \Delta_{tot}\hat{x}_{k+1|k} \end{pmatrix} \leq \begin{pmatrix} \beta & 0 \\ c_2 & \gamma_k \end{pmatrix} \cdot \begin{pmatrix} \Delta_{tot}K_{k-1} \\ \Delta_{tot}\hat{x}_{k|k-1} \end{pmatrix} + \begin{pmatrix} \Delta_k \\ \Delta_x \end{pmatrix}, \tag{59}
$$

where $\beta_k = \|R_{k-1}{}^e \cdot R_k{}^{e-1}\|_2$. Recursive summation of these inequalities, as was done to obtain (58), only converges here – for both $\Delta_{tot}K_\infty$ and $\Delta_{tot}\hat{x}_\infty$ – when the β_k increase sufficiently slowly to 1 as k grows. We remark here that these are only upper bounds (just as the bounds for the other filters), but the fact that they may diverge does indeed indicate that for the CSRF numerical problems are more likely to occur.

Notice that the first-order analysis of this part collapses when $O(\delta^2)$ and $O(\delta)$ errors become comparable. According to Lemma 1, this happens when $\kappa(R_k{}^e) \sim 1/\delta$, but in such cases it is highly probable that divergence will occur for all filter implementations.

IV. ERROR ANALYSIS OF THE PROPAGATION OF MODELING ERRORS

In applying the KF to a specific system, the dynamical system model $\{A_k, B_k, C_k, D_k\}$, noise statistics $\{Q_k, R_k\}$, and *a priori* data $\{x_{0|-1}, P_0\}$ must be specified. Since the system model is usually an approximation of a physical situation, the model parameters and noise statistics are seldom exact. That is, the system model used in constructing the filter differs from the actual system that generates the observations. It is clear that an inexact filter model will *degrade* the filter performances.

In the literature several authors have considered this filter degradation and developed error models for particular modeling errors. Because this effect is very important in practical applications, investigations were performed not long after Kalman's paper [1]. A. H. Jazwinski gave a very nice overview of these different contributions. In his book [2] he combined these results in one general theorem that formulates a single error model for the *propagation* of the different modeling errors. More recently, these results have been reconfirmed by B. D. O. Anderson in [8].

All these investigations are restricted to the study of the propagation of the different kinds of modeling errors in the KF recursion. This was done without taking into account the effect of the numerical implementation chosen. More importantly, the interaction of the errors caused by the implementation used with the propagation of the modeling errors was again not considered. This problem, however, very nicely fits into the framework developed in the previous part. This is demonstrated in this section for the error on the transition matrix

A_k (for the other modeling errors which can be derived in a very similar way we refer to [2] and [8]) and only for the CKF. We also restrict our derivations to the effect on the state error covariance matrix.

Let δA_k be the error on the system matrix in step k, then we denote the transition matrix of the model used in the KF as:

$$\bar{A}_k = A_k + \delta A_k,$$
(60)

where we again use the notation $O(\delta)$ to represent the error $\|\delta A_k\|$.

Since we are no longer working with the real system model, the calculated matrix $\bar{P}_{k+1|k}$, which is computed by:

$$P_{k+1|k} = \bar{A}_k(\bar{P}_{k|k-1}C'_k \bar{R}_k^{e-1} C_k \bar{P}_{k|k-1})\bar{A}'_k$$
$$+ B_k Q_k B'_k$$
(61)

is no longer an error covariance matrix. The real state error covariance matrix, however, satisfies a similar difference equation:

$$P_{k+1|k} = A_k(P_{k|k-1} - P_{k|k-1}C'_k R_k^{e-1} C_k P_{k|k-1})A'_k$$
$$+ B_k Q_k B'_k$$
(62)

The difference between (61) and (62), denoted by $\delta P_{k+1|k}$, can be computed in a similar way, as outlined in Section III,A, where δ is taken as defined in (60).

If we assume that $\delta P_{k|k-1}$ remains symmetric, the following error propagation model results:

$$\delta P_{k+1|k} = F_k \, \delta P_{k|k-1} \, F'_k + \delta A_k \, P_{k|k-1} \, F'_k$$
$$+ F_k P_{k|k-1} \, \delta A'_k + O(\delta^2).$$
(63)

So, the error propagation behaves roughly as:

$$\left\| \delta P_{k+1|k} \right\| \approx \gamma_k^2 \left\| \delta P_{k|k-1} \right\| + c \cdot \gamma_k \left\| P_{k|k-1} \right\| \cdot O(\delta)$$
(64)

with c a constant of the order of unity.

Model (64) again shows that when $\delta P_{k|k-1}$ is symmetric the difference $\delta P_{k|k-1}$ decreases in time when no additional errors are performed.

Remark 1. From [2] and [8] it is observed that a similar stabilization of the errors remains valid for the errors on the other system model matrices, noise statistics, and *a priori* data. This is not true if unknown zero bias errors occur on the input signal u_k of the state space model (1). Their presence can lead to severe deterioration of the reconstructed state variables. A treatment of this kind of error source is given in [7] and [9].

To formulate an upper bound for the errors made during each recursion by the KF implementation used, we can use Corollary 3. If we are restricted to the symmetrized CKF, we are now able in combination with the model of (64) to write down an upper bound for the total error due to δA_k:

$$\left\| \delta_{tot} P_{k+1|k} \right\| \le \gamma_k^2 \left\| \delta P_{k|k-1} \right\| + c \cdot \gamma_k \left\| P_{k|k-1} \right\| \cdot O(\delta) + \overline{\Delta}_p^{\eta}, \tag{65}$$

where $\overline{\Delta}_p^{\eta}$ is the $\overline{\Delta}_p$ used in Theorem 1, first part, with ϵ_i replaced by the relative error on A_k, i.e., $\| \delta A_k \| \le \eta \| A_k \|$.

V.   ERROR ANALYSIS OF THE PROPAGATION OF DISCRETIZATION ERRORS

The discrete system model (1) often results from discretizing a set of differential equations:

$$\dot{x} = \mathscr{A} x + \mathscr{B} u, \tag{66}$$

where we now restrict ourselves to the time-invariant case. This is performed to solve this set of equations on a digital computer. Here, one looks for an approximation of the solution to (66):

$$x(t) = e^{\mathscr{A}(t-t_0)} x(t_0) + \int_{t_0}^{t} e^{\mathscr{A}(t-\tau)} \mathscr{B} u(\tau) \, d\tau. \tag{67}$$

If we consider this solution only over one sample period p, where we denote the values of x at the time instant ip by x_i, (67) can also be written as:

$$x_{k+1} = e^{\mathscr{A} p} x_k + \int_{kp}^{(k+1)p} e^{\mathscr{A}([k+1]p-\tau)} \mathscr{B} u(\tau) \, d\tau. \tag{68}$$

It is common practice to approximate x_{k+1} in (68) by the state $\overline{x}_{k+1}$ of a discrete time system:

a

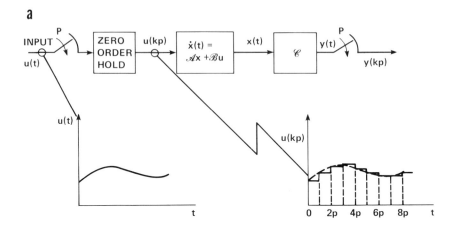

b

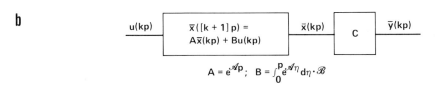

Fig. 1. (a) Discretizing a continuous linear time system by a zero-order hold. (b) Discrete-time equivalent. p is the discretization period.

$$\bar{x}_{k+1} = e^{\mathscr{A}p}\,\bar{x}_k + \int_0^p e^{\mathscr{A}\eta}\,d\eta\,\mathscr{B}u_k. \tag{69}$$

This corresponds to the use of a zero-order hold with no delay for the input signal, as depicted in Fig. 1. This means that:

$$u(\tau) = u(kp) \quad \text{for} \quad kp \le \tau \le (k+1)p.$$

Equation (69) can easily be verified using the above condition for the input signal; see also, e.g., [21].

This approximation, leaving alone the question of the accuracy by which the transition matrix $e^{\mathscr{A}p}$ and the input distribution matrix $\int_0^p e^{\mathscr{A}\eta}\,d\eta\,\mathscr{B}$ can be calculated (see, e.g., [22]) induces an error in the state calculations. The effect of this approximation on any computation involving the discretized system matrices is summarized under the name *discretization error*.

The design of a KF for continuous time systems with a digital computer is based on a discretized system model, as given by (69). In practical applications we are interested in *the influence of the choice of the discretization period* on the performance of the KF. Therefore, we will compare the calculated KF quantities based on the discrete system model as (69) for different choices of discretization period p.

To allow comparison of the computed KF results, two different values of the discretization periods p have to be chosen that are a multiplicity of each other, say Δt and $2\,\Delta t$. For these two different cases, the system models are:

$$\{A, B, C\}, \quad \text{for a discretization period } \Delta t \tag{70}$$

with $A = e^{\mathscr{A}\Delta t}$ and $B = \int_0^{\Delta t} e^{\mathscr{A}\eta}\,d\eta\,\mathscr{B}$, and

$$\{A^2, (A + I)B, C\}, \quad \text{for a discretization period } 2\,\Delta t. \tag{71}$$

First, we consider the difference that results from the calculation of the state error covariance matrix after the first comparable recursion and using the same starting value, denoted as P_0. For two KF recursions with the system model (70) we obtain:

$$P_{2|1}^{\Delta t} = (A - K_1 C)(A - K_0 C)P_0 (A')^2$$
$$+ (A - K_1 C)BQB'A' + BQB'. \tag{72}$$

One recursion with system model (71) gives:

$$P_{1|0}^{2\,\Delta t} = A(A - K_0 C)P_0 (A^2)' + (A + I)BQB'(A + I)'. \tag{73}$$

So, the difference satisfies:

$$\left(P_{1|0}^{2\,\Delta t} - P_{2|1}^{\Delta t}\right) = AP_{1|0}^{\Delta t}C'\left(CP_{1|0}^{\Delta t}C' + R\right)^{-1}CP_{1|0}^{\Delta t}A' + ABQB' + BQB'A \tag{74}$$

Equation (74) shows that the effect of using a larger discretization period can be interpreted as designing a filter with *more input noise*. This is because the right-hand side of (74) is usually *non-negative definite*. This shows that the KF design becomes *more conservative* by using a larger discretization period.

Although the increase of the discretization period can be seen as an induction of extra input noise, the inherent stabilization of the Riccati difference equation, expressed by (31) or (33), under the assumption that the state error covariance matrix will remain symmetric, assures that the KF recursion does not diverge by using a large discretization period.

Remark 2. From the above analysis we observe that the effect of increased input noise by a larger discretization period will cause the calculated state error covariance matrix to remain higher but bounded, with respect to any consistent norm, on comparable sampling intervals.

Second, we discuss the effect on the computation of the reconstructed state quantities. To analyze the discretization error on the reconstructed state variables, we assume that all the signals are deterministic, i.e., we will only consider the mean of the state quantities. Then (10) with the system matrices $\{A, D\}$ equal to $\{e^{Ap}, \int_0^p e^{A\eta} d\eta B\}$, for a particular discretization period p, gives the *reconstructed state* quantity:

$$\hat{x}([k+1]p) = e^{Ap} \hat{x}(kp)$$
$$+ \int_{kp}^{[k+1]p} e^{A([k+1]p-\eta)} Bu(kp) \, d\eta$$
$$+ K_k y_k - K_k C\hat{x}(kp). \tag{75}$$

The *real state* obeys (68). Therefore, the error between the reconstructed state and the real state quantities becomes:

$$[x([k+1]p) - \hat{x}([k+1]p)] = \left(e^{Ap} - K_k C \right)[x(kp) - \hat{x}(kp)]$$
$$+ \int_{kp}^{[k+1]p} e^{A([k+1]p-\eta)} B[u(\eta) - u(kp)] \, d\eta \tag{76}$$

Where the system matrix $(e^{Ap} - K_kC)$ is clearly the KF transition matrix F_x in (30), which tends to a matrix with spectral radius smaller than one [8]. Therefore, the reconstructed error due to the discretization will be *bounded*. From this analysis the following *qualitative* results can be given:

(1) If a *larger* discretization period is used, $\|K_\infty\|$ will normally increase, causing the eigenvalues of the KF transition matrix F_∞ or $\tilde{F}_\infty$ to move more inside the unit disk. Therefore, the reconstructed error due to discretization will *decrease faster*. On the other hand, (76) shows that a larger discretization period causes the second term on the right-hand side to increase, depending on the nature of the input signal. These contradicting facts will determine the (increase or decrease of the) magnitude of the deterministic error on the reconstructed state variables.

(2) It is also well known [8] that a more stable "observer" design, makes the filter calculations more sensitive to the random errors on the processed observations. Hence an increased discretization period also results in an increase of the random errors on the reconstructed state variables.

The practical value of these observations will be verified by experimental analysis in the Section VI,E.

TABLE I. TEST CONDITIONS TO EVALUATE THE DIFFERENT KALMAN FILTER IMPLEMENTATIONS

	Test 1	Test 2	Test 3	Test 4	Test 5	Test 6
$\kappa(A)$	$1.46 \cdot 10^1$	$1.46 \cdot 10^1$	$1.46 \cdot 10^1$	$1.46 \cdot 10^1$	$2.36 \cdot 10^6$	$1.46 \cdot 10^1$
$\kappa(Q)$	1.0	1.0	1.0	1.0	$1.39 \cdot 10^6$	$9.99 \cdot 10^3$
$\kappa(R)$	$9.90 \cdot 10^1$	$9.90 \cdot 10^1$	1.0	1.0	$1.00 \cdot 10^3$	3.4
$\kappa(R_2^e)$	7.53	8.06	1.02	1.02	$1.35 \cdot 10^1$	1.67
c_w	1.0	0.9	1.0	1.0	1.0	1.0
$\rho(F_\infty)$	$9.80 \cdot 10^{-1}$	$9.00 \cdot 10^{-1}$	$9.80 \cdot 10^{-1}$	$9.80 \cdot 10^{-1}$	$9.00 \cdot 10^{-1}$	$9.95 \cdot 10^{-1}$
$P_{0|-1}$	$\neq 0$	$\neq 0$	$\neq 0$	$\neq 0$	$\neq 0$	$\neq 0$
$\|P_\infty\|$	$2.06 \cdot 10^{-2}$	$1.97 \cdot 10^{-3}$	$6.96 \cdot 10^{-2}$	$6.95 \cdot 10^{-2}$	$1.98 \cdot 10^{-1}$	$3.36 \cdot 10^{-3}$
$\|K_\infty\|$	$4.37 \cdot 10^{-1}$	$2.50 \cdot 10^{-1}$	$1.29 \cdot 10^{-1}$	$1.29 \cdot 10^1$	1.21	$1.81 \cdot 10^{-2}$
$\|S_\infty\|$	$1.56 \cdot 10^{-1}$	$4.91 \cdot 10^{-2}$	$2.98 \cdot 10^{-1}$	$2.98 \cdot 10^{-1}$	$4.49 \cdot 10^{-2}$	$6.09 \cdot 10^{-2}$

VI. EXPERIMENTAL EVALUATION OF THE DIFFERENT KALMAN FILTERS

In this section we show a series of experiments reflecting the results of our error analysis. For these examples the upper bounds for numerical roundoff developed in the previous section are reasonably close to the true error buildup. The first set of experiments addresses the propagation of errors due to roundoff errors (Section VI,A–D). The final support (Section VI,E) then presents the experimental evaluation of the propagation of errors due to modeling errors and discretization errors.

A. EXPERIMENTAL SETUP

The simulations are performed for a realistic flight-path reconstruction problem, described in [10]. The *numerical difficulties* observed in a preliminary experimental analysis with the CKF [23] showed that this case study is ideally suites to validate the theoretical analysis of Section III. Conversely, it demonstrated how this first-order perturbation study contributes in understanding and solving these difficulties. In order to shed more light on the trouble spots of some of the filters, we have "artificially" modified the realistic conditions of our problem (see Table I). We then show that the behavior of the different filters can be predicted by the error analysis of Section III. This analysis indicated the following parameters as being relevant for the error propagation in the four different KF implementations we considered:

(1) The initial condition for the error covariance matrix $P_{0|-1}$.

(2) The condition number $\kappa(R_k^e)$ of the innovation signal covariance matrix. In our example, it turns out that $\kappa(R_k)$ approximately determines $\kappa(R_k^e)$ during the whole run. This is partly due to the fact that $\|P_{k|k-1}\|$ is small compared to $\|R_k\|$.

(3) The spectral norm γ_k and radius ρ_k of the matrix F_k. This can be affected by "weighting" the system matrix A_k by a factor c_w.

(4) The condition number $\kappa(Q_k)$ of the process noise covariance matrix.

(5) The condition number $\kappa(A_k)$ of the system state transition matrix. This is affected by the choice of a state space coordinate system.

(6) The condition number $\kappa(S_k)$ of the Choleski factor of the error covariance matrix. This parameter is hard to estimate *a priori*.

These are also the parameters we tried to influence in our experimental setup as given in Table I.

To study roundoff errors in single precision, mixed precision computations were carried out and *double precision* results are considered to be exact. The roundoff errors on three different quantities that result from a KF were considered in the simulations, namely:

(1) On the state error covariance matrix P, denoted by

$$\Delta_{tot}P_{k|k-1} = \left\| P_{k|k-1} - \overline{P}_{k|k-1} \right\| = \left\| \delta_{tot}P_{k|k-1} \right\|$$

(2) On the Kalman gain K, denoted by

$$\Delta_{tot}K_k = \left\| K_k - \overline{K}_k \right\| = \left\| \delta_{tot}K_k \right\|$$

(3) On the reconstructed state quantities $\hat{x}_{k|k-1}$ or $\hat{x}_{k|k}$ denoted by

$$\Delta_{tot}x_k = \left\| \hat{x}_{k|k-1} - \hat{x}_{k|k-1} \right\| \quad or \quad \left\| \hat{x}_{k|k} - \hat{x}_{k|k} \right\|$$

In the experiments, the total roundoff error Δ_{tot} in (57) and (59) is approximated by the Frobenius norm of the difference between the single and double precision quantities which are, respectively, denoted by $\overline{(\cdot)}$ and $(\cdot)$. For the state error covariance matrix $P_{k|k-1}$ this approximation becomes $\Delta_{tot}P_{k|k-1} = \|P_{k|k-1} - \overline{P}_{k|k-1}\| = \|\delta_{tot}P_{k|k-1}\|$. It is noted that the SRIF does not require the Kalman gain K_k explicitly to compute the filtered state quantities. Therefore, the second parameter will not be considered for this implementation.

Since the accuracy of the first two quantities determines the accuracy of the reconstructed state, a first analysis can be *restricted* to these quantities. If conditions can be formulated under which accuracy degradation of these two quantities occurs, extensive simulation tests with input and output time histories of the real (or simulated) system become obsolete.

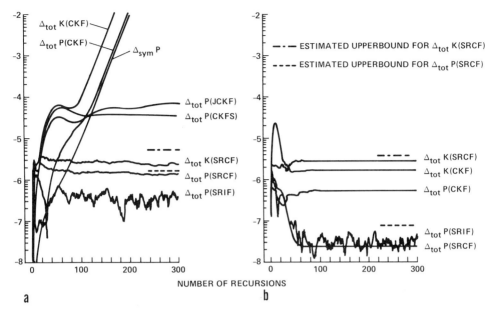

Fig. 2. Comparison of the SRCF/SRIF and the CKF. (a) Test 1; (b) test 2. —·—, estimated upper bound for Δ_{tot}K(SRCF); - - -, estimated upper bound for Δ_{tot}P(SRCF.).

Because of the inclusion of the CSRF, only the *time-invariant* case will be considered here. The SRCF and the SRIF algorithms are closely related from a numerical point of view. They are, therefore, first compared to the CKF and second to the CSRF.

B.   COMPARING THE SRCF/SRIF WITH THE CKF

The experimental conditions of the different tests are listed in Table I. From the theoretical analysis of Section III, it follows that the relevant parameters that influence the reliability of the CKF are $\kappa(R_k^e)$ and $\rho(F_k)$, the spectral radius of F_k. Two tests were performed to analyze their effect. The magnitudes of the variables $\kappa(R)$ and $\rho(A)$ given in Table I. The results of these tests are plotted in Fig. 2. From this figure the following observations are made:

1.   Test 1 – Fig. 2a [$\rho(A) = 1.0$ and $\kappa(R) = 10^2$]

Since symmetry of the error state covariance matrix P is not preserved by the CKF, the roundoff error propagation model for the local error $\delta P_{k|k-1}$, given by (31), shows that divergence of roundoff errors on P and hence on K will occur if the original system is *unstable*. This experiment confirms this divergence phenomenon also when $\rho(A) = 1.0$, as is the case for the considered flight-path reconstruction problem [10]. Furthermore, it is observed from Fig. 2a that the error on P with the CKF is almost completely determined by the *loss of symmetry*, computed by $\|\overline{P}_{k|k-1} - \overline{P}_{k|k-1}'\| = \Delta_{sym}P_{k|k-1}$.

As indicated in the previous section, different methods have been proposed to solve this problem. One particular class of methods consists in forcing the error on the state covariance matrix to become symmetric, which is done here by averaging the off-diagonal elements of P after each recursion. The behavior of $\Delta_{tot}P_{k|k-1}$ for this implementation, denoted by CKF(S) in Fig. 2a, clearly indicates that this implementation again becomes competitive, even when the original system is unstable. A similar effect has also been observed when computing only the upper triangular part of P. On the other hand, the behavior of $\Delta_{tot}P_{k|k-1}$ for Joseph's stabilized CKF, denoted by (J)CKF in Fig. 2a, confirms that the roundoff errors do not diverge even when the symmetry of P is not retained. We also observe from Fig. 2a that the roundoff error on P with these modified CKFs remains higher (a factor of 10) than the SRCF/SRIF combination.

2. Test 2 – Fig. 2b [$\rho(A) = 0.9$ and $\kappa(R) = 10^2$

If we make the original system stable, the CKF is numerically stable. Moreover, the accuracy with which the Kalman gain is computed is of the same order as that of the SRCF. This is in contrast with a general opinion that SRFs improve the calculations of the Kalman gain or filtered estimates [3, 6]. We can state that they do not make the accuracy poorer. From Fig. 2b it is observed that *only* the error covariance matrix P is computed more accurately, which confirms the upper bounds for the roundoff errors as given in Section III. Summarizing these bounds, we obtained in Section III the following recurrences:

$$\Delta_{tot}P_{k+1|k} \leq \gamma_k^2 \cdot \Delta_{tot}P_{k|k-1} + \Delta_p \tag{77}$$

$$\Delta_{tot}K_k \leq c \cdot \gamma_k \cdot \Delta_{tot}P_{k|k-1} + \Delta_k, \tag{78}$$

where the upper bounds for the local errors Δ_p and Δ_k are given in Theorem 1, parts (1) and (2), for the CKF and the SRCF.

A comparison of the (a) and (b) bounds indicates that, when the accuracy of the Kalman gain is considered, no preference should exist for the SRFs to the CKF when A_k is *stable and time-invariant*. [For situations where A_k has eigenvalues *on or outside* the unit circle, the CKF has to be changed, e.g., to the CKF(S) implementation.] However, the experimental results demonstrate that for the latter conditions the loss of accuracy with the CKF(S) is still higher than the SRFs. This is also generally observed for other SRF variants such as the UDU' filters [7]. Here we only want to draw attention to the clear difference to be expected (and also reflected by the experiments) between the accuracy of $P_{k|k-1}$ and K_k in the CKF(S) implementation with respect to those of SRF filters.

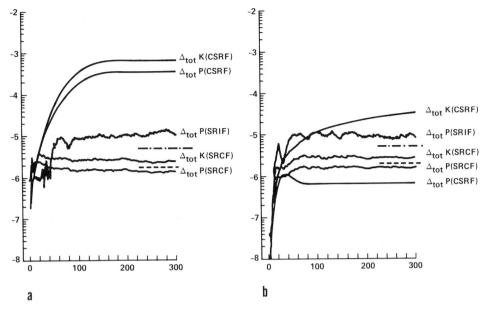

Fig. 3. Comparison of the SRCF/SRIF and the CSRF. (a) Test 3; (b) test 4.

C.   COMPARISON OF SRCF/SRIF WITH CSRF

The upper bound for the roundoff errors of the Kalman gain and the state estimate $\hat{x}_{k+1|k}$ computed by the CSRF (for large k) can be summarized as follows:

$$\Delta_{tot}K_k \le \beta_k \cdot \Delta_{tot}K_{k-1}\Delta_k \tag{79}$$

$$\Delta_{tot}\hat{x}_{k+1|k} \le c \cdot \Delta_{tot}K_{k-1} + \gamma_k \Delta_{tot}\hat{x}_{k|k-1} + \Delta_x, \tag{80}$$

with the upper bounds for the local errors Δ_k and Δ_x given in Theorem 1, part (3). This model indicates that the error propagation is convergent when $\beta_k = \|R_{k-1}^e \cdot (R_k^e)^{-1}\| < 1$, which is the case only if the signature matrix Σ is the identity matrix I. Note that the error variation $\Delta_{tot}K_k$ is now weighted by β_k (instead of γ_k for the other filters), which even for $\Sigma = I$ becomes very close to 1 for large k. This is also the main reason for the poor numerical behavior of this filter. When $\Sigma \ne I$ (which depends on the choice of $P_{0|-1} \ne 0$), β_k is larger than 1 and $\kappa(U_2)$ *may* also become large. Both of these phenomena have a negative influence on the above bounds and may eventually cause divergence. Furthermore, it is remarked that in addition to the *numerical sensitivity* introduced by the choice of $P_{0|-1}$, it also may drastically influence the *efficiency* of the CSRF implementation. This is indicated explicitly by an operation count in [9], but is not presented here for reasons explained at the end of Section VII.

The influence of the choice of $P_{0|-1}$ is analyzed by the following two tests.

1.   Test 3 – Fig. 3a $[P_{0|-1} \neq 0, \rho(A) = 1.0$
      and $\kappa(R) = 1.0]$

The choice of $P_{0|-1} \neq 0$ influences the CSRF implementation *negatively*. The transformations used in each recursion of the CSRF to triangularize the pre-array become Σ-unitary, i.e., having a condition number >1. This is due to the fact that *inc* P_0 is not definite. From Fig. 3a, this negative effect is clearly observed. Both the error levels on P and K are a factor 10^2 larger than for the SRCF or SRIF. For the covariance-type algorithms considered here, it is observed that the error on the Kalman gain is always higher than the error on the state error covariance matrix. This is partly due to the extra calculation $G_k(R_k^e)^{-1/2}$ needed for the Kalman gain, where the condition number of $(R_k^e)^{1/2}$ determines the loss of accuracy.

2.   Test 4 – Fig. 3b $[P_{0|-1} = 0, \rho(A) = 1.0,$
      and $\kappa(R) = 1.0]$

For this case *inc* $P_0 = B \cdot Q \cdot B'$ is positive definite, causing the transformations used in each recursion to be *unitary*. From the experimental results in Fig. 3b, we observe that the error on P is very small, while the error on K is much higher than for the SRCF calculations. Furthermore, the errors on K with the CSRF *increase very slowly* because the coefficient β_k becomes very close to 1. This is due to the fact that for the CSRF roundoff errors are carried along on three matrices, namely G_k, $(R_k^e)^{1/2}$, and L_k, while for the SRCF/SRIF errors are carried along only on the square roots of P or P^{-1}. For the error on L_k (supposing *inc* P_k factored as L_kL_k') this effect does not cause the errors on P_k:

$$P_k = \sum_{i=0}^{k-1} L_i L_i' + P_0 \tag{81}$$

to accumulate because L_k converges rapidly enough to zero such that the accumulated errors on P_k:

$$\Delta_{tot}P_k = \sum_{i=0}^{k} L_i \cdot \Delta_{tot}L_i' + \Delta_{tot}L_i \cdot L_i' \tag{82}$$

also converges if the $\Delta_{tot}L_i$ are not too large. The absolute value of the total error on $(R_k^e)^{1/2}$ and G_k remain much higher. This is clearly reflected in the loss of accuracy in the calculation of K_k by $G_k(R_k^e)^{-1/2}$.

Generally, the CSRF is *less reliable* than the SRCF/SRIF combination. For zero initial conditions of the state error covariance matrix, maximal reliability can be achieved with the CSRF. It is also for this condition that the CSRF is in its most efficient form for the system dimensions at hand [9], so that the CSRF may be preferred because of its increased *computational efficiency* despite its *loss of accuracy*. We stress the fact that this property is only valid for the *time-invariant* case. Modifications of the CSRF exist taking into account certain time-varying effects [15], e.g., for the process noise covariance matrix Q. This, however, induces again an increased computational complexity.

D.   COMPARISON OF THE SRCF AND THE SRIF

In the previous experiments the SRCF/SRIF combination performed equally well. In this section a further analysis is made to compare both implementations. Using the error model that indicates the upper bound for the roundoff errors made during one SRIF recursion:

$$\Delta_{tot}P_{k+1|k+1} \leq \gamma_k^2 \cdot \Delta_{tot}P_{k|k} + \Delta_p \tag{83}$$

$$\Delta_{tot}\hat{x}_{k+1|k-1} \leq \gamma_k \cdot \Delta_{tot}\hat{x}_{k|k} + \mathcal{C}_2\gamma_k \cdot \Delta_{tot}P_{k|k} + \Delta_x \tag{84}$$

with the upper bounds of the local errors Δ_p and Δ_x given in Theorem 1, part (4), teaches that besides $\kappa(R_k)$ and $\rho(F_k)$, other system parameters influence the roundoff error accumulation in the SRIF. The effect of these parameters is analyzed in the following tests.

1.   Test 5 – Fig. 4a

In this test very large condition numbers for A, Q, and R (see Table I), are considered. As expected, this indeed causes the error on P to be much higher (a factor of 10^3) for the SRIF than for the SRCF. As in Test 2, the large value of $\kappa(R)$ again causes a great loss in the accuracy of the Kalman gain calculation in the SRCF. The level of roundoff errors on K indeed becomes a factor of 10^2 larger than the roundoff level of P.

In this test we analyzed the deterioration of the error covariance matrix by the SRIF implementation by (fairly unrealistic) large condition numbers. In many practical situations, the effect of high $\kappa(Q_k^e)$ and $\kappa(R_k^e)$ can be relaxed by scaling, rearranging the system matrices or using scalar measurement and/or input updates [8]. Furthermore, we observed in the experiments that a high $\kappa(Q_k)$

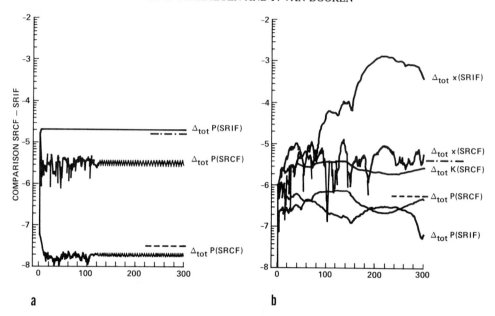

Fig. 4. Comparison of the SRCF and the SRIF. (a) Test 5; (b) test 6.

did not result in a high $\kappa(Q_k^e)$, which is in contrast with what was observed for $\kappa(R_k^e)$. However, the effect of a high $\kappa(A_k)$ is much harder to control and as we have seen may influence the accuracy of the SRIF negatively. We repeat here that this is due to a careful choice of the problem coefficients [here $\kappa(A_k)$ and $\kappa(Q_k)$] in order to put forward the dependency on these parameters.

2. Test 6 – Fig. 4b

For this test, the measurement error statistics were taken from real flight-test measurement calibrations [10]. This results in the following forms for the process noise covariance matrix Q, and, respectively, the measurement noise covariance matrix R:

$$Q = \text{diag}\left\{8 \times 10^{-6}, 5 \times 10^{-5}, 5 \times 10^{-8}\right\},$$
$$R = \text{diag}\left\{5 \times 10^{-2}, 2 \times 10^{-1}\right\}. \tag{85}$$

The relevant parameters for the roundoff error propagation are listed in Table I. In Fig. 4b the simulated error $\Delta_{tot}x$ on the state calculations is plotted for both filter implementations. Here the error level with the SRIF is significantly higher than that for the SRCF, while P is computed with roughly equal accuracy. This is due to the high condition number of T_k (obtained by the test con-

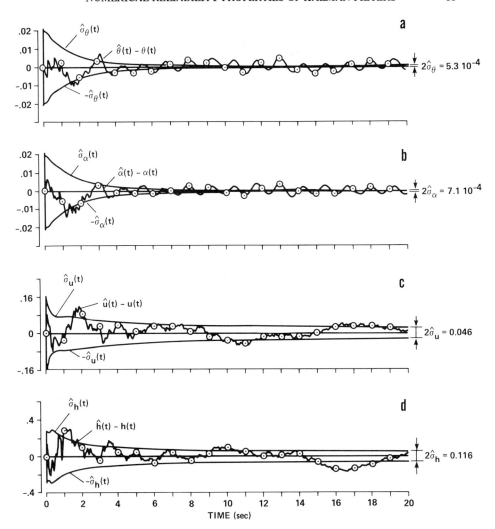

Fig. 5. Errors on the reconstructed flight-path quantities and estimated standard deviations bounds for Δt_1 = 0.05 sec. (a) Flight-path angle θ (rad); (b) angle of attack α (rad); (c) air speed along X, u (m/s); (d) altitude deviation Δh (m).

ditions given in Table I) in the calculation of the filtered state with the SRIF by (23). This latter condition number is again a parameter which is hard to control "externally" by scaling or rearranging the system equations.

E.   THE EFFECT OF MODELING AND DISCRETIZATION ERRORS

According to the analysis given in Section IV, the effect of modeling errors is completely analogous to the effect of rounding errors. As a matter of

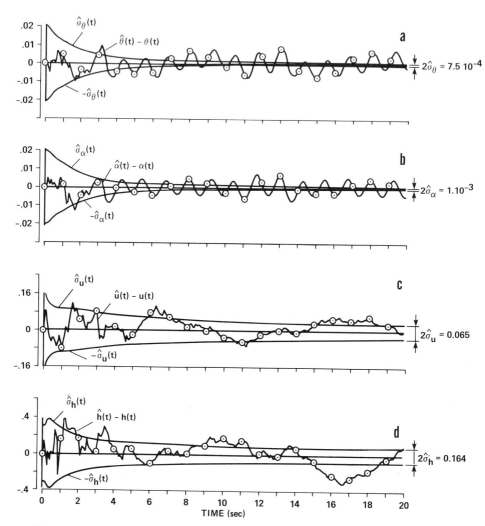

Fig. 6. Errors on the reconstructed flight-path quantities and estimated standard deviations bounds for $\Delta t_2 = 0.1$ sec. Same parts as in Fig. 5.

fact, we came to the conclusion in Section IV that the effect of modeling errors could be demonstrated by working on a computer with machine precision equal to the magnitude of the modeling errors. Therefore, the experimental results concerning modeling errors will be very similar to those presented in the previous subsection.

However, to demonstrate the results related to the discretization error given in Section V, we will perform a separate experiment. Here we focus on the reconstruction of the individual components of the state vector x_k. Again,

TABLE II. DIFFERENT KALMAN FILTER QUANTITIES FOR
TWO DIFFERENT Δt

Quantity	Δt_1	Δt_2
$\rho(F_\infty)$	$9.947 \cdot 10{-}1$	$9.895 \cdot 10{-}1$
$\|P_\infty\|$	$3.385 \cdot 10^{-3}$	$5.824 \cdot 10^{-3}$
$\|K_\infty\|$	$1.965 \cdot 10^{-2}$	$3.926 \cdot 10^{-2}$
$\|S_\infty\|$	$6.223 \cdot 10^{-2}$	$8.833 \cdot 10^{-2}$

the flight-path reconstruction problem, described in [10], will be used as a test vehicle. Instead of referring to the components of the state vector x_k by their corresponding indices, their actual "names" will be used. This is not relevant here, however; for a detailed outline of these individual state quantities we refer to [10]. The state vector of the considered flight-path reconstruction comprises the following four quantities:

(1) The angle of pitch $\theta(t)$;

(2) The angle of attack $\alpha(t)$;

(3) The component of the speed of the aircraft along its X axis, denoted by $u(t)$;

(4) The deviation of the reference altitude $\Delta h(t)$.

In the following experiment these quantities are reconstructed with a SRCF for two different discretization periods, i.e., $\Delta t_1 = 0.05$ sec and $\Delta t_2 = 0.1$ sec. The state reconstruction error, i.e., the difference between the reconstructed state variable and their corresponding true (or simulated) state variable, and the estimated standard deviation ($\hat{\sigma}$), given by the square root of the diagonal element of the error state covariance matrix, are plotted in Fig. 5 for Δt_1 and Fig. 6 for Δt_2. Some important numerical values are given in Table II.

From these experimental results we can make the following observations:

(1) The (Frobenius) norm of the error covariance matrix *increases* with larger Δt; see Table II. Also the estimated standard deviations of the errors on the reconstructed flight-path quantities *increases*, as follows from a comparison between the indicated 2σ values in Figs. 5 and 6. This confirms clearly that the design of a KF becomes *more conservative* by increasing the Δt, as is indicated by (74).

(2) The state reconstruction errors remain *bounded* for a higher Δt; see Fig. 6.

(3) For a larger Δt, $\|K_\infty\|$ increases and at the same time this causes the eigenvalues of $\|F_\infty\|$ to move more inside the unit circle. This is demonstrated by the smaller value of the spectral radius $\rho(F_\infty)$ for Δt_2 than for Δt_1; see Table II. However, the difference is very small. Therefore, the second term on the right-hand side of (76) indicates that the deterministic error will increase due to

the variation in the input signal over the larger discretization period. This can be clearly observed by comparing Figs. 5 and 6.

(4) The experimental results of Figs. 5 and 6 show that the decrease of $\rho(F_\infty)$ for the larger Δt, this results in larger random errors on the reconstructed state quantities. This phenomenon is compensated here by the increase of the estimated standard deviations. However, this influence is only minor.

These experimental results clearly demonstrate the practical value of the qualitative observations made in the analysis given in Section V.

VII. COMPARISON OF THE DIFFERENT FILTERS

In this section we compare the different filter implementations based on the error analysis of Sections III, IV, and V, and strengthened by the simulation study of Section VI.

We first look at the time-varying case (whence excluding the CSRF). According to the error bounds of Theorem 1, it appears that the SRCF has the lowest estimate for the *local* errors generated in a single step k. The *accumulated* errors during subsequent steps are governed by the quantities γ_k for all three filters in a similar fashion (at least for the error on the estimate) – this of course under the assumption that a "symmetrized" version of the CKF or the stabilized CKF is considered. From these modifications, the implementation computing only the upper (or lower) triangular part of the state error covariance matrix is the most efficient. The experiments of Section VI with the realistic flight-path reconstruction problem indeed demonstrate that the CKF, the SRCF, and the SRIF seem to yield a comparable accuracy for the estimates $\hat{x}_{k+1|k}$ or $\hat{x}_{k+1|k+1}$, unless some of the "influential" parameters in the error bounds of Theorem 1 become critical. This is, e.g., true for the SRIF, which is likely to give worse results when choosing matrices A_k, R_k, or Q_k that are hard to invert. As far as R_k or Q_k is concerned, this is in a sense an artificial disadvantage since in some situations the inverses R_k^{-1} and Q_k^{-1} are the given data and the matrices R_k and Q_k then have to be computed. This then would of course be a disadvantage for the SRCF. In [24] it is shown that the problems of inverting covariances can always be bypassed as well for the SRIF as for the SRCF. The problem of inverting A_k and T_k, on the other hand, is always present in the SRIF.

For the time-invariant case, the same comments as above hold for the accuracy of the CKF, SRCF, and SRIF. The fourth candidate, the CSRF, has in general a much poorer accuracy than the other three. This is now not due to pathologically chosen parameters, but to the simple fact that the accumulation of rounding errors from one step to another is usually much more significant than for the three other filters, as was pointed out in Section III. This is particularly the case when the signature matrix Σ is not the identity matrix, which may then lead to divergence, as shown experimentally in Section VI,C.

From the above outline, the SRCF appears to be the most reliable KF implementation for the flight-path reconstruction problem analyzed. What is important here is that this conclusion is drawn "independently" from the theoretical error analysis study given in Section III. The simulation study of Section VI only emphasizes and confirms this conclusion.

For a more detailed comparison the aspect of numerical efficiency should of course also be considered. This algorithmic aspect is much easier to evaluate, e.g., by an operation count or mere timing. This then also depends on the numerical mechanization chosen, the actual computer configuration, etc. Because of all these "practicalities," this topic is not considered here.

VIII. CONCLUDING REMARKS

In this article we have analyzed four different KF algorithms for their reliability. We note here that our implementations may differ substantially from similarly named algorithms described in [7]. The comparison is based on an error analysis.

From the error models a better insight is also obtained into which parameters influence the error propagation in the different KF algorithms that have been investigated. For the CKF and the SRCF these are the condition number of the innovation signal covariance matrix R_k^e and the spectral norm (radius) of the filter state transition matrix F_k, while for the SRIF the relevant parameters are the condition numbers of R_k, Q_k, Q_k^e, A_k, and of the Choleski factor T_k and the spectral norm (radius) of the filter state transition matrix $\tilde{F}_k$. For the CSRF the choice of the initial error covariance matrix $P_{0|-1}$ matrix and of the condition number of the innovation signal covariance matrix R_k^e become critical. This influence is also verified by the simulation study of the flight-path reconstruction problem [10] given in Section VI.

IX. APPENDIX A: ERROR ANALYSIS OF SOME BASIC LINEAR ALGEBRA PROBLEMS

Here we briefly recall the propagation of rounding errors in some basic problems in linear algebra. The norm used is the 2-norm.

Let the matrix–vector pair (A, b) be known with relative precision δ_a and δ_b, respectively:

$$\delta_a = \| \delta A \| / \| A \|, \qquad \delta_b = \| \delta b \| / \| b \|,$$

then we have the following lemma (assuming A to be invertible).

Lemma A.1 [25]. The errors on the products $A \cdot b$ and $A^{-1} \cdot b$ can be bounded by

$$\left\| \overline{(A \cdot b)} - (A \cdot b) \right\| \leq \left(\delta_a + \delta_b \right) \cdot \| A \| \cdot \| b \| + O(\delta^2)$$

$$\left\| \overline{\left(A^{-1} \cdot b\right)} - (A^{-1} \cdot b) \right\| \leq \delta_a \cdot \kappa(A) \cdot \left\| A^{-1} b \right\|$$
$$+ \delta_b \cdot \left\| A^{-1} \right\| \cdot \|b\| + O(\delta^2).$$

When the errors δ_a and δ_b are the backward errors of the above problem solved on a computer with machine precision ϵ, then the above bounds are reasonably well approximated by:

$$\left\| \overline{(A \cdot b)} - (A \cdot b) \right\| \leq \epsilon_1 \cdot \| A \| \cdot \| b \| \approx \epsilon_2 \cdot \| A \cdot b \|$$

$$\left\| \overline{\left(A^{-1} \cdot b\right)} - (A^{-1} \cdot b) \right\| \leq \epsilon_3 \cdot \kappa(A) \cdot \left\| A^{-1} \cdot b \right\|$$

where all ϵ_i are of order ϵ.

The above approximation implies that no serious cancellations occur in the product $A \cdot b$, which in general is a reasonable assumption.

Let A now be an $m \times n$ matrix of rank $n < m$ and transform the compound matrix $[A \mid b]$ by a unitary transformation Q as follows:

$$Q[A \mid b] = \begin{pmatrix} A_1 & \mid & b_1 \\ 0 & \mid & b_2 \end{pmatrix},$$

where A_1 is now invertible. Then we have the following lemma (where the plus superscript denotes the generalized inverse of a matrix).

Lemma A.2 [19]. The errors on the least-squares solution $A^+ \cdot b$ and the residual b_2 can be bounded by

$$\left\| \overline{\left(A^+ \cdot b\right)} - (A^+ \cdot b) \right\| \leq \delta_a \cdot \{\kappa(A) \cdot \left\| A^+ \cdot b \right\|$$
$$+ \kappa(A) \cdot \|A^+\| \cdot \|b_2\|\} + \delta_b \cdot \|A^+\| \cdot \|b\| + O(\delta^2)$$

$$\left\| \overline{(b_2)} - (b_2) \right\| \leq \delta_a \cdot \kappa(A) \cdot \|b\| + \delta_b \cdot \|b\| + O(\delta^2).$$

When the errors δ_a and δ_b are the backward errors of the above problems solved on a computer with machine precision ϵ, then they are both of order ϵ, and the above bounds are reasonably well approximated by:

$$\left\| \overline{(A^+ \cdot b)} - (A^+ \cdot b) \right\| \leq \epsilon_4 \cdot \{\kappa(A) \cdot \left\| A^+ \cdot b \right\|$$

$$+ \kappa(A) \cdot \left\| A^+ \right\| \cdot \left\| b_2 \right\| + \left\| A^+ \right\| \cdot \left\| b_2 \right\| / \cos\varphi\}$$

$$\left\| \overline{(b_2)} - (b_2) \right\| \leq \epsilon_5 \cdot \{1 + \kappa(A)\} \cdot \left\| b_2 \right\| / \cos\varphi,$$

where all ϵ_i are of order ϵ and $\cos\varphi = \|b_2\|/\|b\|$.

We terminate with perturbation bounds on the QR factorization of a matrix A.

Lemma A.3 [26]. Let $A = Q \cdot R$, where A has full column rank n, $Q' \cdot Q = I_n$, and R is upper triangular. Then for a small perturbation $\overline{A}$ of A there exist perturbations $\overline{Q}$ and $\overline{R}$ of the factors, such that

$$\overline{A} = \overline{Q} \cdot \overline{R}$$

and

$$(A - \overline{A}) = Q \cdot (R - \overline{R}) + \Delta$$

with

$$\| \Delta \| \leq \left[\delta_a \cdot \kappa(A) \right]^2 \cdot \| A \|.$$

When the error δ_a is the backward error of the above decomposition solved on a computer with machine precision ϵ, then it is of order ϵ and the above bound becomes

$$\| \Delta \| \leq \epsilon_6^2 \cdot \kappa(A)^2 \cdot \| A \|.$$

A similar result can also be found for a "skew decomposition," i.e., where $Q' \cdot \Sigma \cdot Q = \Sigma$, for some signature matrix Σ.

Although all these bounds are written for the 2-norm, they also hold for several other norms, up to a constant which is close to 1 and can therefore be absorbed in the ϵ_i. This is, e.g., important when deriving the above bounds for a matrix B instead of a vector b. This is done by using the bounds for each column b_i of the matrix B and combining these bounds into a bound involving the norm of B, for which in this case the Frobenius norm is a natural choice [20]. These mixed bounds (as far as norms are concerned) can then again be formulated in terms of one norm only, by again adapting the ϵ_i appropriately.

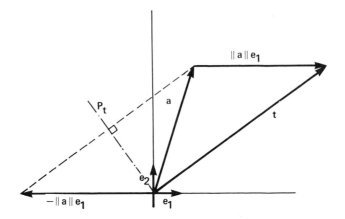

Fig. 7. The Householder transformation in the two-dimensional space. (e_1, e_2) represents the natural orthonormal base.

X.   APPENDIX B: THE SKEW HOUSEHOLDER TRANSFORMATION

A.   THE CLASSICAL HOUSEHOLDER TRANSFORMATION

The "classical" Householder transformation is designed to map a chosen vector a onto a basic vector e_i of the natural orthogonal basis, but reflected from its initial orientation in the direction of that basis vector. This is schematically illustrated in Fig. 7 for the two-dimensional case.

From Fig. 7 we observe that we may start by constructing the vector $t = a + \|a\|e_1$. Thus a vector with the same coordinates as a except for the first coordinate, which is $a_1 + \|a\|$. We then construct the plane P_t, perpendicular to t and passing through the origin. The mapping that reflects all vectors through this plane is given by the transformation

$$H = (I - tt'/t'a), \tag{86}$$

where I denotes the identity matrix of appropriate order. Reflecting an arbitrary vector a towards the i-th basis vector of the natural orthogonal space with the same 2-norm, the vector t in (86) becomes $a + sgn(a_i) \cdot \|a\| \cdot e_i$, with $sgn(a_i)$ denoting the sign of the i-th coordinate of the a vector in the natural orthogonal space. The Householder transformation matrix H in (86) can be written equivalently as:

$$H = I - (2tt'/t't) \tag{87}$$

If we denote $t/\|t\|_2$ by u, then we obtain

$$H = (I - 2uu'), \quad \text{with} \quad \|u\|_2 = 1. \tag{88}$$

B. THE OPERATION OF THE SKEW HOUSEHOLDER TRANSFORMATION

The skew Householder transformation acts in a similar way to the classical Householder transformation, but preserves the Σ-norm of the transformed vector. Let us first define this norm.

Definition B.1. The Σ-norm of a vector x is the product:

$$(x'\Sigma x)^{1/2} \tag{89}$$

for some particular signature matrix Σ and is denoted as $\|x\|_\Sigma$.

Now to reflect a vector to a chosen i-th basis vector of the natural orthogonal space with the same Σ-norm, the transformation matrix H_Σ is chosen as follows:

$$H_\Sigma = I - 2uu'\Sigma, \quad \text{with} \quad \|u\|_\Sigma = 1. \tag{90}$$

That this is the correct solution will be verified in the following. First, we will verify whether the defined transformation H_Σ is Σ-orthogonal. Therefore, the product $H_\Sigma\Sigma H_\Sigma'$ has to be Σ. Using (90) this product becomes:

$$H_\Sigma\Sigma H_\Sigma' = (I - 2uu'\Sigma)\Sigma(I - 2\Sigma uu')$$

$$= \Sigma - 2uu' - 2uu' + 4uu'\Sigma uu'.$$

Since $\|u\|_\Sigma = 1$, the proposed transformation matrix is indeed Σ-orthogonal. Furthermore, it can easily be verified in a similar way that $H_\Sigma^2 = I$.

Second, we will now construct H_Σ transforming a vector a to a vector oriented along e_1 with the same Σ-norm. The construction of the transformation H_Σ goes as follows. Define a vector w accordingly:

$$w = a + \text{sgn}(a_1)\|a\|_\Sigma e_1. \tag{91}$$

In the subsequent derivation, the $\text{sgn}(a_1)$ will be assumed to be $+1$. The Σ-norm of w is

$$\|w\|_\Sigma^2 = 2(\|a\|_\Sigma^2 + \|a\|_\Sigma a_1) \neq 0. \tag{92}$$

Now u in (90) is chosen as $w/\|w\|_\Sigma$. This choice is verified by applying H_Σ to the vector a, where we make use of (91):

$$
\begin{aligned}
H_\Sigma a &= (1 - 2uu'\Sigma)a \\
&= a - 2\frac{ww'\Sigma a}{\|w\|_\Sigma^2} \\
&= a - \frac{\left(a + \|a\|_\Sigma e_1\right)\|w\|_\Sigma^2}{\|w\|_\Sigma^2} \\
&= -\|a\|_\Sigma e_1
\end{aligned}
\tag{93}
$$

which was desired.

ACKNOWLEDGMENTS

The authors would like to thank B. D. O. Anderson for pointing out the use of Lemma 2 in the theoretical error analysis of Section III,A and G. Bierman for many constructive remarks on the first draft.

REFERENCES

1. R. E. KALMAN, *J. Basic Eng.* **82**, 34–45 (1960).
2. A. H. JAZWINSKI, "Stochastic Processes and Filtering Theory," Academic Press, New York, 1970.
3. G. J. BIERMAN and C. L. THORNTON, *Automatica* **13**, 23–35 (1977).
4. A. E. BRYSON, *Int. J. Guidance Control* **1**, No. 1, 71–79 (1978).
5. R. E. BATTIN, "Astronautical Guidance," pp. 303–340. McGraw-Hill, New York, 1964.
6. P. G. KAMINSKI, A. BRYSON, and S. SCHMIDT, *IEEE Trans. Autom. Control* **AC-16**, 727–737 (1971).
7. G. J. BIERMAN, "Factorization Methods for Discrete Sequential Estimation," Academic Press, New York, 1977.
8. B. D. O. ANDERSON and J. B. MOORE, "Optimal Filtering," Prentice-Hall, Information and System Sciences Series, Englewood Cliffs, New Jersey, 1979.
9. M. H. VERHAEGEN, "A New Class of Algorithms in Linear System Theory, with Application to Real-time Aircraft Model Identification," Ph.D. Dissertation, Catholic University of Leuven, Leuven (1985).
10. M. H. VERHAEGEN, *AIAA J. Guidance, Control Dyn.* (1987).
11. G. H. GOLUB, *Numer. Math.* **7**, 206–216 (1965).
12. T. KAILATH, *IEEE Trans. Inf. Theory* **IT-19**, 750–760 (1973).
13. M. MORF and T. KAILATH, *IEEE Trans. Autom. Control* **AC-20**, 487–497 (1975).
14. F. R. GANTMACHER, "The Theory of Matrices," Chelsea, New York, 1960.

15. B. D. O. ANDERSON and J. B. MOORE, *SIAM J. Control Optim.* **19**, No. 1, 20–32 (1981).
16. D. D. SILJAK, "Nonlinear Systems," Wiley, New York, 1969.
17. R. E. BELLMAN, "Matrix Analysis," 2nd ed., McGraw-Hill, New York, 1968.
18. G. W. STEWART, *SIAM Rev.* **19**, 634–662 (1977).
19. A. VAN DER SLUIS, *Numer. Math.* **23**, 241–254 (1975).
20. G. W. STEWART, "Introduction to Matrix Computations," Academic Press, New York, 1973.
21. G. FRANKLIN and J. POWELL, "Digital Control of Dynamic Systems," Addison-Wesley, California, 1980.
22. C. VAN LOAN, *IEEE Trans. Autom. Control* **AC-23**, 395–404 (1978).
23. M. H. VERHAEGEN and P. VAN DOOREN, in "Proceedings of the INRIA Conference on Analysis and Optimization of Systems, Nice," Vol. 62–63, pp. 250–267. Springer-Verlag, Berlin and New York, 1984.
24. C. C. PAIGE, "Special Issue of Contemporary Mathematics on Linear Algebra and its Role in Systems Theory," Am. Math. Soc., Providence, Rhode Island, 1985.
25. J. H. WILKINSON, "The Algebraic Eigenvalue Problem," Oxford Univ. Press (Clarendon), London and New York, 1965.
26. G. W. STEWART, *SIAM J. Numer. Anal.* **14**, 509–518 (1977).

ALGORITHMS FOR SYSTEM FAULT DETECTION THROUGH MODELING AND ESTIMATION TECHNIQUES

HAGOP PANOSSIAN

Rockwell International
Rocketdyne Division
6633 Canoga Avenue
Canoga Park, California 91303

I. INTRODUCTION

The technological leaps of the past decades in computers, electronics, optics, and advanced, high-performance, complex control systems have created the need for extra reliability and safety. An underlying feature of all "safety critical" systems entails a reliable fault-detection (and often isolation and reconfiguration) system. The conventional methods of fault detection, such as use of regular limits, thresholds, and trend checks, are surpassed nowadays by the application of algorithms on modern digital computers and microcomputers with the integration of advanced sensors and actuators. One of the disadvantages of conventional techniques is the frequent occurrence of false alarms when the limits are located below failure points. Also, when the limits or thresholds are close to the failure points, then detection occurs after failure and the resulting damage. Sophisticated measurement systems, with ultrahigh sensitivity sensors, have made early fault detection and isolation possible through the appropriate use of measurable signals and outputs. A whole range of system faults can now be detected and identified via application of computers to analytical process and signal models. Both signal prediction and estimation of nonmeasurable state variables, as well as process parameters (and other characteristic features), can be carried out relatively easily now more than ever. Moreover, performance monitoring through artificial intelligence and expert systems application has opened new doors to future system fault detection and identification [1]. Failure detection through modern techniques of estimation and software implementation via expert systems can predict failures prior to occurrence and thus avoid damage. One important application of digital control instrumentation concerns systems with the requirement of reorganization (reconfiguration) following failures in sensors and actuators. Redundancy of components (hardware redundancy) provides the means of reorganization for sensors via appropriate routing schemes. However, the above-mentioned reorganization can be accomplished only if sufficient duplication of function exists between the actuators or the sensors in a given system [2, 3].

Failure detection and isolation may also be carried out via analytical means, when redundancy exists between dissimilar components. To utilize this form of redundancy, however, one must be fully aware of the dynamic behavior of the whole system as well as its constituent components.

During the past decade, mathematics and engineering have been increasingly involved in the decision-making processes of many complex systems. The underlying inspiration for such a trend is mainly the significant economic benefits that usually result from proper decisions concerning the optimal distribution of costly resources. It has been demonstrated that such problems can often be realistically formulated and mathematically analyzed to obtain the best decision. Computers have played a fundamental role in the development and wide application of the science of decision making. Simultaneously, computers have revolutionized and tremendously extended the application of mathematics and control theory by making the solution of numerous complex problems possible. Analytical redundancy is a good example of these problems [4].

Dynamical systems with uncertainties, or stochastic systems, have to be treated differently from deterministic systems when concerning detection of sudden changes, such as failures [5]. The design methods for failure detection of such systems range from the application of specialized failure-sensitive filters, to the use of filter innovations via statistical data, to the derivations of jump process formulations. When unexpected random changes, such as component failures or abrupt variations in operating conditions, cause appreciable degradation of system performance (enough to cause serious concern), then the situation at hand can be called a "failure." For continued satisfactory performance of a system, a fundamental issue is the prompt detection and identification of such failures and the appropriate correction measures to be taken [6].

Many researchers have treated the problem of fault detection through mathematical modeling and estimation algorithms. Survey papers dealing with various failure modes, different fault detection techniques, and numerous application examples have been written recently [1, 5]. Processes with random transition failures were treated with the application of maximum-likelihood estimation by Friedland [7] and Friedland and Grabowsky [8]. The bias in the linear dynamic system is estimated herein using residuals, and appropriate correction measures are suggested. A generalized likelihood test approach for failure detection and isolation in redundant sensor configurations was presented by Daly et al. [9], following Willsky and Jones [10, 11] and Carlson [12]. The approach in [9] essentially involves formulation of a composite hypothesis testing problem and using generalized likelihood tests for the derivation of the decision functions. An on-board failure-detection and identification method for dual redundant sensors on the NASA F8C digital fly-by-wire aircraft was presented [13]. Mehra and Peschon [14] have come up with a few possible statistical tests that can be performed on the innovations of a process. Among these, the chi-squared test was applied in [15]. Texts that treat various fault-detection and identification methods and that give a relatively wide perspective on the problem are by Van Trees [16], Pau [17], and Himmelblau [18]. Most of the research in the area of fault detection and identification deals with situations where adequate measurement data are available. Less research exists for situations whereby rate variables are not measurable directly. Moreover, even less published literature exists on fault detection and identification for systems with nonmeasurable process parameters and characteristic quantities such as efficiency, energy consumption, etc. [1].

In this article, algorithms will be reviewed that are of general use for system fault detection and identification via mathematical modeling. Some of the recent developments in fault detection for dynamic systems will be briefly discussed, and various approaches to the solution of the generalized failure-detection and identification problem will be presented.

Fault-detection system design involves several complex issues, such as quick response prior to significant performance degradation as well as consideration of system redundancy. Moreover, advanced fault-detection algorithms, based on careful consideration of system dynamic characteristics, can often lead to significant reduction of hardware redundancy. Tradeoff studies that consider hardware redundancy, algorithmic complexity, and computational requirements should be carried out in order to determine an optimal implementation scheme. System complexity versus performance, modular versus parallel implementation, as well as a practical range of implementation options should all be under consideration prior to a final fault-detection methodology.

Classification of failure-detection methods into groups with common characteristics is a nontrivial matter [1, 5]. However, in order to be able to evaluate the most common fault-detection approaches by underlining their advantages and disadvantages, a formal categorization is necessary. System reorganization or reconfiguration subsequent to the detection of a fault and the formal design of "fault-tolerant" control systems, which perform satisfactorily even under significant changes in their operating conditions, are also very important issues that will be treated very briefly in the present article.

There are three main concerns in fault detection and identification. The primary objective is to establish that a failure has occurred. The type and location of failure as well as the extent of degradation are the two remaining tasks that should be addressed appropriately. The principal thrust of the present article concerns the detection problem. However, many research papers exist that deal with problems related to failure analysis, reorganization, and probability of systems with large changes. For closed-loop control systems [19–22] deal with adaptive "fault-tolerant" control system design. Moreover, stochastic system stability under changing characteristics is considered by [23–25]. The interested reader is referred to the above-mentioned articles for details.

II. THE FAULT-DETECTION PROBLEM

Advanced control systems with very high reliability requirements will be a commonplace application in the future, especially those that will have numerous components built to operate a number of years on space vehicles. Systems of this type will probably employ highly sophisticated fault-tolerant control systems with redundancy and reconfiguration capability [26–28]. An active approach to the design of fault-tolerant control systems entails detection and identification of faulty components and reorganization of the control system for failure accommodation. Hence, failure detection and identification form an inseparable part of complex control systems whereby residuals are generated and are utilized for optimal decision [5]. The residual generation approach can be summarized (Fig. 1) as a process where the measurement signals and the command actuation signals are taken as inputs to the residual generator and a vector of residuals is generated with a close to zero magnitude when no failure has occurred and with an appreciable positive magnitude when a component has failed. The above-mentioned process is carried out by simply subtracting the outputs of two identical sensors that measure the same thing. When one of the sensors fails, the residual is used to detect its failure [6]. This is referred to as "direct redundancy."

An alternate approach for residual generation is "temporal redundancy," which manipulates the histories of sensor outputs and actuator inputs. This approach relies heavily on the model of the dynamic system relating sensor outputs and actuator inputs. Actuator failures are assumed to be bias failures [6, 8]. Beard [29] and Jones [30] proposed a different approach to residual generation by designing a special observer that accentuates the influence of failure on the innovation of the observer. Here the observer gain is chosen in such a manner that the direction of the innovation vector in the output space can be used to identify the failed component. In [31] a geometric approach to this problem was described that solves the above-mentioned "Beard–Jones" problem and illustrates its duality with the restricted control decoupling problem.

A.   THE CONTINUOUS-TIME CASE

Consider the following state-space representation of a dynamic system linearized about a nominal operating point for implementation purposes:

$$\dot{x}(t) = Ax(t) + Bu(t) + \xi(t) \tag{1}$$

with a measurement system given by

$$y(t) = Cx(t) + Du(t) + \gamma(t), \tag{2}$$

where $x \in R^n$ is the state vector, $u \in R^m$ is the known input vector, $y \in R^p$ is the measurement vector, A, B, C, D are constant matrices of appropriate dimensions, and ξ and γ are zero-mean, independent, white Gaussian noise vectors with intensities

$$E\left[\xi(t)\xi^T(\tau)\right] = Q\,\delta(t-\tau), \quad E\left[\gamma(t)\gamma^T(\tau)\right] = R\,\delta(t-\tau),$$

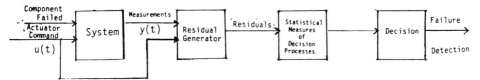

Fig. 1. Residual generator and failure detection.

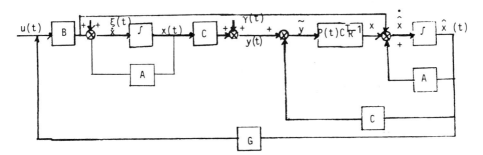

Fig. 2. Continuous-time system compensator model.

where δ is the Kronecker delta operator. The above equations are supposed to represent the normal operation (no failure) of the system at hand. Thus, under normal operating conditions, the optimal state estimates are given by the Kalman filter

$$\dot{\hat{x}}(t) = A\hat{x}(t) + Bu(t) + K(t)[y(t) - C\hat{x}(t)], \quad \hat{x}((0) = \hat{x}_0 \tag{3}$$

$$\dot{P}(t) = AP(t) + P(t)A^T - K(t)RK^T(t) + Q, \quad P(0) = P_0 \tag{4}$$

and the Kalman gain matrix is given by

$$K(t) = PC^T R^{-1}. \tag{5}$$

In the above equations, $P(t)$ is the estimation error covariance matrix of the estimates $\hat{x}(t)$. In the case when a closed-loop control law is utilized for better performance, the linear feedback control law is given by:

$$u(t) = -G(t)\hat{x}(t) \tag{6}$$

then the normal operating condition (Fig. 2) results.

The fault-detection problem of abrupt changes in the system modeled by (1) and (2) can be carried out [5] through

(1) "Fault-sensitive filters," in which the Kalman gain matrix $K(t)$ is so chosen that specific failure modes appear as residuals $\tilde{y}(t)$ [29, 30]. This is a deterministic approach.

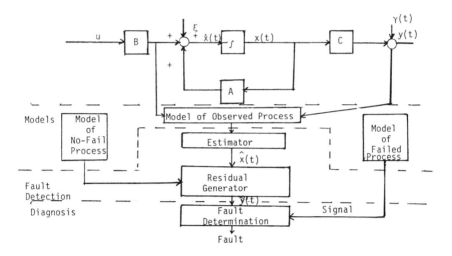

Fig. 3. Fault-detection system with state estimation.

(2) Whiteness and chi-squared tests of the residuals of the regular Kalman filter [14].

(3) A bank of Kalman filters with appropriate likelihood tests to determine the most likely models [2, 3].

(4) Generalized likelihood ratio tests that correlate observed residuals with *a priori* computed filter responses due to a particular failure [10].

The latter two methods are stochastic techniques [32]. All the above-mentioned methods assume a correct model of the system and measurement equations as well as the input signals. A block diagram of state-space techniques for fault detection is depicted in Fig. 3.

B.   THE DISCRETE-TIME CASE

Given the following linear stochastic discrete-time model in the state-space form

$$x(k + 1) = \Phi(k)x(k) + \Gamma(k)u(k) + \omega(k) \tag{7}$$

with the sensor dynamics of:

$$y(k) = \theta(k)x(k) + \nu(k), \tag{8}$$

where x, u, and y are as previously defined, Φ, Γ, and θ are constant matrices of appropriate dimensions, and ω and ν are zero-mean, independent, white Gaussian noise sequences with covariances given by:

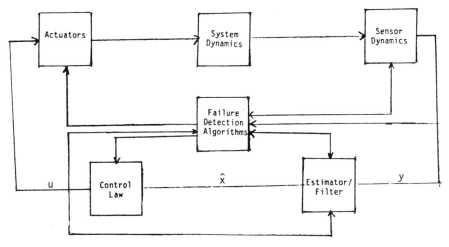

Fig. 4. Failure-detection system.

$$E\left[\omega(i)\omega^T(j)\right] = W\delta_{ij}$$

$$E\left[\nu(i)\nu^T(j)\right] = V\delta_{ij},$$

where δ_{ij} is the Kronecker delta operator. Under no failure, the normal optimal state estimator is the discrete Kalman filter

$$\hat{x}(k + 1/k) = \Phi(k)\hat{x}(k/k) + \gamma(k)u(k) \tag{9}$$

$$\hat{x}(k/k) = \hat{x}(k/k - 1) + K(k)\left[y(k) - \theta(k)\hat{x}(k/k - 1)\right] \tag{10}$$

$$P(k + 1/k) = \Phi(k)P(k/k)\Phi_T(k) + W \tag{11}$$

$$S(k) = \theta(k)P(k/k - 1)\theta^T(k) + V \tag{12}$$

$$K(k) = P(k/k - 1)\theta^T(k)S^{-1}(k) \tag{13}$$

$$P(k/k) = P(k/k - 1) - K(k)\theta(k)P(k/k - 1), \tag{14}$$

where $P(i/j)$ is the covariance of the estimation error, and $S(k)$ is the covariance of the innovations [the quantity in the square brackets in (10)]. The closed-loop control algorithm is normally given by

$$u(k) = G(k)\hat{x}(k/k). \tag{15}$$

As depicted in Fig. 4, when changes occur in the normal functioning of the control system, the detection algorithm will be able to monitor and detect the failure and accordingly induce adjustments. Of course, isolation of failures is a relatively sophisticated software problem. However, a tradeoff between hardware redundancy and software capabilities with the ensuing computational burden should be carried out and the corrective measures should be determined accordingly.

III. VARIOUS APPROACHES TO FAULT DETECTION

Generalized parity checks or analytical redundancy relations are exploited in all fault-detection systems. Time histories of measured outputs are utilized in the form of functions or relations that are very small in magnitude under normal operation. Virtually all approaches to failure detection use a dynamic model for the design of algorithms via the implicit use of the above-mentioned relations.

In order to be able to identify individual relationships of components and functions, an explicit (rather than implicit) use of the "most reliable" redundancy relations is more desirable. This way, a general method can be formulated that, according to some criterion of the degree of reliability of a specific redundancy scheme, will be relatively insensitive to modeling errors and approximations [33]. In this section, a general overview of various approaches that are common in failure detection systems will be presented and briefly discussed. The various techniques involved in fault-detection schemes are based on essentially different failure models, and each method has a different hypothetical model that is a variation of (1), (2) or (7), (8). The differences in the dynamics as well as in the fault models could be significant. One underlying feature of the models is that they indicate the basis for the method used and thus furnish information on the applicability and the advantages of each technique [5].

A.   "FAILURE (FAULT)-SENSITIVE'
     FILTERING ALGORITHMS

This is a deterministic approach whereby the feedback gain matrix K in (3) [or (10)] is so chosen as to make specific failure modes appear as residuals in a given direction or in a known plane. The underlying reason for such an approach is, as has been observed by many researchers [34–37], that the above-mentioned optimal filters perform adequately under insignificant modeling errors and that the state estimates might diverge under appreciable (high) unmodeled dynamics and the singularity of the error covariance matrix P. The filter becomes essentially oblivious to new measurements and relies heavily on old ones for its estimates, thus performing very poorly. It is desirable to develop a filter that will respond promptly to abrupt changes and be amenable to new data. Examples of such filters are the "exponentially age-weighted" filter [34, 35] and the limited memory filter [36]. Other measures that increase the sensitivity of the filter to new data are fixing the gains and artificially increasing the noise covariance. However, this type of artificial remedy causes the filter to become more sensitive to sensor noise and be degraded under normal (no-fault) operation. In such circumstances, it is suggested that a dual mode filtering algorithm be utilized, whereby the regular optimal filter would be the principal filter and a fault-sensitive filter will be activated only under faults [5, 16]. All of the above-mentioned methods yield an indirect approach to fault detection.

Methods that are designed to signal an alert under particular faults have also been developed [39, 40]. Failure modes, such as biases, are considered as state variables and are estimated in this technique. Pronounced difference from a predetermined value is an indication of failure, thus leading to an alarm signal. The "two-ellipsoid overlap" decision rule for fault detection described in [39] and [40] provides estimation (and even fault detection and isolation) at the expense of increased order and some degree of performance degradation (under normal operation).

B.   USE OF MULTIPLE FILTERS

A "bank" of linear observers or filters based on various hypotheses of faulty conditions and one of normal operation condition are often utilized in fault-detection systems. The underlying feature of this approach is the selection of multiple sets of system matrices, with separate filters for each model, and computation of the conditional probabilities for use to identify the correct model [41]. Changes in system performance is reflected in changes in the above-mentioned probabilities.

Methods of fault detection basedon the comparison of multiple hypotheses are also used via multiple filters and appropriate likelihood function s [42]. By assigning the hypotheses H_0 to the normal operation condition (no fault) and H_i, $i = 1, ..., n$, for n different failure modes and by computing and using the residuals of each filter, appropriate likelihood functions (failure probabilities) for H_i are generated that give an indication of fault. Sometimes the innovation of each filter can be utilized and the hypothesis with the maximum likelihood can be chosen as the failure mode [43]. The main concern is usually the detection of abrupt changes in the state variable (or components of it). There is a state-space model of the form given in systems (1), (2) or (7), (8) above. The variations in the states are normally modeled as shifts and the probability density fucntions of the additive noise terms in (1) [$\xi(t)$] or in (7) [w(k)] are so chosen as to reflect the characteristics of the random variations of the states. Implementation of such procedures requires a large number of filters that will grow exponentially as the order of the system states grows. In order to avoid this exponential growth, a number of approximations have been suggested [5, 43].

One of the disadvantages of the multiple filter approach is its extreme complexity. However, considering the recent developments in the computer and software implementation areas involving parallel processing, it is conceivable that a part of the above-mentioned complexities could be overcome. Moreover, utilization of reduced-order observers could increase the practicality of such an approach. Even so, the possibility exists that differences in hypotheses may not be detected, thus leading to sluggish performance of the fault-detection system. Nevertheless, such multiple hypothesis fault-detection schemes are useful in establishing tradeoffs with simpler techniques and in providing insight into the dynamics and characteristics of the fault propagation and identification [15].

Various techniques exist for detecting successive switchings from one model to another [5]. When switching from one model to the next, in a two-model situation (a no-fault model and a faulty model), whereby the two dynamic models have different process noise covariances, one can reduce the exponential growth to a linear growth in the number of filters required [44]. In this technique, the hypothesis is that the process has just changed once. Moreover, the linear growth could also be eliminated, under certain conditions, by utilizing a decision rule based on the sequential probability ratio test [45]. The *a posteriori* probabilities of the two models are computed in this technique, under the assumption that two hypotheses are already given, such as switching of the process (or not) at time k [46]. The ratio of the logarithm of the two probabilities is compared to two predetermined thresholds and, if it is greater than one or less than the other, an appropriate decision rule is followed to stop the process. In [44], an "occasional" test approach was proposed, whereby a single sequential probability ratio test is first performed and, as a decision is made, a new hypothesis is initiated and the test starts all over again. Presumably, a change could occur while a test is in progress and the algorithm may not be able to respond optimally due to the delay in responding during the next test.

Another development in this area is special techniques for the rejection of measurements that have a "great deal" of noise [47]. Each of the measurements has a primary random variable $g(k)$ with a value 1 when it is a "good" measurement and a 0 when "bad" (pure noise). In this reference, a maximum likelihood approach is used to estimate the set of possibilities for all the times k of interest. In all of these types of approaches, a desirable element is of course to be able to remove bad measurements and to give some adaptive characteristic to the filter utilized.

C.   THE INNOVATIONS APPROACH

Anomalous behavior can often be identified through fault-detection methods that monitor the innovations of the filter used for estimating the required states or parameters. This type of approach involves the monitoring of the magnitude of the innovations of the filter in use based upon a predetermined hypothesis of the normal operating condition of the system at hand. Moreover, the overall system with the appropriate feedback controller and the corresponding filter provides desirable characteristics for better performance [14]. Several tests that can be carried out on the innovations process via statistical means, such as the chi-squared, the "whiteness," and the generalized likelihood ratio tests, are of widespread use in various fault-detection systems.

In order to illustrate the use of the innovations process, consider

$$\alpha(y) = y(t) - C\hat{x}(t) \tag{16}$$

in (3) and

$$\beta(k) = y(k) - \theta(k)\hat{x}(k/k - 1) \tag{17}$$

in (10) for the discrete-time case. Then, under normal operation, the above processes are both zero-mean and white with given covariances of $U(t)$ and $V(k)$, respectively. A quadratic weighted sum of the innovations (with the inverses of the covariances as weights) is usually considered as the appropriate chi-squared random variable, whose magnitude is associated with a threshold and a decision-making of a fault-detection criterion [5, 15]. Consequently, using chi-squared tables, the probability of a false alarm is calculated based on the innovations "window length" [15] and the decision threshold. This technique is essentially an alarm or signal alert method. Thus, faults that influence the innovations process the most are detected without being isolated or identified. It is a relatively simple scheme to implement. However, failures that occur due to slow variations, in a rather subtle manner, are very difficult to detect with this approach. In certain situations, fault detection via simultaneous isolation and state (parameter estimation) using the innovations approach lead to more reliable results and better performance than the multiple hypotheses method. Thus, it is possible to evaluate different components of the innovations process (especially for sensor failures) in order to obtain more information that helps isolate the fault [16].

Another, more general innovations-based approach, where the effect of faults on system innovations are utilized in the decision process, is generally known as the generalized likelihood ratio (GLR) method. This technique furnishes a reliable means for making optimal decisions for fault detection. Moreover, with this method, most often failure identification for system reconfiguration after a fault can be successfully carried out, with appropriate tradeoffs between complexity and performance [48–50]. The GLR technique is amenable to a wide variety of actuator and sensor failure-detection and isolation problems.

The underlying features of the GLR method involves extraction of failure information via functional redundancy and monitoring the innovations from the output of a Kalman filter or an appropriate observer (Fig. 5). Multiple threshold comparisons and simple correlation operations based on the filter innovations detect the occurrence of sudden changes in systems with linear characteristics.

In systems of the form of (1), (2) and (7), (8), an additional term can be included that introduces the effects of abrupt changes and biases [5]. Thus, (1) and (2) become:

$$\dot{x}(t) = Ax(t) + Bu(t) + \xi(t) + \rho\ \delta(t - \theta) \tag{18}$$

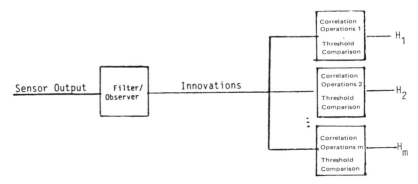

Fig. 5. Generalized likelihood ratio test schematic.

$$y(t) = Cx(t) + Du(y) + \gamma(t) + \rho\ \delta(t - \theta) \tag{19}$$

where ρ is an n-dimensional unknown vector, θ, is the unknown time of failure, and δ is the delta function. Furthermore, in systems of the form of (7) and (8), similar formulations lead to the following:

$$
\begin{aligned}
x(k + 1) &= \Phi(k)x(k) + \Gamma(k)u(k) + \omega(k) \\
&\quad + \rho s(k + 1, \theta)
\end{aligned}
\tag{20}
$$

$$y(k) = \theta(k)x(k) + \nu(k) + \rho\sigma(k, \theta) \tag{21}$$

where $\sigma(i, j)$ takes the value 1 for all $i \geq j$ and zero for $i < j$. The applications of such models are for various changes, such as bias states or actuation system failures [29, 30].

The most general form of the nonwhite residual that might be produced by the failure of a system is given by:

$$\alpha(t) = G_i\ (t, \theta)\rho + \overline{\alpha}(t)$$

$$\beta(k) = G_i\ (k, \theta)\rho + \overline{\beta}(k), \tag{22}$$

where G_i describes the effect of failure α or β that is of type i and that occurs at a time θ on a residual at time k or t. A set of hypotheses is usually established (H_0 = no fault, H_i = faults of type i). (22) is for the discrete time case. Here $\overline{\alpha}(t)$ and $\overline{\beta}(k)$ are the innovations processes under normal operating conditions and G is the failure signature matrix. This matrix can be computed *a priori* [11, 16] and, knowing the residuals, the maximum likelihood estimates are computed (ρ and θ) and then the log-likelihood ratios for failure are derived [51].

Estimating the unknown time-of-failure parameter θ often results in high sensitivity to new data and a great deal of complexity in the fault-detection and isolation process. There are means of partly reducing the complexity by *a priori* restricting θ to a predetermined interval. However, the result of reducing complexity is an increase in the estimation error of ρ [5]. Another problem that is associated with GLR is the time dependency of its monitoring system even for linear time-invariant plants. The reason for such time dependence is the transient effects of the failure signature matrix G. It is possible to utilize steady-state signatures for simplifications; however, there are disadvantages to this approach as well [52].

It is often the case that the value of ρ is not of prominent importance. In such cases, it is possible to preset the value of ρ and perform failure detection and isolation. By the use of several constant values of ρ, high levels of isolation can be achieved with relatively simple algorithms.

Additional types of models that include special effects due to increased process noise, hard-over sensor failures, added sensor noise failures, jumps, steps, and other dynamic effects can be formulated for special situations. Moreover, in cases of false alarms, the likelihood ratios can be interpreted as ratios of conditional probabilities of failure times θ, and perform appropriate changes in the GLR algorithm for simplification as well as adequate performance.

D.   VOTING METHODS

Under analysis of hardware redundancy situations, voting methods are very useful. Hard (or large) failures and some soft failures can be resolved very effectively using this approach [53–55]. Normally, with a minimum of three identical instruments, an appropriate scheme is selected (such as midvalue selection), and simple logic is then utilized for fault detection and isolation. These schemes are generally easy to implement and often provide a quick means of detecting hard failures in systems with a high degree of parallel hardware redundancy. When only single or dual sensors are in use, then the information provided cannot be utilized by such voting schemes, since the data from unlike sensors are usually ignored.

The voting schemes are applicable to original measurements (prior to processing) and to filtered estimates of the sources of potential faults. Parity equations [53] can often be developed (and modified as needed) that can be used with variable decision thresholds for comparison and decision-making purposes. This is done in order to account for differences in accuracies of components and provides enough leeway for expected variations in standard deviation of each participant for noise and maneuvers. Soft failures, such as subtle bias shifts, are very difficult to detect with voting fault-detection systems [5].

E.   ESTIMATION OF PARAMETERS

In general, it is desirable to detect and to diagnose a fault in a process. Thus it is necessary to derive adequate models for the normal, failed, and measured systems with their significant differences characterized appropriately. Even when state-space models are available, parametric models are often very useful in fault detection and isolation. When the parameters are not accurately known, estimation techniques are required to generate adequate approximations [56]. There are various approaches to parameter estimation, some of which will be briefly discussed in the following paragraphs.

Least Squares. Consider a dynamical system of the form given by (1), (2) or by (7), (8). Any stable process that is represented by time-invariant linear ordinary differential/difference equations can be represented by the above-mentioned equations, but a parametric model of such systems will have a general form given by

$$y = \psi\theta + e, \tag{23}$$

where θ is the vector of unknown parameters, ψ is a matrix of appropriate dimensions, and e is the error between the measured and the actual values. Then, the least-squares estimation algorithm involves the derivation of an estimate that minimizes the following squared error functional:

$$J = e^T e, \tag{24}$$

where $e = y - \psi\hat{\theta}$ ($\hat{\theta}$ is the estimate of θ).

The well-known nonrecursive estimate of the parametric vector is now given by:

$$\hat{\theta} = [\psi^T\psi]^{-1}\psi^T\nu. \tag{25}$$

However, in this approach, the parameter estimates usually give a biased value, and the accuracy is meaningful only if the signal-to-noise ratio is large.

The parametric approaches are useful when coefficients in the physical process models are not amenable to direct measurements. The procedure for process fault detection via parameter estimation is as follows [1]: derivation of the analytic representation of the input–output relations, establishment of a relationship between model parameters and the coefficients of the physical process model, and estimation of the parameters from noisy measurements. The use of these parameter estimates as a means of fault detection is then possible through "truth" tables or fault detection logic.

In cases when biased estimates are not acceptable, other "instrumental" variables are generated [57, 58] that are not (essentially) correlated with the pure output. One way is to model the process that generates the "instrumental" variables. This approach to fault detection is started using the least-squares technique, and then a recursive algorithm can be developed to utilize the results and implement the appropriate fault-detection logic [58]. In closed-loop configurations, the estimates obtained suffer from bias due to the correlation of the noise with the input signals. When on-line real-time estimation of critical parameters is needed, then a recursive-type algorithm can be written, and both least-squares and instrumental variables methods can be utilized [59].

Parameter estimation techniques for discrete time processes are widely used. Moreover, it is possible to transform estimates of parameters from discrete-time models into continuous-time models [60, 61].

F. LIMIT/TREND CHECKING AND SIGNAL ANALYSIS

Very often a signal is very clearly and accurately measurable, and maximum and minimum operational values of the signal under normal conditions are available. Under such conditions, "absolute value" checks are used, with appropriate precaution to avoid damage and false alarms. Limit checking and "absolute value" checks can be utilized simultaneously if the limit values are set appropriately and the rate change of variables or parameters are deemed of interest.

One disadvantage of the above-mentioned limit/trend checking approach is that the safeguards one takes for avoidance of false alarms and unnecessary damage could lead to situations when the variation causing concern is removed without any action. This can be avoided by predicting such a variation of the variable via mathematical modeling of the process faults. The parameters that are not directly measurable have to be incorporated in the mathematical models, and recursive parameter estimation techniques should be used in order to identify high-frequency signal models and thus establish process anomalies from variations in the signal model parameters [61–63].

IV. FAILURE ACCOMMODATION

The advent of the modern digital computer has created tremendous potential for greater system flexibility and high performance. The availability of advanced electronics and instrumentation with very high-speed integrated circuits will further expand and extend the utility and power of software to enhance failure-detection systems. Analytical and hardware redundancy used in an integrated manner can create potential advantages in many complex applications [4]. One of the most important potentials brought about by modern advanced computational capabilities is the ability of digital systems to reconfigure themselves and accommodate for failed actuators and sensors [2, 3].

A.   REDUNDANCY MANAGEMENT

Redundancy management is the process whereby proper operation of complex systems are monitored, failures are detected and appropriately isolated, and the operationally normal elements are reconfigured [64]. Thus redundancy management systems are specifically designed to provide a fully redundant configuration with self-contained redundancy management algorithms. These algorithms permit the system at hand to experience an in-operation failure and then automatically detect, isolate, and eliminate the faulty element and continue operation without loss or out-of-specification degradation of its principal function [65].

In high-performance systems, the loss-of-control and abort rates become the main drivers of the design, have a great degree of influence on the system architecture, and make reliability a major factor of the overall system. Initial requirements are assessed to identify candidate architecturs, and then these are evaluated and developed into a final configuration. One of the main requirements is the derivation of a loss-of-control or failure probability equation. Then, an appropriate algorithm is developed that will handle the decision-making process.

Monitors of different forms (software and hardware) are often employed to enhance the failure-detection, isolation, and identification procedure. However, care must always be exercised to prevent excessive monitoring or insufficient monitoring. The main elements that are usually monitored are the inputs, outputs, the processing units, and the interfaces. There is a large body of literature on redundancy management, for which the reader is referred to the above-mentioned references.

B.   ANALYTICAL REDUNDANCY

The high-performance requirements of modern complex control systems based on reconfiguration and redundancy management concepts and characterized by relaxed stability features create the needs for adequate margins of stability and acceptable response. With this type of feature, the high functional reliability of a system becomes an important operational and safety issue [66]. The usual approach to increasing functional reliability has been the use of hardware redundancy. This approach has created the common triple- or quad-redundant schemes that utilize midvalue select logic for sensor fault detection, identification, and isolation [67].

One of the disadvantages of hardware redundancy is (normally) the introduction of penalties in cost, volume, weight, power consumption, and reduction of reliability. Moreover, the additional components created result in more stringent requirements due to the increase of complexity of the selection logic. Thus, the often hypothetical gains in reliability are diminished due to higher failure rates associated with more parts. This is why most modern systems do not exceed quadruple redundancy [68].

The concept of analytical redundancy is related to failure detection and isolation in two respects. First, through this means, additional hardware requirements are eliminated (thus reducing the need for additional fault detection circuits). Second, analytical fault-detection algorithms now replace those that were to be utilized if the analytical redundancy algorithms did not exist and hardware redundancy took its place. Thus there are two advantages to having analytical redundancy in relation to fault detection. First, fault detection is generally simplified and reliability increased. Second, analytical fault detection is performed via software implementation. Whether this type of approach is always advantageous or even feasible is of course another issue that needs to be considered under every new situation.

V. CONCLUSIONS

Major failure-detection methods were presented briefly in the preceding pages. Both unmeasurable parametric quantities as well as state variable approaches were considered and discussed. In the fault-detection process, mathematical models (whether parametric or state-space, state variable models) play a prominent role. Parameter estimation techniques and state estimation techniques, recursive and nonrecursive methods, are all used, and the appropriate approach in a given situation is directly related to the particular case, the measurements available, the constraints (physical and others), and many other factors that have to be analyzed appropriately.

In many situations, accurate models are necessary, and only well-known processes are amenable to such fault-detection schemes. However, since all failure-detection methods are based on some comparison to a "normal" operating condition, changes and parametric, state, or other variations should be utilized intelligently and mechanized into the fault-detection system.

On the other hand, if estimates of very high accuracy are a requirement, then only low-order linear time-invariant models can be utilized efficiently. Once again, there are always tradeoffs that need to be evaluated concerning accuracy, simplicity, practicality, implementation, and safety. For the goal of a fault-detection process is the improvement of the process reliability and safety. The golden mean is often relative computational simplicity, ease of implementation, and reliability.

Failure detection in all situations is a process that involves multidisciplinary engineering knowledge, experience, and insight. Every fault-detection and isolation process should be treated under its own constraints, characteristics, requirements, and merits. Thus modeling, analysis, and estimation will always be helpful tools for the overall system design. However, sometimes simple hardware or software applications give adequate results.

REFERENCES

1. R. ISERMANN, "Process Fault Detection Based on Modeling and Estimation Methods, A Survey," *Automatica* **20**, No. 4, 387–409 (1984).
2. R. C. MONTGOMERY and A. K. CAGLAYAN, "Failure Accommodation in Digital Flight Control Systems by Bayesian Decision Theory," *J. Aircr.* **13** No. 2, 69–75 (1976).
3. R. C. MONTGOMERY and D. B. PRICE, "Failure Accommodaton in Digital Flight Control Systems Accounting For Nonlinear Aircraft Dynamics," *J. Aircr.* **13**, No. 2, 76–82 (1976).
4. E. Y. SHAPIRO and H. V. PANOSSIAN, "Analytical Redundancy for Aircraft Flight Control Sensors," *NATO AGARD 43RD SYMP. ADV. GUIDANCE CONTROL SYST. TECHNOL.*, 53–1, 53–20, OCTOBER, 1986.
5. A. S. WILLSKY, "A Survey of Design Methods for Failure Detection in Dynamic Systems," *Automatica* **12**, 601–611 (1976).
6. E. Y. CHOW and A. S. WILLSKY, "Analytical Redundancy and the Design of Robust Failure Detection Systems," *IEEE Trans. Autom. Control* **AC–29**, No. 7, 603–614 (1984).
7. B. FRIEDLAND, "Maximum-Likelihood Estimation of a Process with Random Transitions (Failures)," *IEEE Trans. Autom. Control* **AC–24**, No. 6, 932–937 (1979).
8. B. FRIEDLAND and S. M. GRABOWSKY, "On Detecting Sudden Changes (Failures) of Biases in Linear Dynamic Systems," *Proc. IEEE 19th Conf. Decis. Control, Albuquerque*, December 1980.
9. K. C. DALY, E. GAI, and J. V. HARRISON, "Generalized Likelihood Test for Fault Detection and Isolation in Redundant Sensor Configuration," *J. Guidance Control* **2**, No. 1, 9–17 (1979).
10. A. S. WILLSKY and H. L. JONES, "A Generalized Likelihood Ratio Approach to the Detection and Estimation of Jumps in Linear Systems Subject to Abrupt Changes," *IEEE Conf. Autom. Control*, November 1974.
11. A. S. WILLSKY and H. L. JONES, "A Generalized Likelihood Ratio Approach to the Detection and Estimation of Jumps in Linear Systems, *IEEE Trans. Autom. Control* **AC–21**, 108–112 (1976).
12. N. A. CARLSON, "Statistical Basis for IMU Failure Detection and Isolation," Intermetrics Shuttle GN and C Memo 03-07, January 1974.
13. M. N. DESAI, J. G. DECKERT, J. J. DYST, A. S. WILLSKY, and E. Y. CHOW, "Dual Redundant Sensor FDI Techniques Applied to the NASA F8C DFBW Aircraft," *Proc. AIAA Conf.*, 502–513, August 1978.
14. R. K. MEHRA and J. PESCHON, "An Innovation Approach to Fault Detection and Diagnosis in Dynamic Systems," *Automatica* **7**, 637–640 (1971).
15. A. S. WILLSKY, J. J. DEYST, JR., and B. S. CRAWFORD, "Two Self-Test Methods Applied to an Inertial System Problem," *J. Spacecr. Rockets* **12**, No. 7, 434–437 (1975).
16. H. L. VAN TREES, "Detection, Estimation, and Modulation Theory." Part I, Wiley, New York, 1971.
17. L. F. PAU, "Failure Diagnosis and Performance Monitoring." Dekker, New York 1981.
18. D. M. HIMMELBLAU, "Fault Detection and Diagnosis in Chemical and Petrochemical Processes," Elsevier, Amsterdam, 1978.
19. B. D. PIERCE and D. D. SWORDER, "Bayes and Minimax Controllers for a Linear System with Stochastic Jump Parameters," *IEEE Trans. Autom. Control* **AC–16**, No. 4, 300–307 (1971).
20. V. G. ROBINSON and D. D. Sworder, "A Computational Algorithm for Design of Regulators for Linear Jump Parameter Systems," *IEEE Trans. Autom. Control* **AL–19**, 47–49 (1974).
21. R. S. RATNER and D. G. LUENBERGER, "Performance Adaptive Renewal Policies for Linear Systems," *IEEE Trans. Autom. Control* **AC–14**, No. 4, 344–351 (1969).
22. M. H. A. DAVIS, "The Application of Nonlinear Filtering to Fault Detection in Linear Systems," *IEEE Trans. Autom. Control* **AC–20**, No. 2, 257–259 (1975).

23. H. PANOSSIAN, "Stochastic Optimal Linear Feedback Control Systems Using Available Measurements," *J. Optim. Theor. Appl.* **7**, No. 2, 248–250 (1984).
24. H. PANOSSIAN, "State and Parameter Estimation in Electrohydraulic Actuation Systems for Failure Analysis," *Int. Symp. Test. Failure Anal., Long Beach*, 228–231 (1985).
25. H. PANOSSIAN, "Reducer Order Observers Applied for State and Parameter Estimation of Hydromechanical Servoactuators," *J. Guidance, Control, Dyn.* **9**, 249–251 (1986).
26. E. V. FANELLI and H. HECHT, "The Fault Tolerant Spaceborne Computer," *Proc. AIAA Conf.*, 73–81, November 1977.
27. M. FERNANDEZ, "A State-of-the-Art Fault-Tolerant Computer," *Proc. IEEE Conf.*, 319–324 (1979).
28. P. FORMAN and K. MOSES, "Multiprocessor Architecture for Software Implemented Fault Tolerance Flight Control and Avionics Computers, *Proc. IEEE Conf.*, 325–329 (1979).
29. R. V. BEARD, "Faulure Accommodation in Linear Systems through Self Reorganization," PhD Dissertation, Massachusetts Institute of Technology (1971).
30. H. L. JONES, "Failure Detection in Linear Systems," Ph.D. Dissertation, Massachusetts Institute of Technology (1973).
31. M. A. Massoumnia, "A Geometric Approach to the Synthesis of Failure Detection Filters," *IEEE TRANS. AUTOM. CONTROL* AC–31, NO. 9, 839–846 (1986).
32. J. S. WILLSKY, "Failure Detection in Dynamic Systems," *NATA AGARDogr.*, No. 109 (1980).
33. X.-C. LOU, J. S. WILLSKY, and G. C. VERGHESE, "Optimally Robust Redundancy Relations for Failure Detection in Uncertain Systems," *Automatica* **22**, No. 3, 333–344 (1986).
34. S. L. FAGIN, "Recursive Linear Regression Theory, Optimal Filter Theory, and Error Analysis of Optimal Systems, *IEEE Int. Conv. Rec.*, 216–240 (1964).
35. T. J. TARN and J. ZABORSKI, "A Practical Nondiverging Filter," *AIAA J.* **8**, 1127–1133 (1970).
36. A. H. JASWINSKI, "Limited Memory Optimal Filtering," *IEEE Trans. Autom. Control* **13**, 557–563 (1968).
37. A. H. JASWINSKI, "Stochastic Processes and Filtering Theory," Academic Press, New York, 1970.
38. T. H. KERR, "Real-Time Failure Detection: A Nonlinear Optimization Problem that Yields a Two-Ellipsoid Overlap Test," *J. Optim. Theory Appl.* **22**, No. 4, 509–535 (1977).
39. T. H. KERR, "Statistical Analysis of a Two-Ellipsoid Overlap Test for Real Time Failure Detection," *IEEE Trans. Autom. Control* AC–25, No. 4, 911–918 (1980).
40. D. G. LAINIOTIS, "Joint Detection, Estimation, and System Identification," *Inf. Control* **19**, 75–92 (1971).
41. R. N. CLARK, D. C. FORTH, and V. M. WALTON, "Detecting Instrument Malfunctions in Control Systems," *IEEE Trans. Aerosp. Electron. Syst.* AES–11, No. 4, 465–473 (1975).
42. A. S. WILLSKY, J. J. DYST, JR., and B. S. CRAWFORD, "Two Self-Test Methods Applied to an Inertial System Problem," *J. Spacecr. Rockets* **12**, No. 7, 434–437 (1975).
43. P. M. NEWBOLD and Y. C. HO, "Detection of Change in the Characteristics of Gauss-Markov Processes," *IEEE Trans. Aerosp. Electron. Syst.* AES–4, No. 5, 707–718 (1968).
44. J. C. HANCOCK and P. A. WINTZ, "Signal Detection Theory," McGraw-Hill, New York, 1966.
45. M. ATHANS, K. P. DUNN, C. P. GREENE, W. H. LEE, N. R. SANDELL, I. SEGALL, and A. S. WILLSKY, "The Stochastic Control of the F–8C Aircraft Using the Multiple Model Adaptive Control Method," *Proc. 1975 IEEE Conf. Decis. Control, Houston* (1975).
46. T. P. McGARTY, "State Estimation with Faulty Measurements: An Application of Bayesian Outlier Rejection," *Proc. 5th Nonlinear Estim. Appl., San Diego* (1974).
47. R. J. McAULAY and E. DEULINGER, "A Decision Directed Adaptive Tracker," *IEEE Trans. Autom. Electron. Syst.* AEX–9, 229–236 (1973).

48. P. SANYAL and C. N. SHEN, "Bayes' Decision Rule for Rapid Detection and Adaptive Estimation Scheme with Space Applications," *IEEE Trans. Autom. Control* AC–19, 228–231 (1974).

49. J. J. DYST and J. C. DECKERT, "RCS Jet Failure Identification for the Space Shuttle," *Proc. IFAC 75, Cambridge, Massachusetts*, August 1975.

50. D. MIDDLETON and E. ESPOSITO, "Simulations for Failure Detection and Estimation of Signals in Noise," *IEEE Trans. Inf. Theory* IT–14, No. 3, 434–444 (1968).

51. T. T. CHIEN, "An Adaptive Technique for a Redundant-Sensor Navigation System," Rep. T–560, C. S. Draper Labs, Cambridge, Massachusetts, 1972.

52. R. B. BROEN, "A Nonlinear Voter-Estimator for Redundant Systems," *Proc. 1974 IEEE Conf. Decis. Control, Phoenix*, 747–748 (1974).

53. R. McKERN and J. GILMORE, "A Redundant Strapdown Inertial System Mechanization," *AIAA Guidance Control Flight Mech. Conf., Santa Barbara*, August 1970.

54. J. E. POTTER and M. C. SUMAN, "Extension of Midvalue Selection Technique for Redundancy Management of Inertial Sensors," *J. Guidance, Control*, Dyn. 9, No. 1, 37–44 (1986).

55. P. C. YOUNG, "Parameter Estimation for Continuous-Time Models – A Survey," *Automatica* 17, 23–30 (1981).

56. P. C. YOUNG, "An Instrumental Variable Method for Realtime Identification of a Noisy Process," *Automatica* 6, 271–275 (1970).

57. P. C. YOUNG and A. JAKEMAN, "Refined Instrumental Variable Methods of Recursive Time-Series Analysis. Part III. Extensions," *Int. J. Control* 31, 741–751 (1980).

58. R. ISERMANN, "Digital Control Systems," Springer, Berlin, 1981.

59. N. K. SINHAN and G. J. LASTMAN, "Identification of Continuous Time Multivariable Systems from Sampled Data," *Int. J. Control* 35, 117–122 (1982).

60. S. STRMENICK and F. BREMSAK, "Some New Transformation Algorithms in the Identification of Continuous-Time Multivariable Systems Using Discrete Identification Methods," in "Identification and Systems Parameter Estimation," Pergamon Press, Oxford, 1979.

61. R. M. C. DE KEYSER and VAN CANWENBERGHE, "A Self Tuning Multistep Predictor Application," *Automatica* 17, 167–169 (1981).

62. G. C. ZWINGELSTEIN and B. R. UPHADYAYA, "Identification of Multivariate Models for Noise Analysis of Nuclear Plant," in "Identification and System Parameter Estimation," Pergamon Press, Oxford, 1979.

63. J. H. WATSON, W. J. YOUSEY, and J. M. RAILEY, "Redundancy Management Considerations for a Control-Configured Fighter Aircraft Triplex Digital Fly-By-Wire Flight Control System," *NATO AGARD Conf. Proc.*, No. 272 (1980).

64. R. A. BAUM, G. E. S. MORRISON, and R. C. PETERS, "A Redundant Inertial Navigation System for IUS," *NATO AGARD Conf. Proc.*, No. 272 (1980).

65. R. F. STENGEL, "Equilibrium Response of Flight Control Systems," *Automatica* 18, No. 3, 343–348 (1982).

66. J. E. POTTER and M. C. SUMAN, "Extension of Midvalue Selection Technique for Redundancy Management of Inertial Sensors," *J. Guidance, Control, Dyn.* 9, No. 1, 37–44 (1986).

67. E. Y. SHAPIRO, "Software Techniques for Sensor Redundancy Management of Flight Control Systems," *J. Aircr.* 15, No. 7, 632–638 (1977).

ARRANGING COMPUTER ARCHITECTURES TO CREATE HIGHER-PERFORMANCE CONTROLLERS

STEPHEN A. JACKLIN

NASA Ames Research Center
Moffett Field, California 94035

I. INTRODUCTION

Our ability to create faster and more reliable real-time, computer-based control systems is being constantly challenged by the ever-increasing demands for higher-performance controllers. The guidance and control of aircraft and spacecraft, the direction of robotic automation equipment, and the stabilization of dynamic structures are just a few of the many application fields asking for controllers having higher throughput and greater computation rates. These applications need controllers that can acquire data from many sensors, precondition the input data stream, perform numerous control computations, and output multiple control signals at high speed. The control computations will most likely include on-line systems identification, since for many applications the parameters describing the system dynamics will likely be uncertain or subject to time variation. This, of course, makes the control computations more lengthy, and requires a higher computation rate of the control system. In addition, the control system may also be tasked to perform activities that are indirectly related to control, such as database management and on-line interaction with the control engineer.

Though few people today are ignorant of the power that microprocessors have given control systems, many are unaware or uninformed of how computer system architectures can be manipulated to yield higher-performance controllers. These controllers integrate microprocessors, array processors, and other intelligent devices to offer real-time computation and throughput gains. Higher performance is achieved through arranging the many system components to form a distributed or parallel-processing control system. These systems distribute the real-time work load over many microprocessors, data paths, intelligent peripherals, and specialized communication interfaces. Though these designs are

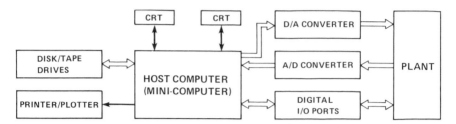

Fig. 1. The classical design of many computer-based controllers is to attach all of the peripheral devices directly to the central computer.

sometimes more expensive than classical designs, in many cases, it is possible to simply reorganize the system components (or to specify different components) so that increased performance may be achieved at roughly the same cost. Moreover, in that there exists a multitude of system expansion components available today, creating multimicroprocessor, distributed control systems need not be difficult.

The design considerations given here will discuss how computer architectures can be arranged to yield controllers having higher performance than those designed in the classical fashion. First, the classical design will be examined to see why its design is not optimal for real-time control. Then, ways to improve the classical design without changing the basic structure of the control system will be examined. The array processor will be introduced as a coprocessing peripheral which can be used to greatly increase the computation speed of a classically designed computer at a very reasonable cost. Then a better way to use the array processor for real-time control will be presented which involves a rearrangement of the computer architectures. This will be followed by a discussion of the many ways in which intelligent peripherals and interfaces can be used to further distribute the real-time burden to achieve maximum throughput and computation speeds. Finally, an example will be presented to show how these design considerations were applied in an actual design study. Though the high performance controller of this example was designed to actively reduce rotorcraft vibration and increase rotor system stability, its architecture is sufficiently general to be applicable to a wide range of automatic control applications.

II. COMPUTER ARCHITECTURES – THEY ARE NOT ALL THE SAME!

The term "computer architecture" can have many meanings. In one sense, this term can be correctly applied to mean the actual design of a computer or to specify the layout of a computer board. In another sense, computer architecture can refer to the intricate details associated with the design of a microprocessor and its internal workings. For this article, however, it is desired to broaden the term to mean an integration of all components of the computer system to form an integrated control system. In doing this, computer architecture is viewed not from the perspective of the electrical engineer, but from the viewpoint of the control systems engineer who seeks an arrangement of board-level devices (and up) to form a computer-based control system as a whole.

The objective of this section is to show how changes in computer architecture can be used to form higher-performance controllers over that found using a classical design approach. More often than not, the architecture of the average computer-based control system is a rather straightforward integration of a mini or a mainframe computer with several peripheral devices, as illustrated in Fig. 1. With this classical design, all of the peripheral devices connect directly to the central computer's bus. The bus is the main path over which data are passed from one element to another inside the computer. By plugging each board of the computer into a chassis containing all of the bus lines, the elements of each board have access to all of the other devices. This chassis is called the "backplane" of the computer, and extra slots in it allow the connection of other boards or devices to the central computer. The peripheral devices connected in this fashion to the central computer may include printer/plotter units, disk or tape drives, terminals, analog-to-digital (A/D) converter units, digital-to-analog (D/A) converter units, digital input/output ports, video cameras, and countless other devices. The central computer is often referred to as the "host" computer because it is host to all of the peripheral devices and is responsible for controlling their operation. Many control systems have this type of architecture because it was the way in which the manufacturer of the central computer envisioned the interfacing of the computer to the real world, of which control applications are only a small part. Hence, although it seems prudent that an analog-to-digital converter should not be attached in the same manner as a line printer, the typical host computer treats them the same. Nevertheless, this design has flourished because of the ease with which modules may be connected to the host.

This ease with which the host can be expanded by plugging modules into the backplane, however, may cause considerable problems for those control system designers who attempt to form their own computer-based controller. The main problem is in knowing what hardware to use out of the myriad devices available for connection to the host computer. Many computer hardware product vendors provide documentation on how their individual devices improve a given aspect of computer performance, but cannot provide specific suggestions as to whether the hardware product is appropriate for the intended control system, since they do not know what host the user has chosen or what will be the target application. This often leaves the control system designer in a state of uncertainty, and prompts many designers to feel that the system with the most options and devices will be the best. But this may actually fall short of satisfying the user's needs.

Moreover, the control systems engineer must usually work with a limited budget in designing the control system. If the design effort is not properly focused, a control system with inferior performance may be chosen instead of one costing about the same, but with much higher capability. An awareness of computer architecture design considerations is therefore useful in finding ways to

TABLE I. SOME MICROPROCESSOR CHARACTERISTICS

Processor CPU make or model	Data bus word size (bits)	CPU word size (bits)	CPU clock frequency (MHz)	Maximum MIPS	Number of interrupts	Memory CPU can address (bytes)
Intel 8080-A	8	8	2.0	0.67	1	65K
National INS8048	8	8	11.0	0.74	1	4K
TI TMS7002	8	8	8.0	1.0	6	64K
Zilog Z8-108	8	8	25.0	2.0	2	500K
GTE Micro G65SC802	8	16	8.0	1.0	2	16M
Intel iAP 88/10	8	16	8.0	5.0	1	1M
NEC PD70208	8	16	8.0	1.0	8	1M
TI SPB9989	8	16	4.4	0.73	17	128K
Fairchild F9450	16	16	20.0	4.0	16	2M
Immos IMST202	16	16	20.0	20.0	1	64K
Intel 80188	16	16	8.0	4.0	256	1M
Zilog Z8001B	16	16	10.0	1.0	5	8M
DEC DCJ11-AA	16	32	15.0	3.0	7	4M
Fairchild F16032	16	32	6.0	2.5	256	16M
Motorola MC68012	16	32	12.5	2.5	7	2G
NEC V-60	16	32	16.0	3.5	8	4G
AT&T WE32100	32	32	18.0	6.0	16	4G
Inmos IMST414	32	32	20.0	20.0	1	4G
Motorola MC68020	32	32	16.0	2.52	7	256M
NEC V-70	32	32	16.0	6.0	256	4G

increase system performance at no or very minimal additional costs. Alternatively, for a loosely constrained budget, this knowledge is helpful in making sure that the most performance per dollar will be obtained. These design considerations will be presented in the ensuing discussion, starting from the most basic ideas and ending with more advanced concepts.

III. EXPANDING THE POWER OF THE HOST COMPUTER

A good starting point for our discussion will be to examine what performance gains can be obtained through modification (or selection) of the host computer. Though this modification process can entail replacing the host computer with a new computer, many basic improvements to system performance can be made by simply expanding the existing host system in the appropriate manner. These suggestions apply to those choosing a new system as well as to those who already have a host computer they wish to modify. The first topic to be discussed concerns what properties are desirable for a host microprocessor.

A. FINDING THE RIGHT HOST MICROPROCESSOR

The single most important factor governing the performance of the host computer is the type of microprocessor upon which it is based. The microprocessor is typically a single chip device which forms the "brain" of the host computer and performs all computations. As such, computer system performance is very closely tied to microprocessor performance. With a good system design, the performance of the system will be close to that of its microprocessor. Because many computers use the same microprocessor, it is more important to discuss microprocessor selection, rather than computer make and model selection. The first point, therefore, when selecting a host computer is to find out what microprocessor it uses to perform computations. This is the key to determining what will be the host computer system's ultimate performance.

Of the 600 to 700 commercially available microprocessors, Table I lists only a few to provide some examples for the following discussion. Though this table is not intended to be comprehensive, it does list some of the basic factors that tend to categorize microprocessor performance. These include the width of the microprocessor's data bus, its computation word size, its maximum clock cycle speed, the rate it can execute instructions, its interrupt structure, and its capacity to directly address memory. The factor(s) which are most important depend upon the specific application.

If numerical precision is very important, the width of the data bus and the computation word size of the microprocessor are important. The microprocessors in Table I have been arranged in order of increasing width of the data path. Only 8, 16, and 32 bit widths are listed (4, 38, 64 and others exist). Computers using narrower-width data buses do not lose numerical accuracy, but do take longer to transmit data. This is because narrower data paths require more words to represent a single number. The 32-bit-wide buses have the advantage of being able to transmit 32-bit numbers directly between memory and the microprocessor in a single clock cycle. To transmit the same number over an 8-bit width would require four cycles, leading to a commensurate reduction in computation. Viewing the computation word size column, one can see that some microprocessors with a 16-bit bus width can perform 32-bit computations within the microprocessor to maintain internal precision. Though these microprocessors are sometimes labeled as 32-bit machines, it is important to recognize that the data flow within the computer is still limited to 16-bit words. In general, 32-bit microprocessor-based systems cost more than 16-bit systems, and 16-bit systems cost more than those systems based on 8-bit microprocessors. If the intended control application involves acquisition and manipulation of numbers having many significant figures, the selection of a 16-bit or 32-bit microprocessor over an 8-bit processor is usually very advantageous and cost effective.

If speed is a primary consideration, the maximum clock frequency of the microprocessor and degree of computational parallelism of the microprocessor and its environment are important. Each instruction executed by a microprocessor is composed of several smaller actions which can each be performed on a single clock pulse. Microprocessors which can operate at higher clock speeds can therefore potentially perform more computations per second. But this is not always true. Another factor, the degree of parallelism existing in the computer and computer's software, is also important. Parallelism is the degree to which all the computer components function to support numerical computation. Since there can be so many ways to realize parallel computation, parallelism is a difficult term to directly quantify. Another term, MIPS, designates the millions of instructions which can be executed per second. A microprocessor with a high clock speed, situated in a computer emphasizing parallel computation, will have a high MIPS rate. Similarly, a microprocessor with a high clock rate situated in a computer lacking parallelism will tend to have a lower MIPS rate. Though the MIPS rate is generally indicative of microprocessor performance, the other microprocessor support chips also play an important role. In general, they must be capable of parallel operation as well. For the end user, it often suffices to find out what the MIPS rate is for a candidate microprocessor. This is often given as a range, rather than as a single number, since it depends on the type of operations being done. Comparing the clock and MIPS columns of Table I, one can see than a 10 MHz processor does not necessarily have a fivefold increase in computation speed over a 2 MHz processor.

If it is desired that the host computer respond quickly to a number of predefined events, the interrupt structure of the microprocessor is important. An interrupt implements the same thing that a software conditional branch statement (like a FORTRAN "IF' statement) does, but in hardware. In order for a microprocessor to possess interrupt capability, it must have physical interrupt line connections. When it receives an interrupt signal from an external device, the microprocessor's program is forced to branch to a specific memory location that contains the first instruction of the subroutine which dictates how the microprocessor is to respond to the interrupt. Viewing Table I, it is seen that some microprocessors support only a single interrupt, while others support 256 separate interrupts. For event-driven control tasks requiring lighting quick response, interrupt support capability is essential. Interrupts are fast because a microprocessor can respond at any time to an interrupt signal, whereas a branch done in software can only be made when the statement is executed. Moreover, interrupts can be ordered to form an execution hierarchy by using a combination of maskable and nonmaskable interrupts, another trick not possible in software. Maskable interrupts are those interrupts which are disregarded if a "disable interrupt" command is executed in the program software. Maskable interrupts are useful because there are certain times when it is desirable to avoid interrupt response. For example, when responding to an interrupt generated by an external device, it is useful to disable subsequent interrupts from other devices until the first interrupt has been processed. This effectively puts the other devices on hold. Nonmaskable interrupts cannot be ignored by the processor and are usually reserved for very high priority functions, such as an emergency stop of the control system.

For control tasks requiring a fairly large amount of memory (e.g., video transformations and analysis), the ability of the microprocessor to directly address memory is important. The ability of the microprocessor to directly address memory is a function of how many address lines it has to specify memory locations. For example, a 16-bit address bus can access 2^{16} or 64K bytes of memory, and a 32-bit address bus can access 4G (gigabytes) of memory. A microprocessor which cannot address enough memory for a given control task must use mass storage devices, which have very slow response times compared to core memory. It is usually a good idea to select a microprocessor which can address more memory than that needed for the intended application. Then, when it is recognized later on that more core memory is needed (which is almost always the case), no costly system modifications will be needed.

There are several other factors which can be important in selecting the right microprocessor which are not referenced in Table I. One notable feature is the ability of the microprocessor to support DMA (direct memory access) data transfers. In DMA transfers, an attached device can gain access to the host computer's core memory without interaction of the host microprocessor. (This is advantageous in supporting parallel operations, as will be discussed in a later section.) Although most 16-bit and 32-bit processors have DMA capability, some do not. Moreover, some microprocessors support only visible DMA operations, in which the host microprocessor's operation must be suspended while the DMA data transfer takes place. Other microprocessors use the more efficient "cycle stealing" DMA method, in which the data are transferred to memory any time the host processor is not using core memory [1]. Another important consideration governing microprocessor selection is the structure and type of software it can support. All microprocessors do not speak the same languages. Some are only assembly level language programmable, while others support higher-level languages like FORTRAN, BASIC, and Pascal. More importantly, some microprocessors can support multitasking environments, which are very useful for real-time control, as will be shown below. The number of instructions in the microprocessor's repertoire also varies widely (40–165), and can have ramifications on the programming options left open to the end user. Some microprocessors can determine which program statements are to be executed next. This is advantageous for cache memory applications, as will be mentioned later. Some microprocessors lend themselves well to system expansion (e.g., coprocessor addition, memory addition), while others do not. For those interested, several references are available to provide detailed and up-to-date information on microprocessor characteristics [2, 3].

Once a microprocessor and host computer are identified, the host computer as a whole can be evaluated to see what features will enhance its performance. These considerations also apply to those wishing to enhance the performance of an existing host computer and are presented below.

B.   INCREASING THE POWER OF THE HOST MICROPROCESSOR

Because different microprocessors have different numbers of address lines, data lines, power connections, and pin assignments, it is normally not possible to increase the power of the host microprocessor by simply replacing the old microprocessor. What can be done in some cases is to add an additional processor to the system called a coprocessor. The idea is to let this processor share the computation burden. In some cases, the addition of a coprocessor is very easy and inexpensive, and requires only the connection of another board module to the system. In other cases, the cost of adding a coprocessor is higher because, along with the extra microprocessor, some rewiring of the host backplane and addition of various utility boards must also be done. Though some systems allow the addition of more than one coprocessor (e.g., Intel 80286's 80287 coprocessor or Motorola 68020's 68881 coprocessor), many do not have provisions to attach a coprocessor. Whether or not a system can support a coprocessor is often something to consider when selecting a host system. Both the system hardware and software must exist to support a coprocessor.

Since a coprocessor is physically no different than another microprocessor, a list of coprocessor characteristics is not provided. In fact, many of the processors in Table I could serve as a coprocessor. The real task in adding a coprocessor to an existing system lies in software modification. Though the high-level languages like FORTRAN remain the same, the assembler or compiler must be written with logic capable of dividing the processing workload between the two processors. This is not an easy task, since parallel operation of the processors is desired to maximize the total computation rate. Hence the assembler or compiler must sequence as many operations to occur in parallel before a common product is needed, and add timing or wait loops to the processor that finishes first. This task is so involved that most systems offering a coprocessor option were designed with that in mind, and not as a retrofit, though that's sometimes the case. The capability of the assembler or compiler to interweave the processor's operations is the key to increasing the computer's aggregate computation rate.

One thing to keep in mind when considering addition of a coprocessor is that the manufacturer's advertised increase in computation speed may not be attainable most of the time. This is because many manufacturers add the processing speed of the coprocessor to the speed of the host microprocessor to arrive at a peak processing speed. This peak speed is possible only when both microprocessors are operating at their maximum rate. Since one processor must usually wait some of the time for the other processor in order to synchronize joint processing, this maximum rate is attainable only some of the time. This makes the aggregate computation rate much lower. Moreover, it should be recognized that, prior to coprocessor addition, the original host microprocessor did not have the burden of supervising a coprocessor. This task subtracts from the performance of the host processor. Hence, when figuring computation speed, it is usually a good idea to find out what the speed of the coprocessor itself is and to try to assess to what degree the processors can perform their designated operations at the same time. This is often difficult to do, since the characteristics of the assembler or compiler may not be published. The manufacturer must therefore be questioned to determine the manner in which their compiler or assembler optimizes parallel operation.

A second factor to consider when adding a coprocessor is that they can also be used to increase system throughput. Throughput is a term used to designate the total rate at which data can flow into and out of the computer. It is dependent upon the number of operations which must be performed to input the data, the number of computations which must be done between input and output, and the number of operations necessary to output the control signals. A system having a 2 MHz processor cannot usually maintain a throughput rate of even 100 kHz [4]. This is because the host microprocessor must perform numerical computations and supervise data transfer operations between the system peripherals at the same time. Both activities must be done to maintain throughput, though only one operation can be done at a time. In the cases where throughput is to be maximized, a coprocessor can largely take over the control computation aspect, leaving the host microprocessor more time to arbitrate data transfer operations between the system components. A coprocessor used in this fashion can increase system throughput greatly and increase the aggregate computation rate modestly at the same time. The increase in computation rate is slight, because the coprocessor must still be supervised by the host microprocessor, and also because the processors are performing different roles. In Section IV, array processors will be presented as coprocessing peripherals that can operate independently of the host processor, leading to a great increase in computation speed and throughput if coupled in the right manner.

C.   INCREASING THE HOST MEMORY SIZE

The type and size of host core memory can have a very important effect upon system performance. A computer's core memory is composed of several random access memory (RAM) board modules, whose memory locations can be directly addressed by the host microprocessor. This is distinguished from the computer's mass memory storage devices (like floppy disk drives, hard disk drives, and tape drives), which are used to store operating system software, user written programs, and archived data. Mass memory devices cannot typically be used in real-time control applications because of the slow data access times these devices have. For real-time applications, all required control software and data should be copied into core memory before beginning controller operation. A core memory which is too small to hold all of the control software will impede the real-time performance of the controller.

If a control program is too large to fit into memory, then the technique of overlaying must be used. In this technique, only part of the program is held in core memory. The remainder is stored on the mass storage disks. When that part of the program stored on disk is needed, it is swapped into memory or "overlaid" onto that part of core memory the old program segment used. The problem with this procedure is that reading data from a disk involves a significant time delay, which can seriously degrade controller performance. The time delay involved with disk seek and access times is usually specified in milliseconds. For real-time control programs, in which operations are timed to the microsecond, and even nanosecond, a delay of milliseconds is often intolerable.

A better solution is to expand the size of core memory. This is where having a microprocessor which can directly address a large core memory space is desirable. However, even microprocessors which can only directly address a small amount of memory can be expanded to address more memory by using the appropriate additional hardware. [These devices effectively add an extra data line(s) and thus expand the address space.] Increasing the size of core memory is usually cost effective, because additional computer memory is very inexpensive. Often, core memories can be doubled and even quadrupled from the "standard" size, for less than 10% of the overall computer cost. High-speed memory, however, is an exception to the low-cost aspect of RAM memory expansion.

High-speed memory costs more because it is made from more costly semiconductor materials needing much less time to energize and discharge the memory locations. The memory access or cycle time is typically measured in nanoseconds and designates the amount of time required to read data from or write data to the memory. Though cycle times of 250–500 ns are commonly used for minicomputer and mainframe designs, some systems use memory with cycle times as low as 1–3 ns [5]. Using fast-responding memory is of course only possible with microprocessors having an appropriately fast clock rate. (That is, nothing is gained by using a memory device which can accept and produce memory values faster than the microprocessor can give or acquire them.) Assuming the host microprocessor has a high enough cycle speed itself, faster-responding memory can be used to increase host performance.

To keep costs down, many computers implement a cache memory concept. The cache memory is usually small, containing only 2–4 kbytes of very fast memory. The idea is that, if the program statements to be executed soon can always be moved into the cache memory before they are needed, then all the benefits of fast memory can be obtained by acquiring only a small quantity of expensive fast memory. The problem is that the system look-ahead software or address anticipation hardware cannot always predict which subroutines will be executed, since they may be conditioned on an external event. The percentage of the time the computer can do this is referred to as the "hit" rate, and gets better with increased cache memory size, since that increases the probability that the next executable line will already be held in fast memory. If the cache memory specified is too large, the cost may be prohibitive, and memory coherency problems may be encountered [6]. Coherency problems occur when data values are changed in regular core memory, but not in the copy stored in cache memory. Since most computers come configured with a small cache memory, it is generally a good idea to expand cache memory. Many manufacturers limit the cache memory expansion size (say from 2 to 8K) so that coherency will not become a problem.

When sizing the core memory for a host system, it is useful to remember that core memory space can rarely be specified too large. This is because even the most experienced programmers have difficulty projecting how much core memory space will be needed to hold a given program. One reason for this is that not all core memory is available to hold user-written control programs. The operating system of the computer must always reside in core memory, and some operating systems are quite large. Another reason is that, although the remainder of core memory is potentially available to hold user-written programs, other software may compete for this space. This software may comprise device drivers (software to communicate with peripherals), graphic routine software, and other numerical computation routines which must coexist in core memory with the control program, not to mention data. In fact, the amount of core memory used to hold the actual control program is usually very small compared with the space needed to hold the auxiliary graphics and numerical computation routines. This space is commonly neglected, underestimated, or altogether unknown, as commonly occurs when controller acquisition precedes control program formulation. If the memory space required by the programs is greater than the available memory, the host system's performance will be memory bound. Unfortunately, many control systems in use today are in exactly this position, yet function without hardware modification through the use of complex overlay software.

D.   USING MULTITASKING SOFTWARE ON THE HOST

The concept of multitasking is an important software advantage which can be implemented by certain types of microprocessors. Multitasking software increases controller performance by preventing the host microprocessor from waiting for some even to take place. For example, the host processor may have to wait for an analog-to-digital conversion, or for the results to be obtained from a coprocessor. When this happens, the processor enters the wait state and performs no operations. This waiting represents a loss of performance.

To retrieve these lost processing cycles, some host operating systems are multitasking. These operating systems allow the processor to run more than one program at a time. They are especially common on large systems whose many users simultaneously compete with with each other to get a slice of the main processor's time. From the control standpoint, multitasking allows a control program to be divided into two or more subprograms which can be executed simultaneously. One advantage of doing this is that when one program becomes blocked, waiting for an external event, the other program(s) can still be executed by the processor (one at a time). This strategy tends to ensure that the host processor will always have something to do. Moreover, multitasking often allows the assignment of priorities to the subprograms, so that the subprogram with the highest priority gets the attention of the host microprocessor first. This is particularly important when all the real-time control tasks have been grouped into one program. By defining priorities, the real-time control tasks are always done before the lower-priority tasks. Multitasking is also nice in that it permits more than one person to write controller software at the same time.

IV. USING ARRAY PROCESSORS TO CUT COMPUTATION TIME

An array processor can be attached to a host computer to dramatically increase its real-time control performance. Array processors are attached computers which have been designed with specialized hardware to optimally process vector and array-type data. Array processors are computers in their own right in that they have microprocessors, memories, and the internal structure of a computer. However, array processors are usually not designed to operate by themselves as would a general-purpose minicomputer. Instead, array processors must rely on a host computer to perform all software development functions and file manipulation for the array processor. Though array processors require some capital outlay (about $50,000), they can give a small host computer the computation speed of a much larger machine, but at a fraction of the cost. Array processors accomplish this feat by specializing their hardware to perform numerical calculations, leaving the peripheral device supervision, data management, and file manipulation tasks to the host computer. Array processors have no means to permanently store, retrieve, or modify programs. But, by delegating these functions to a host computer, array processors can be designed with relatively expensive computing hardware, and still be very reasonably priced.

Unlike host computers, which typically have one microprocessor and only one or two buses (data paths) for data flow, array processors use several microprocessors and several buses to facilitate high speed computation. Most array processors have at least one I/O processor to coordinate data flow, an interface processor to talk to the host, a control processor to sequence mathematical operations, and one or more arithmetic processors to perform numerical computations. Some array processors have separate multiplication and addition processors. These microprocessors are usually custom designed and typically use data and computation word sizes ranging from 32 to 64 bits. The many microprocessors within the array processor communicate with each other and with memory over a network of four to seven data paths. These buses usually include an address bus, an input/output data bus, one or more multiplication buses, one or more addition buses, and a control bus, as illustrated in Fig. 2. The data paths themselves also range from 32 to 64 bits in width [7].

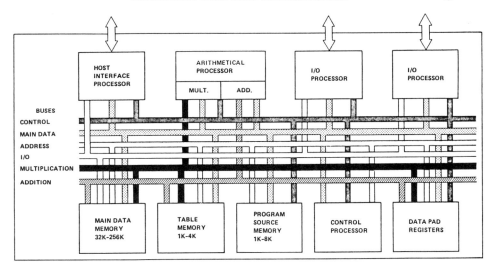

Fig. 2. Array processors are computers that use multiple microprocessors, multiple buses (or data paths), and multiple memories to facilitate high-speed operation.

In addition to the multiple microprocessors and multiple buses, most array processors utilize multiple memories. Because array processor memory is commonly made of memory having a faster cycle time than most host system cache memories, the cache memory concept is not widely used. Rather, the program source and main data memories are chosen to have access speeds which represent a compromise between performance and cost. Most array processors have separate memories for program storage, data storage, and table constant storage. Separation allows the memories to be accessed by different processors at the same time. Separation also allows these memories to be made of semiconductor materials having different response times. Though slower responding memory is never desired, fast-responding array processor memory is very expensive. Therefore, a compromise between cost and performance is usually required when specifying array processor memory, since the choice of memory can often double the cost of an array processor. Because of cost considerations, most array processors are designed with small memories. Program source memories of 2–4K words (32–64 bit), and data memories of 32–64K words are common. Though seemingly small, it should be remembered that array processors do not store operating systems or need to perform any software development. Moreover, an instruction or program word of 64 bits often contains 6–10 operands, allowing many operations to be commanded by a single instruction. The smaller the memory becomes, the less expensive it is to acquire the fastest memory for the array processor. However, the smaller memory becomes, the greater are the chances that the programs and data will not fit into array processor memory. Since this has the greatest potential to degrade array processor performance, it is usually a good idea to size array processor memory on the basis of the space the application will need to avoid program overlays and copying of

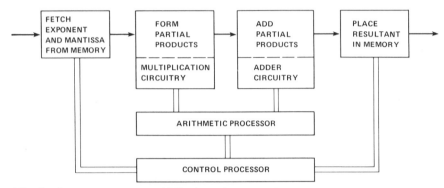

Fig. 3. An array processor multiplication scheme showing the summation of partial products to form the outputs in a parallel-processing pipeline.

TABLE II. SOME ARRAY PROCESSOR COMPU-
TATION RATES

Array processor make or model	Peak processing speed (MFLOPS)
CDC STAR-100	50
Datawest MATP	120
FACOM 230/75	22
FPS AP-120B	12
FPS 164	12
IBM 3838	30
MAP 6400	5
TI-ASC	30
VAX 11/780[a]	2

[a]Used for comparison only.

data, and not on the basis of memory response time. After the basic space requirements are met, the advantages of faster-responding memory can be considered relative to the application and budget.

More than just architecture is optimized to maximize array processor speed. Array processors are designed to use their several microprocessors, data paths, and memories in a highly coordinated fashion, so that vast amounts of parallel processing can be performed. The many microprocessors perform their programmed operations and communicate with each other simultaneously through use of multiple data paths between the different processors and memory. This design facilitates the implementation of a type of parallel processing known as "fast math" or pipelining" [8]. Pipelining is a technique used to perform array-type numerical computations in parallel at the microprocessor level. Though multiplication, for example, is often thought of as a single-step operation, it actually involves several steps consisting of the summation of partial products of mantissa and exponent to form the final output on the microprocessor level. For a scalar multiplication, array processors hold no advantage over ordinary minicomputers. But for matrix multiplication, array processor software uses the many microprocessors to form a processing pipeline. As shown in Fig. 3, while the multiplication processor is forming the partial products of one set of numbers, the addition processor is adding the partial products of the previous multiplication, and the control processor is passing new vector elements to the multiplier while storing the results obtained from the adder. Neglecting the first two multiplications, pipelined operation produces a new product every machine cycle, rather than every eight or ten cycles as would be done by a typical host computer. For this reason, the pipelined mathematics of array processors makes them extremely efficient in performing the repetitive multiplication, addition, array-indexing, and loop-counting operations needed to process large arrays.

The high-speed multimicroprocessor, multibus, and multimemory architecture combines with the performance gains attained by parallel processing, allowing most array processors to attain speeds of at least 12–15 million floating point operations per second (MFLOPS). In fact, some special-purpose parallel processors have been reported to achieve computation speeds of up to 800 million multiply/add operations per second [9]. Table II presents some of the commercially available array processors along with their peak processing speeds. It can be noted from this table that array processors perform numerical operations 3 to 60 times faster than most mainframe computers, depending on the type of array processor.

Array processors greatly expand the computation and throughput speeds of their host computers to perform operations far beyond the scope of the host machine. For example, a controller using an array processor as a coprocessing peripheral might allow the computation of a robotic arm's kinematic equations of motion to be done in real time. Motion control of robotic arms today, if done by computer, usually involves placing the computer in a teaching mode and then digitizing the arm position at rates up to 50 times per second as it is manually moved through the desired trajectory [10]. For arms with more than one or two degrees of freedom, the amount of memory required for a fairly detailed motion can be considerable. The addition of an array processor to a robotic arm control system could allow the solution of the kinematic equations, which cannot be done fast enough using a minicomputer alone. More importantly, by using the array processor to solve the kinematic equations of motion, subject to various performance constraints, the computation of optimal paths becomes possible. In this way array processors can be used to beneficially boost control system computation speed for robotic controllers, and other control systems where the application scope is limited by signal processing efficiency [11–13]. Also, by freeing the host from computation, the host is left more free to supervise throughput requests made by the peripheral devices. Throughput rates of several 100 kHz are attainable using array processors as coprocessing peripherals, depending on the application.

The disadvantage of using array processors is that they represent another computer to program. Typically, array processor programs are written in assembly language with several operands per instruction line so that more than one operation can be done at a time. The user or assembler (depending on the array processor) must determine which instructions can be executed simultaneously by the different microprocessors. Though the speed of array processors is most directly attained using assembly-level languages, many array processors can be purchased with translator programs to translate FORTRAN or BASIC programs into assembly language. These programs usually generate a great deal of superfluous code (owing to its generalized nature) and may create a control program too large to fit into the limited array processor's program source memory. A technique for overlaying program segments from main data memory can then be used, but is much less efficient for real-time control. A middle of the road solution is to chain together a sequence of factory-written mathematical routines which have already been optimized in assembly language for a particular machine. The importance of these routines is that they have been optimized to use the many microprocessors and data paths to facilitate parallel processing. These FORTRAN-like chainer programs permit indexing and conditional statements to be mixed with calls to the mathematical routines. The user does not have to work with assembly language nor worry about which operations need to be done in parallel, but does assume the responsibility of manipulating array processor variables by the literal locations they occupy in array processor memory. This technique is quite efficient, but restricts the user from performing operations not in the library, unless the user wishes to write a custom subroutine for the library.

In the next section, a way to increase system throughput and computation rates is presented which does not necessarily require the use of an array processor, but benefits greatly by the use of one.

V. USING DIFFERENT COMPUTER SUBSYSTEMS TO SEPARATE REAL-TIME EVENTS FROM NON-REAL-TIME EVENTS

A controller design technique which can increase both computer throughput and computation speeds is that of using two or more dedicated computer subsystems to separate the real-time events from the non-real-time events. In the last section, it was seen how an array processor could be used as a coprocessing peripheral device to greatly increase the computation and throughput speeds of the host computer. However, though this controller design allowed the computation speed to increase to the computation rate of its array processor, the system throughput speed was limited to that of the host computer's bus. In this section it will be shown how an array processor or other computer can be used to greatly increase system throughput as well as the computation rate. This requires only a restructuring of the control system from that system using an array processor as a coprocessing peripheral.

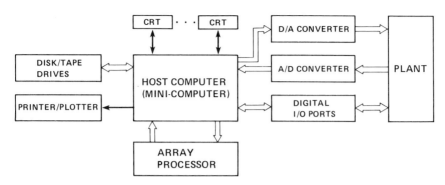

Fig. 4. A minicomputer-based controller using an array processor as a coprocessing peripheral can perform computations as fast as a much larger mainframe computer.

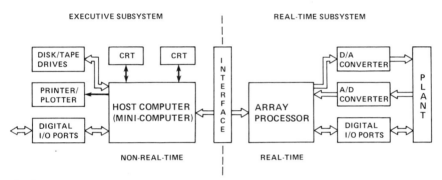

Fig. 5. A controller design using an array processor to form a separate real-time computer subsystem can support high throughput and high computation rates.

To understand this, it is useful to consider the architecture of a controller having an array processor attached as a coprocessing peripheral, as illustrated in Fig. 4. The important aspect of this design is that all of the data acquisition devices and system peripherals are directly attached to the host computer. Even though the host computer can delegate a large portion of the processing tasks to the array processor (or another coprocessing computer), it must still sequence the control program actions while coordinating data flow from the measurement and actuation hardware. If no array processor or coprocessor is attached to the host (as in Fig. 1), the situation is much worse. Then the central host computer must not only perform all of the numerical computations, but it must also control all of the peripheral devices. It is, in fact, the burdensome task of supervising the peripheral devices which bogs down the performance of most host computers. Even peripheral devices which have a microprocessor must still communicate with the host by using a handshaking protocol, whereby the host signals an external device to perform an operation and the device acknowledges the host when the task has been completed. These peripheral devices rely upon the host computer to synchronize their operation with the rest of the system. As the throughput or computation demands increase, a point is eventually reached where the host computer becomes so burdened down with the supervision of the peripheral devices that it does not have enough time to perform the control calculations in real time, even with an array processor.

This situation is greatly improved by using two separate computers to effect a separation of the real-time events from the non-real-time events. Figure 5 illustrates this arrangement, in which one computer is of a general purpose nature, while the other is an array processor. Using another computer, such as an array processor, to perform all of real-time computation and throughput tasks conveniently divides the control system into two microprocessor-based subsystems. These subsystems are identified in Fig. 5 as the executive subsystem and the real-time subsystem. The executive subsystem consists of the host computer, the printer/plotter units, the host disk drives, and the computer terminals. The function of the executive computer is to supervise its own peripherals and the array processor and to perform all software development. The real-time subsystem consists of the array processor, the A/D converters, the D/A converters, and possibly other real-time devices.

The real-time subsystem's task is to perform all of the real-time control functions. Because the data acquisition and actuation devices shown in Fig. 5 are directly attached to the array processor, it can transfer data to and from these devices at speeds much higher than those which could be supported by the typical host computer. Throughput rates of 8–12 MHz may be achieved using an array processor as the core of the real-time subsystem. Moreover, by programming an array processor to perform all closed-loop control operations, the computation rate can exceed that speed attainable using the array processor as a peripheral. This is possible because the real-time subsystem does not have to wait for any non-real-time events, nor does it have to wait for some action from the executive subsystem. Though always under the control of the executive subsystem, the real-time subsystem operates independently of it. If another general-purpose minicomputer is used as the real-time computer, a throughput rate of about 2 MHz is attainable if control computation is kept to a minimum. This is still much faster than the 100 kHz limiting throughput rate attainable on most host systems. The disadvantage of using most minicomputers for real-time control is that their data buses cannot usually support a data transmission rate faster than about 2 MHz [14].

The executive processor subsystem serves to implement the operating system and to coordinate all non-real-time activities. It is called the executive subsystem because it controls the real-time subsystem, which operates independently of it. Asynchronous operation of these two systems is made possible through the use of an interface placed between them. No longer burdened with heavy I/O or intensive numerical analysis, the executive computer system is freed to monitor system performance, update on-line graphical displays, record processed run data to disk, interact with the user, and perform all file manipulation functions. These tasks are designated as being non-real-time because nothing critical happens if they are placed on hold for a few milliseconds, which is generally not true of real-time control operations.

At the same time, using the array processor to decouple the real-time events from the non-real-time events allows closed-loop control computations and throughput operations to proceed at extremely high continuous rates. This results from the real-time subsystem not having to contend with any slow or non-real-time events. The important thing to see from Fig. 5 is that the real-time data acquisition and control devices are connected to the array processor, rather than the host computer. Though another minicomputer could be used instead of an array processor, the data buses of array processors commonly support throughput rates of 6–12 MHz, and sometimes up to 50 MHz in some cases [15]. Nevertheless, even if the second computer is not an array processor, a considerable throughput gain can still be made using the second computer to perform all closed-loop control computations and all real-time data transfer operations, rather than the host computer. Obviously, the controller design using an array processor to form a real-time subsystem (Fig. 5) is not any more expensive to construct than the design using the array processor as a coprocessing peripheral device (Fig. 4). What is probably not obvious is that the controller design using the array processor to form a real-time subsystem is not necessarily any more expensive than the design having a single host computer (Fig. 1). The reason is that the host computer in Fig. 5 does not need to be as capable as the host computer in Fig. 1, since the real-time computation burden has been shifted to the array processor. This division of labor can also be realized using two minicomputers of identical make, though to a lesser extent. However, if an array processor is used to form the real-time subsystem, then the host computer could be replaced by a personal computer, and yet possess a closed-loop control performance exceeding that of many mainframe computers. In fact, some very high-speed mainframe computers (e.g., Cray-1, Cyber-205) are essentially composed of a smaller front-end host machine attached to a vector or array processor of some kind [7].

VI. USING INTELLIGENT DEVICES TO SHARE THE REAL-TIME BURDEN

Though using an array processor to form a real-time subsystem increases system throughput very greatly, intelligent devices and interfaces must be used to maximize throughput speed to meet very demanding applications. For example, a robotic arm control system needing to process data from a video camera requires a very high throughput rate. Video cameras, which are really massive analog-to-digital converters, break an analog image into horizontal vectors (called lines) which are composed of so many 8-bit elements (called pixels). The resulting matrix of data is referred to as a frame. Commercially available video cameras can transmit up to 30 frames of data per second [16]. Now, if a controller needed to process only one (512 line × 512 pixel) frame per second, a minimum throughput rate of about 264 kHz 8-bit bytes would be required, eliminating all minicomputers except those with coprocessors. However, to transfer data at 30 frames per second, a throughput rate of about 7.9 MHz 8-bit bytes (for the camera only) would be required. Though this rate may at first seem to fit the capability of the control system described in the previous section, it actually does not. The reason is that processing video data into a form suitable for control requires a fairly massive amount of numerical analysis. The controller described in the previous section can support throughput rates of 8–12 MHz, but only if the computation load is very minimal, which is not the case here. For this application, the throughput rate must be a good deal faster than 8 MHz to allow time for the numerous imaging and control computations which must be done at the same time. What is really needed is a way to maintain a 12 MHz computation rate concurrently with 12 MHz throughput rate. This need is met by controller designs incorporating intelligent devices and interfaces.

If intelligent devices and interfaces are used, throughput rates of 8–12 MHz (8-bit bytes) with substantial parallel processing can be achieved, with faster speeds attainable by some types of hardware [17, 18]. The word intelligent is used to mean microprocessor-based devices or interfaces which can be programmed to perform user-defined functions. (Though some people refer to any device having a microprocessor as being intelligent, the emphasis here is on user programmability, so that the device can be intelligent in the eyes of the user.) Intelligent devices and interfaces serve to distribute the real-time control burden, in much the same way an array processor can take the real-time burden away from a host computer. By distributing the real-time workload over many microprocessors, the ability of the controller to perform parallel processing operations increases, thereby increasing the performance of the control system. Intelligent devices will be discussed in this section, leaving the discussion of intelligent interfaces to the next.

In order to provide a clearer discussion, a rough comparison will be made of the operations required of an array processor using a nonprogrammable and a programmable analog-to-digital converter. Figures 6 and 7 illustrate how the distribution of the real-time workload changes when an intelligent converter is used instead of a nonprogrammable one. As shown in Fig. 6, when the array processor needs new data, it signals the converter to get a data sample. The microprocessor of the converter (which is not user programmable) then initiates a conversion and signals the array processor that a data sample is ready for transmission. At this point, the converter has the data values from the n data channels in n single word buffers. Upon receiving a signal from the converter that data are ready, the array processor transfers the data to its own core memory. The converter cannot acquire new data until the old data have been transferred. If there are to be m samples taken per input record, then this cycle must be repeated m times. Some converters place the data from every channel into a single buffer, requiring the data words for each channel to be multiplexed sequentially into the buffer memory location. To obtain a single record, the array processor must perform (n × m) operations, since it must initiate conversion and read data from n channels m times. This places a substantial overhead on the array processor when n and m are large.

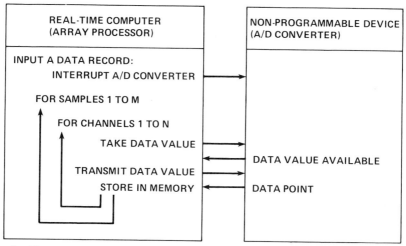

Fig. 6. Nonprogrammable devices place a considerable burden on their real-time computer hosts.

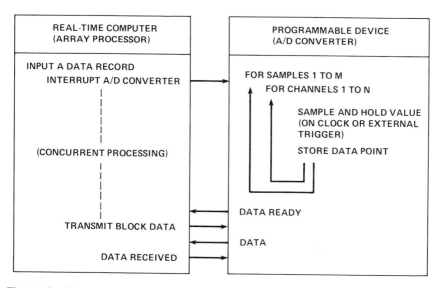

Fig. 7. Intelligent or user-programmable devices share the real-time processing burden with their real-time host controller.

An intelligent or user-programmable digital-to-analog converter allows the converter to share the real-time throughput burden with the array processor, as shown in Fig. 7. This can be done by downloading the converter with a program to make it gather data in parallel with the array processor. When a data record is desired, the array processor need only send an interrupt signal to the converter to make it acquire an entire record of data while the array processor performs other computations. The converter already knows the values of n, m, the sampling format, and the sampling rate from the program which was downloaded by the host computer (through the array processor) prior to the start of closed-loop control operations. The formatted n × m samples are typically stored in a memory provided in the converter. When all samples are obtained, the converter signals the array processor, and all of the data can be transferred to the core memory of the array processor using a block data transfer mode. In this fashion, an intelligent converter reduces the overhead commands to only two, shortens the data transfer time, and leaves the array processor free to perform concurrent processing while the converter is supervising data acquisition.

Real-time throughput and computation speeds are thereby both increased through the use of intelligent devices. From the above example, it is seen that the throughput rate of a system using intelligent devices is essentially limited by the rate at which the attached devices can support block data transfers. If an intelligent device's bus can only support a 2 MHz transmission rate, throughput rates higher than 2 MHz cannot be achieved by directly connecting the device to the array processor. To avoid this problem, another hardware improvement must be made, and this is to add an intelligent interface between the device and the array processor or real-time computer.

VII. USING INTELLIGENT INTERFACES TO INCREASE COMMUNICATION SPEEDS

Intelligent interfaces are microprocessor-controlled communication data paths which can be programmed to perform automated data transfer operations between two or more intelligent devices. Intelligent interfaces allow block data transfer operations to occur between a real-time intelligent device and its real-time host computer (or array processor), without the intervention of either the device's or host's microprocessor. Moreover, because intelligent interfaces can transfer data over their own high-speed buses, the data transmission rate is not limited to the operation speeds of the devices.

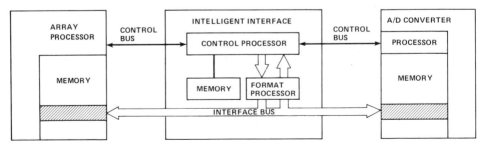

Fig. 8. An intelligent interface is a microprocessor-controlled data path between two or more devices.

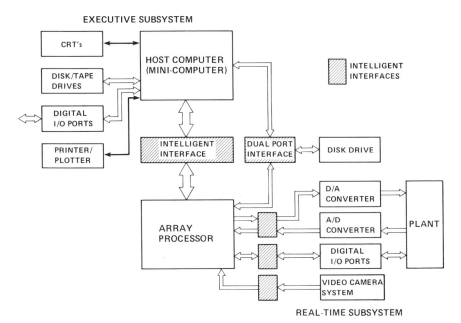

Fig. 9. Intelligent interfaces maximize system throughput by coordinating data transfer operations and by asynchronously connecting devices having different operation speeds.

As shown in Fig. 8, intelligent interfaces have one or two microprocessors, one or more high-speed data paths, and, optionally, memory. The control processor serves to control the flow of data between the devices connected to the interface. The interface is intelligent because the control processor is downloaded with a user-written program prior to the start of real-time operations. This program specifies the addresses (or memory locations) where data are to be obtained and where they are to be delivered. When a device needs to transfer data, it makes a request to the interface control processor, instead of the other device's microprocessor. These signals are usually interrupt signals which force the control processor to jump to a specialized subroutine, known as an interrupt service routine. The interrupt service routines specify the source addresses, destination addresses, and manner in which the data are to be transferred between the devices it connects (see Ref. [1] for details). Usually, a direct memory access transfer is used to transfer the data at high speed. During DMA transfers, the control processor of the interface transfers data from the memory of one device to the memory of the other device without needing the assistance of either device's microprocessor. The only requirement is that devices must have the hardware ports necessary to attach the interface, as is the case with many intelligent devices. Though all interfaces have a control processor, some also have a processor to format the data as they are being transferred. Some interfaces use their format processor, for example, to pack three 12-bit A/D words into one 38-bit array processor word, leading to a threefold increase in throughput. In this manner, intelligent interfaces can transfer data at rates approaching 30 MHz, leaving the real-time subsystem's computer free to perform other computations [19].

Intelligent interfaces are very important devices in terms of increasing controller performance, and they have widespread application in the real-time control world. For example, consider Fig. 9, which illustrates the connection of an analog-to-digital converter, a digital-to-analog converter, an array processor, a disk, and a host computer through intelligent interfaces. The interface between the host computer and the array processor allows data to be transmitted between the host system and the array processor without stopping the operation of either. This could be very useful in changing control gains within the array processor or for sending data from array processor memory to the host for archiving. Without this interface, all data from the host would have to be transferred to the array processor before the start of real-time control, and all data from the array processor could be transferred back to the host only after the end of closed-loop control.

The interfaces between the array processor and the A/D and D/A converter units shown in Fig. 9 have a different role. These interfaces can be programmed to transfer data in a double buffered mode of operation, especially useful in video and other high-throughput applications. The double buffering technique sets up two memory buffers in each device to allow the devices to work with one memory buffer, while the array processor uses the other. Thus, while the digital-to-analog converter outputs the control commands of one buffer, its other buffer is available for new control data from the array processor. When the new control data are ready, the array processor generates an interrupt to the interface. The interface, in turn, transfers the data to the free buffer of the A/D converter and then generates an interrupt to the device so that it switches buffers and outputs the new commands. This leaves the old buffer free to be refilled by the array processor. A similar process can be used in reverse for the analog-to-digital converter and video camera. Switching buffers and transferring data require only that the A/D converter and array processor (for D/A switching) generate the appropriate interrupt signals to the interfaces. The interfaces supervise all data transfer operations, leaving both the array processor and intelligent devices free to perform operations in parallel with the interface.

Also seen in Fig. 9 is an interface placed between the host computer, the array processor, and a disk. In this application, the use of the interface is to connect devices having vastly different operation speeds, another important use of interfaces. Though the disk's data transfer rate is much slower than the array processor's, by connecting the disk through an intelligent interface the array processor is allowed to operate at its maximum speed. When the array processor needs to store data onto the disk, the array processor sends an interrupt signal to the interface, but continues on with its own computations. The interface transfers the data from array processor memory to the disk without the assistance of the array processor. Actually, the interface placed between the executive subsystem and the real-time subsystem also served to connect two computers of different speeds and allowed asynchronous operation. Programmable interfaces thus allow system components to be decoupled from each other to allow them to operate at their maximum speeds. The devices then communicate with each other by making requests to their connecting interfaces, and thereby do not have to halt their operation, waiting for the response of other devices.

One caution on the use of intelligent interfaces and devices is to remember that each of these devices requires the user to write a program to control their operation. With the introduction of every intelligent interface and device, the real-time control burden is further distributed, but at the expense of having another device to program. For example, in the double-buffered conversion application mentioned above, four programs would need to be written: a control program for the analog-to-digital converter, a control program for the digital-to-analog converter, and two more programs for the interfaces connecting them to the array processor. The writing of these programs is usually fairly involved, since the logic needed to supervise the orderly transfer of data involves precise coordination of the interrupt service routines within the real-time subsystem. These routines must usually be written in a special kind of machine-oriented assembly language, making programming difficult and prone to error. To aid this situation somewhat, many interfaces and devices can be purchased with interrupt drivers. These routines provide the user with a few factory-designed control modes, which may be used as is or used in a user-customized format. In all cases, however, there does exist a very real software cost associated with distributing the real-time processing. For applications not requiring high throughput, the programming burden may outweigh the benefits associated with these devices.

One nice thing about programmable interfaces is that they are usually inexpensive. Since most interfaces are single-board devices which offer much less flexibility than a personal computer, they are usually priced very reasonably. Interfaces having sophisticated processors and memory boards may be priced higher, but this is often not the case. The real cost of using intelligent interfaces lies not in their purchase price, but rather in the time it takes to program them for successful operation.

VIII. APPLICATION EXAMPLE: HELICOPTER CONTROLLER USED TO SUPPRESS VIBRATION AND TO AUGMENT STABILITY

In this last section, an application example is presented to give the reader an understanding of how the design considerations given above were applied to an actual control system design task. This example concerns the design of a high-speed controller at the NASA Ames Research Center used to suppress helicopter vibration and to augment helicopter stability. Because the architecture of this controller is of a sufficiently general nature, its design can be applied to a wide range of other automatic control applications as well.

The task of this controller is to compute the control signals needed to reduce helicopter vibration and/or to increase helicopter stability. Owing to the possible unsteadiness of the helicopter vibration and stability dynamics, it was

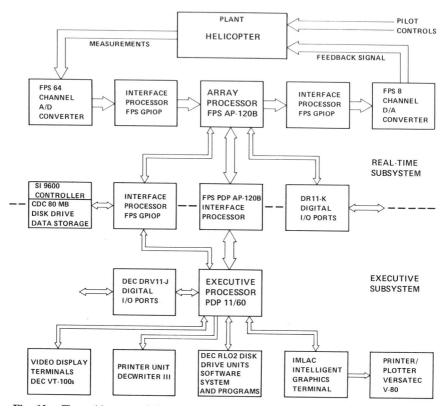

Fig. 10. The architecture of the helicopter vibration and stability controller used at the NASA Ames Research Center.

felt that computation of these control signals might be required once every rotor revolution. The tasks to be performed within this time interval were analog-to-digital conversion of up to 64 input accelerometer signals, identification of the system's dynamic model, computation of control commands to drive at least three blade pitch control actuators, and digital-to-analog conversion of the control signals. It was additionally required that the controller be able to monitor its performance and be able to permanently store selected data for post-test analysis. Since typical helicopter rotors rotate at 4–5 Hz, the tasks needed to be done by the controller are great, relative to the time allowed for their completion (0.20–0.25 s).

The overall architecture of this controller is essentially that shown in Fig. 9 (minus the video camera). The details of the design are shown in Fig. 10, with a line drawn to indicate the division of the controller into two subsystems. These two subsystems are designated as the executive subsystem and the real-time subsystem. This division separates the real-time, closed-loop control functions, from those tasks which do not need to be done in real time. The real-time subsystem is composed of a Floating Point Systems (FPS) AP-120B array processor, a Data Translation 64 channel A/D converter, a Data Translation 8-channel D/A converter, a System Industries 9600 disk controller interfaced to a Control Data Corporation (CDC) 80-megabyte disk drive unit, and 4 DEC DRV11-K digital I/O interfaces. The analog-to-digital and the digital-to-analog converters are intelligent devices. They are connected to the array processor through intelligent interfaces made by Floating Point Systems, called General Purpose Input/Output Processors (GPIOPs). The executive or non-real-time subsystem is integrated around a Digital Equipment Corporation (DEC) PDP 11/60 computer. This computer serves as the host for the array processor and several non-real-time devices. These devices include two RLO2 disk drives, a Versatec V-80 printer/plotter unit, a Decwriter III printer, an IMLAC Intelligent graphics terminal, a DEC VT-100 terminal, and 4 DEC DRV11-J digital I/O ports. All program development and file manipulation is done by the PDP 11/60, which implements the operating system of the controller. The real-time and executive subsystems are discussed separately below.

A. REAL-TIME SUBSYSTEM DESCRIPTION

The real-time subsystem is used to perform intensive, closed-loop rotor system identification and control calculations. The heart of this subsystem is an FPS AP-120B array processor. This array processor has seven buses, an I/O processor, a control processor, two adder units, two multiplier units, and separate program source, main data, and table memories. For the present application, the AP-120B has been configured with a 64K word main data memory, 4K word program source memory, and 1K table memory. These memories all have access times of 167 ns and use words which are 38 bits in width. The AP-120B does have a program overlay facility, in case the control program is larger than 4K words, but it is not needed in the present application. (Initially, the array processor had only 2K of program source memory. This was found to be too small for the control program if overlays were not to be used to avoid slowing the computation rate. This underscores the need to double check memory requirements and to order more than that thought needed if the memory requirements are uncertain.) Intelligent devices and interfaces have been used to distribute the real-time control burden over many microprocessors. This optimizes computation and throughput capability at the expense of having a greater programming task. Aside from the array processor, programs for the analog-to-digital converter, digital-to-analog converter, and the intelligent interfaces also needed to be written. Another programming task was to write a subprogram for an 80 MB disk which had also been attached to the array processor through an intelligent interface. This disk is used to store test data which are acquired or produced by the array processor during the course of a control session.

Distributing the real-time burden is the key which the real-time subsystem uses to maximize control computation and throughput rates. A first application of this principle, of course, was to separate the real-time and non-real-time events by using two computers (a host and array processor). A further extension of distributing the real-time processing burden is demonstrated in the way in which analog-to-digital and digital-to-analog converters are made to operate in parallel with the array processor. This parallelism in operation deserves comment because it is noteworthy how the burdensome task of data I/O is removed from the array processor. This task is cumbersome because many data points per input record for several channels must be obtained, and because data may be desired at a specified sampling rate or on trigger from a pulse generator slaved to the rotor position. In either case, it is preferable that some device other than the array processor perform the sampling task, so that the array processor can be used to perform other computations. The devices which do this are the fully programmable converters and intelligent interfaces. The converters are programmed to sample (or output) data on cue from either a programmable clock generator or rotor tachometer pulse to allow for either time-domain or frequency-domain sampling. Prior to starting the control system, the programs for the converters and interfaces are downloaded by the host (PDP 11/60) computer through the array processor. Once in operation, the converters are programmed to gather (or output) one record of data for all of the channels each time the array processor makes a request. Not only are the converters programmable, but they also have 512 words of on-board RAM for each channel, so that an entire record of data may be stored prior to transmission to or from the array processor.

Moreover, the interfaces and converters have been programmed to provide a continuous, double-buffered stream of data to the array processor. The converters are programmed to set up two memory buffers, allowing up to 2×256 words per channel. The interfaces then transfer data in parallel with array processor operation. In the case of data acquisition, when one buffer of the analog-to-digital converter is filled, the converter generates an interrupt to the interface, specifying which buffer is full, and the data are transferred to array processor memory under the direction of the intelligent interface's program. The interface's program knows the location where the input data are to reside inside the array processor's main data memory. The interface is also programmed to send an error signal to the executive subsystem if the converter has a second sample of data ready for input before transfer of the first sample has been completed. This might happen, for example, if the array processor was programmed to perform too much computation between samples. Hence, the intelligent interface and intelligent converter take the burden of data acquisition away from the array processor. The array processor can then work with the input data as it would any other data stored in its memory. Digital-to-analog conversion for control output is handled in an exactly analogous fashion. The only difference is that the interface for the digital-to-analog converter is programmed to transfer data from the array processor's main data memory to the memory of the converter. When the array processor finishes computing the control commands for a given iteration, it generates an interrupt to the interface, which then transfers the data to one of the digital-to-analog converter's buffers. The converter then switches buffers, begins to output the new control signals, and makes the old buffer available to be refilled by the array processor.

Also attached to the array processor are a CDC 80 MB disk drive unit and four digital interface ports. The disk has been interfaced to the array processor through another FPS GPIOP intelligent interface. The interface is needed to connect the disk to the array processor so that the relatively slow speed of the disk does not impair array processor performance. When the disk's interface receives an interrupt signal from the array processor, it transfers the data from array processor memory to disk, without halting the operation of the array processor. It can further be noted that the interface is dual ported, and has its other port connected to the executive subsystem. This path is desirable for off-line data reduction of data stored on the disk. The digital interface ports are not utilized in the present application, but may be useful if further expansion of the controller is done. The function of these ports is to accept digitized data from another computer or digital device. They can also be programmed to accept serial data on each bit or to sense up to 64 events of the on/off type.

All real-time identification and closed-loop control computations are performed by the FPS AP-120B array processor. The array processor is programmed to optionally perform a Kalman filter or least mean square (LMS) type on-line system identification with every rotor revolution. This identification subroutine is coupled with a minimum variance type of control law to calculate the vibration and stability control commands. The array processor can perform these calculations up to a maximum rate of 12 million floating point operations per second. By programming the intelligent interfaces to pack three 12-bit words into one 38-bit array processor word, this system can support a 36 MHz throughput rate if control computations are kept small. Though this throughput rate is well above the application's maximum required throughput rate of about 1 MHz, a vast amount of computation needs to be done at the same time. A 12 MHz data transmission speed is actually used to leave the majority of array processor time free for identification and control computations. Typically, Kalman filter or LMS filter identification and minimum variance control law calculation can be done at rotor speeds of up to about 1500 rpm (25 Hz), with higher speeds attainable if on-line identification is not done. Though these rpms are not encountered by real world heliocopters, small-scale models of these rotors used for wind tunnel testing rotate much faster. Small-scale rotors must turn four to five times faster than their full-scale counterparts to generate the equivalent aerodynamic forces and moments. After the controller in this example was acquired, it was used to test active control concepts on a small-scale rotor which could rotate up to 2000 rpm. This is mentioned only to point out that high-speed controller designs can have unforeseen benefits, since one is never quite sure what future applications might arise.

B.   EXECUTIVE SUBSYSTEM DESCRIPTION

The executive computer subsystem is built around a DEC PDP 11/60 computer, which serves as host computer to the AP-120B array processor and executive subsystem peripherals. The executive subsystem operates independently, yet maintains control of the real-time subsystem. Independent operation of these subsystems is provided by the multitasking nature of the executive subsystem's operating system and by having an interface between the two subsystems. The executive subsystem functions to monitor system control performance and to pass data to and from the array processor. The PDP 11/60 has a DEC FP11-E floating point processor which can directly address 256K bytes of memory and support up to 256 vectored interrupts. This processor has a maximum MIPS rate of 3 MHz and a maximum throughput rate of 2 MHz. The PDP 11/60 was configured with a 2K cache memory and 128K of core RAM memory. This computer uses a 16-bit bus but can perform mathematical computations in 32-bit or 64-bit precision. The executive subsystem peripherals include two RLO2 10MB disk drives, a Decwriter III printer, a Versatec V-80 printer/plotter, an IMLAC Intelligent Graphics terminal, a VT-100 terminal, and four digital interface ports. The structure of the executive subsystem is not one which distributes the non-real-time burden, since the peripherals cannot operate independently of the host computer. For the current application this is acceptable, because the executive subsystem performs no numerical computations. Hence, it is largely free to fulfill its role as a supervisor of the peripheral devices.

The executive computer subsystem provides the means to edit and permanently store the system software. Since the array processor has no such capability, all software development, including programs for the real-time subsystem's intelligent devices, intelligent interfaces, array processor, and the PDP 11/60, must be done on the executive subsystem. The controller uses one of the 10MB RLO2 disks to store the operating system, linker, editor, and other program utilities, while using the other disk to hold program software for all of the controller's many devices.

The operating system of the host computer, RSX-11M, supports a multitasking environment. This not only allows the executive computer to host several terminals, but also supports the running of more than one program at a time. In the present application, multitasking is used to run two programs at once. One program communicates with the operator of the control system and handles all non-real-time events, while the other program supervises the real-time needs of the array processor. The non-real-time program offers a menu of options to the user so that various plot and printout functions can be done by the PDP 11/60 while the array processor handles real-time control. These plots and printouts assist the operator in determining whether the controller is operating as planned. This program also provides the user with a software on/off switch for the array processor. When this start option is selected, the second (real-time) program is activated in the PDP 11/60. This program downloads the array processor and all of the intelligent devices and intelligent interfaces with their control programs. After the programs are downloaded, it activates the real-time subsystem, and closed-loop control operation is begun. When the array processor needs to pass data to or accept data from the executive subsystem, the array processor generates an interrupt of the interface connecting the two subsystems and the second PDP 11/60 program receives the data. This interface allows both the executive and the real-time subsystems to operate at their maximum speeds, which is necessary to maximize controller performance. Moreover, the multitasking environment respects the user-defined priorities, so that the real-time de-

TABLE III. COMPARISON OF COMPUTATION AND THROUGHPUT RATES

Controller Architecture	Max. computation rate (MFLOPS)	Max. throughput rate (8-bit bytes)
Classical design	1.0–2.0	100 kHz
Coprocessor board in host computer	3.0–5.0	1.5 MHz
Array proc. used as a coprocessor	12–15	1.5–3.0 MHz
Array proc. forms a real-time subsystem	12–15	6–8 MHz
Above with intelligent devices and interfaces	12–120[a]	24–36 MHz

[a]800 MFLOPS and faster rates are possible using custom designed intelligent devices and interfaces.

mands are attended to first, before meeting less important needs, such as the updating of graphic displays and printouts.

IX. CONCLUDING REMARKS

In summary, Table III presents a rough comparison of what average performance gains in computation and throughput may result from applying the above design considerations. When viewing the table, it is important to keep in mind that throughput tasks tend to compete with computation tasks for processor time. If intelligent interfaces and devices are not used to aid throughput, then the maximum throughput rate and maximum computation rate cannot be achieved at the same time. By using intelligent devices and interfaces, however, this restriction is relaxed considerably. Though the rates cited in Table III will probably increase with advances in technology, the design considerations used to increase controller computation and throughput rates will likely still apply. When attempting the design of a high-speed controller, or considering whether an existing controller can be made to function better, it may be useful to consider the following questions:

(1) Can the performance characteristics of the current (or proposed) computer be improved upon? If the computer will support more core or cache memory, expansion of the memory may be desirable to avoid program overlaying and make more room for additional (or yet unknown) control software. If the computer has not yet been acquired, it is wise to consider whether its processor has a high enough MIPS rate, if it has the right interrupt structure, if it has DMA capability, if it can perform computations in the desired precision, if its bus is wide enough, and if it can support a multitasking or other desired operating system.

(2) Has an array processor or other coprocessor been used to share the computation burden placed on the host computer? This processor could be a coprocessor board for the host, another minicomputer, or an array processor. In the above discussion, it has been shown that an array processor can be added to a host minicomputer as a peripheral device to free the host from intensive numerical calculation. This leaves the host or central computer more time to supervise the peripheral devices, thereby increasing system throughput as well.

(3) Have two or more computers been used to effect a separation of the real-time events from the non-real-time events? Separation allows real-time devices to operate at their maximum computation and throughput speeds by not coupling them to the operation of slower devices or non-real-time events.

(4) Is it possible to use an array processor as the basis for a real-time subsystem? A small minicomputer can attain the closed-loop speed of a large mainframe computer, if an array processor is used to form the real-time computer subsystem.

(5) Have intelligent devices and interfaces been used where appropriate to distribute the real-time control burden? Intelligent devices can be used to perform simple, yet tedious, operations such as data acquisition, thereby leaving the closed-loop control computer free to perform other computations in parallel with the devices. Intelligent interfaces further enhance controller performance by allowing all data transfer operations to be conducted in parallel with the operations of the intelligent devices and real-time computer.

Even if no further hardware acquisition is contemplated, great improvements in controller performance can be made by simply rearranging the control system components or by changing the way in which data flows through the computer system. Controllers that implement all of the design considerations given above will most likely be able to maintain very high control throughput and computation rates at the same time. Though this may not be required for every control system today, future applications will likely rely on control systems having higher throughput and computation speeds. It is possible that minicomputer and mainframe computer manufactures will recognize this trend and will add to their product lines those devices which can increase system computation and throughput rates. If this is done, the task of structuring a high-speed control system will be made much easier, since many of the devices to be integrated into the control system will be made by the same vendor. This will then shift a large portion of the component integration burden from the control system designer to the manufacturer. However, it is also possible that the manufacturers of host systems will spend their time designing more advanced computing machines, but of a general-purpose nature. If this happens, the task of integrating real-time coprocessing computers, intelligent interfaces, and intelligent devices will be left to the control system designer.

REFERENCES

1. H. GARLAND, "Introduction to Microprocessor System Design," McGraw-Hill, New York, 1979.
2. Hearst Business Publication, "IC Master," Hearst, 1988.
3. D.A.T.A. Inc., "D.A.T.A. Book Microprocessor Integrated Circuits," *Electron. Inf. Ser.*, 9th ed., Vol. 30, Book 8, D.A.T.A., Inc., March 1985.
4. CSPI, INC., "Array Processors," CSPI, Inc., Billerica, Massachusetts, 1983.
5. B. K. GILBERT, B. A. NAUSED, D. J. SCHWAB, and R. L. THOMPSON, "The Need for a Wholistic Design Approach," *Computer* 19, No. 10, October 1986.
6. D. MacGREGOR and J. RUBINSTEIN, "A Performance Analysis of MC68020-based Systems," *IEEE Micro* 5, No. 6, December 1985.
7. K. HWANG and F. A. BRIGGS, "Computer Architectures and Parallel Processing," McGraw-Hill, New York, 1984.
8. P. ALEXANDER, "Array Processors," *Mach. Des.*, August 1979.
9. H. MORRIS, "Industry Begins to Apply Vision Systems Widely," *Control Eng.*, January 1985.
10. H. MORRIS, "Robotic Control Systems: More Than Simply Collections of Servo Loops," *Control Eng.*, May 1984.
11. Floating Point Systems, "A Real-Time Digital Filter Subsystem," Idaho National Energy Lab, FPS Rep. 360470, FPS, Inc., Portland, Oregon, 1980.
12. CSPI, INC., "Using the Array Processor for Finite Element Modeling," CSPI APN 9.0, CSPI, Inc., Billerica, Massachusetts, October 1980.
13. P. ALEXANDER, "The Array Processor as an Intelligent Simulation Compressor," *Proc. Summer Comput. Simul. Conf., Toronto,* 345–351 (1979).
14. Digital Equipment Corporation, "VAX Hardware Handbook," Digital's New Product Marketing, DEC, Santa Clara, California, 1981.
15. Floating Point Systems, Inc., "AP-120B Array Processor Hardware Reference Manual," FP Doc. No. 860-7431-000A, FPS, Inc., Portland, Oregon, 1982.
16. Data Translation, Inc., "Goldbook Catalog of Microcomputer I/O Boards and Software," Data Translation, Inc., Marlboro, Massachusetts, 1987.
17. CSPI, INC., "Array Processors in Image Analysis Applications," CSPI   12.0, CSPI, Inc., Billerica, Massachusetts, 1980.
18. CSPI, INC., "Video Tracking," CSPI APN 10.1, CSPI, Inc., Billerica, Massachusetts, 1981.
19. CSPI, INC., "Guide to MAP Family of I/O Interfaces," CSPI Doc. S-12, CSPI, Inc., Billerica, Massachusetts, 1979.

COMPUTATIONAL TECHNIQUES IN ANGLE-ONLY TRACKING FILTERING

CHAO-YIN HSIAO

Mechanical Engineering Department
Feng Chia University
Seatwen, Taichung, Taiwan

I. INTRODUCTION

This article covers some of the most commonly used ideas and techniques for angle-only tracking (AOT) filtering and the most promising ideas and techniques that may be used in the future. Four topics are outlined and discussed: two major AOT properties, possible additional information, Kalman filters and maneuvering target-tracking techniques, and some other useful AOT filtering techniques.

Observability and angular sensitivity are two major AOT properties. During tracking, there are no measurement range data; the range between the target and the observer must be estimated, which always makes the target trajectory undeterminable. This is the problem of observability, which is serious in AOT, especially in single-sensor angle-only tracking (SSAOT). Here single-sensor angle-only means that the observer has only one sensor, and this sensor can only measure the direction of the target. On the other hand, if the observer has more than one sensor, and each of those sensors can only measure the direction of the target, it is called multisensor angle-only tracking (MSAOT). The observability is less serious in MSAOT. The problem of observability of SSAOT will be discussed in Section II. It has been discovered that the relationship between the target velocity and the angular rate of the line of sight of the target with respect to a fixed observer can be used to construct a field called the field of angular sensitivity [1], which will be discussed in Section III. Basically, AOT is a kind of information extraction process. In order to get better tracking results, it is useful to collect extra information, and to get some kind of *a priori* knowledge about the target. By doing this, some cases may still be considered "wide-sense AOT" (only angles and time derivatives of the angle are measured). Some of them may not be AOT any longer, but may still belong to "passive tracking." Cases belonging to either of these are outlined and discussed in Section IV. Kalman filter techniques and maneuvering target-tracking techniques are the most common tracking techniques. They are not limited to AOT and will be discussed in Section V. There are many other AOT techniques which are more or less specially designed or frequently used. These will be discussed in Section VI. In Section VII some comments, conclusions, and future research topics are given.

II.   OBSERVABILITY OF SINGLE-SENSOR ANGLE-ONLY TRACKING

Without the range data, and without any *a priori* knowledge about the target's kinematic behavior, it is impossible to determine the unique target trajectory from the measured data. Actually, for a given set of measured data, there are infinite target trajectory solutions. If some *a priori* knowledge is obtained about the target's kinematic behavior, such as that the target is fixed, is running with constant velocity, is running with constant acceleration, or is running with some kind of time function, then a unique target solution may exist. Based on these assumptions, the problem of observability can then be discussed.

In this section, the cases of fixed target, targets with constant velocity trajectory, with constant acceleration trajectory, and with constant-coefficient n-th-order time polynomial trajectory in general are discussed. Also, at the end of this section, two illustrations are given to show the possible shapes of the covariances of estimation of two observable MSAOT cases.

A.   FIXED TARGET

It is not difficult to see that if the observer is also fixed, or the observer always moves along a straight line that passes through the fixed target, then the line of sight (LOS) of the observation does not change with time; so the range of the target is unable to be estimated. On the other hand, if some measurements are taken with the observer not on the same line, then the target's location can be estimated by trigonometric theory. Also, if the target's location can be estimated by trigonometric theory, some measurements must be taken when the observer is not on the same line. This proves the necessary and sufficient conditions of the observability of the fixed target case, stated as follows: "A moving observer, and the observer trajectory and the fixed target are non-collinear" [1].

B.   TARGET WITH CONSTANT VELOCITY

Murphy [2] determined that, in the case of constant-velocity straight-line target trajectory, the necessary condition of observability is observer acceleration. Later, the necessary and sufficient conditions of the unique target trajectory solution of this constant-velocity target case were derived by Nardone and Aidala [3], as follows: Own-ship accelerates, subject to the constraint,

$$\int_0^t (t - \tau)[a_{ox}(\tau) \cos \beta (t)$$
$$- a_{oy}(\tau) \sin \beta(t)] \, d\tau \neq 0.$$

Here, own-ship is the observer, $a_{ox}(\tau)$ and $a_{oy}(\tau)$ are the x and y acceleration components of the observer, and $\beta(t)$ is the angle of the LOS measured at time t.

C.   TARGET WITH CONSTANT ACCELERATION

1.   System Description

At time t the target trajectory is

$$x_t(t) = l_{tx} + v_{tx}(t) + 1/2a_{tx}t^2 \tag{1}$$

$$y_t(t) = l_{ty} + v_{ty}t + 1/2a_{ty}t^2. \tag{2}$$

The sensor trajectory is

$$x_s(t) = l_{sx} + v_{sx}(t) + 1/2a_{sx}t^2 + H_x(t) \tag{3}$$

$$y_s(t) = l_{sy} + v_{sy}(t) + 1/2a_{sy}t^2 + H_y(t). \tag{4}$$

The target trajectory with respect to the coordinates attached to the sensor is

$$x_r(t) = x_t(t) - x_s(t)$$
$$= r_x + v_{rx}(t) + 1/2a_{rx}t^2 - H_x(t) \tag{5}$$

$$y_r(t) = yx_t(t) - y_s(t)$$
$$= r_y + v_{ry}y + 1/2a_{ry}t^2 - H_y(t), \tag{6}$$

where l_{tx}, l_{ty}, v_{tx}, v_{ty}, a_{tx}, and a_{ty} are the x and y components of the target's location, velocity, and acceleration, respectively, at time 0; l_{sx}, l_{sy}, v_{sx}, v_{sy}, a_{sx}, and a_{sy} are the x and y components of the sensor's location, velocity, and acceleration, respectively, at time 0; $H_x(t)$, $H_y(t)$ are higher-order time polynomials representing the x and y components of the sensor's kinematic behavior; and r_x, r_y, v_{rx}, v_{ry}, a_{rx}, a_{ry} are the x and y components of the target's location, velocity, and acceleration, respectively, with respect to the coordinates attached to the sensor at time 0.

2. Noise-Free Measurement

At time t

$$\tan \beta = \frac{x_r(t)}{y_r(t)} \tag{7}$$

$$\frac{\sin \beta_t}{\cos \beta_t} = \frac{x_t(t) - x_s(t)}{y_t(t) - y_s(t)} \tag{8}$$

$$y_t(t)\sin \beta_t + x_t(t)\cos \beta_t$$

$$= y_s(t) \sin \beta_t - x_s(t) \cos \beta_t \tag{9}$$

$$1/2t^2 \sin \beta_t\, a_{ty} - t \sin \beta_y\, v_{ty} + \sin \beta_t\, l_{ty}$$

$$- 1/2t^2 \cos \beta_t\, a_{tx} - t \cos \beta_t\, v_{tx} - \cos \beta_t\, l_{tx}$$

$$= 1/2t^2 \sin \beta_t\, a_{sy} + t \sin \beta_t\, v_{sy}$$

$$+ \sin \beta_t\, l_{sy} - 1/2t^2 \cos \beta_t\, a_{sx} - t \cos \beta_t\, v_{sx} - \cos \beta_t\, l_{sx}$$

$$+ \sin \beta_t\, H_y(t) - \cos \beta_t\, H_x(t), \tag{10}$$

with N measurements taken at $t_1, \ldots, t_N$. Using β_i to represent β_{ti}, it follows that

$$A_N x_t = A_N x_s + b, \tag{11}$$

in which

$$A_N = \begin{bmatrix} 1/2t_1^2 \sin \beta_1 & t_1 \sin \beta_1 & \sin \beta_1 & -1/2t_1^2 \cos \beta_1 & -t_1 \cos \beta_1 & -\cos \beta_1 \\ 1/2t_2^2 \sin \beta_2 & t_2 \sin \beta_2 & \sin \beta_2 & -1/2t_2^2 \cos \beta_2 & -t_2 \cos \beta_1 & -\cos \beta_2 \\ \vdots & \vdots & \vdots & \vdots & \vdots & \vdots \\ 1/2t_N^2 \sin \beta_N & t_N \sin \beta_N & \sin \beta_N & -1/2t_N^2 \cos \beta_N & -t_N \cos \beta_N & -\cos \beta_N \end{bmatrix} \tag{12}$$

$$x_t = [a_{ty}\ v_{ty}\ l_{ty}\ a_{tx}\ v_{tx}\ l_{tx}]^T \tag{13}$$

$$x_s = [a_{sy} \; v_{sy} \; l_{sy} \; a_{sx} \; v_{sx} \; l_{sx}]^T \tag{14}$$

$$b = \begin{bmatrix} H_y(t_1) \sin \beta_1 & - & H_x(t_1) \cos \beta_1 \\ H_y(t_2) \sin \beta_2 & - & H_x(t_2) \cos \beta_2 \\ \vdots & & \vdots \\ H_y(t_N) \sin \beta_N & - & H_x(t_N) \cos \beta_N \end{bmatrix} \tag{15}$$

3.   Solution

With x and b assumed known and β_i coming from measurements, if $A_N^T A_N$ is nonsingular, then

$$x_t = x_s + \left(A_N^T A_N \right)^{-1} A_N^T \, b. \tag{16}$$

From (16) it is clear that the necessary and sufficient conditions of a unique and nontrivial solution are: $A_N^T A_N$ nonsingular and $(A_N^T A_N)^{-1} A_N^T b$ a nonzero vector.

4.   Comments

The condition $(A_N^T A_N)^{-1} A_N^T b \neq 0$ in (16) implies $b \neq 0$, which implies neither $H_x(t_i) = 0$ and $H_y(t_i) = 0$ nor $H_y(t_i) \sin \beta_i - H_x(t_i) \cos \beta_i = 0$, which means not only the observer (the sensor) should be more active than the target $[H_x(t_i) \neq 0$ or $H_y(t_i) \neq 0]$ but also the condition $[H_y(t_i) \sin \beta_i - H_x(t_i) \cos \beta_i \neq 0]$ should be satisfied. Of course, the condition $A_N^T b \neq 0$ should also be satisfied.

D.   TARGET WITH CONSTANT-COEFFICIENT
TIME POLYNOMIAL TRAJECTORY

1.   System   Description

At time t the target trajectory is

$$x_t(t) = \sum_{i=0}^{n} x_{ti} t^i \tag{17}$$

$$y_t(t) = \sum_{i=0}^{n} y_{ti} t^i ; \tag{18}$$

the sensor trajectory is

$$x_s(t) = \sum_{i=0}^{n} x_{si} t^i + H_x(t) \tag{19}$$

$$y_s(t) = \sum_{i=0}^{n} y_{si} t^i + H_y(t) \tag{20}$$

where x_{ti}, y_{ti} are unknown constant coefficients, some of which can be zero, but

$$x_{tn}^2 + y_{tn}^2 \neq 0. \tag{21}$$

n can be zero or some larger integer. n = 0 means a fixed target; n = 1, a constant-velocity target trajectory; n = 2, a constant-acceleration target trajectory, etc. x_{si}, y_{si} are assumed known exactly. $H_x(t)$, $H_y(t)$ are higher-order time polynomials (higher than n) representing the x and y components of the sensor's kinematic behavior. Both are assumed known exactly.

2. Noise-Free Measurement

At time t

$$\tan \beta_t = \frac{x_t(t) - x_s(t)}{y_t(t) - y_s(t)}, \tag{22}$$

with N measurements taken at $t_1, \ldots, t_N$, and using β_i to represent β_{ti}, it then follows that

$$A_N x_t = A_N x_s + b, \tag{23}$$

where

$$A_N = \begin{bmatrix} t_1^n \sin \beta_1 & t_1^{n-1} \sin \beta_1 & \cdots & \sin \beta_1 & -t_1^n \cos \beta_1 & -t_1^{n-1} \cos \beta_1 & \cdots & -\cos \beta_1 \\ t_2^n \sin \beta_2 & t_2^{n-1} \sin \beta_2 & \cdots & \sin \beta_2 & -t_2^n \cos \beta_2 & -t_2^{n-1} \cos \beta_2 & \cdots & -\cos \beta_2 \\ \vdots & \vdots & & \vdots & \vdots & \vdots & & \vdots \\ t_N^n \sin \beta_N & t_N^{n-1} \sin \beta_N & \cdots & \sin \beta_N & -t_N^n \cos \beta_N & -t_N^{n-1} \cos \beta_N & \cdots & -\cos \beta_N \end{bmatrix} \tag{24}$$

$$x_t = \begin{bmatrix} y_{tn} & y_{tn-1} & \cdots & y_{t0} & x_{tn} & x_{tn-1} & x_{t0} \end{bmatrix}^T \tag{25}$$

$$x_s = \begin{bmatrix} y_{sn} & y_{sn-1} & \cdots & y_{s0} & x_{sn} & x_{sn-1} & x_{s0} \end{bmatrix}^T \qquad (26)$$

$$b = \begin{bmatrix} H_x(t_1) \sin \beta_1 & - & H_x(t_2) \cos \beta_1 \\ H_y(t_2) \sin \beta_2 & - & H_x(t_2) \cos \beta_2 \\ \vdots & & \vdots \\ H_y(t_N) \sin \beta_N & - & H_x(t_N) \cos \beta_N \end{bmatrix} \qquad (27)$$

3.   Solution

With x_s and b assumed known and β_i coming from measurements, if $A_N^T A_N$ is nonsingular, then

$$x_t = x_s + \left(A_N^T A_N \right)^{-1} A_N^T b. \qquad (28)$$

From (28) it is clear that the necessary and sufficient conditions for a unique and nontrivial solution are $A_N^T A_N$ nonsingular and $(A_N^T A_N)^{-1} A_N^T b$ a nonzero vector.

E.   DISCUSSION

(1) From Subsections II, A–D it can be seen that, in order to be observable, the observer (sensor) should always be more "active" than the target:

(i) When the target is fixed, the observer should be moving.

(ii) When the target moves with constant velocity, the observer should have acceleration.

(iii) When the target moves with constant acceleration, the observer should have t^3 or higher-order terms.

(iv) When the target trajectory is a constant-coefficient n-th-order time polynomial in general, the observer should have nonzero $H_x(t_i)$ or $H_y(t_i)$.

(2) As indicated in subsection II,D, the necessary and sufficient conditions of observability are $A_N^T A_N$ nonsingular and $(A_N^T A_N)^{-1} A_N b$ a nonzero vector, but how to make $A_N^T A_N$ nonsingular is not known. It is not sufficient but it usually works to design the observer's maneuvering strategy based on maximizing the trace of the predicated $A_N^T A_N$ [4] or minimizing the trace of the predicated $(A_N^T A_N)^{-1}$ [1].

(3) During tracking, usually the target's states are unknown a priori, and it is reasonable to assume that the target is running with constant acceleration for each short period of time, and to treat it as a constant-acceleration case.

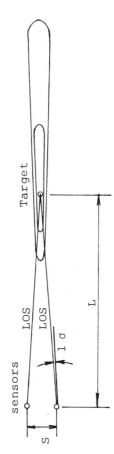

Fig. 1. The possible covariance contours of estimation in the case of two sensors (not exact curves).

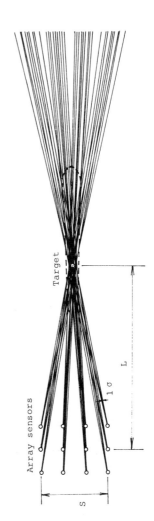

Fig. 2. The closed dashed curve enclosed the area which is most likely to be estimated as the real target location in the case of array sensors.

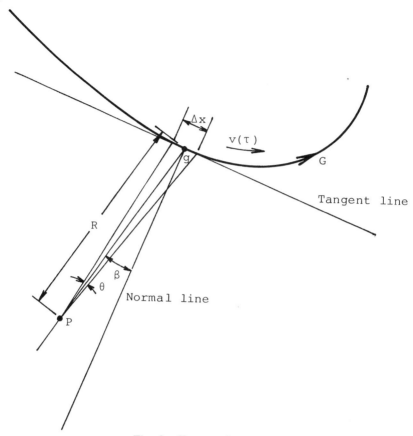

Fig. 3.   Target trajectory.

(4) In the case of MSAOT it is not difficult to infer from trigonometric theory that, if the target and all sensors are not located on the same line, then at any instance the target's location can always be determined. In particular, in 2D cases, is the sensors are not all collinearly located, then the system is always observable.

(5) In some observable tracking systems, if the shape of the covariance of estimation is overelongated, and if the elements of the related covariance matrix are truncated during matrix transformations, then the covariance matrix may have negative eigenvalues. These negative eigenvalues will cause the Kalman filter to diverge. This kind of matrix is called ill-conditioned.

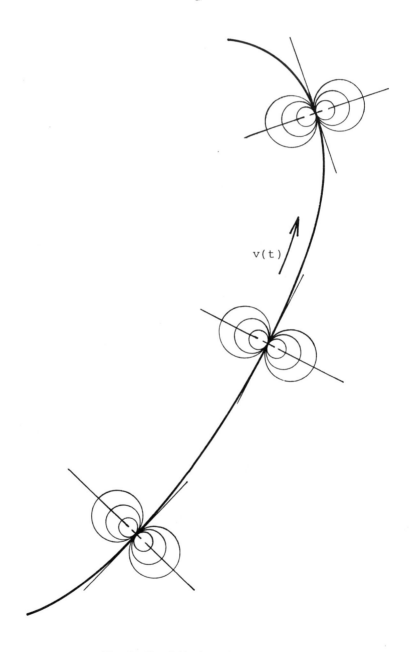

Fig. 4. The field of angular sensitivity.

(6) In Fig. 1 the possible shape of the covariance of estimation in the case of two sensors is indicated, in which σ is the standard deviation of the measurement error. In Fig. 2 the possible shape of the covariance of estimation of the sensor array is indicated. From both Figs. 1 and 2 it can be seen that, if the L/S ratio is large, then it will have an elongated covariance of estimation.

III. ANGULAR SENSITIVITY

As shown in Fig. 3, in two-dimensional space, assuming all sensor locations are fixed, when the target is moving along a trajectory G with a velocity v(t), then to each sensor the direction of the line of sight of the target with respect to sensor will change with time.

Assume the target velocity is v(t), the range between the target and a given sensor p is R(t), and the angle between the LOS and the normal line of the target trajectory is β(t). Then the angular sweeping rate $\dot{\theta}$ (θ is shown in Fig. 3) of the target with respect to this sensor is

$$\dot{\theta} = \lim_{\Delta t \to 0} \frac{\Delta x}{\Delta t} \frac{\cos \beta (t)}{R(t)}$$

$$= \frac{v(t)}{R(t)} \cos \beta (t)$$

(29)

Based on this definition, when the target is running with velocity v(t), a field called "the field of angular sensitivity" can be defined [1] with $\dot{\theta}$ as its strength. An example of this field is shown in Fig. 4, in which the circles represent the locations that have equal strength $\dot{\theta}$.

Comments.

(1) In Section IV "the field of angular sensitivity" of Hsiao [1], a more detailed derivation, some phenomena, and some strategy investigations can be found.

(2) The extention to a three-dimensional case is straightforward, and can also be found in Hsiao [1].

(3) The application of this field is still an open-ended research area.

IV. ADDITIONAL INFORMATION

In order to improve the observability of the tracking system, additional information, as well as *a priori* knowledge, has been used. With extra information and knowledge, some cases may still be considered as "wide-sense AOT" (having only angles and time derivatives of angles in the measured data). Some cases may not be AOT any longer, but they still belong to one of the "passive-tracking" cases, as illustrated below.

A. DOPPLER SHIFT OF THE CENTRAL
NOISE FREQUENCY [5–7]

In addition to the angular information, the Doppler shift information (the angular rate) is also measured. There is no range or range rate measured. Tenney *et al.* used this angular rate data together with angles to track a maneuvering target, finding it very powerful.

Based on Tenney's simulation results [5], when there is target maneuvering, the angle of the LOS changes sluggishly, but the angular rate of the LOS changes immediately. This property is highly suitable for tracking a maneuvering target. It is necessary that the measuring instrument is able to measure the Doppler shift.

B. TIME DELAY IN SONARY DATA [8, 9]

In shallow water, for a given sonar source, and with a given receiver, the receiver will receive the sonar data in three different ways: directly from the source through water to the receiver; directly from the source, hitting the water surface and reflected to the receiver; directly from the source, hitting the bottom ground and reflected to the receiver. These three paths of translation have different translation lengths, and so have different delay times of arrival. These delay times were included with other data used to determine the location of the target. By doing this, the target maneuvering can also be determined.

This is good because the location of the target can be determined immediately when the signal with the largest delay time is received, and with this capability the maneuverability of the target can be determined.

A prerequisite for this is that the entire distribution of the depth of the water must be known *a priori*, or at least known when the data are being processed. This is a kind of passive tracking, but does not belong to AOT.

C. ARRAY OF PASSIVE SENSORS [10, 11]

Based on the discussion given in Section II, it can be seen that in a multisensor case the system can always be made observable by properly arranging the location of the sensors. Based on trigonometric theory, the target trajectory can be determined instantaneously. It is obvious that a linear array is much better than a single sensor. Murphy [10] successfully used a linear array to track a maneuvering target, and a similar technique was used by Liu and Bongiovanni [4].

From the two illustrations given in Section II,B, it can be inferred that when the L/S ratio is large, then the shape of the estimated covariance will appear elongated.

D. GEOMETRIC ORIENTATION OF THE TARGET

The idea of adding the geometric orientation of the target to track the target trajectory was originated by Maybeck [11–13]. This technique was neither used in AOT, nor used in passive tracking. However, if the target has two or more noise sources, each of them has a different pattern of frequencies, and there are fixed distances among them, and all these things are known by the observer *a priori*, then the orientation of the target can be estimated, and Maybeck's idea can be applied.

E.   A PRIORI KNOWLEDGE OF CONSTRAINTS

A more general concept of adding deterministic *a priori* constraints to statistical measurements to improve the estimation result was given by Chang and Sherman [14]. Later, the *a priori* knowledge of velocity constraint was used by Change [15] in doing AOT. He demonstrated that adding this *a priori* velocity constraint does improve the tracking performance. Following this idea, if the *a priori* knowledge of range constraint, energy constraint, acceleration constraint, or a combination is available, then the tracking performance can be improved.

F.   COMMENTS

The addition of extra constraints, information, or *a priori* knowledge does improve the tracking performance, and is essential in the case of weak observability, such as in AOT.

V.   KALMAN FILTERS AND MANEUVERING TARGET-TRACKING TECHNIQUES

Kalman filters and maneuvering target-tracking techniques are the most commonly used tracking techniques.

In the case of linear systems and Gaussian stochastic processes, the Kalman filter will provide a minimum variance unbiased estimate. In order to handle nonlinear, non-Gaussian cases, and for computational convenience, many variations have been created. In this section, some important variations are outlined and discussed.

In order to track a maneuvering target, many techniques have been created, and these will also be outlined and discussed here. The ideas discussed in this section are for tracking in general, and are not limited to AOT.

A.   THE DISCRETE-TIME KALMAN FILTER [16–18]

1.   System Model

$$x(k + 1) = \Phi(k + 1, k)x(k) + \Gamma(k + 1, k)w(k) \tag{30}$$

$$z(k + 1) = H(k + 1x)(k + 1) + v(k + 1), \tag{31}$$

where $k = 0, 1, 2, ...,$ is the discrete-time index; x is the n-state vector with initial state x(0); x(0) is a zero mean n vector with $E[x(0)x^T(0)] = P(0)$; $E[\cdot]$ is the expected operator; P(0) is an n × n positive semidefinite covariance matrix; Φ is the n × n-state transition matrix; Γ is the n × p disturbance transition matrix; w is the Γ disturbance vector; w(k) is the Γ-dimensional zero-mean Gaussian white sequence with $E[w(j)w^T(k)] = Q(k)\delta_{jk}$, $j, k = 0, 1, 2, ...$; Q(k) is a positive semidefinite p × p matrix; δ_{jk} is the Kronecker delta; z is the m measurement vector; H is the m × m measurement matrix; v is the m measurement error vector; v(k + 1) is an m-dimensional zero-mean Gaussian white sequence with $E[v(j + 1)v^T(k + 1)] = R(k + 1)\delta_{jk}$; R(k + 1) is a positive semidefinite m × m matrix; x(0), w(k), v(k + 1) are independent of each other, for all k;

$E[x(j)w^T(k)] = 0$, for all $k \geq j$, $j = 0, 1, ...$;
$E[z(j)w^T(k)] = 0$, for all $k \geq j$, $j = 0, 1, ...$;
$E[x(j)v^T(k)] = 0$, for all j and k, $j = 0, 1, ...$ and $k = 1, 2, ...$;
$E[z(j)v^T(k)] = 0$, for all $k \geq j$, $j, k = 1, 2, ...$

2.   Kalman Filter

For the system described in Subsection V,A,1, the optimal state estimate $\hat{x}(k + 1 \mid k + 1)$ of x(k + 1), and the estimated covariance matrix P(k + 1 | k + 1) of the stochastic process $\tilde{x}(k + 1 \mid k + 1) = x(k + 1) - \hat{x}(k + 1 \mid k + 1)$, are given by the following recursive relation:

$$x(k + 1 \mid k + 1) = \Phi(k + 1, k)x(k \mid k) + K(k + 1)[z(k + 1) \\ - H(k + 1)\Phi(k + 1, k)\hat{x}(k \mid k)] \tag{32}$$

$$K(k + 1) = P(k + 1 \mid k)H^T(k + 1) \\ \times [H(k + 1)P(k + 1 \mid k)H^T(k + 1) + R(k + 1)]^{-1} \tag{33}$$

$$P(k + 1 \mid k) = \Phi(k + 1, k)P(k \mid k)\Phi^T(k + 1, k) \\ + \Gamma(k + 1, k)Q(k)\Gamma^T(k + 1, k) \tag{34}$$

$$P(k + 1 \mid k + 1) = [I - K(k + 1)H(k + 1)]P(k + 1 \mid k) \tag{35}$$

for $k = 0, 1, 2, ...,$ where I is the n × n identity matrix; and K(k + 1) is the n × m gain matrix. This computational algorithm is the famous discrete-time Kalman filter (KF).

3.   Comments

(1) Basic condition of running KF.
    (i) Linear dynamic system.
    (ii) Linear measurements in the state variables.
    (iii) Full knowledge of the system parameters and noise statistics.
    (iv) All stochastic processes are Gaussian.

If it satisfies the above four conditions, a state estimation problem is optimally solved by KF.

(2) Characteristics of KF..

　　(i) Provides the minimum variance unbiased estimate.

　　(ii) Filter structure is linear.

　(iii) Gain and covariance can be processed off-line.

　　(iv) Has finite states.

　(v) The estimation is determined by conditional mean and conditional covariance.

　(vi) During the processing, only the m × m matrix needs to be inverted, instead of the n × n matrix, in which m is the dimension of the measurements and n is the dimension of the states, and usually m is much smaller than n.

　(vii) Because of its recursive nature, it can be run on-line in real time.

B.　　MODIFIED KALMAN FILTERS [18–33]

In the literature of this field, many modified Kalman filters have been investigated. However, for the purpose of modification, they can be classified into three categories:

(1) Modification for nonlinearity.

(2) Modification for non-Gaussian process.

(3) Modification for computational convenience.

1. Modification for Nonlinearity

When the state equations and/or the measurement equations are nonlinear, then the Kalman filter mentioned in Section V,A should be modified. The most common modification is linearizing the nonlinear equations about a trajectory determined by the last state estimate $\hat{x}(k \mid k)$. Then by using an algorithm similar to that mentioned in Section V,A to run the filter, the well-known extended Kalman filter (EKF) is obtained.

In the following, the general form of the EKF and the EKF for the AOT are formulated, and then other advanced EKFs are discussed.

　　a. *Extended Kalman Filter [19–23, 31]*. For a given nonlinear system, with the dynamic equation and the measurement equation given below:

$$x(t) = f(x(t), t) + w(t) \tag{36}$$

$$z(t) = h(x(t)) + v(t), \tag{37}$$

where $w(t)$ and $v(t)$ are zero-mean Gaussian white stochastic processes. Defining $k \triangleq t$; $k + 1 \triangleq t + \Delta t$, Δt being a small time step; $\hat{x}(k \mid j) \triangleq$ the estimate of $x(k)$ based on all measurements up to time j; and $P(k \mid j) \triangleq$ the error covariance matrix associated with $\bar{x}(k \mid j)$.

$$\tilde{x}(k \mid j) = x(k) - \hat{x}(k \mid j).$$ (38)

Then the extended Kalman filter will be

$$\hat{x}(k + 1 \mid k) = \hat{x}(k \mid k) + \int_t^{t+\Delta} f(x(\tau \mid t), \tau) \, d\tau$$ (39)

$$\begin{aligned} \hat{x}(k + 1 \mid k + 1) = &\hat{x}(k + 1 \mid k) + K(k + 1)[z(k + 1)] \\ &- h(\hat{x}(k + 1 \mid k))] \end{aligned}$$ (40)

$$\begin{aligned} k(k + 1) = &P(k + 1 \mid k)H^T(k + 1)[H(k + 1) \\ &\times P(k + 1 \mid k)H^T(k + 1) + R(k + 1)]^{-1} \end{aligned}$$ (41)

$$P(k + 1 \mid k) = \Phi(k + 1, k)P(k \mid k)\Phi^T(k + 1, k) + Q(k)$$ (42)

$$\Phi(k + 1, k) = I + \frac{\partial f}{\partial x} \hat{x}(k \mid k) \, \Delta t$$ (43)

$$H(k + 1) = \frac{\partial h}{\partial x} \hat{x}(k \mid k)$$ (44)

$$P(k + 1 \mid k + 1) = [I - K(k + 1)H(k + 1)]P(k + 1 \mid k)$$ (45)

with the initial conditions

$$\hat{x}(0 \mid 0) = x(0)$$
$$P(0 \mid 0) = P(0)$$

are assumed given, where $Q(k)$ and $R(k + 1)$ are the covariance matrices associated with $w(k)$ and $v(k + 1)$, respectively.

$$E[w(k)w^T(j)] = Q(k)\delta_{kj}$$ (46)

$$E[v(k + 1)v^T(j + 1)] = R(k + 1)\delta_{kj}.$$ (47)

All the modeling errors and truncating errors are assumed to be absorbed by $w(k)$ and $v(k + 1)$.

    b. *Extended Kalman Filter for AOT.* Consider a two-dimensional constant target velocity case. Assume that the time of consideration the target located at (r_{tx}, r_{ty}) moves with constant velocity (v_{tx}, v_{ty}), and the sensor (observer) located at (r_{sx}, r_{sy}) moves with velocity (v_{sx}, v_{sy}) and has acceleration $(a_{sx}(t), a_{sy}(t))$. This can be defined as:

$$x_t(t) = [r_{tx} \quad r_{ty} \quad v_{tx} \quad v_{ty}]^T$$ (48)

$$x_s(t) = [r_{sx} \quad r_{sy} \quad v_{sx} \quad v_{sy}]^T \tag{49}$$

$$x(t) = x_t(t) - x_s(t)$$
$$= [r_x \quad r_y \quad v_x \quad v_y]^T, \tag{50}$$

where $x_t(t)$ is the target-state vector; $x_s(t)$ is the sensor-state vector; and $x(t)$ is the relative-state vector. The time indexes of all elements of $x_t(t)$, $x_s(t)$, $x(t)$ are omitted for simplicity.

The discrete-time state equation is

$$x(k + 1) = \Phi(k + 1, k)x(k) + u(k) + w(k), \tag{51}$$

where

$$\Phi(k + 1, k) = \begin{pmatrix} I & (t_{k+1} - t_k)I \\ 0 & I \end{pmatrix} \tag{52}$$

$$I = \begin{pmatrix} 1 & 0 \\ 0 & 1 \end{pmatrix} \tag{53}$$

$$u(k) = [0 \quad 0 \quad u_x(k) \quad u_y(k)] \tag{54}$$

$$u_x(k) = -\int_{t_k}^{t_{k+1}} a_{sx}(\tau) \, d\tau \tag{55}$$

$$u_y(k) = -\int_{t_k}^{t_{k+1}} a_{sy}(\tau) \, d\tau \tag{56}$$

$w(k)$ is a zero-mean Gaussian white sequence with

$$E[w(k)w^T(j)] = Q(k)\delta_{kj}.$$

The measurement taken at time $k + 1$ will be

$$\beta(k + 1) = \theta(k + 1) + v(k + 1) \tag{57}$$

$$\theta(k + 1) = \tan^{-1}\left(\frac{r_x(k + 1)}{r_y(k + 1)}\right). \tag{58}$$

$v(k + 1)$ is a zero-mean Gaussian white measurement error process with

$$E[v(k+1)v^T(j+1)] = R(k+1)\delta_{kj}. \tag{59}$$

Then

$$H(k+1) = \frac{\partial \theta(k+1)}{\partial x} \bigg|_{\hat{x}(k+1)|k)}$$

$$= \left[\frac{r_y(k+1|k)}{r_x^2(k+1|k) + r_y^2(k+1|k)} \quad \frac{-r_x(k+1|k)}{r_x^2(k+1|k) + r_y^2(k+1|k)} \quad 0 \quad 0 \right]$$

$$= \left[\cos \hat{\beta}(k+1|k) \quad -\sin \hat{\beta}(k+1|k) \quad 0 \quad 0 \right] \tag{60}$$

Then the extended Kalman filter will be

$$\hat{x}(k+1|k) = \Phi(k+1,k)\hat{x}(k|k) + u(k) \tag{61}$$

$$\hat{x}(k+1|k+1) = \hat{x}(k+1|k) + K(k+1)$$
$$\times \left[\beta(k+1) - \tan^{-1}\left(\frac{\hat{r}_x(k+1|k)}{\hat{r}_y(k+1|k)} \right) \right] \tag{62}$$

$\hat{r}_x(k+1|k)$ and $\hat{r}_y(k+1|k)$ come from $\hat{x}(k+1|k)$; see (50).

$$K(k+1) = P(k+1|k)H^T(k+1)[H(k+1)P(k+1|k)$$
$$\times H^T(k+1) + R(k+1)]^{-1} \tag{63}$$

$$P(k+1|k) = \Phi(k+1,k)P(k|k)\Phi^T(k+1,k) + Q(k) \tag{64}$$

$$P(k+1|k+1) = [I - K(k+1)H(k+1)]P(k+1|k) \tag{65}$$

with initial conditions

$$\hat{x}(0 \mid 0) = x(0)$$
$$P(0 \mid 0) = P(0)$$

assumed to be given.

    c. *Comments on Some Other Nonlinear Modifications.*
    (1) With variances in the way of state extrapolation, covariance matrix extrapolation, and the weighting matrix computation, many different KFs are created [19–23, 31].

(2) In our EKF of Subsection V,B,1,a if, before advanced to k + 2, the $\hat{x}(+ 1|k + 1)$ is used to replace $\hat{x}(k|k)$, and we run the EKF again iteratively until some stop criterion is met, then it is advanced to k + 2. This is called the iterative EKF. Iterative EKF may improve the filtering performance, but n iterative requires n times of computational effort. On the other hand, if the time interval Δt of the simple EKF is reduced to be $\Delta t/n$, then during the same time interval Δt both will have used the same amount of computational effort. It may be hard to say which one will be better before actual comparison.

(3) In our EKF of Section V,B,1,a, $f(\hat{x}(k \mid k))$ is used to replace $\hat{f}(x(t), t)$. This is equal to expanding $\hat{f}(x(t), t)$ about $\hat{x}(k|k)$ and keeping the linear term. If more terms are kept and used to run the filter, they are called the higher-order EKFs. Higher-order EKFs can reduce the error of nonlinearity, but they do require more computational effort in handling those extra terms. On the other hand, if the time interval Δt of the simple EKF is reduced, then the nonlinearity can also be reduced. By using the same computation effort, it is hard to say which one is better before actual comparison.

(4) Based on the arguments given above, it can be seen that in most cases the simple EKF may be the best choice.

(5) All the techniques mentioned above, which include Taylor series expansion and iterative relinearization, are local techniques. There is a global iterative technique called the quasilinear approach [19, 24] which has been investigated. The way of implementation is to replace F and H_k, the Jacobian matrices of f and h of (36) and (37), with the describing functions N_f and N_h, respectively, and to replace $f(\hat{x}(t), t)$ and $h(\hat{x}_k)$ with $\hat{f}(x(t), t)$ and $\hat{h}_k(x)$, respectively (in which k indicates the k-th iterative, while the caret indicates the best estimation of x). The result is global optimization, but the price to pay for this is a significantly greater computational requirement.

2. Modification for Non-Gaussian Processes [23]

In case the conditional probability density function is non-Gaussian, there are some techniques that have been investigated, three of which are outlined below. For a more detailed description, one can look in the cited references.

   a. Gaussian Sum Approximation [25, 26]. The non-Gaussian conditional probability density function is approximated by a finite weighted sum of Gaussian density functions with different means and covariances. The resulting Gaussian sum filter is actually a bank of Kalman filters working in parallel, and the outputs of each KF are then weighted and summed together to form the output of the system.

   b. Orthogonal Series Expansion [27, 31]. In handling a nonlinear non-Gaussian problem, Sorenson and Stubberud [27] used the Edgeworth series expansion to approximate the *a posteriori* density function (the probability density function for the estimated state, conditioned on all available measurement data). They then use the nonlinear perturbation approach to describe the system. This Edgeworth series,, consisting of Hermite orthogonal polynomials, is useful for densities which are nearly Gaussian [31].

c. Finite Set of Moments Approximation. A non-Gaussian density function can be represented as an infinite set of moments. Thus, the non-Gaussian density can be approximated by a truncated finite set of moments. This idea has been used by Kushner [28] in handling nonlinear, non-Gaussian estimation.

3. Modification for Computational Convenience

In order to obtain computational convenience or improve computational efficiency, some modifications have been made.

a. Alternate Gain Expression [18]. Using the formulas given in Subsection V,A,2, the normal sequence of Kalman filter computation is $P(k + 1|k) \rightarrow K(k + 1) \rightarrow P(k + 1|k + 1)$. If

$$K(k+1) = P(k + 1|k + 1)H^T(k + 1)R^{-1}(k + 1) \tag{66}$$

and

$$
\begin{aligned}
P(k+1|k+1) = {} & P(k + 1|k) - P(k + 1|k)H^T(k + 1) \\
& \times [H(k + 1)P(k + 1|k)H^T(k + 1) \\
& + R(k + 1)]^{-1}H(k + 1)P(k + 1|k)
\end{aligned}
\tag{67}
$$

are used, then the sequence of computation can be changed to $P(k + 1|k) \rightarrow P(k + 1|k + 1) \rightarrow K(k + 1)$. This change offers no computational advantage over the original one. However, if only an error covariance analysis is desired, with no regard for the time history of $K(k + 1)$, one can calculate $P(k + 1|k)$ and $P(k + 1|k + 1)$ alternately without computing $K(k + 1)$, by using this changed formula. Also, if only the history of $P(k|k)$ is of interest, then $P(k + 1|k)$ can be substituted into this changed $P(k + 1|k + 1)$ formula to obtain a first-order matrix relationship between $P(k + 1|k + 1)$ and $P(k|k)$.

b. Inverse Covariance Matrix Filter [33]. The inverse covariance matrix $M(k|k) = P^{-1}(k|k)$ is calculated and updated, instead of the $P(k|k)$ matrix. It is desirable in the case of nearly ill-conditioned $P(k|k)$ matrix.

c. Square-Root Filter [32]. Instead of calculating or updating the $P(k|k)$ matrix, the $S(k|k)$, in which $P(k|k) = S^T(k|k)S(k|k)$, is calculated and updated.

d. U–D Covariance Factorization Filter [33]. Rather than decomposing the covariance into its square-root factor $S(k|k)$ as mentioned above, the P matrix is expressed as $P = UDU^T$, in which the U matrix is an upper triangular and unitary matrix (with ones along the diagonal), and the D matrix is a diagonal matrix.

The use of either a square-root filter or U–D covariance factorization filter can save some computational effort by virtue of matrix algebra properties.

C.   MANEUVERING-TARGET TRACKING TECHNIQUES

A maneuvering target is a target in which the velocity is no longer constant. There are many maneuvering-target tracking techniques. Most of them differ from each other in the following way.

(1) Whether to model the target parametrically or not.

(2) Whether to use a detecting scheme or not.

(3) Whether to use a single filter, two filters, or parallel filters.

(4) Whether to use an adaptive filter, a fading memory filter, or a limited memory filter.

The following discussion is not limited to AOT.

1.   Parametric or Nonparametric Models of the Target

In a parametric model of the target, the random variables and processes have been known density functions (*a priori* statistical description). The nonparametric statistics approach tries to develop estimates that do not depend on the density function.

1.1. *Parametric Models [31, 34–40].* Among the parametric models, the most famous may be Singer's first-order autoregressive model, Moose's semi-Markov process model, and Zhou's modified Rayleigh "current" statistical model. Besides these three approaches, the traditional simple increase in the level of the Q matrix and Jazwinski's adaptive Q can be included as well.

a. Singer's Autoregressive Model [34, 35]. Underlying Assumptions.

(1) The target has a probability P_1 of maximum positive acceleration $+A$, a probability P_1 of maximum negative acceleration $-A$, a probability P_2 of no acceleration at all, and an assumed uniform probability distribution of amplitudes $[1 - (2p_1 + p_2)]/2A$ of acceleration between $-A$ and $+A$.

(2) The maneuvering in one sampling period is correlated with the maneuvering in the previous (or the next) sampling period.

Based on the above information, the target's acceleration was modeled as a random process with known exponential autocorrelation; then the state equation was augmented with this acceleration term.

Characteristics.

(1) No detector is required.

(2) Can use a single Kalman filter.

(3) Additional state variables are required.

b. Moose's Semi-Markov Process Model [36–38].

Modeling.

(1) n certain discrete states are chosen; these n states then act as mean values around which the state of the target randomly varies.

(2) The target acceleration is modeled as a semi-Markov process. That is, the state transitions behave according to the probability matrix of a Markovian process, while the time spent in any state i before the next transition to state k is a random variable.

(3) A single Kalman filter, augmented by a Bayesian estimation scheme that automatically learns the maneuver command of the target, is developed.

Characteristics.

(1) No detector is required.

(2) An automatic learning scheme is included.

c. *Zhou's Modified Rayleigh "Current" Statistical Model [39].*

Modeling.

(1) A modified Rayleigh density function is proposed to describe the maneuvering target's acceleration.

(2) Set the mean values of random acceleration to be equal to the current acceleration.

(3) The maneuver is time correlated.

(4) The acceleration is drive by a white noise with mean value $\alpha \bar{a}$. Here, α is the reciprocal of the maneuver (acceleration) time constant, and $\bar{a}$ the current acceleration.

Characteristics.

(1) No detector is required.

(2) Can use a single Kalman filter.

(3) Additional state variables are required.

d. *Increases in the Level of Q.* Q is the covariance matrix of the modeling error. Usually, the nonlinearity of the dynamic equation or the modeling error of the dynamic equation is included in the Q matrix. If the level of Q is large enough to cover the modeling error, then the divergence in the Kalman filter can be avoided. But a larger Q means more uncertainty about the dynamic equation, which will make the P matrix of the output of the Kalman filter larger; a larger P matrix means poor performance (see Section V,A).

In the maneuvering-target environment, if the level of Q can be increased to cover the magnitude of the maneuver, then the Kalman filter will be convergent and the maneuver can be updated automatically into the state variables. But the performance may be too poor to be useful.

e *Jazwinski's Adaptive Q [31, 40].* The values of the Q matrix can be adaptively adjusted based on the residual sequence. This adaptive Q approach has the advantages of a simple structure, no augmented state variables (as in Singer's model), no detector scheme requirement, and the performance being good when there is no target maneuvering.

1.2 *Nonparametric Model [41, 42].* Without modeling the target maneuver stochastically, using a least-squares estimator is used to estimate the acceleration input vector. In the following section, the techniques used by Chan *et al.* [41], and Bar-Shalom and Birmiwal [42] are introduced.

a. Chan *et al.* [41]. At the beginning, the target is assumed to be non-maneuvering and a simple Kalman filter is used. A least-squares estimator is used to estimate a constant-acceleration input vector I. If |U|, the norm of the estimated U, is greater than a preset threshold, then a maneuver is declared. Assuming that the number of measurements used to estimate U is s, and if at time $k + s$ the maneuver is declared, then $\hat{x}(k + s + 1)$, as well as the covariance matrix $P(k + s + 1)$, will be corrected.

b. Bar-Shalom and Birmiwal [42]. The major difference between this approach and that of Chan et al. [41] is that if, at time k + s, the maneuver is declared, then the correction will start from time k + 1. With this refinement of Chan's approach, some improvement has been achieved.

2. The Use of a Detecting Scheme

a. No Detecting Scheme. In many cases, when the *a priori* statistical information is included in the Q matrix, such as constant Q, adaptive Q, or Singer's model, no detecting scheme is required. Also, in other cases, when using a bank of N Kalman filters, and output the weighted output of these N Kalman filters, then the detecting scheme can be avoided.

b. Detecting Scheme [43]. Usually this scheme includes one detector and two filters, one of which is a simple filter that assumes a constant-velocity target. The other is a higher-order filter, which assumes a maneuvering target. As long as no maneuver has been declared by the detector, the simple filter is used. When a maneuver is detected, the covariance matrix is reinitialized, or the state variables are changed using stored data updated to the present time; the higher-order filter is used when the new data arrive. The detector can also bring the tracker back to the simple filter model, when the data show the maneuver has disappeared. A filter with Singer's model has been used as a higher-order filter by McAulay [43]. Chan *et al.* [41] and Bar-Shalom and Birmiwal [42] also used a detecting scheme.

3. Use of a Single Filter, Two Filters, or Parallel Filters

In cases such as adaptive Q, Singer's model with augmented state vector, Moose's semi-Markov model with an automatic learning scheme attached, etc., one single filter is good enough to handle a maneuvering-target situation.

However, it has been determined that, if the target maneuver only happens occasionally, it is better to use a detecting scheme such that a lower-order filter is used when no maneuver is detected, and a higher-order filter when the maneuver is detected. The advantage of using two filters can be found in subsection V,C,2.

It can be found from the work of Moose *et al.* [36–38], and McAulay and Denliger [43] that, at the beginning of deriving the filter algorithm, one always requires a bank of N filters or a growth of N, N^2, and N^3, ..., filters to obtain optimal performance. Then, under some assumptions, this was reduced to a single filter. However, with improvement in computer hardware, parallel or peripheral array systems are available, in which systems there are multi-CPUs and each CPU can run independently. With parallel filters running in these systems, better performance can be expected.

4. Adaptive Filter, Fading Memory Filter, and Limited Filter [40, 44]

In a maneuvering-target environment, the old data are no longer reliable in determining target maneuverability. Some ideas have been created to handle this situation.

The idea of adaptive Q has been mentioned in Subsection V,C,1. Depending on the residual sequence, the Q matrix is (adaptively) adjusted to fit the changed environment. As a result of this, the effect of the old data disappears gradually.

If at each time, before processing the new data and updating the filter, the result of the old data is weighted by a factor which is less than unity, then the overall result is equal to forgetting the old data exponentially. Based on this idea, the fading-memory filters are created.

Instead of forgetting the old data gradually or exponentially, the limited-memory filter simply truncates all the old data which are older than N time intervals, in which N is the window width of the filter.

All three approaches have one thing in common: the old data are forgotten. Which approach is better depends on the situation.

5. Comments on Maneuvering-Target AOT

In the case of a weak observability problem, such as AOT, the system is heavily dependent on the old data to obtain a better estimation result. On the other hand, in the maneuvering-target environment, the old data are no longer reliable in determining the maneuverability of the target.

It is better to collect more information, and to use the data as efficiently as possible, which requires a heavier computational algorithm.

IV. SOME OTHER USEFUL AOT FILTERING TECHNIQUES

In addition to Kalman filters and maneuvering-target tracking techniques, there are some other useful AOT filtering techniques, such as:

(1) Observer maneuver strategy design.
(2) Pseudostate measurement approach.
(3) Modified polar coordinates approach.
(4) Monte Carlo simulation.
(5) Cramer–Rao lower-bound simulation.

These will be discussed in the following subsections.

A. THE IDEA OF OBSERVER MANEUVER

Murphy [2] discovered that, in the case of SSAOT, with a constant-velocity target, if the observer is also moving with constant velocity, it is unable to determine the target trajectory. This means that the observer maneuver is required to force the system to be observable.

Subsequently, an optimum observer maneuver strategy that minimized the trace of the predicated information matrix was proposed by Liu and Bongiovanni [4].

B. PSEUDO-STATE MEASUREMENTS [46, 47]

Pseudo-state measurements z_p are constructed as nonlinear functions of the actual measurements z and the *a priori* state estimate $\overline{x}$ as

$$z_p = z_p(z, \overline{x}), \tag{68}$$

and the state variables are constructed as

$$\begin{aligned}
x_p &= x_p(\overline{x}) \\
&= A\overline{x}, \tag{69}
\end{aligned}$$

which are linear functions of the *a priori* state estimate $\overline{x}$. Here A is an $n \times n$ matrix. The pseudo-state residual is then

$$\Delta\gamma_p = z_p(z, \overline{x}) - A\overline{x}. \tag{70}$$

Using z_p, x_p, and $\Delta\gamma_p$ instead of z, $\overline{x}$, and $z - h(\overline{x})$ the EKF can be implemented, where $z - h(\overline{x})$ is the actual residual.

Characteristics [46, 47].

(1) The pseudo-state measurements z_p are linear functions of the state variables x.

(2) The filter is linear in construction, and all nonlinearity in the measurement model is restricted to the computation of the covariance and variance error matrices.

(3) Computation of nonlinear residuals is avoided, and nonlinear propagation of the states is used as in EKF.

(4) The filter estimates minimize the usual weighted least-squares cost function with correlated state and pseudo-state measurements.

(5) When this is applied to bearings-only tracking, the estimated range vectors are unbiased, while the estimated velocity vector becomes asymptotically unbiased after the observer's maneuver. Under the same condition, the general EKF will be unstable or even divergent.

(6) It is much simpler in structure than the modified polar coordinates approach (next subsection).

C. MODIFIED POLAR COORDINATES [5, 48]

The state vector is defined as

$$y(t) = \left[\beta(t) \quad \dot{r}(t)r(t) \quad \beta(t) \quad 1/r(t)\right]^{-1}, \tag{71}$$

where r is the range; $\dot{r}$ is the range rate; β is the bearing; and $\dot{\beta}$ is the bearing rate. Characteristics [5, 48].

(1) The measurement equation is very simple

$$H_y(y(t)) = [0 \quad 0 \quad 1 \quad 0] \cdot y(t), \tag{72}$$

but the dynamic equation is much more complex than that of the pseudo-state measurement or that of the extended Kalman filter in Cartesian coordinates (Section V,B,1,a).

(2) When applied to bearing-only tracking using EKF, the output of the EKF is both stable and asymptotically unbiased.

(3) Automatic decoupling of observable and unobservable components of the estimated state vector prevents the covariance matrix from ill-conditioning, which is the primary cause of filter instability.

(4) Prediction accuracy in Cartesian coordinates is completely preserved.

(5) Choice of $1/\gamma$ as the fourth state is optimal from the viewpoint of minimizing system nonlinearity.

(6) $1/\gamma$ remains unobservable until the observer-maneuver requirement is satisfied.

D.   MONTE CARLO SIMULATION

For a given system with the following dynamic equation and measurement equation:

$$x(k+1) = f(x(k),k) + w(k) \tag{74}$$

$$z(k+1) = h(x(k+1)) + v(k+1) \tag{75}$$

With a given initial condition x(0) and with signal generators to generate the stochastic sequence w(k) and v(k + 1), then x(k + 1) and z(k + 1) can be obtained, in which k = 0, 1, 2, ..., is the time index; w(k) is a zero-mean n-vector Gaussian white sequence with $E[w(k)w^T(j)] = Q(k)\delta_{kj}$; and v(k + 1) is a zero-mean m-vector Gaussian white sequence with $E[v(k+1)v^T(j+1)] = R(k+1)\delta_{kj}$.

If one inputs the measured sequence z(k + 1) into an EKF as described in Section V, then the estimated state sequence $\hat{x}(k + 1|k + 1)$ as well as the covariance matrix sequence P(k + 1|k + 1) can be obtained.

The Monte Carlo simulation can be conducted as the block diagram shown in Fig. 5, in which x(k + 1) is generated by (73) and N measurements $z_i(k + 1)$ are generated by (74) with a different measurement error sequence $v_i(k +$

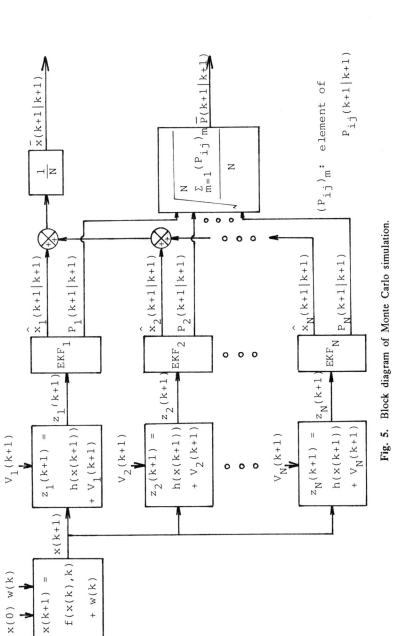

Fig. 5. Block diagram of Monte Carlo simulation.

1). All $v_i(k + 1)$ are zero-mean Gaussian white sequences with the same constant covariance matrix R. All EKF_i in the figure are assumed identical. Then the outputs of each EKF_i are averaged to get $\bar{x}(k + 1|k + 1)$ and the root-mean squares are taken to get $\bar{P}(k + 1|k + 1)$, respectively. Here $\bar{x}(k + 1|k + 1)$ and $\bar{P}(k + 1|k + 1)$ are the results of Monte Carlo simulation. They represent the typical values of $x(k + 1|k + 1)$ and $P(k + 1|k + 1)$ that may be obtained by the EKF of Fig. 5.

E.   THE CRAMER–RAO LOWER-BOUND SIMULATION [49–52]

For any unbiased estimate $\hat{x}$ of x, the covariance matrix $E[(\hat{x} - x)(\hat{x} - x)^T = M^{-1}$, where M^{-1} is the Cramer–Rao lower-bound (CRLB) of the estimation, while M is the Fisher information matrix. In our problem,

$$M = E\left[\left(\frac{\partial \ln p(\beta_m|x)}{\partial x}\right)\left(\frac{\partial \ln p(\beta_m|x)}{\partial x}\right)^T\right],$$
(75)

where $E(\cdot)$ is the expectation operator; ln is the natural logarithm function; and $P(\beta_m|x)$ is the conditional probability density function of β_m given x.

$$P(\beta_m|x) = \left[(2\pi)^k |w|\right]^{-1/2}$$
$$\times \exp\left[-\frac{1}{2}(\beta_m - \beta)^T w^{-1}(\beta_m - \beta)\right],$$
(76)

in which

$$\beta = \begin{bmatrix} \beta_1 & \beta_2 & \cdots & \beta_k \end{bmatrix}^T$$
(77)

is the vector of true angles from time 1 to time k.

$$\beta_m = \begin{bmatrix} \beta_{m1} & \beta_{m2} & \cdots & \beta_{mk} \end{bmatrix}^T$$
(78)

is the vector of measured (noise-corrupted) angles from time 1 to time k.

$$\beta_{mi} = \beta_i + \mu_i,$$
(79)

where μ_i is the measurement noise at time i and is assumed to be zero-mean Gaussian white noise and with a constant standard deviation $\sigma_{\mu_i} = \sigma$

$$w = \text{diag} \left[\sigma_{\mu_i} \right] = \sigma^2 I, \tag{80}$$

where diag [·] stands for a diagonal matrix; I is a k × k identity matrix; and with

$$x = \begin{bmatrix} r_x & r_y & v_x & v_y \end{bmatrix}^T \tag{81}$$

the state vector at time i. Now evaluate

$$\frac{\partial \ln p(\beta_m | x)}{\partial x} = \left[\frac{\partial \beta}{\partial x} \right]^T w^{-1} (\beta_m - \beta) \tag{82}$$

for k measurements

$$\left[\frac{\partial \beta}{\partial x} \right] = \begin{bmatrix} \frac{1}{r_1} \cos \beta_1 & - \frac{1}{r_1} \sin \beta_1 & \frac{t_1}{r_1} \cos \beta_1 & - \frac{t_1}{r_1} \sin \beta_1 \\[2mm] \frac{1}{r_2} \cos \beta_2 & - \frac{1}{r_2} \sin \beta_2 & \frac{t_2}{r_2} \cos \beta_2 & - \frac{t_2}{r_2} \sin \beta_2 \\[2mm] \frac{1}{r_3} \cos \beta_3 & - \frac{1}{r_3} \sin \beta_3 & \frac{t_3}{r_3} \cos \beta_3 & - \frac{t_3}{r_3} \sin \beta_3 \\[2mm] \vdots & \vdots & \vdots & \vdots \\[2mm] \frac{1}{r_k} \cos \beta_k & \frac{1}{r_k} \sin \beta_k & \frac{t_k}{r_k} \cos \beta_k & \frac{t_k}{r_k} \sin \beta_k \end{bmatrix} \tag{83}$$

where r_i represents the true range between the target and the observer at time i; and β_i represents the true angle of the target with respect to the observer at time i; so that

$$
\begin{aligned}
M &= E \left(\left[\frac{\partial \beta}{\partial x} \right]^T w^{-1} [\beta_m - \beta][\beta_m - \beta]^T w^{-1} \left[\frac{\partial \beta}{\partial x} \right] \right) \\[2mm]
&= \left[\frac{\partial \beta}{\partial x} \right]^T w^{-1} E[\beta_m - \beta][\beta_m - \beta]^T w^{-1} \left[\frac{\partial \beta}{\partial x} \right] \\[2mm]
&= \left[\frac{\partial \beta}{\partial x} \right]^T w^{-1} w w^{-1} \left[\frac{\partial \beta}{\partial x} \right] \\[2mm]
&= \left[\frac{\partial \beta}{\partial x} \right]^T w^{-1} \left[\frac{\partial \beta}{\partial x} \right] \\[2mm]
&= \sigma^{-2} \left[\frac{\partial \beta}{\partial x} \right]^T \left[\frac{\partial \beta}{\partial x} \right]
\end{aligned}
\tag{84}
$$

$M = \sigma^{-2}$

$$\times \begin{bmatrix} \Sigma\dfrac{1}{r_i^2}\cos^2\beta_i & -\Sigma\dfrac{1}{r_i^2}\cos\beta_i\sin\beta_i & \Sigma\dfrac{t_i}{r_i^2}\cos^2\beta_i & -\Sigma\dfrac{t_i}{r_i^2}\cos\beta_i\sin\beta_i \\[2ex] -\Sigma\dfrac{1}{r_i^2}\cos\beta_i\sin\beta_i & \Sigma\dfrac{1}{r_i^2}\sin^2\beta_i & -\Sigma\dfrac{t_i}{r_i^2}\cos\beta_i\sin\beta_i & \Sigma\dfrac{t_i}{r_i^2}\sin^2\beta_i \\[2ex] \Sigma\dfrac{t_i}{r_i^2}\cos^2\beta_i & -\Sigma\dfrac{t_i}{r_i^2}\cos\beta_i\sin\beta_i & \Sigma\dfrac{t_i^2}{r_i^2}\cos^2\beta_i & -\Sigma\dfrac{t_i}{r_i^2}\cos\beta_i\sin\beta_i \\[2ex] \Sigma\dfrac{t_i}{r_i^2}\cos\beta_i\sin\beta_i & \Sigma\dfrac{t_i}{r_i^2}\sin^2\beta_i & -\Sigma\dfrac{t_i}{r_i^2}\cos\beta_i\sin\beta_i & \Sigma\dfrac{t_i}{r_i^2}\sin^2\beta_i \end{bmatrix}$$

$$(85)$$

Some illustrations of using the trace of this M^{-1} as the objective function can be found in Hsiao [1].

F.   COMMENTS

The idea of maneuvering the observer to get a better tracking performance is a kind of input optimization technique. However, this idea is not commonly used in other tracking situations, where the tracking performance will also be changed when the observer maneuvers, but this change of performance may not be so large. On the other hand, in the case of single-sensor angle-only tracking without observer maneuvering, it will be unobservable. This is why observer maneuvering is so serious in the case of SSAOT.

The pseudo-state measurements approach and the modified polar coordinates approach are no more than state variable recombination techniques. However, both approaches have been found very useful in AOT in reducing the nonlinearity of the measurement equation. This nonlinearity of the measurement equation will cause serious problems in AOT, but will cause less serious problems in some other tracking situations.

Monte Carlo and Cramer–Rao lower-bound simulations are off-line techniques. Monte Carlo simulation can indicate typical performance, while the Cramer–Rao lower-bound simulation can indicate the best average performance. The results of both simulations can be used as a reference to adjust the filter algorithm to improve the tracking performance.

VII. DISCUSSION, CONCLUSION, AND FURTHER RESEARCH TOPICS

A.   DISCUSSION

Because of weak observability, it is difficult to do AOT, and it is more difficult to do maneuvering-target AOT. This is because, in the case of AOT, the system is heavily reliant on old data to get better filter performance. On the other hand, in the maneuvering-target environment, the old data are not reliable in evaluating the maneuvering-target kinematic. Based on all the materials given in the previous six sections, some suggestions are given below to reduce the difficulty of doing maneuvering-target angle-only tracking.

(1) It is better to use a sensor array to improve observability.

(2) The sensor must be able to detect the Doppler shift.

(3) Based on the concept of the field of angular sensitivity, it is better to move the observer to a "better" position.

(4) All possible *a priori* information, knowledge, and constraints about the target must be included.

(5) Parallel filters on parallel computers or peripheral array computers are preferred.

(6) Reduce the time intervals of the discrete-time EKF as much as possible.

(7) If necessary, move the observer to get better performance.

B.   CONCLUSIONS

(1) In the case of SSAOT, the observer (or the sensor) must be more "active" than the target to make the system observable.

(2) From the observability point of view, an array sensor is better than a single sensor. However, if L/S is large (large range), then the estimated covariance will appear elongated.

(3) Obtaining Doppler shift information is a good approach for tracking maneuvering targets.

(4) The field of angular sensitivity is a good reference for measuring the quality of the observer's location with respect to the moving target.

(5) In the case that the target only occasionally maneuvers, using a detecting scheme with two filters will be better than using a single filter without a detecting scheme.

(6) If possible, the implementation of parallel filters on a parallel computer system or on a peripheral array computer system is preferable to using a single filter.

(7) The time intervals of the EKF should be reduced as much as possible.

(8) Longer computer word lengths are preferred for truncation error reduction.

C.   FUTURE RESEARCH TOPICS

There are many topics that require further study. Some important ones are:

(1) Deriving the necessary and sufficient conditions of observability in various cases of SSAOT.

(2) Further investigating the field of angular sensitivity.

(3) Finding more efficient ways of doing maneuvering-target angle-only tracking.

(4) Developing parallel filters on parallel and peripheral array computer systems.

(5) Finding more *a priori* information, knowledge, and constraints about the anticipated target.

ACKNOWLEDGMENTS

The author wishes to express his deepest gratitude to C. T. Leondes and C. T. Russell at the University of California, Los Angeles, for their guidance, encouragement, and support during his graduate studies.

REFERENCES

1. C. Y. HSIAO, "On Maneuver of Bearings Only Tracking," Ph.D Dissertation, Department of MANE, University of California, Los Angeles (1986).
2. D. J. MURPHY, "Noise Bearing-Only Target Motion Analysis," Ph.D. Dissertation, Department of Electrical Engineering, Northeastern University, Boston, Massachusetts (1970).
3. S. C. NARDONE and V. J. AIDALA, "Observability Criteria for Bearings-Only Target Motion Analysis," *IEEE Trans. Aerosp. Electron. Syst.* AES-17, No. 2, 162–166, March 1981.
4. P. T. LIU and P. L. BONGIOVANNI, "Optimal Platform Maneuver for Passive Tracking with Time Delay Measurements," *MIT/ONR Workshop c^3 Proc.*, 1982.
5. R. R. TENNEY, "A Passive Tracking System for Maneuvering Sources," Master's Thesis, Massachusetts Institute of Technology, February 1976.
6. R. R. TENNEY, R. S. HEBBERT, AND N. R. SANDELL, JR., "Tracking A Maneuvering Acoustical Source with A Single Frequency-Bearing Sensor," *Proc. 1976 IEEE Conf. Decis. Control*, 420–427, December 1976.
7. R. R. TENNEY, R. S. HEBBERT, AND N. R. SANDELL, JR., "A Tracking Filter for Maneuvering Sources," *IEEE Trans. Autom. Control* AC-22, 246–251, April 1977.
8. D. H. McCABE and R. L. MOOSE, "Passive Source Tracking Using Sonar Time Delay Data," *IEEE Trans. Acoust., Speech, Signal Process.*, June 1981.
9. R. L. MOOSE, "Adaptive Range Tracking of Underwater Maneuvering Targets Using Passive Measurements," in "Statistical Signal Processing" (D. B. Owen, ed.), 1984.
10. D. J. MURPHY, B. W. GUIMOND, and D. W. MOORE, "Linear Array Tracking of A Maneuvering Target," *IEEE, 15th Asilomar Conf. Circuits, Syst., Comput., Pacific Grove*, 416–423, November 1981.
11. P. S. MAYBECK, J. E. NEGRO, S. J. CUSUMANO, and M. DE PONTE, JR., "A New Tracker for Air to Air Missile Targets," *IEEE Trans. Autom. Control*, AC-24, No. 6, December 1979.
12. J. D. KENDRICK, P. S. MAYBECK, and J. G. REID, "Estimation of Aircraft Target Motion Using Orientation Measurement," *IEEE Trans. Aerosp. Electron. Syst.*, AES-17, No. 2, 254–260, March 1981.
13. P. S. MAYBECK, R. L. JENSEN, and D. A. HARNLY, "An Adaptive Extended Kalman Filter for Target Image Tracking," *IEEE Trans. Aerosp. Electron. Syst.*, AES-17, No. 2, 173–180, March 1981.

14. C. B. CHANG and J. W. SHERMAN, "The Combination of a Statistical Measurement with Deterministic A Priori Constraint," *Proc. 4th Symp. Nonlinear Estim. Theory Appl., San Diego*, September 1973.

15. C. B. CHANG, "Optimal State Estimation of Ballistic Trajectories with Angle-Only Measurements," Note 1979-1, Lincoln Laboratory, Massachusetts Institute of Technology, January 1979.

16. R. E. KALMAN, "A New Approach to Linear Filtering and Prediction Problems," *J. Basic Eng.* **82**, 35–45 (1960).

17. R. E. KALMAN and R. S. BUCY, "New Results in Linear Filtering and Prediction Theory," J. Basic Eng. **83**, 95–108 (1961).

18. J. S. MEDITCH, "Stochastic Optimal Linear Estimation and Control," McGraw-Hill, New York, 1969.

19. A. GEIB (ed.), *Applied Optimal Estimation*, Analytic Sciences Corporation, M.I.T. Press, Cambridge, Massachusetts, 1974.

20. R. P. WISHNER, R. E. LARSON, and M. ATHANS, "Status of Radar Tracking Algorithms," *IEEE Symp. Nonlinear Estim. Theory Appl., San Diego*, September 1970.

21. C. T. LEONDES (ed.), "Control and Dynamic Systems: Advances in Theory and Applications, Vol. 19, Academic Press, New York, 1983

22. C. T. LEONDES (ed.), "Control and Dynamic Systems: Advances in Theory and Applications, Vol. 20, Academic Press, New York, 1983.

23. C. T. LEONDES (ed.), "Control and Dynamic Systems: Advances in Theory and Applications, Vol. 21, Academic Press, New York, 1984.

24. J. W. AUSTIN and C. T. LEONDES, "Statistically Linearized Estimation of Reentry Trajectories," *IEEE Trans. Aerosp. Electron. Syst.* **AES-17**, 54–61 (1981).

25. H. W. SORESON and D. L. ALSPASH, "Recursive Bayesian Estimation Using Gaussian Sums," *Automatica* **7**, 465–479 (1971).

26. D. L. ALSPASH and H. W. SORENSON, "Nonlinear Bayesian Estimation Using Gaussian Sum Approximations," *IEEE Trans. Autom. Control* **AC-17**, NO. 4, 439–448, AUGUST 1972.

27. H. W. SORENSON and A. R. STUBBERUD, "Nonlinear Filtering by Approximation of the A Posteriori Density," *Int. J. Control* **8**, No. 1, 33–51 (1968).

28. H. J. KUSHNER, "Approximation to Optimal Nonlinear Filters," *IEEE Trans. Autom. Control* **AC-12**, 546–556, October 1967.

29. R. K. MEHRA, "A Comparison of Several Nonlinear Filters for Reentry Vehicle Tracking," *IEEE Trans. Autom. Control* **AC-16**, No. 4, 307–319, August 1971.

30. R. K. MEHRA, "On the Identification of Variances and Adaptive Kalman Filtering," *IEEE Trans. Autom. Control* **AC-15**, No. 2, 175–184, April 1970.

31. A. H. JAZWINSKI, "Stochastic Processes and Filtering Theory, Academic Press, New York, 1969.

32. P. G. KAMINSKI, A. E. BRYSON, JR., and S. F. SCHMIDT, "Discrete Square Root Filtering: A Survey of Current Techniques," *IEEE Trans. Autom. Control* **AC-16**, No. 6, December 1971.

33. P. S. MAYBECK, "Stochastic Models, Estimation and Control," Vol. 1, Academic Press, New York, 1979.

34. R. A. SINGER, "Estimating Optimal Tracking Filter Performance for Manned Maneuvering Targets," *IEEE Trans. Aerosp. Electron. Syst.* **AES-6**, 473–483, July 1970.

35. R. A. SINGER and K. W. BEHNKE, "Real Time Tracking Application," *IEEE Trans. Aerosp. Electron. Syst.* **AES-17**, 100–110, January 1971.

36. R. L. MOOSE, "Adaptive State Estimation Solution to the Maneuvering Target Problem," *IEEE Trans. Aerosp. Electron. Syst.* **AC-20**, 359–362, June 1975.

37. R. L. MOOSE and N. H. GHOLSON, "Adaptive Tracking of Abruptly Maneuvering Targets," *Proc. 1976 IEEE Conf. Decis. Control*, 804–808, December 1976.

38. R. L. MOOSE, H. F. VANLANDINGHAM, and D. H. McCABE, "Modeling and Estimation for Tracking Maneuvering Targets," *IEEE Trans. Aerosp. Electron. Syst.* **AES-15**, No. 3, 448–455, May 1979.

39. H. ZHOU and K. S. P. KUMAR, "A 'Current' Statistical Model and Adaptive Algorithm for Estimating Maneuvering Targets," *J. Guidance* **7**, No. 5, 596–602, October 1984.

40. A. H. JAZWINSKI, "Adaptive Eiltering," *Automatica* **5**, 475–485 (1969).

41. Y. TL CHAN, A. G. C. HU, and J. B. PLANT, "A Kalman Filter Based Tracking Scheme with Input Estimation," *IEEE Trans. Aerosp. Electron. Syst.* **AES-15**, No. 2, 237–244, March 1979.

42. Y. BAR-SHALOM and K. BIRMIWAL, "Variable Dimension Filter for Maneuvering Target Tracking," *IEEE Trans. Aerosp. Electron. Syst.* **AES-18**, No. 5, 621–629, September 1982.

43. R. J. McAULAY and E. J. DENLINGER, "A Decision-Directed Adaptive Tracker," *IEEE Trans. Aerosp. Electron. Syst.* **AES-9**, 229–236, March 1973.

44. A. H. JAZWINSKI, "Limited Memory Optimal Filtering," *Proc. 1968 J. Autom. Control Conf., Ann Arbor*, 383–393, June 1968.

45. H. W. SORENSON and J. E. SACKS, "Recursive Fading Memory Filtering," pp. 101–119, Information Sciences, 1971.

46. D. W. WHITCOMBE, "Pseudo-State Measurements Applied to Recursive Nonlinear Filter," *Proc. 2nd Symp. Nonlinear Estim. Theory Appl.*, 278–281, 1972.

47. V. J. AIDALA and S. C. NARDONE, "Biased Estimation Properties of the Pseudolinear Tracking Filter," *IEEE Trans. Aerosp. Electron. Syst.* **AES-18**, No. 4, 432–441, July 1982.

48. V. J. AIDALA and S. E. HAMMEL, "Utilization of Modified Polar Coordinates for Bearings-Only Tracking," *IEEE Trans. Aerosp. Electron. Syst.* **AC-28**, No. 3, 283–294, March 1983.

49. H. L. VAN TREES, "Detection, Estimation and Modulation Theory, Part 1," Wiley, New York 1968.

50. S. C. NARDONE, A. G. LINDGREN, and K. F. GONG, "Fundamental Properties and Performance of Conventional Bearings-Only Target Motion Analysis," *IEEE Trans. Autom. Control* **AC-29**, No. 9, 775–787, September 1984.

51. J. H. TAYLOR, "The Cramer–Rao Estimation Error Lower Bound Computation for Deterministic Nonlinear Systems," *IEEE Trans. Autom. Control* **AC-24**, 343–344, April 1979.

52. R. W. MILLER, "A Lower Bound on Angle-Only Tracking Accuracy," Proj. Rep. RMP-149, Lincoln Laboratory, Massachusetts Institute of Technology, May 1978.

GRADIENT PROJECTION METHODS
FOR SYSTEMS OPTIMIZATION PROBLEMS

JOSEPH C. DUNN

Mathematics Department
North Carolina State University
Raleigh, North Carolina 27695

I.   INTRODUCTION

Variable metric gradient algorithms for unconstrained minimization amount to generalized steepest-descent iterations,

$$u \rightarrow u + \sigma v \tag{1a}$$

$$v = - S \, \nabla J(u), \tag{1b}$$

where u is a vector in a real hilbert space $\mathscr{U}$ with inner product $\langle u, v \rangle$, S is a positive-definite bounded linear transformation on $\mathscr{U}$, σ is a positive real number, and S and σ are determined at each stage by auxiliary rules designed to decrease the continuously differentiable real-valued function J, to drive $\|\nabla J(u)\|$ to zero, and to ensure rapid convergence to any nearby nonsingular relative minimizer for J. The quantity $S \, \nabla J(u)$ appearing in (1b) may be viewed as the gradient of J in the metric derived from the weighted inner product $\langle u, v \rangle_S = \langle u, S^{-1} v \rangle$; hence the name "variable metric" gradient method for (1).

A related family of constrined minimization algorithms is obtained from (1) by adding a projection step, i.e., by implementing the recursion

$$u \rightarrow P_\Omega (u + \sigma v) \tag{2a}$$

$$v = - S \, \nabla J(u), \tag{2b}$$

where Ω is a given nonempty set in which the minimizers of J are sought, P_Ω denotes nearest point projection into Ω relative to the ground metric $\|u\|^2 = \langle u, u \rangle$ in $\mathscr{U}$, and S and σ are chosen to decrease J, to force some appropriate constrained minimization counterpart of $\|\nabla J(u)\|$ to zero, and to induce rapid local convergence to nonsingular relative minimizers of J in Ω. When S is the identity operator I on $\mathcal{U}$, the iteration (2) reduces to the ordinary gradient projection method first considered by Goldstein [1] and Levitin and Polyak [2] in the 1960s and subsequently investigated in [3–13]. On the other hand, when $S \neq I$, the scheme (2) becomes a variable metric gradient projection algorithm in which the projector P_Ω and the scaled gradient $S \nabla J(u)$ are computed in *different* metrics. Bertsekas [14] developed the first useful (S, σ) selection rules for "two-metric" projection methods of this sort in simple polyhedral convex sets Ω (e.g., orthants and boxes). Gafni and Bertsekas [15] later proposed a class of iterations similar to (2), but utilizing positively homogeneous nonlinear scaling operators S derived from an explicit linear inequality representation for Ω. The algorithms in [15] are quite general since any closed convex set in $\mathcal{U}$ can be represented by a (typically infinite) system of linear inequalities; however, they seem best suited to polyhedra, and the convergence rate analysis in [15] is actually limited to this special case. In the present article, we outline a different two metric projection scheme that behaves asymptotically like the iterative methods in [15] when Ω is polyhedral, and produces something entirely new in convex feasible sets prescribed by finitely many smooth nonlinear inequalities. The new method uses a Gafni–Bertsekas step length rule and the Lagrangian scaling operators recently proposed and analyzed by Gawande and Dunn [10, 16, 17].

By definition, the projection $P_\Omega(w)$ is obtained by solving the constrained minimization problem,

$$\min_{\hat{w} \in \Omega} \|\hat{w} - w\|^2, \qquad w \in \mathcal{U}. \tag{3}$$

The Hilbert space projection theorem [18] ensures that (3) has a unique solution when Ω is a nonempty closed convex set; however, finding this solution may prove to be as difficult as solving the original problem of minimizing f over Ω. In such cases (2) has no practical computational value. On the other hand, (3) is readily solved for a large class of feasible sets Ω commonly encountered in optimal control, network flow, and other structured systems optimization problems. For these problems, gradient projection methods can be very effective.

Example 1. Let $u = (u_1, ..., u_k) \in R^k = \mathcal{U}$, with any diagonally weighted inner product

$$\langle u, v \rangle = \alpha_1 u_1 v_1 + ... + \alpha_k u_k v_k, \qquad \alpha_i > 0 \tag{4}$$

and associated squared norm

$$\|u\|^2 = \langle u, u \rangle = \alpha_1 u_1^2 + ... + \alpha_k u_k^2. \tag{5}$$

Let Ω be the unit cube in R^k, i.e.,

$$\Omega = \left\{ \left(u_1, \ldots, u_k \right) : \left| u_i \right| \le 1, \quad i = 1, \ldots, k \right\}. \tag{6}$$

Since the squared norm is separable, the corresponding projection problem (3) now splits into k uncoupled one-dimensional problems,

$$\min_{\hat{w}_i \in [-1,1]} \left| \hat{w}_i - w_i \right|^2, \qquad w_i \in R^1 \tag{7}$$

with self-evident solutions

$$\hat{w}_i = P_{[-1,1]}(w_i) = SAT_{[-1,1]}(w_i), \tag{8}$$

where

$$SAT_{[a,b]}(x) \overset{\Delta}{=} a, \qquad x < a$$
$$\overset{\Delta}{=} x, \qquad a \le x < b \tag{9}$$
$$\overset{\Delta}{=} b, \qquad b < x.$$

In short,

$$P_\Omega(w) = \left(\hat{w}_1, \ldots, \hat{w}_k \right) \tag{10a}$$

with

$$\hat{w}_i = P_{[-1,1]}(w_i), \qquad i = 1, \ldots, k. \tag{10b}$$

Furthermore, relative to the inner product (4), the gradient of any differentiable function $J : R^k \to R^1$ is just

$$\nabla J(u) = \left(\alpha_1^{-1} \frac{\partial J(u)}{\partial u_1}, \ldots, \alpha_k^{-1} \frac{\partial J(u)}{\partial u_k} \right). \tag{11}$$

Hence, the right-hand side of (2a) becomes

$$P_\Omega(u + \sigma v) = \hat{w} = {}_1 \left(\hat{w}_1, \ldots, \hat{w}_k \right) \tag{12a}$$

with

$$\hat{w}_i = \text{SAT}_{[-1,1]}(u_i + \sigma v_i) \tag{12b}$$

and

$$-v_i = S_{i1}\alpha_1^{-1}\frac{\partial J(u)}{\partial u_1} + \ldots + S_{ik}\alpha_k^{-1}\frac{\partial J(u)}{\partial u_k} \tag{12c}$$

for $i = 1, \ldots, k$, where S_{ij} is the i,j-th entry in the $k \times k$ matrix representor for S relative to the standard basis for R^k. In particular, if S is the identity operator on R^k and $\alpha_i = 1$ for all i, then (2) reduces to a simple unscaled gradient projection iteration

$$u \rightarrow P_\Omega(u + \sigma v) = \left(\hat{w}_1, \ldots, \hat{w}_k\right) \tag{13a}$$

with

$$\hat{w}_i = \text{SAT}_{[-1,1]}\left(u_i - \sigma\frac{\partial J(u)}{\partial u_i}\right). \tag{13b}$$

Equation (10) is merely a special case of the general projection decomposition rule,

$$P_\Omega(w) = \left(\hat{w}^1, \ldots, \hat{w}^k\right) \tag{14a}$$

$$\hat{w}^i = P_{U_i}(w^i) \qquad i = 1, \ldots, k \tag{14b}$$

for k-fold Cartesian products

$$\Omega = U_1 \times \ldots \times U_k \tag{15a}$$

$$\stackrel{\Delta}{=} \cdot\left\{\left(u^1, \ldots, u^k\right) : u^i \in U_i, \qquad i = 1, \ldots, k\right\}, \tag{15b}$$

where each U_i is a nonempty closed convex set in some Hilbert space $\mathcal{U}_i$ with inner product $\langle\cdot, \cdot\rangle_i$ and associated norm $\|\cdot\|_i = \langle\cdot, \cdot\rangle_i^{1/2}$, where scalar multiplication and vector addition are defined componentwise in the space $\mathcal{U}$ of k-tuples $u = (u^1, ..., u^k)$, i.e.,

$$\alpha u = \left(\alpha u^1, ..., \alpha u^k \right) \tag{16a}$$

$$u + v = \left(u^1 + v^1, ..., u^k + v^k \right), \tag{16b}$$

and where $\mathcal{U}$ is equipped with the separable inner product

$$\langle u, v \rangle = \langle u^1, v^1 \rangle_1 + ... + \langle u^k, v^k \rangle_k \tag{16c}$$

and corresponding separable squared norm

$$\|u\|^2 = \|u^1\|_1^2 + ... + \|u^k\|_k^2 \tag{16d}$$

In view of (15) and (16), the projection problem (3) reduces to k uncoupled constrained minimizations

$$\min_{\hat{w} \in U_i} \|\hat{w}^i - w^i\|_i^2, \qquad i = 1, ..., k, \tag{17}$$

and this decomposition immediately produces the component-wise projection rule (14). Notice that the unit cube (6) is a k-fold product of intervals $U_i = [-1, 1] \subset \mathcal{U}_i = R^1$; hence (10) is in fact a special case of (14). More generally, the importance of (14) is clear whenever each component projection $P_{U_i}(w^i)$ is easy to compute, e.g., when U_i is an interval, half-line, orthant, simplex, ball, ellipsoid, circular cone, ball–ball, or ball–cone intersection, etc., and when $\langle \cdot, \cdot \rangle_i$ is a suitably matched inner product. Products of such sets are often seen in a system optimization context.

Example 2 (discrete-time optimal control). A fleet of m trawlers works a prescribed fishing ground, harvesting a particular species of fish over a period of k days. If x_i fish are present on the i-th day and if u_i boats are sent after them, the fleet can expect to catch about $r(x_i, u_i)$ fish on that day, where $r(x, u)$ is a smooth function of the real variables x and u (r is typically increasing and concave in each argument. On the other hand, when no fish are taken, the net daily increase in the population is roughly proportional to its present size. The following difference equation therefore provides an approximate population dynamics model over the time interval in question:

$$x_{i+1} - x_i = \lambda x_i - r(x_i, u_i), \qquad i = 1, ..., k. \tag{18}$$

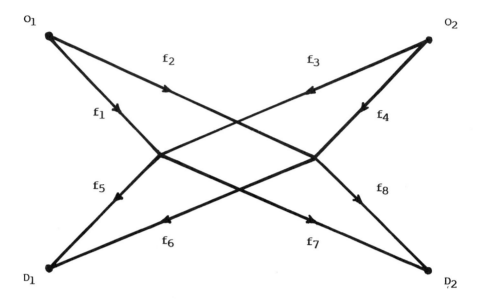

Fig. 1. Multicommodity flow in a network.

In this equation, λ is a positive real constant, and x_i and u_i are real variables, with

$$0 \le u_i \le m, \quad i = 1, \ldots, k. \tag{19}$$

Suppose now that each boat costs c dollars per day to operate and each fish brings p dollars at the market. The net profit earned over the k-day period is then

$$J(u) = \sum_{i=1}^{k} \left[pr\left(x_i, u_i\right) - cu_i \right], \tag{20}$$

where x_i is obtained from x_1 with (18). Given x_1, the problem is to maximize J (or minimize –J) over all real k-tuples $u = (u_1, \ldots, u_k)$ satisfying the constraints (19). Equivalently, let

$$U_i = [0, m] \subset R^1 = \mathcal{U}_i \tag{21a}$$

and

$$\Omega = U_1 \times \ldots \times U_k. \tag{21b}$$

Then J is to be maximized over k-dimensional cube Ω in the space $\mathscr{U}$ of real k-tuples u (see [18] for an unconstrained continuous-time version of this example). With reference to (14) and Example 1, it can be seen that

$$P_\Omega = \left(\hat{w}_1, \ldots, \hat{w}_k \right) \tag{22a}$$

$$\hat{w}_i = SAT_{[0,\,m]}(w_i), \qquad i = 1, \ldots, k \tag{22b}$$

when $\mathscr{U}$ is equipped with the inner product (4).

   Example 3 (multicommodity network flow). The directed network in Fig. 1 has four origin–destination pairs that may be indexed as follows:

Pair No.	1	2	3	4
Pair	(O_1, D_1)	(O_1, D_2)	(O_2, D_1)	(O_2, D_2)

In a given interval of time, r_i units of a certain commodity are to be sent from origin to destination in the i-th (O, D) pair. If $u_1{}^i$ and $u_2{}^i$ are the portions of r_i assigned to the leftmost and rightmost paths joining the i-th (O, D) pair, then

$$u^i_j \geq 0,$$
$$u^i_1 + u^i_2 = r_i, \qquad i = 1,2,3,4; \quad j = 1,2 \tag{23}$$

and the combined flow rates in the eight links of the network are proportional to the numbers

$$f_1 = u^1_1 + u^2_1, \qquad f_2 = u^1_2 + u^2_2, \qquad f_3 = u^3_1 + u^4_1$$
$$f_4 = u^3_2 + u^4_2, \qquad f_5 = u^1_1 + u^3_1, \qquad f_6 = u^1_2 + u^3_2$$
$$f_7 = u^2_1 + u^4_1, \qquad f_8 = u^2_2 + u^4_2. \tag{24a}$$

   Suppose that the total cost J(u) of a particular set of routing decisions u = (u^1, u^2, u^3, u^4) depends only on the resulting link flows f_i, i.e.,

$$J(u) = D(f(u)),$$
(24b)

where D is a given function of the real 8-tuple $f = (f_1, ..., f_8)$. Then the problem is to minimize J over all (vector-valued) 4-tuples u satisfying the constraints (23). Equivalently, let U_i be the two-dimensional simplex

$$U_i = \{(u^i_1, u^i_2) \in R^2 : u^1_i \geq 0, \quad u^i_2 \geq 0,$$

$$u^i_1 + u^i_2 = r_i\}$$
(25a)

and let

$$\Omega = U_1 \times U_2 \times U_3 \times U_4.$$
(25b)

Then $J(u)$ is to be minimized over the Cartesian product Ω in the space $\mathscr{U}$ of 4-tuples (u^1, u^2, u^3, u^4) with each u^i in $\mathscr{U}_i = R^2$ (larger versions of this problem are treated in [15]).

References [15] and [19] describe projection algorithms for general m-dimensional simplexes U_i in the space $\mathscr{U}_i = R^m$ with standard inner product

$$\langle u^i, v^i \rangle = u^i_1 v^i_1 + ... + u^i_m v^i_m;$$
(26)

however, in the present case (m = 2) we may use the simple projection formula

$$P_{U_i}(w^i) = (\hat{w}_1, \hat{w}_2), \qquad w^i \in R^2$$
(27a)

$$\hat{w}^i_1 = SAT_{[0, r_i]}\left(\frac{r_i + w^i_1 - w^i_2}{2}\right)$$
(27b)

$$\hat{w}^i_2 = r_i - w^i_2.$$
$$\hat{w}^i_2 = r_i - \hat{w}^i_1.$$
(27c)

Furthermore, if the inner product in $\mathscr{U}$ is

$$\langle u, v \rangle = \alpha_1\left(u^1_1 v^1_1 + u^1_2 v^1_2\right) + ... + \alpha_4\left(u^4_1 v^4_1 + u^4_2 v^4_2\right)$$

$$\alpha_i > 0$$
(28)

and if scalar multiplication and vector addition are defined by the usual componentwise rule (16), then (14) gives

$$P_\Omega(w) = \left(P_{U_i}(w^1), \ldots, P_{U_4}(w^4) \right). \tag{29}$$

The projection decomposition rule for k-fold Cartesian products can be extended further to certain classes of functions u: $\mathscr{S} \to \mathscr{U}$ with infinite domain sets $\mathscr{S}$. For instance, let $\mathscr{U} = \mathscr{L}^2([a, b], R^m)$ denote the Hilbert space of square integrable functions u : [a, b] $\to R^m$ with inner product

$$\langle u, v \rangle = \int_a^b \left[u_1(t)v_1(t) + \ldots + u_m(t)v_m(t) \right] dt \tag{30}$$

and let

$$\Omega = \left\{ u \in \mathscr{U} : u(t) \in U_0, \ a \le t \le b \right\}, \tag{31}$$

where U_0 is a given nonempty closed convex set in R^m. Then it can be shown that Ω is closed and convex in $\mathscr{U}$, and that

$$P_\Omega(w) = \hat{w}, \quad w \in \mathscr{U} \tag{32a}$$

$$\hat{w}(t) = P_{U_0}(w(t)), \quad t \in [a, b]. \tag{32b}$$

This rule is important in the applications of (2) to continuous-time optimal control problems.

Example 4 (continuous-time path follower). The instantaneous shaft angular position $x_1(t)$, shaft angular velocity $x_2(t)$, and applied current u(t) for a dc motor are related by the differential equations

$$\dot{x}_1 = x_2 \tag{33a}$$

$$\dot{x}_2 = -w_2 + u(t) \tag{33b}$$

with initial conditions

$$x_1(0) = 0, \quad x_2(0) = 0. \tag{34}$$

In addition, the current u(t) is amplitude-restricted by

$$|u(t)| \le 1, \quad t > 0. \tag{35}$$

Roughly stated, the problem is to choose an admissible current schedule that makes the angle $x_1(t)$ follow the desired profile

$$x_1(t) = t, \quad 0 \le t \le t_f \tag{36}$$

with small mean-squared error

$$\int_0^{t_f} (x_1 - t)^2 \, dt \tag{37a}$$

and small power consumption

$$\int_0^{t_t} u^2 \, dt \tag{37b}$$

on the fixed interval $[0, t_f]$. Since these goals are in conflict, we form the single weighted objection function

$$J(u) = \int_0^{t_f} \left[\lambda \left((x_1 - t)^2 + u^2 \right) \right] dt \tag{38}$$

with positive weight factor λ. For each square integrable function $u : [0, t_f] \to R^1$. there is a unique solution $x : [0, t_f] \to R^2$ of (33) and (34), and a corresponding value for $J(u)$. The problem then is to minimize J over square integrable u's satisfying (35). Equivalently, let $\mathcal{U} = \mathcal{L}^2([0, t_f], R^1)$, and

$$\Omega = \left\{ u \in \mathcal{U} : u(t) \in U_0, \quad 0 \le t \le t_f \right\} \tag{39a}$$

with

$$U_0 = [-1, 1] \subset R^1. \tag{39b}$$

Then J is to be minimized over the feasible set Ω.

Conditions (39) define an infinite-dimensional analog of the hypercube in Example 1, and we note that the projection decomposition rule (32) yields the expected counterpart of (10) for this set, namely

$$P_\Omega(w) = \hat{w}, \quad w \in \mathcal{U} \tag{40a}$$

$$\hat{w}(t) = \mathrm{SAT}_{[-1,1]}(w(t)), \quad t \in [0, t_f] \tag{40b}$$

Examples 1–4 suggest the wide range of interesting constrained minimization problems for which the projection computation in (2) is either trivial or at least very much easier than the original optimization problem itself. Additional material on projection can be found in [3, 5, 14, 15, 19]; however, the remainder of this article is concerned mainly with the construction of suitable scaling transformations S and step lengths σ for (2). Here again, it is possible to exploit the product form in sets like (15) or (31), and to achieve further significant computational advantages for structured objective functions like (20), (24), or (38).

We begin with a brief examination of the unconstrained variable metric gradient scheme (1) in Section II, since the general factors that govern the selection of S and σ are well understood and readily accessible in this special case. A modified step length rule suitable for unscaled gradient projection (S = I) is described next in Section III, and the resulting iteration (2) is seen to behave much like the ordinary steepest-descent method for unconstrained problems. Sections II and III provide a paradigm for the subsequent extension to scaled gradient projection; however, certain new considerations enter at this level of generality. To see what is at issue here, recall that if Ω is convex and $\bar{u}$ is a relative minimizer of J in Ω, then the differential of J at $\bar{u}$ must be non-negative in the direction of any line segment leading from $\bar{u}$ to other points in Ω; thus

$$\langle \nabla J(\bar{u})u - \bar{u} \rangle \geq 0, \qquad u \in \Omega \tag{41}$$

In geometric terms, this condition says that $-\nabla J(\bar{u})$ lies in the cone of exterior normals to Ω at $\bar{u}$, i.e.,

$$-\nabla J(\bar{u}) \in K(\bar{u}), \tag{42a}$$

where

$$K(u) = \left\{ w \in \mathcal{U} \colon \langle w, v - u \rangle \leq 0, \quad v \in \Omega \right\}. \tag{42b}$$

According to (42), the ray $\left\{ v : v = P_\Omega(\bar{u} - \sigma \nabla J(\bar{u})), \quad (\exists \sigma > 0) \right\}$ extends outward from $\bar{u}$, normal to Ω; hence each of its points must project backward onto $\bar{u}$ (by the Hilbert space projection theorem [18]); in other words, for each $\bar{\sigma} > 0, \bar{u}$ satisfies the corresponding fixed-point equation

$$\bar{u} = P_\Omega\left(\bar{u} - \bar{\sigma} \nabla J(\bar{u})\right). \tag{43}$$

Conversely, (43) implies the stationarity requirement (42), and so the two conditions are actually equivalent. Furthermore, it can be shown that the strict descent condition

$$J\left(P_\Omega(u - \sigma \nabla J(u))\right) < J(u), \qquad \text{small } s > 0 \tag{44}$$

holds at every nonstationary point $u \in \Omega$ (see Section III). Thus, the projection scheme (2) makes sense as a descent method when S = I and σ is sufficiently small and positive. Unfortunately, this is not necessarily true if I is replaced by an arbitrary positive-definite scaling operator S in (2). Without further restrictions on S, the iteration (2) may halt at a nonstationary point, and the initial portion of the corresponding feasible path

$$w(\sigma) = P_\Omega\big(u - \sigma S \, \nabla J(u)\big), \quad \sigma > 0 \tag{45}$$

may actually lead *uphill* [14].

     Example 5. In $\mathcal{U} = R^2$ let

$$\Omega = \big\{(u_1, u_2) : u_1 \le 0, \quad u_2 \le 0\big\}$$

and put

$$J(u) = -(u_1 + u_2).$$

Relative to the standard unweighted inner product in R^2, we then have

$$\nabla J(u) = -(1, 1), \quad u \in R^2.$$

With reference to (42), the function J has $\overline{u} = (0, 0)$ as its only stationary point (and global minimizer) in Ω. However, if we let $S : R^2 \to R^2$ be the positive-definite operator with matrix representor

$$S = \begin{bmatrix} 1 & -1 \\ -1 & 2 \end{bmatrix}$$

in the standard basis for R^2, then

$$-S \, \nabla J(u) = (0, 1), \quad u \in R^2$$

and, therefore,

$$P_\Omega\big((u_1, 0) - \sigma S \, \nabla J(u_1, 0)\big) = (u_1, 0),$$
$$0 \ge u_1, \quad \sigma > 0,$$

i.e., for each $\sigma > 0$, *every* point on the nonpositive u_1 axis is a fixed point for the iteration (2). On the other hand, if

$$S = \begin{bmatrix} 2 & -3 \\ -3 & 5 \end{bmatrix}$$

then

$-S \, \nabla J(u) = (-1, 2)$

and therefore

$$P_\Omega\big((u_1, 0) - \sigma S \, \nabla J(u_1, 0)\big) = (u_1 - \sigma, 0),$$
$$0 \geq u_1, \quad \sigma > 0.$$

Evidently, (2) will *not* halt at $\bar{u} = (0, 0)$ even though this point is stationary; furthermore, if $u_1 < 0$, then $(u_1, 0)$ is not stationary and yet

$$J\big(P_\Omega\big((u_1, 0) - \sigma S \, \nabla J(u_1, 0)\big)\big) = -u_1 + \sigma$$

$$> -u_1$$

$$= J(u_1, 0), \quad \sigma > 0,$$

i.e., the feasible path (45) leads uphill at nonstationary points $(u_1, 0)$.

The undesirable circumstances illustrated in Example 5 cannot arise if the scaling transformations S admitted at each $u \in \Omega$ are required to have the form

$$S = s_N P_N + S_T P_T, \tag{46}$$

where (N, T) is any pair of complementary orthogonal closed subspaces of $\mathscr{U}$ with $N \supset K(u)$, s_N is a positive number, S_T is a positive-definite bounded linear transformation on T, and P_N and P_T are bounded linear projection maps of $\mathscr{U}$ onto N and T. By construction, every transformation in the class (46) has the normal cone $K(u)$ and its complement $\hat{K}(u)$ as invariant sets at every $u \in \Omega$ (notice that this is *not* true for the two scaling operators in Example 5). As an immediate consequence, we find that for each $\sigma > 0$, $\bar{u}$ is stationary iff $\bar{u}$ is a fixed point of the map in (2). With some additional effort, it can be shown that the feasible path (45) is initially downhill. Finally, if the step length rule of Section III is modified to suit (46), and if N, s_N, and S_T are chosen in the right way at each iteration, then the resulting two metric gradient projection processes can retain at least some of the desirable global convergence properties of unscaled gradient projection sequences, and at the same time exhibit the accelerated local asymptotic convergence rates of a Newton iteration near nonsingular relative minimizers $\bar{u}$. This point is developed further in Section IV for closed convex sets Ω prescribed by finitely many linear or smooth nonlinear inequalities; in such cases, it is possible to describe suitable choices for N, T, s_N and S_T in terms of the gradients and Hessians of J and the constraint functions, and (in $\mathscr{U} = R^n$) to compute corresponding matrix representations for P_N, P_T and $-S \, \nabla J(u)$ with standard algebraic procedures (e.g., QR and Cholesky decompositions). Substantial computational reductions are possible here when Ω is a Cartesian product defined by separable constraints, since P_N and P_T then have sparse block-diagonal matrix representors. Furthermore, it is possible to achieve major simplifications in the calculation of $-S \nabla J(u)$ for the kind of structured objective functions commonly seen in optimal control problems. Specialized variable metric gradient projection methods that capitalize on this structure are formulated in Section V for discrete-time optimal control problems and their continuous-time limits.

II. UNCONSTRAINED VARIABLE METRIC GRADIENT METHODS

For unconstrained minimization problems, the feasible set Ω coincides with the entire underlying Hilbert space $\mathcal{U}$, and the first-order stationary condition (43) therefore reduces to

$$\nabla J(u) = 0. \tag{47}$$

Every relative minimizer $\bar{u}$ must satisfy (47). In addition, if J is twice differentiable, then

$$\langle w, \nabla^2 J(\bar{u}) w \rangle \geq 0, \qquad w \in \mathcal{U}, \tag{48a}$$

Conversely, if J is twice continuously differentiable at $\bar{u}$, if $\bar{u}$ satisfies (47), and if there is a positive constant c such that

$$\langle w, \nabla^2 J(\bar{u}) w \rangle \geq c\|w\|^2, \qquad w \in \mathcal{U}. \tag{48b}$$

then $\bar{u}$ is a proper relative minimizer. By definition, (47) and (48b) comprise the *standard second-order sufficiency conditions* for unconstrained minimization; any relative minimizer that satisfies these conditions is said to be *nonsingular*.

When $\Omega = \mathcal{U}$, the scheme (2) reduces to an unconstrained variable metric gradient iteration (1), since P_Ω is just the identity map I in this case. If S is any invertible linear transformation on $\mathcal{U}$, then $S \nabla J(\bar{u}) = 0$ iff $\nabla J(\bar{u}) = 0$, and therefore

$$\nabla J(\bar{u}) = 0 \Leftrightarrow \bar{u} = \bar{u} - \sigma S \ \nabla J(\bar{u}), \qquad \sigma > 0. \tag{49}$$

i.e., the iteration (1) stops at $\bar{u}$ iff $\bar{u}$ is stationary. More specifically, suppose that S is self-adjoint and positive-definite in the sense that

$$\langle u, Sv \rangle = \langle Su, v \rangle, \qquad w \in \mathcal{U}, \tag{50a}$$

and for some $\mu > 0$

$$\langle w, Sw \rangle \geq \mu \|w\|^2, \qquad w \in \mathscr{U}. \tag{50b}$$

Then condition (49) holds and also

$$\nabla J(u) \neq 0 \Rightarrow \frac{d}{d\sigma} J(u - \sigma S \nabla J(u)) \bigg|_{\sigma=0} \tag{51}$$
$$= - \langle \nabla J(u), S \nabla J(u) \rangle < 0.$$

Consequently, if S is any self-adjoint positive-definite transformation, then

$$\nabla J(u) = 0 \Rightarrow J((u - \sigma S \nabla J(u)) = J(u), \qquad \sigma < 0 \tag{52a}$$

and

$$\nabla J(u) \neq 0 \Rightarrow J(u - \sigma S \nabla J(u)) < J(u), \tag{52b}$$
$$\text{small } \sigma > 0.$$

According to (52), the scheme (1) with decrease J at a nonstationary iterate $u^{(i)}$ if the step length $\sigma^{(i)}$ is sufficiently small; on the other hand, if the $\sigma^{(i)}$s are consistently *too* small, the sequence $\{u^{(i)}\}$ need not converge to a relative minimizer and may not even approach the set of stationary points for J. The step length rule described below achieves a proper balance in this respect and is also easy to implement. This rule was originally proposed for ordinary steepest descent (S = I) by Armijo [20].

A.   ARMIJO'S STEP LENGTH RULE

Condition (51) and the mean value theorem readily yield the following sharper version of the descent condition (52b): if δ is any fixed positive number less than 1 and if S satisfies (50), then

$$J(u) - J(u - \sigma S \nabla J(u)) \geq \delta\sigma \langle \nabla J(u), S \nabla J(u) \rangle \tag{53}$$
$$\geq \delta\mu\sigma \|\nabla J(u)\|^2, \qquad \text{small } \sigma > 0.$$

This estimate improves on (52b) by establishing a key link between the nonstationarity measure ‖∇J(u)‖ and achievable decrements in J at u. Several desirable convergence properties can be established for sequences generated by (1) and any step length rule that selects sufficiently *large* values of $\bar{\sigma}$ satisfying (53). One of the simplest of these rules may be formulated as follows. Fix constants $\alpha_1 \geq \alpha_0 > 0$, $\beta \in (0, 1)$, $1 > \delta_1 \geq \delta_0 > 0$. Suppose that positive-definite scaling trans-formations $S^{(i)}$ are given for i = 1, 2, ... (the precise nature of the $S^{(i)}$s does not matter at present). At the i-th iteration of (1), choose $a^{(i)} \in [a_0, a_1]$, $\delta^{(i)} \in [\delta_0, \delta_1]$, and set

$$u = u^{(i)}, \quad S = S^{(i)}, \quad \sigma = a^{(i)}, \quad \delta = \delta^{(i)}. \tag{54}$$

Then compute $J(u)$, $\nabla J(u)$, $v = -S \nabla J(u)$, $\langle \nabla J(u), v \rangle$, and enter the following loop:

Step 1. Compute $J(u + \sigma v)$.

Step 2. If $J(u) - J(u + \sigma v) \geq - \delta\sigma\langle \nabla J(u), v \rangle$, go to step 3; otherwise replace σ by $\beta\sigma$ and go to Step 1.

Step 3. Put $\sigma^{(i)} = \sigma$ and stop.

In view of (53), this loop must terminate after finitely many passes, with

$$\sigma^{(i)} = \max \sigma \tag{55a}$$

subject to

$$\sigma/a^{(i)} \in \{ 1, \beta, \beta^2, \dots \} \tag{55b}$$

and

$$J\left(u^{(i)}\right) - J\left(u^{(i)} + \sigma v^{(i)}\right) \tag{55c}$$
$$\geq - \delta^{(i)}\sigma\langle \nabla J\left(u^{(i)}\right), v^{(i)} \rangle,$$

where

$$v^{(i)} = - S^{(i)} \nabla J\left(u^{(i)}\right). \tag{55d}$$

The iteration (1) then produces

$$u^{(i+1)} = u^{(i)} + \sigma^{(i)} v^{(i)}. \tag{55e}$$

According to (53), the sequences $\{J(u^{(i)})\}$ generated by (55) are surely nonincreasing and hence convergent to some limit $\geq \inf J \geq -\infty$; however, this does not imply that $\{u^{(i)}\}$ actually converges to some relative minimizer of J, or even that $\{\nabla J(u^{(i)})\}$ approaches zero. To reach such conclusions, we must impose further restrictions on $\{S^{(i)}\}$ and J.

Theorem 1. Suppose that J is continuously differentiable, that $\{u^{(i)}\}$ is generated by (55), and that the scaling operators $S^{(i)}$ are uniformly bounded and uniformly positive-definite; i.e., for some constants $\mu_1 \geq \mu_0 > 0$,

$$\mu_1 \|w\|^2 \geq \langle w, S^{(i)} s \rangle \geq \mu_0 \|w\|^2, \qquad w \in \mathscr{U}$$

$$i = 1, 2, \ldots$$

(56)

Then the following assertions are true:

(a) If $\nabla J(u^{(i)}) \neq 0$ for all i, then $\{J(u^{(i)})\}$ is strictly decreasing.

(b) Every subsequential limit of $\{u^{(i)}\}$ is a zero of ∇J, and J assumes a common value on all such limits.

(c) If J is bounded below and ∇J is uniformly continuous, then

$$\lim_{i \to \infty} \nabla J(u^{(i)}) = 0$$

(57)

and

$$\lim_{i \to \infty} \left\| u^{(i+1)} - u^{(i)} \right\| = 0.$$

(58)

(d) If the level sets

$$L_c = \{ u \in \mathscr{U} : J(u) \leq c \}$$

(59)

are compact, then conditions (57) and (58) hold, and, in addition, $\{u^{(i)}\}$ converges to the set of stationary points

$$Z = \{ \overline{u} \in \mathscr{U} : \nabla J(\overline{u}) = 0 \};$$

(60)

i.e.,

$$\lim_{i \to \infty} \min_{\overline{u} \in Z} \left\| u^{(i)} - \overline{u} \right\| = 0.$$

(61)

Furthermore, if Z is a finite set, then $\{u^{(i)}\}$ converges to some $\overline{u} \in Z$.

(e) If J is bounded below and convex, and if ∇J is Lipschitz continuous on each level set L_c, then

$$J(u^{(i)}) - \inf J = O(i^{-1}).$$

(62)

Moreover, if $\{u^{(i)}\}$ also converges to some limit $\overline{u}$, then $\overline{u}$ is an absolute minimizer of J and

$$J(u^{(i)}) - \inf J = o(i^{-1}).$$

(63)

(f) If $\overline{u}$ is a nonsingular relative minimizer for J, then

$$\lim_{i \to \infty} u^{(i)} = \overline{u} \tag{64}$$

provided $u^{(1)}$ is sufficiently close to $\overline{u}$. Furthermore, if $\{u^{(i)}\}$ converges to $\overline{u}$, then the rate of convergence is linear (or geometric); i.e., for some positive number $\rho < 1$, the inequalities

$$\left\| u^{(i+1)} - \overline{u} \right\| \le \rho \left\| u^{(i)} - \overline{u} \right\| \tag{65}$$

eventually hold for i sufficiently large.

Parts (b)(d) and (f) of Theorem 1 can be proved with standard arguments (e.g., see [21] and recent refinements in [12]); part (e) is established in [7]. An asymptotic convergence theory for singular proper relative minimizers is developed in [8].

Note 1. With minor alterations, Theorem 1 and its proof remain valid for variable metric gradient processes generated by a Goldstein step length rule [22]. In fact, all of the algorithms and associated convergence theories in this article have obvious counterparts for step length rules of the Goldstein type.

B.   NEWTONIAN SCALING

The local linear convergence rate estimate in Theorem 1 is actually observed for "most" operator sequences $\{S^{(i)}\}$ in the class defined by (56); in particular, this is true for the prototype sequence

$$S^{(i)} = I, \quad i = 1, 2, \ldots \tag{66}$$

employed in ordinary steepest descent. Nevertheless, it is possible to attain *superlinear* asymptotic convergence rates with properly constructed sequences $\{S^{(i)}\}$ satisfying (56). In fact, (55) can be made to behave asymptotically like Newton's method for the equation $\nabla J(u) = 0$, i.e., like the iteration

$$u^{(i+1)} = u^{(i)} + v^{(i)}, \tag{67a}$$

where $v^{(i)}$ is obtained by solving the linear equation

$$\nabla^2 J(u^{(i)})v^{(i)} = -\nabla J(u^{(i)}). \tag{67b}$$

We may derive (67) from elementary considerations as follows: put $\sigma = 1$ in (1) and imagine that S is obtained from some rule that assigns one–one onto scaling transformations $S = S(u)$ to each vector $u \in \mathcal{U}$. In this case, (1) reduces to an iteration of the map

$$u \to \phi(u) = u - S(u) \nabla J(u) \tag{68}$$

whose fixed points coincide with the stationary points $\bar{u}$ of J. We may now ask whether $S(u)$ can be chosen to ensure rapid local convergence to stationary points $\bar{u}$. More specifically, we ask if $S(u)$ can be chosen to make

$$\phi(u) - \bar{u} = o(\|u - \bar{u}\|) \tag{69}$$

where $\bar{u}$ is a nonsingular stationary point, i.e., when J is twice continuously differentiable at $\bar{u}$ and $\nabla^2 J(\bar{u})$ is one–one onto. If so, then any ϕ-iterate sequence $\{u^{(i)}\}$ that converges to $\bar{u}$ must converge superlinearly, since either

$$\lim_{i \to \infty} \frac{\left\| u^{(i+1)} - \bar{u} \right\|}{\left\| u^{(i)} - \bar{u} \right\|} = \lim_{i \to \infty} \frac{\left\| \phi(u^{(i)}) - \bar{u} \right\|}{\left\| u^{(i)} - \bar{u} \right\|} = 0 \tag{70}$$

or else $u^{(i)} = \bar{u}$ eventually; in either case, there is a sequence of positive numbers $\rho^{(i)}$ such that

$$\lim_{i \to \infty} \rho^{(i)} = 0 \tag{71a}$$

and

$$\left\| u^{(i+1)} - \bar{u} \right\| \le \rho^{(i)} \left\| u^{(i)} - \bar{u} \right\| \qquad i = 1, 2, \ldots. \tag{71b}$$

What is more, if (69) holds, then ϕ contracts small neighborhoods of $\bar{u}$ and therefore $\{u^{(i)}\}$ must converge to $\bar{u}$ from nearby starting points $u^{(1)}$. Observe now that $\nabla J(\bar{u}) = 0$ and therefore

$$\begin{aligned} \phi(u) - \bar{u} = u - \bar{u} &= S(u)[\nabla^2 J(u)(u - \bar{u}) \\ &+ o(\|u - \bar{u}\|)], \end{aligned} \tag{72}$$

since $\nabla^2 J$ is continuous at $\bar{u}$. Furthermore, by continuity, the operators $\nabla^2 J(u)$ are one–one onto near $\bar{u}$, and their inverses are locally uniformly bounded. Hence, the obvious choice,

$$S(u) = \nabla^2 J(u)^{-1} \tag{73}$$

is (locally) admissible, and yields the desired result

$$\phi(u) - \bar{u} = - \nabla^2 J(u)^{-1} o(\|u - \bar{u}\|) = o(\|u - \bar{u}\|). \tag{74}$$

When (73) is used in (68), the resulting iteration is theoretically equivalent to (67); i.e., the two schemes generate identical sequences $\{u^{(i)}\}$ when $\nabla^2 J(u)^{-1}$ exists [nevertheless, (67) is superior from a computational standpoint since the solution of the linear equation (67b) generally costs much less than the inversion of the linear operator $\nabla^2 J(u)$].

In general, the inverse Hessian in (73) is sign-indefinite and hence inadmissible as a scaling operator for variable metric gradient descent schemes such as (55); however, (73) can be used with (55) in the vicinity of a nonsingular relative minimizer $\bar{u}$. Under these circumstances, (55) is equivalent to a relaxed Newton method with Armijo steps, namely

$$u^{(i+1)} = u^{(i)} + \sigma^{(i)} v^{(i)} \tag{75a}$$

$$\nabla^2 J(u^{(i)}) v^{(i)} = - \nabla J(u^{(i)}) \tag{75b}$$

$$\sigma^{(i)} = \max \sigma \tag{75c}$$

subject to

$$\frac{\sigma}{\alpha^{(i)}} \in \{1, \beta, \beta^2, ...\} \tag{75d}$$

and

$$J(u^{(i)}) - J(u^{(i)} + \sigma v^{(i)}) \tag{75e}$$

$$\geq - \delta^{(i)} \sigma \langle \nabla J(u^{(i)}), v^{(i)} \rangle.$$

Moreover, it can be shown that (75) eventually reduces to (67) if $\alpha^{(i)}$ and $\delta^{(i)}$ are suitably restricted.

    Theorem 2. Suppose that $\bar{u}$ is a nonsingular relative minimizer for J, and that $\alpha^{(i)} = 1$ and $\delta^{(i)} \in [\delta_0, 1/2)$ in (75) for $i = 1, 2, ...$ If $u^{(1)}$ is sufficiently close to $\bar{u}$, then (75) generates a corresponding sequence $\{u^{(i)}\}$ that converges to $\bar{u}$; furthermore, for sufficiently large i, the inverse Hessians $\nabla^2 J(u^{(i)})$ are positive-definite and the step lengths $\sigma^{(i)}$ are equal to 1. Thus (75) eventually reduces to (67), and hence $\{u^{(i)}\}$ converges superlinearly to $\bar{u}$.

    Theorem 2 can be proved with a modification of Goldstein's argument in [23].

C.   QUASI-NEWTON METHODS

The so-called quasi-Newton methods for unconstrained minimization consist of a basic descent scheme such as (55), together with an auxiliary recursion that generates positive-definite scaling transformations (or their inverses) as the iteration unfolds. In practice, the best of these methods produce $S^{(i)}$s that often meet requirement (56) in Theorem 1, and also satisfy the conditions

$$\lim_{i \to \infty} \frac{\left\| \left[S^{(i)} - \nabla^2 J\left(u^{(i)}\right)^{-1} \right] \nabla J\left(u^{(i)}\right) \right\|}{\left\| \nabla J\left(u^{(i)}\right) \right\|} \tag{76a}$$

and

$$\lim_{i \to \infty} \sigma^{(i)} = 1 \tag{76b}$$

when $\left\{ u^{(i)} \right\}$ converges to a nonsingular relative minimizer $\overline{u}$. Condition (76a) merely says that the $S^{(i)}$s asymptotically approximate the inverse Hessians $\nabla^2 J(u^{(i)})^{-1}$ on one-dimensional subspaces generated by the gradients $\nabla J(u^{(i)})$. Nevertheless, (76a) and (76b) imply the superlinear convergence rate estimate (71); this follows easily from (72) and the fact that $\|\nabla J(u)\| \, \|u - \overline{u}\|^{-1}$ is bounded away from zero near nonsingular stationary points $\overline{u}$. Furthermore, for large-scale problems with unstructured objective functions, the accumulated cost of computing the quasi-Newton direction vectors $-S^{(i)} \nabla J(u^{(i)})$ is typically much less than the cost of calculating $\nabla^2 J(u^{(i)})$ and solving the linear equation (75b). References [24] and [25] develop this important topic at some length for minimization problems in R^n and in Hilbert space.

III. ORDINARY GRADIENT PROJECTION METHODS

When Ω is a convex set, every relative minimizer of J in Ω must satisfy the first-order stationarity condition (41). As explained earlier, condition (41) is equivalent to the fixed-point equation (43) for any fixed $\sigma > 0$, and in particular for $\sigma = 1$. Hence $\overline{u}$ is stationary iff $\overline{u}$ is a zero of the continuous function

$$d(u) = \left\| u - P_\Omega(u - \nabla J(u)) \right\|. \tag{77}$$

Evidently, $d(u)$ may serve as a constrained minimization counterpart of the nonstationarity measure $\|\nabla J(u)\|$ in Section II [in fact, $d(u) = \|\nabla J(u)\|$ when $\Omega = \mathcal{U}$]. The equivalence between (41) and (43) also quickly suggests the iteration

$$u \to P_\Omega(u + \sigma v) \tag{78a}$$

$$v = - \nabla J(u) \tag{78b}$$

with positive step lengths σ chosen at each stage to decrease J and drive d(u) to zero. Bertsekas [5] proposed a suitable step length rule of the Armijo type for (78), and the convergence properties of the resulting gradient projection algorithm are by now fairly well understood [5–13].

Convergence theories for (78) begin with a simple geometrical observation: according to the projection theorem [18], the vector $w - P_\Omega(w)$ is perpendicular to Ω at the point $P_\Omega(w)$, i.e.,

$$w - P_\Omega(w) \in K\left(P_\Omega(w)\right), \qquad w \in \mathscr{U}. \tag{79}$$

Condition (79) produces a sequence of key inequalities leading directly to an analog of the decrement estimate (53) for unconstrained minimization. Thus, if we put

$$\varphi(\sigma) = P_\Omega(u + \sigma v), \qquad \sigma \geq 0, \quad u \in \Omega, \quad v \in \mathscr{U}, \tag{80}$$

then it follows immediately from (79) and the definition of K in (42b) that

$$\langle u + \sigma v - \varphi(\sigma), w - \varphi(\sigma) \rangle \leq 0, \qquad w \in \Omega \tag{81}$$

and therefore

$$\sigma \langle v, \varphi(\sigma) - u \rangle \geq \| \varphi(\sigma) - u \|^2. \tag{82}$$

With (82) and the Cauchy inequality, we obtain

$$\| \varphi(\sigma) - u \| \leq \sigma \| v \|. \tag{83}$$

Furthermore, it can be shown that

$$\sigma > \tau > 0 \Rightarrow \| \varphi(\sigma) - u \| \geq \| \varphi(\tau) - u \| \tag{84}$$

$$\sigma > \tau > 0 \Rightarrow \frac{\| \varphi(\sigma) - u \|}{\sigma} \leq \frac{\| \varphi(\tau) - u \|}{\tau}. \tag{85}$$

The latter result is derived from (81) in [11], and (84) can be obtained with a similar argument {(85) was originally proved in [15] by a different method; for yet another recent proof of this estimate, see [12]}. Now put $v = -\nabla J(u)$ in (82) and use (84)–(85) to obtain the inequality

$$\left\langle \nabla J(u), u - P_\Omega(u - \sigma \nabla J(u)) \right\rangle \geq \min\{1, 1/\alpha\} d^2(u)\sigma, \tag{86}$$

$$\sigma \in [0, \alpha].$$

When u is not stationary, the quantity $d(u)$ is positive, and $0 < \|u - P_\Omega(u - \sigma \nabla J(u))\| = O(\sigma)$ for $\sigma > 0$ [see (83)]. Consequently, for any fixed $\delta \in (0, 1)$, we have

$$
\begin{aligned}
J(u) - J\Big(P_\Omega\big((u - \sigma \nabla J(u))\big)\Big) &\geq \left\langle \nabla J(u), u - P_\Omega(u - \sigma \nabla J(u)) \right\rangle \\
&\quad + o(\sigma) \\
&\geq \delta \left\langle \nabla J(u), u - P_\Omega(u - \sigma \nabla J(u)) \right\rangle \\
&\geq \delta d^2(u)\sigma, \quad \text{small } \sigma > 0.
\end{aligned}
\tag{87}
$$

This estimate establishes the strict descent property for (78) at nonstationary points and justifies Bertsekas' modification of the Armijo step length scheme.

A.   THE BERTSEKAS STEP LENGTH RULE

Bertsekas [5] proposed the following rule for selecting a sufficiently large value of σ satisfying (87). Fix constants $\alpha_1 \geq \alpha_0 > 0$, $\beta \in (0, 1)$, $1 > \delta, \geq \delta_0 > 0$. At the i-th iteration of (78), choose $\alpha_{(i)} \in [\alpha_0, \alpha_1]$, $\delta^{(i)} \in [\delta_0, \delta_1]$ and set

$$u = u^{(i)}, \quad \sigma = \alpha^{(i)}, \quad \delta = \delta^{(i)}. \tag{88}$$

Then compute $J(u)$ and $v = -\nabla J(u)$, and enter the loop described below.

Step 1.   Compute $P_\Omega(u + \sigma v)$, $J(P_\Omega(u + \sigma v))$, and $\langle \nabla J(u), u - P_\Omega(u + \sigma v)\rangle$.

Step 2.   If $J(u) = J(P_\Omega(u + \sigma v)) \geq \delta\langle \nabla J(u), u - P_\Omega(u + \sigma v)\rangle$, go to step 3; otherwise, replace σ by $\beta\sigma$ and go to Step 1.

Step 3.   Put $\sigma^{(i)} = \sigma$ and stop.

According to (87), this loop will terminate after finitely many passes with

$$\sigma^{(i)} = \max \sigma \tag{89a}$$

subject to

$$\frac{\sigma}{\alpha^{(i)}} \in \left\{ 1, \beta, \beta^2, \dots \right\} \tag{89b}$$

and

$$J\left(u^{(i)} \right) - J\left(P_\Omega \left(u^{(i)} + \sigma v^{(i)} \right) \right)$$
$$\wedge \delta^{(i)} \left\langle \nabla J\left(u^{(i)} \right), \ u^{(i)} - P_\Omega \left(u^{(i)} + \sigma v^{(i)} \right) \right\rangle \tag{89c}$$

where

$$v^{(i)} = -\nabla J\left(u^{(i)} \right). \tag{89d}$$

The next iterate generated by (78) is then

$$u^{(i+1)} = P_\Omega \left(u^{(i)} + \sigma^{(i)} v^{(i)} \right). \tag{89e}$$

The gradient projection method (89) behaves essentially like an unconstrained steepest-descent iteration with Armijo steps. Several basic nonlocal convergence properties of (89) are described below, while local asymptotic results are developed separately in Section III,B.

Theorem 3. Suppose that J is continuously differentiable, that Ω is closed and convex, and that $\{u^{(i)}\}$ is generated by (89). Let d(u) be the nonstationarity measure in (77). Then the following assertions are true.

(a) If $d\left(u^{(i)}\right) > 0$ for all i, then $\{J(u^{(i)})\}$ is strictly decreasing.

(b) every subsequential limit of $\{u^{(i)}\}$ is a zero of $d(\cdot)$, and J assumes a common value on all such limits.

(c) If J is bounded below, and ∇J is uniformly continuous, then

$$\lim_{i \to \infty} d\left(u^{(i)} \right) = 0 \tag{90}$$

and

$$\lim_{i \to \infty} \left\| u^{(i+1)} - u^{(i)} \right\| = 0. \tag{91}$$

(d) If the level sets

$$L_c = \left\{ u \in \Omega : J(u) \le c \right\} \tag{92}$$

are compact, then conditions (90) and (91) hold, and, in addition, $\{u^{(i)}\}$ converges to the set of stationary points

$$Z = \{\bar{u} \in \Omega : d(\bar{u}) = 0\};$$ (93)

i.e.,

$$\lim_{i \to \infty} \min_{\bar{u} \in Z} \left\| u^{(i)} - \bar{u} \right\| = 0.$$ (94)

Furthermore, if Z is a finite set, then $\{u^{(i)}\}$ converges to some $\bar{u} \in Z$.

(e) If J is bounded below and convex, and if ∇J is Lipschitz continuous on each level set L_c, then

$$J\left(u^{(i)}\right) - \inf_{\Omega} J = o\left(i^{(i)}\right).$$ (95)

Moreover, if $\{u^{(i)}\}$ also converges to some limit $\bar{u}$, then $\bar{u}$ is an absolute minimizer of J and

$$J\left(u^{(i)}\right) - \inf_{\Omega} J = o\left(i^{(i)}\right).$$ (96)

Parts (b) and (c) of Theorem 3 are straightforward corollaries of results proved in [12]; similar theorems have been established in [7–9] for (89), and certain variable (one) metric extensions of (89), under stronger Lipschitz continuity conditions on ∇J. Part (d) of Theorem 3 follows from parts (b) and (c) by standard arguments (e.g., see [21]). Part (e) is proved in [7]. Notice that Theorem 3 subsumes parts (a)–(e) of Theorem 1 for $\Omega = \mathcal{U}$.

B.   ASYMPTOTIC CONVERGENCE PROPERTIES

The local behavior of (89) near a relative minimizer $\bar{u}$ is controlled mainly by the growth properties of J and the defect function d in Ω near $\bar{u}$ [8, 11]. In a number of important cases it is possible to derive these properties and associated convergence theorems from local structural features of Ω and the differentials of J at $\bar{u}$. In particular, local asymptotic stability and convergence rate theorems are proved in [8] for proper relative minimizers $\bar{u}$ lying in open facets $\mathcal{F} \subset \Omega$ and satisfying the *nondegenerate stationarity condition*

$$-\nabla J(\bar{u}) \in \text{ri } K(\bar{u}),$$ (97)

where ri means relative interior (roughly speaking, "open facet" is a generalization of "polyhedral face"). Thus, if ∇J is locally Lipschitz continuous, if J grows uniformly (with respect to directions) in Ω near $\bar{u}$, and if d grows uniformly in $\mathcal{F}$ near $\bar{u}$, then iterate sequences $\{u^{(i)}\}$ generated by (89) will converge to $\bar{u}$ from nearby starting points $u^{(1)}$, and all such convergent sequences must eventually enter and remain within the facet $\mathcal{F}$. The latter condition implies that (89) eventually reduces to an ordinary Armijo steepest descent process in $\mathcal{F}$, and this makes it possible to extract asymptotic convergence rate estimates for $\{J(u^{(i)})\}$ and $\{u^{(i)}\}$ from the local growth rates of J and d restricted to $\mathcal{F}$. More specifically, if J is twice continuously differentiable and if $\bar{u}$ is *nonsingular* in the sense that (97) holds and the Hessian of the restriction $J|_{\mathcal{F}}$ and is positive-definite, then $\{u^{(i)}\}$ converges linearly to $\bar{u}$ from nearby starting points $u^{(1)}$ in Ω. Convergence rate estimates for singular minimizers are also derived in [8], and related technical refinements are developed in [13] for nondegenerate stationary points in quasipolyhedral faces (open facets are the relative interiors of quasipolyhedral faces).

Asymptotic convergence theorems have also been proved recently for proper relative minimizers $\bar{u}$ in closed convex sets of the form

$$\Omega = \left\{ u \in \mathcal{U} : g_i(u) \le 0, \quad i = 1, ..., m \right\}, \tag{98}$$

where the g_i's are typically affine or smooth convex nonlinear real-valued functions on $\mathcal{U}$. At each $u \in \Omega$, let $\mathcal{F}_0(u)$ denote the set of active constraint indices, i.e.,

$$\mathcal{F}_0(u) = \left\{ i : g_i(u) = 0 \right\}. \tag{99}$$

A point $u \in \Omega$ is said to be *normal* if $\mathcal{F}_0(u) = \varnothing$ or the corresponding active constraint gradient set

$$\mathcal{G}_0(u) = \left\{ \nabla g_i(u) \right\}_{i \in \mathcal{F}_0(u)} \tag{100}$$

is linearly independent. At a normal point, it can be shown that the normal cone $K(u)$ consists of all non-negative linear combinations of vectors in $\mathcal{G}_0(u)$. Hence at a normal *stationary* point $\bar{u}$, (42) implies the first-order Kuhn–Tucker–Lagrange (KTL) conditions, namely: for some $\bar{\lambda} \in R^m$ and for $i = 1, ..., m$,

$$\nabla_u l(\bar{u}, \bar{\lambda}) = 0 \tag{101a}$$

$$\nabla_\lambda l(\bar{u}, \bar{\lambda}) = 0 \tag{101b}$$

$$\lambda_i \ge 0 \tag{101c}$$

$$\lambda_i > 0 \;\Rightarrow i \in \mathcal{J}_0(\overline{u}\,), \tag{101d}$$

where l is the Lagrangian function

$$l\;(u,\lambda) = J(u) + \sum_{i=1}^{m} \lambda_i g_i(u). \tag{101e}$$

Every normal relative minimizer $\overline{u}$ must satisfy the first-order KTL conditions. Furthermore, if J and the g_i's are twice continuously differentiable at $\overline{u}$, then the second-order KTL condition must also hold, i.e.,

$$\left\langle v, \nabla_{uu}^2 l(\overline{u},\, \overline{\lambda}) v \right\rangle \geq 0, \quad v \in T_0(u), \tag{102a}$$

where

$$T_0(\overline{u}) = N_0(\overline{u})^{\perp} \tag{102b}$$

and

$$N_0(\overline{u}) = \mathrm{span}\; \mathcal{G}_0(\overline{u}) = \mathrm{span}\; K(\overline{u}). \tag{102c}$$

Conversely, if J and the g_i's are twice continuously differentiable, and if (101d) and (102a) are replaced by the strengthened conditions

$$\lambda_i > 0 \;\Leftrightarrow i \in \mathcal{J}_0(\overline{u}) \tag{101e}$$

and

$$(\exists\,\mu > 0)\;\left\langle v,\; \nabla_{uu}^2 \; l(\overline{u},\overline{\lambda}) v \right\rangle \geq \mu \|v\|^2, \quad v \in T_0(\overline{u}), \tag{102d}$$

then $\overline{u}$ is a proper relative minimizer {26}. These expressions and the remaining portions of (101) and (102) comprise the Kuhn–Tucker–Lagrange sufficient conditions for relative minimality.

In the present context, a relative minimizer is said to be *nonsingular* iff it is normal and satisfies the KTL sufficient conditions. At a nonsingular minimizer, the so-called strict complementarity condition (101e) has the equivalent geometric expression (97). Furthermore, $T_0(\overline{u})$ is the subspace tangent to the smooth manifold

$$\mathcal{A}(\overline{u}) = \left\{ v \in \Omega : \mathcal{J}(v) = \mathcal{J}_0(u) \right\} \tag{103}$$

defined by the active constraints at $\bar{u}$, and condition (102d) says that the second differential of the restriction of J to $\mathscr{A}(\bar{u})$ must be positive-definite. These conditions are enough to ensure that iterates of (89) beginning near $\bar{u}$ must eventually enter the manifold $\mathscr{A}(\bar{u})$ and converge to $\bar{u}$.

Theorem 4. Suppose that Ω is a closed convex set with representation (98), that J and the functions g_i are twice continuously differentiable, and that $\{u^{(i)}\}$ is generated by (89). Let $\bar{u}$ be a nonsingular relative minimizer of J in Ω, with corresponding active constraint manifold $\mathscr{A}(\bar{u})$. If $u^{(1)}$ is sufficiently near $\bar{u}$, then

$$\lim_{i \to \infty} u^{(i)} = \bar{u} \tag{104a}$$

and

$$\left\| u^{(i)} - \bar{u} \right\| = o(\lambda^i) \tag{104b}$$

for some $\lambda \in [0, 1)$; moreover

$$u_{(i)} \in \mathscr{A}(\bar{u}) \tag{104c}$$

for sufficiently large i.

Theorem 4 follows easily from the analysis in [11] for a related variable (one) metric gradient projection scheme with Goldstein steps. Reference [8] also establishes a local asymptotic stability theorem for more general (i.e., possibly singular) relative minimizers. Notice that Theorem 4 essentially reduces to Theorem 1, part (f), when $\mathscr{J}_0(\bar{u}) = \emptyset$ (i.e., when $\bar{u}$ lies in the interior of Ω). Furthermore, when the constraint functions g_i are affine, Theorem 4 overlaps with previously quoted results for minimizers in polyhedral faces; however, the latter results do not require a "normality" assumption, and are in fact representation-free (i.e., they do not depend on the particular system of inequalities used to define Ω). Affine constraints are also treated in [5], and a result similar to Theorem 4 is obtained there in this special case.

IV. TWO METRIC GRADIENT PROJECTION METHODS

We have seen that a proper choice for the scaling transformation sequence $\{S^{(i)}\}$ in unconstrained variable metric gradient iterations (2) can accelerate local asymptotic convergence and still preserve the desirable nonlocal convergence properties of the basic steepest-descent method. This is also true of (1) relative to the ordinary gradient projection method in Section III; however, the correct forms for $S^{(i)}$ and the step length rule for $\sigma^{(i)}$ are now harder to determine.

A.   THE SUPERNORMAL-SUBTANGENT SCALING DECOMPOSITION RULE

The following result indicates one possible way around the difficulties explained in Example 5 of Section I; this theorem is a corollary of Lemma 4.1 in [17], and can also be obtained with a simple modification of the argument in Section 2 of [16].

Theorem 5. Let K(u) denote the normal cone (42b) at the point u in the closed convex set Ω, let N be any closed subspace containing K(u), and let T = $N^\perp$. Suppose that σ and s_N are positive numbers, and that $S_T : T \to T$ is a positive-definite bounded linear transformation on T. Then the operator

$$S = s_N P_N + S_T P_T$$

in (46) is a positive-definite bounded linear transformation on $\mathcal{U}$, and

$$\bar{u} = P_\Omega(\bar{u} - \sigma S \, \nabla J(\bar{u})) \tag{105}$$

if and only if $\bar{u}$ is a stationary point for J in Ω [i.e., $\bar{u}$ satisfies (41), or equivalently (42)].

According to Theorem 5, the stopping points for (2) are precisely the stationary points of J, provided S is given by (46) at each iteration. However, the following basic questions remain. First, does the strict descent property hold at nonstationary points u, i.e., can we show that

$$J(u) - J\left(P_\Omega(u - \sigma S \, \nabla J(u))\right) > 0, \qquad \text{small } \sigma > 0 \tag{106}$$

when u is nonstationary and S is in the class (46)? Better still, can we derive a counterpart of the estimate (87) that will lead us to an appropriate modification of the step length rule in Section III for scaling operators S in (46)? Finally, if such a rule is found, can we choose the "supernormal" and "subtangent" subspaces N and T and the scaling parameters s_N and s_T at each iteration so as to accelerate local asymptotic convergence while maintaining acceptable nonlocal convergence behavior? The main theorems and conjectures bearing on these points are outlined in the balance of this section.

B.   THE DESCENT CONDITION

Suppose that S is given by (46), and write

$$\varphi(\sigma) = P_\Omega(u + \sigma v) \tag{107a}$$

with

$$v = -S \, \nabla J(u) = v_N + v_T \tag{107b}$$

$$v_N = -s_N P_N \, \nabla J(u) \tag{107c}$$

$$v_T = -S_T P_T \, \nabla J(u). \tag{107d}$$

Guided by the development leading to (87) in Section III, we now use (82) to obtain

$$\sigma s_N \langle \nabla J(u), u - \varphi(\sigma) \rangle \geq \| u - \varphi(\sigma) \|^2 - \sigma \langle v_T, \varphi(\sigma) - u \rangle$$
$$- \sigma s_N \langle P_T \nabla J(u), \varphi(\sigma) - u \rangle. \tag{108}$$

The last two terms on the right-hand side of (108) are of the form $\langle x, \varphi(\sigma) - u \rangle$ with $x \in T$. Since $\langle x, v_N \rangle = 0$, we may therefore write

$$\langle x, \varphi(\sigma) - u \rangle = \langle x, v_T \rangle \sigma - \langle x, \psi(\sigma) \rangle, \tag{109a}$$

where

$$\psi(\sigma) = u + \sigma v - \varphi(\sigma) \in K(\varphi(\sigma)) \tag{109b}$$

$$\| \varphi(\sigma) - u \| \leq \| v \| \sigma \tag{109c}$$

$$\| \psi(\sigma) \| \leq 2 \| v \| \sigma \tag{109d}$$

for $\sigma > 0$ [see (79) and (83)]. Evidently, $\varphi(\sigma) \to u$ and $\varphi(\sigma) = O(\sigma)$ as $\sigma \to 0^+$; moreover, (109b) suggests that the unit vectors $\|\varphi(\sigma)\|^{-1}\varphi(\sigma)$ approach the normal cone $K(u) \subset N = T^\perp$ as $\sigma \to 0^+$. Hence, it is plausible that

$$\langle x, \psi(\sigma) \rangle = o(\sigma), \qquad x \in T. \tag{110}$$

[This can be deduced rigorously from weak closure of the set-valued map $u \to K(u)$.] In particular, if Ω is *polyhedral*, it is not hard to see that

$$K(u') \subset K(u) \subset N, \qquad u' \text{ near } u \tag{111a}$$

and therefore

$$\langle x, \psi(\sigma) \rangle = 0, \quad \text{small } \sigma > 0, \; x \in T. \tag{111b}$$

With (108)–(111) we now obtain the key estimates in the following lemma.

Lemma 6. Let Ω be a closed convex set in $\mathcal{U}$. At $u \in \Omega$ let N and T be complementary orthogonal closed subspaces in $\mathcal{U}$ with $N \supset K(u)$. Suppose that S is a bounded linear operator in the class (46), and define $\varphi(\sigma)$ by (107). Then

$$\langle \nabla J(u), u - \varphi(\sigma) \rangle \geq \frac{1}{\sigma S_N} \left\| u - \varphi(\sigma) - \sigma S_T P_T \nabla J(u) \right\|^2 \tag{112}$$

$$+ \langle P_T \nabla J(u), S_T P_T \nabla J(u) \rangle \sigma + o(\sigma)$$

Furthermore, if Ω is polyhedral, then for some $\sigma > 0$

$$\langle \nabla J(u), u - \varphi(\sigma) \rangle \geq \frac{1}{\sigma S_N} \left\| u - \varphi(\sigma) - \sigma S_T P_T \nabla J(u) \right\|^2$$
$$+ \langle P_T \nabla J(u), S_T P_T \nabla J(u) \rangle \sigma \qquad \sigma \in (0, \sigma 1]. \tag{113}$$

Note 2. Variants of the inequality (113) were first obtained by Bertsekas [14] for simple polyhedral convex sets Ω, and later by Gafni and Bertsekas [15] for a general two-metric gradient projection scheme that differs somewhat from the method under consideration here. In [15], the negative gradient $-\nabla J(u)$ is first decomposed with respect to a special pair of dual closed convex supernormal-subtangent *cones* (N, T) whose description is based explicitly on a linear inequality representation for Ω. The resulting normal component $P_N(-\nabla J(u))$ is then left unscaled, while $P_T(-\nabla J(u))$ is first transformed by a suitable positive-definite linear transformation on the subspace

$$\Gamma_T = \text{span} \left[\{P_N(-\nabla J(u))\}^{\perp} \cap T \right]. \tag{114}$$

and then projected back to the generating cone in (114).

This construction is designed to force the inequality (113) to hold even in *non-polyhedral* sets Ω; however, the weaker estimate (112) is adequate for our immediate purposes.

The inequality (112) leads directly to the descent condition (106) as follows. Observe first that if $P_T \nabla J(u) \neq 0$, then

$$\langle P_T \nabla J(u), S_T P_T \nabla J(u) \rangle \geq \mu_T \left\| P_T \nabla J(u) \right\|^2 > 0, \tag{115a}$$

where

$$\mu_T = \inf_{v \in T, \|v\|=1} \langle v, S_T v \rangle.$$

(115b)

On the other hand, if $P_T \nabla J(u) = 0$, then (84) and (85) imply that

$$\frac{\left\| u - \varphi(\sigma) - \sigma S_T P_T \nabla J(u) \right\|^2}{\sigma^2 s_N^2} = \frac{\left\| u - P_\Omega(u - \sigma s_N) \nabla J(u) \right\|^2}{\sigma^2 s_N^2}$$

$$\geq c \left\| u - P_\Omega(u - \nabla J(u)) \right\|^2$$

$$= c d^2(u), \qquad \sigma \in (0, \alpha],$$

(115c)

where

$$c = \min\{1, s_N/\alpha\} > 0.$$

(115d)

Consequently,

$$\frac{1}{\sigma^2 s_N} \left\| u - \varphi(\sigma) - \sigma S_T P_T \nabla J(u) \right\|^2 + \left\langle P_T \nabla J(u), S_T P_T \nabla J(u) \right\rangle$$

$$\geq d_1^2(u), \qquad \sigma \in (0, \alpha]$$

(116a)

with

$$d_1^2(u) = \mu_T \left\| P_T \nabla J(u) \right\|^2, \qquad \text{if } P_T \nabla J(u) \neq 0$$

$$= c s_N d^2(u), \qquad \text{if } P_T \nabla J(u) = 0.$$

(116b)

Since $\| P_T \nabla J(u) \| \neq 0 \Leftrightarrow -\nabla J(u) \notin N \Rightarrow -\nabla J(u) \notin K(u) \Leftrightarrow d(u) > 0$, we see that

$$d_1(u) > 0 \Leftrightarrow u \text{ is not stationary.}$$

(117)

Hence if u is not stationary, it follows from (83), (112), and (115) that for any fixed $\delta \in (0, 1]$,

$$J(u) - J(\varphi(\sigma)) = \left\langle \nabla J(u), u - \varphi(\sigma) \right\rangle + O(\sigma)$$

$$\geq \delta \left\{ \frac{1}{\sigma s_N} \| u - \varphi(\sigma) - \sigma S_T P_T \nabla J(u) \|^2 \right.$$

$$+ \left\langle P_T \nabla J(u), S_T P_T \nabla J(u) \right\rangle \sigma \Big\}$$

$$\geq \delta d_1^2(u)\sigma, \quad \text{small } \sigma > 0.$$

(118)

This counterpart of (87) establishes the strict descent condition (106) at nonstationary points, and shows that the step length rule devised for the dual cone decomposition scheme in [15] is at least feasible for the simpler subspace decomposition rule in (46).

C. A BERTSEKAS–GAFNI STEP LENGTH RULE

Fix constants $\alpha_1 \geq \alpha_0 > 0$, $\beta \in (0, 1)$, $1 > \delta_1 \geq \delta_0 > 0$. Suppose that at the i-th iteration of (2) we are given a positive-definite scaling transformation

$$S^{(i)} = s_N^{(i)} P_N^{(i)} + S_T^{(i)} P_T^{(i)},$$

(119a)

where $N^{(i)}$ and $T^{(i)}$ are supernormal-subtangent closed subspaces, $s_N^{(i)}$ is a positive real number, $S_T^{(i)} : T^{(i)} \to T^{(i)}$ is a bounded linear positive-definite operator, and $P_N^{(i)}$ and $P_T^{(i)}$ signify projection into $N^{(i)}$ and $T^{(i)}$. Choose $\alpha^{(i)} \in [\alpha_0, \alpha_1]$, $\delta^{(i)} \in [\delta_0, \delta_1]$ and set

$$u = u^{(i)}, \quad T = T^{(i)}, \quad N = N^{(i)}, \quad s_N = s_N^{(i)},$$

$$S_T = S_T^{(i)}, \quad \delta = \delta^{(i)}, \quad \sigma = \alpha^{(i)}.$$

(119b)

Compute $J(u)$, $P_N \nabla J(u)$, $P_T \nabla J(u)$, $v_N = -s_N P_N \nabla J(u)$, $v_T = -S_T P_T \nabla J(u)$, $v = v_N + v_T$, $\langle P_T \nabla J(u), v_T \rangle$, and enter the following loop:

Step 1. Compute $\varphi(\sigma) = P_\Omega(u + \sigma v)$, $J(\varphi(\sigma))$, and

$$\theta(\sigma) = \frac{1}{\sigma s_N} \left\| u - \varphi(\sigma) + v_T \sigma \right\|^2 - \left\langle P_T \nabla J(u), v_T \right\rangle \sigma.$$

Step 2. If $J(u) - J(\varphi(\sigma)) \geq \delta\theta(\sigma)$, go to Step 3; otherwise, replace σ by $\beta\sigma$ and go to Step 1.
Step 3. Put $\sigma^{(i)} = \sigma$ and stop.
In view of (118) this loop will eventually terminate with

$$\sigma^{(i)} = \max \sigma$$

(119c)

subject to

$$\frac{\sigma}{\alpha^{(i)}} \in \left\{1, \beta, \beta^2, \dots\right\} \tag{119d}$$

and

$$J\left(u^{(i)}\right) - J\left(P_\Omega\left(u^{(i)} + \sigma v^{(i)}\right)\right)$$

$$\geq \delta^{(i)} \left\{\left(1/\sigma s_N^{(i)}\right)\left\|u^{(i)} - P_\Omega\left(u^{(i)} + \sigma v^{(i)}\right) + v_T^{(i)}\sigma\right\|^2 \right.$$

$$\left. - \left\langle P_T^{(i)} \nabla J\left(u^{(i)}\right), v_T^{(i)}\right\rangle \sigma \right. \tag{119e}$$

where

$$v^{(i)} = v_N^{(i)} + v_T^{(i)} \tag{119f}$$

$$v_N^{(i)} = -s_N^{(i)} P_N^{(i)} \nabla J\left(u^{(i)}\right) \tag{119g}$$

$$v_T^{(i)} = -s_T^{(i)} P_T^{(i)} \nabla J\left(u^{(i)}\right). \tag{119h}$$

The next iterate in (2) is then

$$u^{(i+1)} = P_\Omega\left(u^{(i)} + \sigma^{(i)} v^{(i)}\right). \tag{119i}$$

D.   NONLOCAL CONVERGENCE PROPERTIES

The basic estimate (112) is sufficient to establish the descent property for (119); however, a closer examination of the o(σ) term in (112) is needed in order to prove counterparts of the convergence theorems in Sections II and III. In fact, suitable choices for $N^{(i)}$ are actually dictated in part by the implicit dependence of this term on N at each u, and by its corresponding effect on the nonlocal convergence behavior of (119). We develop this point further below for polyhedral sets

$$\Omega = \left\{u \in \mathscr{U}: \langle a^i, u\rangle - b_i \leq 0, \quad i = 1, \dots, m\right\} \tag{120}$$

and then formulate a conjecture for the larger class of closed convex feasible sets (98) defined by finitely many smooth nonlinear inequalities.

When Ω is polyhedral, the active constraint index and gradient sets in (99) and (100) become

$$\mathscr{I}_0(u) = \{ i: \langle a^i, u \rangle - b_i = 0 \} \tag{121}$$

$$\mathscr{G}_0(u) = \{ a^i \}_{i \in \mathscr{I}_0(u)}. \tag{122}$$

Furthermore, at any point $u \in \Omega$, the normal cone $K(u)$ is composed of $0 \in \mathscr{U}$ and all non-negative linear combinations of $\mathscr{G}_0(u)$, regardless of whether $\mathscr{G}_0(u)$ is linearly independent or empty (i.e., regardless of whether u is a "normal" point). By analogy with the dual cone constructions introduced in [15], we are now led to consider supernormal spaces defined by the ϵ-active constraints at $u \in \Omega$, i.e.,

$$N_\epsilon(u) = \text{span } \mathscr{G}_\epsilon(u) \supset K(u), \tag{123a}$$

where

$$\mathscr{G}_\epsilon(u) = \{ a^i \}_{i \in \mathscr{I}_0(u)}. \tag{123b}$$

and

$$\mathscr{I}_\epsilon(u) = \{ i : \langle a^i, u \rangle - b_i \geq -\epsilon \| a^i \| \} \supset \mathscr{I}_0(u) \tag{123c}$$

for $\epsilon > 0$.

Lemma 7. For all $\epsilon > 0$ and all $u, u' \in \Omega$,

$$\| u' - u \| \leq \epsilon \Rightarrow K(u') \subset N_\epsilon(u). \tag{124}$$

Lemma 7 is a simple consequence of Cauchy's inequality and the normal cone representation at u'. By using (109c) together with (124) in place of (111), we obtain the following key refinement of the estimate (113).

Lemma 8. Let Ω be a polyhedral convex set (120) in $\mathscr{U}$, let ϵ be a fixed positive number, and let N and T be complementary orthogonal closed subspaces in $\mathscr{U}$, with

$$N \supset N_\epsilon(u) \supset N_0(u) = \text{span } K(u). \tag{125}$$

Suppose that S is a bounded linear operator in the class (46), and define $\varphi(\sigma)$ by (108). Then the estimate (113) is valid with any positive σ_1 satisfying

$$\sigma_1 \| v \| < \epsilon. \tag{126}$$

According to Lemma 8, the estimate (113) can be made to hold in arbitrarily big intervals $(0, \sigma_1]$ by enlarging the supernormal space N assigned to u;

in particular, in the extreme case $N = \mathcal{U}$, Lemma 8 produces the inequality (86) obtained earlier for ordinary gradient projection processes. Since (86) supplies key steps in the proofs of parts (b) and (c) in Theorem 3, we are now led to ask how *small* $N^{(i)}$ can be made in (119) without destroying suitably modified non-local convergence proofs based on (113); this question is important because smaller $N^{(i)}$'s mean larger domains $T^{(i)}$ for the scaling operators $S_T^{(i)}$, and hence greater opportunities for convergence acceleration. The following theorem provides a partial answer to our question.

Theorem 9. Suppose that J is continuously differentiable, that Ω is a polyhedral convex set (120), and that $N_\epsilon(u)$ is defined by (123). Fix $\epsilon_0 > 0$ and put

$$\varepsilon(u) = \min\left\{\varepsilon_0, d(u)\right\} \tag{127a}$$

$$\mathcal{J}(u) = \mathcal{J}_\epsilon(u)\Big|_{\varepsilon=\varepsilon(u)} \tag{127b}$$

and

$$N(u) = N_\varepsilon(u)\Big|_{\varepsilon=\varepsilon(u)} \tag{127c}$$

$$T(u) = N(u)^\perp, \tag{127d}$$

where $d(u)$ is the nonstationarity measure (77). Let $\{u^{(i)}\}$ be generated by (119) with

$$N^{(i)} \supset N\big(u^{(i)}\big) \tag{127e}$$

$$\mu_1\|w\|^2 \geq \left\langle w, S_T^{(i)} w\right\rangle \geq \mu_0\|w\|^2, \qquad w \in T^{(i)} \tag{127f}$$

and

$$\mu_3 \geq s_N^{(i)} \geq \mu_2 \tag{127g}$$

for some constants $\mu_1 \geq \mu_1 > 0$, $\mu_3 \geq \mu_2 > 0$, and all $i = 1, 2, \ldots$. Then the following assertions are true:

(a) If $d(u^{(i)}) > 0$ for all i, then $\{J(u^{(i)})\}$ is strictly decreasing.

(b) Every subsequential limit point of $\{u^{(i)}\}$ is a zero of $d(\cdot)$ (and hence a stationary point), and J assumes a common value on all such limits.

(c) If J is bounded below on Ω, and if the level sets of J in Ω are compact, then $\{u^{(i)}\}$ converges to the stationary point set Z in (93), and

$$\lim_{i \to \infty} d\left(u^{(i)}\right) = 0. \tag{128}$$

Part (a) of Theorem 9 is an immediate consequence of (118); part (b) can be established with an adaptation of the proof for Proposition 2 in [15]; part (c) is obtained from (b) with standard compactness arguments [21].

The following counterpart of the supernormal space N(u) in Theorem 9 arises naturally in an extension of the Newtonian scaling principle for gradient projection in feasible sets (98) defined by finitely many smooth nonlinear inequalities (Section IV,E). Fix $\epsilon_0 > 0$ and $\theta > 1$. Let u be a normal point in (98) (Section III) and put

$$\mathcal{J}_\epsilon(u) = \left\{ i : g_i(u) \geq -\theta \left\| \nabla g_i(u) \right\| \epsilon \right\} \tag{129a}$$

$$\mathcal{G}_\epsilon(u) = \left\{ \nabla g_i(u) \right\}_{i \in \mathcal{J}_\epsilon(u)} \tag{129b}$$

$$N_\epsilon(u) = \operatorname{span} \mathcal{G}_\epsilon(u) \supset K(u) \tag{129c}$$

$$\epsilon(u) = \min \left\{ \epsilon_0, d(u) \right\} \tag{129d}$$

$$\mathcal{J}(u) = \mathcal{J}_\epsilon(u) \Big|_{\epsilon = \epsilon(u)} \tag{129e}$$

$$N(u) = N_\epsilon(u) \Big|_{\epsilon = \epsilon(u)} \supset K(u) \tag{129f}$$

$$T(u) = N(u)^\perp. \tag{129g}$$

If $\{u^{(i)}\}$ is a sequence of normal points generated by (119) in the set (98), with $N^{(i)} \supset N(u^{(i)})$, then part (a) of Theorem 9 is still true simply because $N^{(i)}$ is a supernormal space at each $u^{(i)}$. Furthermore, while Lemma 8 is no longer valid in nonpolyhedral sets (98), it seems possible that a different proof scheme can be formulated for part (b) of Theorem 9, based on (112) and estimates for the associated $o(\sigma)$ term.

Note 3. The dual cone projection scheme employed in [15] produces variants of Lemma 8 and part (b) of Theorem 9 in *arbitrary* closed convex sets Ω (see Propositions 1 and 2 in [15]); however, this generality comes at a certain price. For one thing, the cone projection method is computationally more difficult than subspace projection. More significantly, for nonpolyhedral sets Ω, the subtangent spaces (114) employed in [15] seem too small to support scaling operators S_T capable of inducing local superlinear convergence to nonsingular minimizers (this is readily apparent when Ω is the unit ball in R^3); in any case, the sole convergence rate result in [15] holds only in polyhedra.

E.   ASYMPTOTIC CONVERGENCE PROPERTIES

It can be shown that near any nondegenerate stationary point $\bar{u}$ in a polyhedral set (120), the subspace pairs $(N(u), T(u))$ in Theorem 9 and the analogous dual cones in [15] produce identical decompositions of $-\nabla J(u)$; moreover, the subspaces $\Gamma_T(u)$ in (114) coincide with $T(u)$. These observations and some further elaborations on the proof of Proposition 3 in [15] lead directly to the following result.

Theorem 10. Suppose that Ω is a polyhedral convex set (120), that $\bar{u}$ is a nonsingular relative minimizer of J in Ω, and that $N(u)$ and $T(u)$ are defined by (123) and (127) at $u \in \Omega$. Let $\{u^{(i)}\}$ be generated by (119), with supernormal spaces

$$N^{(i)} = N\left(u^{(i)}\right) \tag{130}$$

and scaling parameters $s_N^{(i)}$ and $S_T^{(i)}$ that satisfy conditions (127f) and (127g). Then the following assertions are true:

(a) If $\{u^{(i)}\}$ has $\bar{u}$ as one of its subsequential limit points, then

$$\lim_{i \to \infty} u^{(i)} = \bar{u}. \tag{131}$$

(b) If (131) holds, then $\{u^{(i)}\}$ eventually enters and remains within the active constraint manifold

$$\mathscr{A}(\bar{u}) = \text{ri} \left\{ \left[\bar{u} + T_0(\bar{u}) \right] \cap \Omega \right\} \tag{132}$$

at $\bar{u}$, the iteration (119) eventually reduces to an "unconstrained" variable metric descent process (55) for J restricted to the linear variety $\bar{u} + T_0(\bar{u})$, and $\{u^{(i)}\}$ converges linearly to $\bar{u}$, i.e.,

$$\left\| u^{(i+1)} - \bar{u} \right\| \le \rho \left\| u^{(i)} - \bar{u} \right\| \tag{133}$$

for some $\rho \in [0, 1)$ and all sufficiently large i.

Notice that Theorem 10 does not assert that $\{u^{(i)}\}$ must converge to a nonsingular minimizer $\bar{u}$ from all nearby starting points [cf. Theorem 1, part (f), and Theorem 4]. Asymptotic stability results of this kind for (119) are almost certainly valid in polyhedra but have not yet been proved. Further extensions for feasible sets (98) also seem likely in light of [8, 11], but again, no proofs can be cited here.

F. NEWTONIAN SCALING

Prototype convergence–accelerating transformations S for (1) were derived in Section II,B by setting $\sigma = 1$ and imposing the condition (69). This approach also works for (2) in (98); however, the analysis is less transparent due to the intervening nondifferentiable projection map P_Ω.

As in [17], we let (129) define the supernormal space $N(u)$ and its subtangent orthogonal complement $T(u)$ at each normal point u in the set (98). If $\bar{u}$ is a normal nondegenerate extremal (Section III), then the construction (129) ensures that $N(\bar{u}) = N_0(\bar{u}) = \text{span } K(\bar{u})$ and that $T(\bar{u}) = T_0(\bar{u}) =$ the space tangent to the smooth manifold $\mathscr{A}(\bar{u})$ at $\bar{u}$ [see (103)]; moreover, the map $u \to (N(u), T(u))$ is "continuous" in a certain sense in $\bar{u}$, and therefore,

$$"\lim"_{u \to \bar{u}} \ (N(u), T(u)) = (N(\bar{u}), T(\bar{u})) \tag{134}$$

$$= \left(N_0(\bar{u}), T_0(\bar{u}) \right).$$

We now consider associated mappings

$$u \to \phi(u) = P_\Omega(u - S(u) \nabla J(u)) \tag{135a}$$

with

$$S(u) = s_N(u)P_{N(u)} + S_T(u)P_{T(u)}, \tag{135b}$$

where $S_N(u)$ is a positive number and $S_T(u)$ is a bounded linear transformation on $T(u)$. In view of (134), every normal nondegenerate extremal $\bar{u}$ is a fixed point of the map ϕ. In addition, the following fundamental conditions are also met if the numbers $S_N(u)$ are merely bounded away from zero and ∞ near $\bar{u}$, and the operators $S_T(u)$ are uniformly bounded near $\bar{u}$:

$$\lim_{u \to \bar{u}} \phi(u) = \phi(\bar{u}) = \bar{u} \tag{136a}$$

$$\phi(u) \in \mathscr{A}(\bar{u}), \quad u \text{ near } \bar{u} \tag{136b}$$

$$T(u) = T_0(u) \quad u \in \mathscr{A}(\bar{u}), \quad u \text{ near } \bar{u}. \tag{136c}$$

According to (136a) and (136b), we need only require that

$$\phi(u) - \bar{u} = o(\|u - \bar{u}\|), \quad u \in \mathscr{A}(\bar{u}) \tag{137}$$

to ensure that ϕ-iterates beginning sufficiently near $\overline{u}$ must eventually enter and remain within the active constraint manifold $\mathscr{A}(\overline{u})$ and converge superlinearly to $\overline{u}$. Furthermore, since $T_0(u)$ is the tangent space for $\mathscr{A}(\overline{u})$ at $u \in \mathscr{A}(\overline{u})$ near $\overline{u}$, condition (136c) and the analysis in Section II,B suggest that (137) can indeed be achieved with locally uniformly bounded scaling operators $S_T(u)$ derived from the second differential of the restriction of J to the smooth manifold $\mathscr{A}(\overline{u})$, provided this differential is continuous and one–one onto at $\overline{u}$. All essential details of the foregoing argument are developed in [17]; however, here we can only describe the resulting projected Newton algorithm and indicate why and how it should work.

The following construction is dictated by condition (137). At each normal point u in the set (98), let $\mathscr{A}(u)$ and N(u) be given by (129), and choose $\lambda(u) \in R^m$ so that

$$\sum_{i=1}^{m} \lambda_i(u) \nabla g_i(u) = - P_{N(u)} \nabla J(u), \tag{138a}$$

$$\lambda_i(u) = 0, \quad i \notin \mathscr{A}(u). \tag{138b}$$

These conditions uniquely prescribe a continuous map $u \to \lambda(u)$ on the set of normal points in (98) [this set is open in (98)]. Given $S_N(u) > 0$, form the corresponding bounded linear operators

$$L(u) = \nabla^2 J(u) + \sum_{i=1}^{m} \lambda_i(u) \nabla^2 g_i(u) = \nabla_{uu}^2 l(u, \lambda(u)) \tag{138c}$$

$$E(u) = I + s_N(u) \sum_{i-1}^{m} \lambda_i(u) \nabla^2 g_i(u) \tag{138d}$$

and their projected restrictions,

$$L_T(u) = P_{T(u)} L(u) \Big|_{T(u)} \tag{138e}$$

$$E_T(u) = P_{T(u)} E(u) \Big|_{T(u)}. \tag{138f}$$

Now let

$$\phi(u) = P_{\Omega}(u + v) \tag{138g}$$

with

$$v = v_N + v_T \tag{138h}$$

$$v_N = -s_N(u)P_{N(u)} \nabla J(u) \tag{138i}$$

and

$$v_T = E_T(u)w_T, \tag{138j}$$

where w_T is obtained by solving the linear equation

$$L_T(u)w_T = - P_{T(u)} \nabla J(u). \tag{138k}$$

Finally, given $u^{(1)}$ in the set (98), construct $\{u^{(i)}\}$ recursively with

$$u^{(i+1)} = \phi(u^{(i)}), \quad i = 1,2,.... \tag{138l}$$

The iterative scheme (138) is well-posed in the vicinity of any nonsingular stationary points $\bar{u}$ in (98), i.e., any normal nondegenerate stationary point at which J and g are twice continuously differentiable and the associated second differential

$$P_{T_0(\bar{u})} \nabla^2_{uu} l\ (\bar{u},\bar{\lambda})\Big|_{T_0(\bar{u})} : T_0(\bar{u}) \to T_0(\bar{u}) \tag{139}$$

is one–one onto (notice that every nonsingular relative minimizer is automatically a nonsingular stationary point). All points in (98) near $\bar{u}$ are also normal, and, in view of (129) and (134), it can be shown that

$$\lim_{u \to \bar{u}} \lambda(u) = \bar{\lambda} \tag{140}$$

and

$$\lim_{u \to \bar{u}} L_T(u) = L_T(\bar{u}) = P_{T_0}(\bar{u}) \nabla^2_{uu} l\ (\bar{u},\bar{\lambda})\Big|_{T_0(\bar{u})}, \tag{141}$$

where $\bar{\lambda}$ is the unique Lagrange multiplier vector satisfying (101) with $\bar{u}$. Therefore, "by continuity," the operators $L_T(u)$ are one–one onto with uniformly bounded inverses $L_T(u)^{-1} : T(u) \to T(u)$ defined near $\bar{u}$ [17]. Under these circumstances (138j) and (138k) have the unique solution

$$v_T = - S_T(u)P_T \nabla J(u), \tag{142a}$$

where

$$S_T(u) = \left[I + s_N(u) \Lambda_T(u) \right] L_T(u)^{-1} \tag{142b}$$

with

$$\Lambda_T(u) = P_{T(u)} \sum_{i=1}^{m} \lambda_i(u) \left. \nabla^2 g_i(u) \right|_{T(u)}. \tag{142c}$$

Moreover, if the numbers $s_N(u)$ are bounded away from zero and ∞ near $\bar{u}$, then the operators $S_T(u)$ are uniformly bounded near $\bar{u}$, and conditions (136) and (137) can be verified.

Theorem 11. Let $\bar{u}$ be a nonsingular stationary point of J in the set (98), let (129) define a family of supernormal-subtangent spaces $N(u)$ and $T(u)$ near $\bar{u}$, and suppose that the positive numbers $s_N(u)$ are bounded and bounded away from zero near $\bar{u}$. Then for each $u^{(1)}$ sufficiently near $\bar{u}$, the projected Newton iteration scheme (138) generates a corresponding sequence $\{u^{(i)}\}$ that eventually enters and remains within the active constraint manifold $\mathscr{A}(\bar{u})$ in (103), and converges superlinearly to $\bar{u}$.

For unconstrained minimization problems, the Newtonian scaling operators $S(u) = \nabla^2 Ju)^{-1}$ produce descent directions $-S(u) \nabla J(u)$ when u is sufficiently near a nonsingular minimizer $\bar{u}$. This also happens for the Newtonian operators

$$S(u) = s_N(u) P_{N(u)} + \left[I + s_N(u) \Lambda_T(u) \right] L_T(u)^{-1} P_{T(u)} \tag{143a}$$

described above, provided the normal scaling parameters $s_N(u)$ are suitably matched to the operators $\Lambda_T(u)$ and $L_T(u)^{-1}$. For instance, if we let

$$\gamma(u) = \left\langle P_{T(u)} \nabla J(u), L_T(u)^{-1} P_{T(u)} \nabla J(u) \right\rangle \tag{143b}$$

$$\omega(u) = \left\langle P_{T(u)} \nabla J(u), \Lambda_T(u) L_T(u)^{-1} P_{T(u)} \nabla J(u) \right\rangle \tag{143c}$$

and put

$$
\begin{aligned}
s_N(u) &- 1, \quad &&\text{if} \quad \omega(u) \geq 0 \\
&= \min\left\{ 1, -\frac{1}{2} \frac{\gamma(u)}{\omega(u)} \right\}, \quad &&\text{if} \quad \omega(u) < 0
\end{aligned}
\tag{143d}
$$

then

$$\left\langle P_{T(u)} \nabla J(u), S_T(u) P_{T(u)} \nabla J(u) \right\rangle = \gamma(u) + s_N(u) \omega(u) \tag{144}$$

$$\geq \frac{1}{2} \gamma(u).$$

Near a nonsingular relative minimizer $\overline{u}$ in the set (98), the operators $\Lambda_T(u)$ are uniformly bounded, and the inverse operators $L_T(u)^{-1}$ are uniformly bounded and positive definite. Hence, the normal scaling parameters $s_N(u)$ are locally bounded away from zero and ∞, and

$$\mu_1 \left\| P_{T(u)} \nabla J(u) \right\|^2 \geq \left\langle P_{T(u)} \nabla J(u), S_T(u) P_{T(u)} \nabla J(u) \right\rangle$$

$$\geq \mu_0 \left\| P_{T(u)} \nabla J(u) \right\|^2 \tag{145}$$

for some constants $\mu_1 \geq \mu_0 > 0$ and all u sufficiently near $\overline{u}$. The construction (143) therefore satisfies the hypotheses of Theorem 11 and ensures the descent property (106) near nonsingular minimizers.

When Ω is a polyhedral set (120), the constraint Hessians $\nabla^2 g_i(u)$ vanish identically, the multiplier vectors $\lambda(u)$ are not needed, and the tangential component of the Newtonian scaling operator $S(u)$ in (143) reduces to

$$S_T(u) = P_{T(u)} \nabla^2 J(u) \Big|_{T(u)}^{-1}. \tag{146}$$

In view of Theorems 2 and 10, we may now formulate the following asymptotic convergence result for relaxed projected Newton processes with Bertsekas–Gafni step lengths.

Theorem 12. Suppose that Ω is a polyhedral set (120), that $\overline{u}$ is a nonsingular relative minimizer of J in Ω, and that $N(u)$ and $T(u)$ are defined by (123) and (127) at $u \in \Omega$. Let $\{u^{(i)}\}$ be generated by (119) with $\alpha^{(i)} = 1$, $\delta^{(i)} \in [\delta_0, 1/2)$, and with supernormal spaces $N^{(i)}$ and scaling parameters $s_N^{(i)}$ and $S_T^{(i)}$ satisfying (127f), (127g), and (130). In addition, suppose that $\overline{u}$ is a subsequential limit point of $\{u^{(i)}\}$ and that

$$S_T^{(i)} = P_{T^{(i)}} \nabla^2 J\left(u^{(i)}\right) \Big|_{T^{(i)}}^{-1} \tag{147}$$

eventually. Then $\{u^{(i)}\}$ eventually enters and remains within the active constraint manifold (132), the iteration (139) eventually reduces to an unconstrained relaxed Newton process (75) for J restricted to the linear variety $\overline{u} + T_0(\overline{u})$, the step lengths $\sigma^{(i)}$ are eventually equal to 1, and $\{u^{(i)}\}$ converges superlinearly to $\overline{u}$.

Theorem 12 does not claim that nonsingular relative minimizers are stable local attractors for relaxed projected Newton processes (cf. Theorem 2), although this is almost certainly true in polyhedral sets (120). Still more general local stability/convergence rate results will hold in closed convex sets (98) if it can be shown that

$$\lim_{u \to \bar{u}} \sigma(u) = 1 \qquad (148)$$

when $\bar{u}$ is a nonsingular minimizer in (98) and $\sigma(u)$ is produced by the step length rule in (119) with $\alpha^{(i)} = 1$, $\delta^{(i)} \in [\delta_0, 1/2)$ and the scaling operators S in (143); however, at present, this question is unresolved.

G.   IMPLEMENTATION IN R^n

We now briefly consider finite-dimensional implementations of the previously described subspace decomposition scaling techniques. In this setting, vectors are identified with column matrices, operators with rectangular matrices, and operators action and composition with matrix multiplication. In several important special cases, suitable matrix representations for the required gradient decompositions, multiplier functions, and Newtonian scaling equations can be written down easily once the index set $\mathcal{J}(u)$ in (127) or (129) has been computed. This is true when Ω is a Cartesian product of low-dimensional balls [16] or cylinders [17], and the simplest case of all occurs when Ω is a standard orthant or box in the space R^n with standard inner product

$$\langle u, v \rangle = u^t v \qquad (149)$$

(see [14]). The vectors a^i in (120) are then just nonzero multiples of elements in the standard orthonormal basis

$$\{e^1, ..., e^n\} \qquad (150a)$$

with

$$\begin{aligned} e^i_j &= 1, \qquad j = i \\ &= 0, \qquad j \neq i. \end{aligned} \qquad (150b)$$

Under these circumstances, there is an index set

$$\mathcal{J}(u) \subset \{1, 2, ..., n\}$$

derived from $\mathcal{J}(u)$ in (127b), such that

$$N(u) = \text{span } \{e^i\}_{i \in \mathcal{J}(u)} \qquad (151a)$$

$$T(u) = \text{span } \{e^i\}_{i \in \{1, \ldots, n\} \sim \mathscr{F}(u)} \qquad (151b)$$

$$\left(P_{N(u)} \nabla J(u)\right)_i = \frac{\partial J(u)}{\partial u_i}, \qquad i \in \mathscr{F}(u) \qquad (152a)$$

$$= 0, \qquad i \in \{1, \ldots, n\} \sim \mathscr{F}(u)$$

$$\left(P_{T(u)} \nabla J(u)\right)_i = 0, \qquad i \in \mathscr{F}(u) \qquad (152b)$$

$$= \frac{\partial J(u)}{\partial u_i}, \qquad i \in \{1, \ldots, n\} \sim \mathscr{F}(u)$$

The Newtonian scaling equations that determine the vector v_T in (138) also have a comparable simplicity in this special case. In particular, if

$$\{1, \ldots, n\} \sim \mathscr{F}(u) = \{i_1, i_2, \ldots, i_{n-v}\}, \qquad (153)$$

then

$$v_T = Q_T \alpha, \qquad (154a)$$

where

$$Q_T = \left[\begin{array}{ccccc} & | & & | & \\ e^{i_1} & | & \cdots & | & e^{i_{n-v}} \\ & | & & | & \end{array} \right] \qquad (154b)$$

and α is obtained by solving the $(n - v) \times (n - v)$ linear system

$$L_T(u)\alpha = \beta \qquad (155a)$$

with right-hand side

$$\beta = - Q_T^t \, \nabla J(u)$$

and coefficient matrix

$$L_T(u) = Q_T^t \, \nabla^2 J(u) Q_T.$$

Evidently, β is just the $(n - \nu) \times 1$ column matrix with entries

$$\beta_k = \frac{\partial J(u)}{\partial u_{i_k}}, \qquad 1 \le k \le n - \nu \tag{155b}$$

and $L_T(u)$ is the $(n - \nu) \times (n - \nu)$ submatrix of $\nabla^2 J(u)$ with entries

$$L_T(u)_{k,l} = \frac{\partial^2 J(u)}{\partial u_{i_k} \partial u_{i_l}}, \qquad 1 \le k, \quad l \le n - \nu. \tag{155c}$$

More generally, if Ω is represented by (98) in the space R^n with inner product (149), then orthonormal bases for the subspaces $N(u)$ and $T(u)$ in (129) may be obtained from a QR decomposition of the active constraint gradient matrix. Specifically, if the set $\mathcal{A}(u)$ in (129) consists of $\nu \le n$ indices

$$\mathcal{A}(u) = \{j_1, j_2, \ldots, j_\nu\},$$

we compute an $n \times n$ orthogonal matrix

$$Q = [Q_N \vdots Q_T]$$

and an $\nu \times \nu$ upper triangular matrix R such that

$$\left[\nabla g_{j_1}(u) \vdots \ldots \vdots \nabla g_{j_\nu}(u) \right]$$
$$[Q_N \vdots Q_T] \begin{bmatrix} R \\ -- \\ 0 \end{bmatrix}.$$

(This is always possible when u is sufficiently near a normal extremal [17].) The columns of the $n \times \nu$ and $n \times (n - \nu)$ matrices Q_N and Q_T supply orthonormal bases for $N(u)$ and $T(u)$, and therefore:

$$P_{N(u)} \nabla J(u) = Q_N Q_N^t \nabla J(u)$$
$$P_{T(u)} \nabla J(u) = Q_T Q_T^t \nabla J(u).$$

Furthermore, the multipliers $\lambda(u)$ in (138) are obtained by solving the $\nu \times \nu$ upper triangular linear system,

$$R\lambda(u) = -Q_N^t \nabla J(u),$$

and the Newtonian scaling equations (138j) and (138k) become

$$v_T = Q_T Q_T^t E(u) Q_T \alpha, \tag{156a}$$

where α is obtained by solving the $(n - v) \times (n - v)$ linear system

$$L_T(u)\alpha = \beta \tag{156b}$$

with right-hand side

$$\beta = - Q_T^t \, \nabla J(u) \tag{156c}$$

and coefficient matrix

$$L_T(u) = Q_T^t L(u) Q_T. \tag{156d}$$

Near a nonsingular minimizer $\overline{u}$ in (98), the matrix $L_T(u)$ is positive-definite and (156b) can therefore be solved by Cholesky decomposition. We also note that the matrices $E(u)$, R, Q, $Q_N Q_N^t$, and $Q_T Q_T^t$ are block diagonal when Ω is a Cartesian product defined by separable constraints (see Section I); however, $L_T(u)$ typically is not sparse unless J also has special structure. For further details, see [17].

V. NEWTONIAN SCALING FOR OPTIMAL CONTROL PROBLEMS

Example 2 in Section I is a representative of the class of discrete-time optimal control problems with objective function

$$J(u) = c_{k+1}\left(x^{k+1}\right) + \sum_{j=1}^{k} c_j\left(x^j, u^j\right), \tag{157a}$$

and state equations

$$x^1 = a \tag{157b}$$

$$x^{j+1} = f^j\left(x^j, u^j\right), \qquad j = 1, ..., k \tag{157c}$$

and control input constraints

$$g_l^j \ (u^j) \le 0, \quad j = 1, \dots, k; \quad l = 1, \dots, \mu_j. \tag{158a}$$

In general, u^j and x^j are vectors in real Hilbert spaces $\mathscr{U}_j$ and $\mathscr{X}_0$ with inner products $\langle \cdot, \cdot \rangle_j$ and $(\cdot, \cdot)_0$, respectively. For present purposes, the functions c_j, f^j, and g^j are assumed to be twice continuously differentiable, and the corresponding admissible control input sets

$$U_j = \left\{ u_j \in \mathscr{U}_j : g^j \le 0 \right\} \tag{158b}$$

are required to be convex. If control input vector sequences are viewed as ordered k-tuples $u = (u_1, \dots, u^k)$ in the Hilbert space $\mathscr{U}$ with scalar multiplication, vector addition, inner product, and norm defined by (16), then the admissible control sequences comprise the closed convex Cartesian product set

$$\begin{aligned}
\Omega &= U_1 \times \dots \times U_k \\
&= \left\{ (u^1, \dots, u^k) \in \mathscr{U} : g(u^1, \dots, u^k) \le 0 \right\}
\end{aligned} \tag{158c}$$

with separable constraint function

$$g(u^1, \dots, u^k) = \left(g^1(u^1), \dots, g^k(u^k) \right) \tag{158d}$$

and associated projector decomposition formula (14). The computational significance of (14) has already been discussed in Section I, and we have also just indicated in Section IV,G how constraint separability in R^n leads to block diagonal structure in matrix representations for the operators $P_{N(u)}$, $P_{T(u)}$, and $E(u)$, and attendant simplifications in the Newtonian scaling equations (138). Our purpose now is to outline a further major simplification in the computation of the scaled subtangential gradient component v_T in (138) when J is defined by (157).

A.   DISCRETE-TIME OPTIMAL CONTROL PROBLEMS

The Newtonian scaling equation (138k) is satisfied by $w_T \in T(u)$ if and only if w_T is a stationary point of the quadratic function $\varphi(u; \cdot)$ defined by

$$\varphi(u; v) = \langle \nabla J(u), v \rangle + \frac{1}{2} \langle v, L(u)v \rangle \tag{159}$$

with v restricted to $T(u)$. If J is defined by (157), it turns out that φ is itself the objective function for an accessory optimal control problem with linear state equations and linear equality constraints on the control inputs. This kind of control problem can be treated effectively with the Riccati substitution method described in [27] or with closely related dynamic programming techniques. In either approach, w_T is computed without ever actually assembling the linear operator $L_T(u)$ in (138k), and the associated computational cost typically increases only like the first power of k. Since the cost of computing $\nabla J(u)$ and the remaining steps in (138) are also O(k) for typical problems in the class (157) and (158) (because of constraint separability), we now see that the overall per iteration cost for the projected Newton scheme (138) should be roughly a fixed multiple of the per iteration cost for the ordinary unscaled projected gradient method (89), *regardless of the number of stages in (157) and (158)*. Bertsekas appears to have used dynamic programming in the numerical example in [14]. Gawande and Dunn [10, 16] employed differential dynamic programming techniques [28] in conjunction with projected Newton methods for control problems in Cartesian products of balls, and Dunn [17, 28] later applied the standard dynamic programming principle directly to a general accessory optimal control problem with quadratic objective function (159). Since the latter approach has certain theoretical and computational advantages, we limit further consideration to this case, and merely list the basic recursions here; for additional information, see [17] and [29]. For still another DP-based approach to discrete-time optimal control problems, see [30].

Given $u = (u^1, ..., u_k)$ in (158c) and the initial condition (157b), construct $(x^1, ..., x^{k+1})$ with the forward recursion (157c) and compute the corresponding differentials

$$A^j = \frac{\partial f^j}{\partial x}\left(x^j, u^j\right) \tag{160a}$$

$$B^j = \frac{\partial f^j}{\partial u}\left(x^j, u^j\right). \tag{160b}$$

Then set

$$p^{k+1} = \nabla c_{k+1}\left(x^{k+1}\right) \tag{161a}$$

and construct $(p^2, ..., p^{k+1})$ with the backward recursion

$$p^j = A^{j*} p^{j+1} + \nabla_x c_j\left(x^j, u^j\right), \qquad j = k, ..., 2, \tag{161b}$$

where A^{j*} is the adjoint of the operator A^j relative to the inner product $(\cdot, \cdot)_0$ in $\mathscr{X}_0$ (note that if $\mathscr{X}_0 = R^\nu$ with standard basis and inner product, then the matrix representor for A^{j*} is just the transpose of the matrix for A^j). For $j = 1, ..., k$, $p \in \mathscr{X}_0$, $x \in \mathscr{X}_0$, and $u \in \mathscr{U}_j$, define the Hamiltonians,

$$H_j(p,x,u) = \left(p, f^j(x,u)\right)_0 + c_j(x,u) \tag{162}$$

and compute

$$r^j = \nabla_u H_j\left(p^{j+1}, x^j, u^j\right), \qquad j = 1,...,k. \tag{163a}$$

Then

$$\nabla J(u) = \left(r^1,...,r^k\right). \tag{163b}$$

At a normal point $u = (u^1, ..., u^k)$ in (158c), the subspaces $N(u)$ and $T(u)$ in (129) are direct sums of subspaces in $\mathscr{U}_1, ..., \mathscr{U}_k$, namely

$$N(u) = N_1 \oplus ... \oplus N_k \tag{164a}$$

$$T(u) = T_1 \oplus ... \oplus T_k \tag{164b}$$

with

$$T_j = N_j^\perp \quad (= \text{orthogonal complement of } N_j \text{ in } \mathscr{U}_j) \tag{164c}$$

$$N_j = \text{span} \left\{\nabla g_l^j(u^j)\right\}_{l \in \mathscr{J}_j} \tag{164d}$$

$$\mathscr{J}_j = \left\{l : g_l^j(u^j) \geq -\theta\|\nabla g_l^j(u^j)\|_j \, \varepsilon(u)\right\} \tag{164e}$$

$$\varepsilon(u) = \min\left\{\varepsilon_0, d(u)\right\} \tag{164f}$$

$$d(u)^2 = \sum_{j=1}^{k} \left\|u^j - P_{U_j}\left(u^j - r^j\right)\right\|_j^2. \tag{164g}$$

The corresponding multiplier vector in (138) can then be written as

$$\lambda(u) = \left(\lambda^1, \ldots, \lambda^k\right),$$ (165a)

where the vector-valued components $\lambda^j \in R^{\mu_j}$ are obtained by solving k uncoupled subsystems for (138a) and (138b), namely

$$\sum_{l=1}^{\mu_j} \lambda_l^j \nabla g_l^j(u) = -P_{N_j} r^j,$$ (165b)

$$\lambda_l^j = 0, j \notin \mathcal{J}_j$$ (165c)

for j = 1, ..., k. In this notation, the operators E(u) and L(u) in (138) are given by

$$E(u) = I + s_N(u)\Lambda(u)$$ (166a)

$$L(u) = \nabla^2 J(u) + \Lambda(u)$$ (166b)

with

$$\Lambda(u)v = \left(\Lambda^1 v^1, \ldots, \Lambda^k v^k\right)$$ (166c)

and

$$\Lambda^j = \sum_{l=1}^{\mu_j} \lambda_l^j g_l^j(u^j)$$ (166d)

for $v = (v^1, \ldots v^k) \in \mathcal{U}$ and j = 1, ..., k. If we now set

$$Q^j = \nabla_{xx}^2 H_j\left(p^{j+1}, x^j, u^j\right)$$ (167a)

$$R^j = \nabla_{xu}^2 H_j\left(p^{j+1}, x^j, u^j\right)$$ (167b)

$$S^j = \nabla_{uu}^2 H_j\left(p^{j+1}, x^j, u^j\right) + \Lambda^j,$$ (167c)

then the quadratic functional $\varphi(u; \cdot)$ in (159) has the following control theoretic representation: for $v = (v^1, ..., v^k) \in \mathcal{V}$,

$$\varphi(u;v) = q_{k+1}\left(y^{k+1}\right) + \sum_{j=1}^{k} q_j\left(y^j, v^j\right) \tag{168a}$$

with

$$q_{k+1}\left(y^{k+1}\right) = \frac{1}{2}\left(y^{k+1}, \nabla^2 c_{k+1}\left(x^{k+1}\right) y^{k+1}\right)_0 \tag{168b}$$

and

$$q_j\left(y^j, v^j\right) = \left\langle r^j, v^j \right\rangle_j \\ + \frac{1}{2}\left[\left(y^j, Q^j y^j\right)_0 + 2\left(y^j, R^j v^j\right)_0 + \left\langle v^j, S^j v^j \right\rangle_j\right], \tag{168c}$$

where $(y^1, ..., y^k)$ is generated by the linear state equations

$$y^1 = 0 \tag{168d}$$

$$y^{j+1} = A^j y^j + B^j v^j, \qquad j = 1, ..., k. \tag{168e}$$

We have earlier noted that w_T is a solution of the Newtonian equation (138k) if and only if w_T is a stationary point of the quadratic function $\varphi(u; \cdot)$ restricted to the subspace $T(u)$. When u is sufficiently near a nonsingular relative minimizer $\bar{u}$ for the control problem (157) and (158), the operator $L_T(u)$ in (138k) is positive-definite and hence $\varphi(u; \cdot)$ has a proper global minimizer (and unique stationary point) w_T in $T(u)$. Under these circumstances, an application of the dynamic programming principle of optimality to (164b) and (168) produces the following well-posed and efficient recursive scheme for computing w_T.

With reference to (164)–(166), we put

$$\Theta^{k+1} = \nabla^2 c_{k+1}\left(x^{k+1}\right) \tag{169a}$$

$$\beta^{k+1} = 0 \in \mathcal{X}_0 \tag{169b}$$

and construct $(\Theta^2, ..., \Theta^{k+1})$ and $(\beta^2, ..., \beta^{k+1})$ with the backward recursions

$$\Theta^j = Q^j + A^{j*} \Theta^{j+1} A^j + \left(R^j + A^{j*} \Theta^{j+1} B^j \right) \Gamma^j \tag{169c}$$

$$\beta^j = \Gamma^{j*} r^j + \left(A^j + B^j \Gamma^j \right)^* \beta^{j+1}, \tag{169d}$$

where the operators $\Gamma^j : \mathscr{X}_0 \to \mathscr{U}_j$ are obtained by solving the linear equations

$$D^j \Gamma^j = -P_{T_j} \left(R^{j*} + B^{j*} \Theta^{j+1} A^j \right), \tag{169e}$$

with

$$D^j = P_{T_j} \left(S^j + B^{j*} \Theta^{j+1} B^j \right) \Big|_{T_j}. \tag{169f}$$

Now solve the related system of linear equations

$$D^j \gamma^j = -P_{T_j} \left(r^j + B^{j*} \beta^{j+1} \right) \tag{169g}$$

for $\gamma^j \in \mathscr{U}_j$ and find $y = (y^1, \ldots, y^k)$ and $w_T = (w_T{}^1, \ldots, w_T{}^k)$ with the forward recursions

$$y_1 = 0 \tag{169h}$$

$$y^{j+1} = A^j y^j + B^j w_T{}^j, \qquad j = 1, \ldots, k, \tag{169i}$$

where

$$w_T{}^j = \Gamma^j y^j + \gamma^j. \tag{169j}$$

When $(u^1, \ldots, u^k)$ is close enough to a nonsingular minimizer for (157) and (158), the operators D^j are positive-definite (and hence one–one onto), and the foregoing construction yields the unique solution w_T of the Newtonian equation (138k). The quantities v_T and v_N in (138) are then readily obtained from

$$v_T = \left(v_T{}^1, \ldots, v_T{}^k \right) \tag{170a}$$

$$v_N = \left(v_N^1, \ldots, v_N^k \right) \tag{170b}$$

with

$$v_T^j = P_{T_j} \left(I + s_N(u) \Lambda^j \right) w_T^j \tag{170c}$$

and

$$v_N^j = -s_N(u) P_{N_j} r^j. \tag{170d}$$

B.   CONTINUOUS-TIME OPTIMAL
      CONTROL PROBLEMS

If the finite sum and recursions in (157) are replaced by

$$J(u) = c_f\left(x\left(t_f \right) \right) + \int_0^{t_f} c(t, x(t), u(t)) \, dt \tag{171a}$$

and

$$x(0) = a \tag{171b}$$

$$\frac{dx(t)}{dt} = f(t, x(t), u(t)), \qquad 0 \le t \le t_f, \tag{171c}$$

the result is a continuous-time objective functional of the Bolza type. We now derive a formal projected Newton scheme for minimizing $J(u)$ over a set Ω of square integrable functions u with range in a given closed convex set prescribed by finitely many inequality constraints, i.e.,

$$\Omega = \mathscr{L}^2([0, t_f], U_0), \tag{172a}$$

where

$$U_0 = \left\{ u(t) \in \mathscr{U}_0 : g_l(u(t)) \le 0, \quad l = 1, \ldots, \mu \right\} \tag{172b}$$

and $\mathscr{U}_0$ is a Hilbert space with inner product $\langle \cdot, \cdot \rangle_0$. In these expressions, $x(\cdot)$ is supposed to be (an absolutely continuous) map from $[0, t_f]$ to another Hilbert space $\{ \mathscr{X}_0, (\cdot, \cdot)_0 \}$, the functions c_f, c, f, and g are assumed to be twice continuously differentiable, and the Hilbert space $\mathscr{L}^2([0, t_f], \mathscr{U}_0)$ is equipped with the "separable" inner product,

$$\langle u, v \rangle = \int_0^{t_f} \langle u(t), v(t) \rangle_0 \, dt \tag{173}$$

and a projection decomposition formula for (172a) analogous to (30). In a formal sense, these conditions admit a large variety of continuous-time optimal control problems with ordinary or partial differential equations of state (cf. Example 4 in Section I).

The development in Sections IV,F and V,A requires an explicit representation for Ω in terms of finitely many inequality constraints, and is therefore not immediately applicable to continuous-time optimal control problems {notice that the functions $u(\cdot)$ in (172a) must satisfy the constraints in (172b) at the infinitely many values of t in $[0, t_f]$}. On the other hand, (171) and (172) may be viewed as a "limit" of specially structured versions of (157) and (158), and this suggests the following heuristic approach to guessing a suitable continuous-time projected Newton method. We first select a mesh

$$\left\{ 0 = t_1 < t_2 < \ldots < t_{k+1} = t_f \right\} \tag{174a}$$

for the interval $[0, t_f]$, and put

$$\Delta t_j = t_{j+1} - t_j. \tag{174b}$$

In place of (171)–(173), we next consider the Riemann–Euler approximation,

$$J(u) = c_f\left(x^{k+1}\right) + \sum_{j=1}^{k} c\left(t_j, x^j, u^j\right) \Delta t_j \tag{175a}$$

$$x^1 = a \tag{175b}$$

$$x^{j+1} = x^j + f\left(t_j, x^j, u^j\right) \Delta t_j, \qquad j = 1, \ldots, k \tag{175c}$$

and the feasible set

$$\Omega = U_0 \times \ldots \times U_0, \qquad k \text{ times} \tag{176a}$$

$$U_0 = \left\{ u^j \in \mathscr{U}_0 : g_l(u^j) \leq 0, \quad l = 1, \ldots, \mu \right\} \tag{176b}$$

in the space

$$\mathscr{U} = \mathscr{U}_0 \oplus \dots \oplus \mathscr{U}_0, \qquad \text{k times} \tag{177a}$$

with separable inner product

$$\langle u, v \rangle = \sum_{j=1}^{k} \langle u^j, v^j \rangle_0 \Delta t_j. \tag{177b}$$

Equations (175) and (176) are clearly a special case of (157) and (158), with $c_{k+1} = c_f$, $c_j(x^j, u^j) = c(t_j, x^j, u^j) \Delta t_j$, $f^j(x^j, u^j) = x^j + f(t_j, x^j, u^j) \Delta t_j$, etc. Moreover, the corresponding Newtonian scaling equations in Section V,A are readily seen as discrete-time first-order approximations to certain continuum equations on $[0, t_f]$. We describe the limiting continuous-time equations below, and briefly comment on related higher-order finite difference implementation schemes and unanswered technical questions.

Given u in the set (172a), solve the initial value problem (171b) and (171c) for x(t) on $[0, t_f]$ and compute the corresponding differentials

$$A(t) = \frac{\partial f}{\partial x}(t, x(t), u(t)) \tag{178a}$$

$$B(t) = \frac{\partial f}{\partial u}(t, x(t), u(t)). \tag{178b}$$

Solve the backward initial value problem

$$p({}^t{}_f) = \nabla c_f\big(x({}^t{}_f)\big) \tag{179a}$$

$$\frac{dp}{dt}(t) = - A(t)^* p(t) - \nabla_x c(t, x(t), u(t)) \tag{179b}$$

for p(t) on $[0, t_f]$. For $t \in [0, t_f]$, $p \in \mathscr{X}_0$, $x \in \mathscr{X}_0$, $u \in \mathscr{U}_0$, let

$$H(t, p, x, u) = (p, f(t, x, u))_0 + c(t, x, u) \tag{180}$$

and compute

$$r(t) = \nabla_u H(t, p(t), x(t), u(t)). \tag{181}$$

Define the following subspaces in $\mathscr{U} = \mathscr{L}^2([0, t_f], \mathscr{U}_0)$:

$$N(u) = \big\{ v \in \mathscr{U} : v(t) \in N_t, \quad t \in [0, t_f] \big\} \tag{182a}$$

$$T(u) = \{ v \in \mathcal{U} : v(t) \in T_t, \quad t \in [0, t_f] \},$$ (182b)

where

$$T_t = N_t^\perp \quad (= \text{orthogonal complement of Nt in } \mathcal{U}_0)$$ (182c)

$$N_t = \text{span} \{ \nabla g_l(u(t)) \}_{l \in \mathcal{J}_t}$$ (182d)

$$\mathcal{J}_t = \{ l : g_l(u(t)) \geq -\theta \| \nabla g_l(u(t)) \|_0 \, e(u) \}$$ (182e)

$$e(u) = \min \{ \epsilon_0, d(u) \}$$ (182f)

$$d^2(u) = \int_0^{t_f} \left\| u(t) - P_{U_0} (u(t) - r(t)) \right\|_0^2 dt$$ (182g)

and ϵ_0 and θ are fixed real numbers independent of u, with $\epsilon_0 > 0$ and $\theta > 1$. At each $t \in [0, t_f]$ solve the linear equations

$$\sum_{l=1}^{\mu} \lambda_l(t) \nabla g_l(u(t)) = -P_{N_t} r(t)$$ (183a)

$$\lambda_l(t) = 0, \quad l \notin \mathcal{J}_t$$ (183b)

For $\lambda(t) = (\lambda_1(t), \dots \lambda_u(t)) \in R^\mu$, and compute the following operators:

$$\Lambda(t) = \sum_{l=1}^{\mu} \lambda_l(t) \nabla^2 g_l(u(t))$$ (184a)

$$Q(t) = \nabla_{xx}^2 H(t, p(t), x(t), u(t))$$ (184b)

$$R(t) = \nabla_{xu}^2 H(t, p(t), x(t), u(t))$$ (184c)

$$S(t) = \nabla_{uu}^2 H(t, p(t), x(t), u(t)) + \Lambda(t).$$ (184d)

Solve the backward initial value problem

$$\Theta\left(t_f\right) = \nabla^2 c_f\left(x\left(t_f\right)\right) \tag{185a}$$

$$\beta(t_f) = 0 \in \mathcal{X}_0 \tag{185b}$$

$$\frac{d\Theta}{dt}(t) = -\left\{ Q(t) + A(t)^*\Theta(t) + \Theta(t)A(t) \right. \tag{185c}$$
$$+ \left[R(t) + \Theta(t)B(t) \right] \Gamma(t) \left. \right\}$$

$$\frac{d\beta}{dt}(t) = -\left\{ A^*(t)\beta(t) + \left[R(t) + \Theta(t)B(t) \right] \gamma(t) \right\} \tag{185d}$$

for $t \in [0, t_f]$, where $\Gamma(t) : \mathcal{X}_0 \to \mathcal{U}_0$ and $\gamma(t) \in \mathcal{U}_0$ are obtained by solving the linear equations

$$D(t)\Gamma(t) = -P_{T_t} \left(R(t)^* + B(t)^* \Theta(t) \right) \tag{185e}$$

and

$$D(t)\gamma(t) = -P_{T_t} \left(r(t) + B^*(t)\beta(t) \right) \tag{185f}$$

with

$$D(t) = P_{T_t} S(t) \Big|_{T_t}. \tag{185g}$$

Now construct $y(t)$ and $w_T(t)$ on $[0, t_f]$ by solving the forward initial value problem

$$y(0) = 0 \tag{186a}$$

$$\frac{dy}{dt}(t) = A(t)y + B(t)w_T(t) \tag{186b}$$

with

$$w_T(r) = \Gamma(t)y(t) + \gamma(t) \tag{186c}$$

for $t \in [0, t_f]$. Finally, choose $s_N(u) > 0$, put

$$v(t) = v_N(t) + v_T(t) \tag{187a}$$

with

$$v_N(t) = -s_N(u)P_{N_t} r(t) \tag{187b}$$

$$v_T(t) = P_{T_t}\left(I + s_N(u)\Lambda(t)\right) w_T(t) \tag{187c}$$

and construct the projected Newton map

$$u \rightarrow \dot{w} = \phi(u) = P_\Omega(u + v), \tag{187d}$$

where

$$\dot{w}(t) - P_{U_0}(u(t) + v(t)) \tag{187e}$$

for $t \in [0, t_f]$.

In practice, the integrals and initial value problems in (178)–(187) must be approximated with quadrature and finite-difference equations on a mesh (174a) for $[0, t_f]$. In the crudest such scheme, integrals are replaced by Riemann sums, differential equations are replaced by first-order Euler difference equations, and the resulting O(k) approximate continuous-time PN algorithm is nothing more than (160)–(170) specialized for (175)–(177) (numerical results for an algorithm of this type are presented in [10, 16]). On the other hand, suitable higher-order quadrature and difference equations yield new and presumably more efficient O(k) approximate continuous-time algorithms different from (160)–(170). We note that for unconstrained continuous-time optimal control problems ($U_0 = \mathcal{U}_0$), the scheme (178)–(187) reduces to a "full step" version of the "second variation" method [31], and is also similar to the Riccati substitution treatment of quasilinearization boundary value problems [32]. Finite-difference implementations of a related pointwise quasi-Newton method for unconstrained continuous-time problems are investigated in [33], and [34] formulates an algorithm that amounts to a specialized projected quasi-Newton method for constrained continuous-time problems with $U_0 = [-1, 1] \subset R^1 = \mathcal{U}_0$. In the latter study, projection into Ω is accomplished implicitly by "clipping," variants of the subspaces N_t and T_t are defined implicitly by a "saturation function," the normal component of ∇J is left unscaled, and the tangential scaling operators are generated by a quasi-Newton recursion of the Davidon type; we note that the scaling subspaces in this scheme are determined "pointwise" by the active (as opposed to almost active) control input constraints, and also that the quasi-Newton computational costs increase like the *square* of the number of "unsaturated" mesh points t_j associated with the interior subarcs of the current control function iterate $u^{(i)}$. Numerical results are presented in [34] for control problems with singular subarcs in their solutions.

While finite-difference implementations of (178)–(187) are formally applicable to a large class of continuous-time optimal control problems, our heuristic derivation completely ignores a number of essential technical points, e.g., the existence and uniqueness of solutions for the various vector and operator-valued initial value problems in (171), (179), (185), and (186); differentiability conditions on $J(u)$ derived from analogous conditions on c_f, c, and f; suitable interpretations of the terms "normal point," "nondegenerate stationary point," and "nonsingular stationary point," for (171) and (172); supernormality conditions on $N(u)$ inferred from similar conditions on the cross sections $N_t(u)$; continuity properties of the maps $\rightarrow (N(u), T(u))$, $u \rightarrow E_T(u)$, $u \rightarrow L_T(u)$, and $u \rightarrow \phi(u)$ implicit in (178)–(187); local stability, active constraint identification, and convergence rate properties of the map $u \rightarrow \phi(u)$ near nonsingular relative minimizers; the relationship between convergence properties of the limiting continuous-time algorithm (178)–(187) and its finite-difference implementations. These questions must be treated on a case-by-case basis, and in any event cannot be resolved here.

ACKNOWLEDGMENT

The author's contributions to the convergence theories in Sections III–V grew out of several investigations sponsored by the National Science Foundation (Grants DMS 8702929, DMS 8503746, and ENG 7803385).

REFERENCES

1.   A. A. GOLDSTEIN, "Convex Programming in Hilbert Space," *Bull. Am. Math. Soc.* 70, 709–710 (1964).
2.   E. S. LEVITIN and B. T. POLYAK, "Constrained Optimization Methods," *USSR Comput. Math. Math. Phys. (Engl. Transl.)* 6, 1–50 (1966).
3.   V. F. DEMYANOV and A. M. RUBINOV, "Approximate Methods in Optimization Problems," Am. Elsevier, New York, 1971.
4.   B. N. PSHENICHNY and YU. M. DANILOV, "Numerical Methods in Extremal Problems," MIR Publishers, Moscow, 1978.
5.   D. Bertsekas, "On the Goldstein–Levitin–Poljak Gradient Projection Method," *IEEE Trans. Autom. Control* AC-21, 174–184 (1976).
6.   G. P. McCORMICK and R. A. TAPIA, "The Gradient Projection Method Under Mild Differentiability Conditions," *SIAM J. Control* 10(1), 93–98 (1972).
7.   J. C. DUNN, "Global and Asymptotic Convergence Rate Estimates for a Class of Projected Gradient Processes," *SIAM J. Contr. Optim.* 19, 368–400 (1980).
8.   J. C. DUNN, "On the Convergence of Projected Gradient Processes to Singular Critical Points," *J. Optim. Theor. Appl.* 55, 2, 203–215 (1987).
9.   G. C. HUGHES and J. C. DUNN, "Newton–Goldstein Convergence Rates for Convex Constrained Minimization Problems with Singular Solutions," *Appl. Math. Opt.* 12, 203–230 (1984).
10.   M. GAWANDE, "Projected Gradient and Projected Newton Algorithms for Specially Structured Constrained Minimization Problems," Ph.D. Dissertation, North Carolina State University (1986).

11. M. GAWANDE and J. C. DUNN, "Variable Metric Gradient Projection Processes in Conves Feasible Sets Defined by Nonlinear Inequalities," *Appl. Math. Opt.*, 17, 103–119 (1988).

12. P. H. CALAMAI and J. J. MORÉ, "Projected Gradient Methods for Linearly Constrained Problems," Tech. Memo. MCM-73, Argonne National Laboratory, May 1986.

13. J. V. BURKE and J. J. MORÉ, "On the Identification of Active Constraints," Tech. Memo. MCM-82, Argonne National Laboratory, September 1986.

14. D. BERTSEKAS, "Projected Newton Methods for Optimization Problems With Simple Constraints," *SIAM J. Control. Optim.* 20(2), 221–246 (1982).

15. E. M. GAFNI and D. BERTSEKAS, "Two-Metric Projection Methods for Constrained Optimization," *SIAM J. Control Optim.* 22(6), 936–964 (1984).

16. M. GAWANDE and J. C. DUNN, "A Projected Newton Method in a Cartesian Product of Balls," *J. Optim. Theor. Appl.* (in press).

17. J. C. DUNN, "A Projected Newton Method for Minimization Problems with Nonlinear Inequality Constraints," *Numer.. Math.* (in press).

18. D. G. LUENBERGER, "Optimization by Vector Space Methods," Wiley, New York, 1969.

19. P. H. CALAMAI and J. J. MORÉ, "Quasi-Newton Updates with Bounds (to be published).

20. L. ARMIJO, "Minimization of Functionals Having Continuous Partial Derivatives," *Pac. J. Math.* 16, 1–3 (1966).

21. J. M. ORTEGA and W. C. RHEINBOLDT, "Iterative Solution of Nonlinear Equations in Several Variables," Academic Press, New York, 1970.

22. A. A. GOLDSTEIN, "On Steepest Descent," *SIAM J. Control* 3, 147–151 (1965).

23. A. A. GOLDSTEIN, "On Newton's Method," *Numer. Math.* 7, 391–393 (1965).

24. J. E. DENNIS, JR. and R. B. SCHNABEL, "Numerical Methods for Unconstrained Optimization and Nonlinear Equations," Prentice-Hall, Englewood Cliffs, New Jersey, 1983.

25. W. A. GRUVER and E. SACHS, "Algorithmic Methods in Optimal Control," Pitman Advanced Publishing Program, Boston, Massachusetts, 1980.

26. M. HESTENES, "Calculus of Variations and Optimal Control Theory," Robert E. Krieger Publ., Huntington, New York, 1980.

27. E. POLAK, "Computational Methods in Optimization," Academic Press, New York, 1971.

28. J. C. DUNN, "Efficient Dynamic Programming Implementation of Newton's Method for Unconstrained Optimal Control Problems," *J. Optim. Theor. Appl.* (in press).

29. D. H. JACOBSON and D. Q. MAYNE, "Differential Dynamic Programming," Am. Elsevier, New York, 1970.

30. K. OHNO, "Differential Dynamic Programming and Separable Programs," *J. Optim. Theor. Appl.* 24(4), 617–637 (1978).

31. C. W. MERRIAM, III, "An Algorithm for the Iterative Solution of a Class of Two-Point Boundary Value Problems," *SIAM J. Control Optim., Ser A* 2(1), 1–10 (1964).

32. S. K. MITTER, "Successive Approximation Methods for the Solution of Optimal Control Problems," *Automatica* 3, 135–149 (1966).

33. C. T. Kelley and E. W. SACHS, "Quasi-Newton Methods and Unconstrained Optimal Control Problems ," *SIAM J. Control. Optim.* 25, 1503–1517 (1987).

34. E. R. EDGE and W. F. POWERS, "Function Space Quasi-Newton Algorithms for Optimal Control Problems with Bounded Controls and Singular Arcs," *J. Optim. Theor. Appl.* 20(4), 455–479 (1976).

OPTIMAL CONTROL, ESTIMATION, AND COMPENSATION OF LINEAR DISCRETE-TIME SYSTEMS WITH STOCHASTIC PARAMETERS

W. L. DE KONING

Department of Applied Mathematics
Delft University of Technology
2628 BL Delft, The Netherlands

I. INTRODUCTION

There are two main reasons why discrete-time systems with stochastic parameters are important. First, these systems arise naturally in the field of digital control systems where some of the parameters may be stochastic, such as the sampling period [1], the controller parameters due to the finite word length of the computer [2], or the parameters of the plant [3]. In all three cases it is possible to convert such a digital control system to an equivalent discrete-time system with stochastic parameters. Inherent discrete-time systems, such as economic systems, may also have stochastic parameters.

Second, the parameters of an equivalent or inherent discrete-time system may be *assumed* to be stochastic for the purpose of a robust control system design. It is well known that the standard LQG design does not lead in general to a robust control system with respect to parameter deviations [4]. Stochastic parameters may be exploited to *automatically* desensitize the design to actual parameter variations [5]. The uncertainties regarding the parameters are represented in a stochastic manner which fits naturally in the LQ design context.

The robustness defect of the standard LQG design may have been foreseen by the fact that the first moments of the relevant variables play the main role in spite of the quadratic optimality of the designed control system. It appears that the second moments of the relevant variables play a definitive role in the control system design when the parameters are assumed to be stochastic [6–8]. According to this generalization of the "first moments approach" to the "second moments approach," the usual notions of stabilizability and detectability have to be generalized to the notions of so-called mean-square stabilizability and mean-square detectability [6, 7]. Another effect of stochastic parameters is that the separation principle breaks down [9]. Control and estimation has to be done simultaneously in the case of parameter uncertainties.

In this article the problems of optimal control, estimation, and compensation will be considered in the context of systems with stochastic parameters from a second moments point of view. Descriptive algorithms will be given to calculate the different results.

II. STABILITY, STABILIZATION, AND DETECTABILITY

Consider the open loop system

$$x_{i+1} = \Phi_i x_i + \Gamma_i u_i, \qquad i = 0, 1, \ldots, \tag{1}$$

where $x_i \in R^n$ is the state, $u_i \in R^m$ the control, and Φ_i, Γ_i are real matrices of appropriate dimensions. The processes $\{\Phi_i\}$ and $\{\Gamma_i\}$ are sequences of independent random matrices with constant statistics and the initial value x_0 is deterministic. System (1) is characterized by (Φ_i, Γ_i). Suppose

$$u_i = -Lx_i, \tag{2}$$

where L is a real matrix of appropriate dimensions. Then from (1) we have the closed loop system

$$x_{i+1} = (\Phi_i - \Gamma_i L)x_i. \tag{3}$$

System (3) is characterized by $(\Phi_i - \Gamma_i L)$. Let ms denote mean square and let an overbar denote expectation.

Definition 1. $(\Phi_i - \Gamma_i L)$ is called ms-stable if $\overline{\left\| x_i \right\|^2} \to 0$ as $i \to \infty$ for all x_0.

Let S^n denote the linear space of real symmetric $n \times n$ matrices and define the transformation $A_L : S^n \to S^n$ by

$$A_L X = \overline{(\Phi - \Gamma L)^T X (\Phi - \Gamma L)}, \qquad X \in S^n, \tag{4}$$

where the index i is deleted without ambiguity because $A_L X$ is independent of i. Let ρ denote the spectral radius.

Theorem 1. $(\Phi_i - \Gamma_i L)$ is ms-stable if and only if $\rho(A_L) < 1$.

Proof. See [6].

Let $\otimes$ denote Kronecker product [10].

Algorithm 1. The ms-stability of $(\Phi_i - \Gamma_i L)$ may be checked by cal-culation of $\rho(A_L)$. It is easy to show that the eigenvalues of A_L and of $\overline{(\Phi - \Gamma L) \otimes (\Phi - \Gamma L)}$ are the same. Hence $\rho(A_L) = \rho(\overline{(\Phi - \Gamma L) \otimes (\Phi - \Gamma L)})$, which is easy to calculate with standard software.

Definition 2. $(\Phi_i - \Gamma_i)$ is called ms-stabilizable if there exists an L such that $(\Phi_i - \Gamma_i L)$ is ms-stable.

Define the recursive equation

$$A_{i+1} = \overline{\Phi^T A_i \Phi} - \overline{\Phi^T A_i \Gamma} \; (\overline{\Gamma^T A_i \Gamma})^+ \overline{\Gamma^T A_i \Phi}, , \qquad A_0 = I, \tag{5}$$

where the plus superscript denotes the Moore–Penrose pseudoinverse [11]. Denote the spectral norm by $\|\cdot\|$.

Theorem 2. (Φ_i, Γ_i) is ms-stabilizable if and only if

$$\bar{\rho} = \lim_{i \to \infty} \left\| A_i \right\|^{1/i} < 1.$$

Proof. See [6].

Algorithm 2. The ms-stabilizability of (Φ_i, Γ_i) may be checked by calculation of $\bar{\rho}$. Therefore we need to iterate (5) until convergence is reached. In (5) there arise terms like $\overline{\Phi^T X \Gamma}$ for some matrix X which may equally be written as $st^{-1}\left[\overline{(\Gamma \otimes \Phi)}^T st(X)\right]$, where st denotes the stack operator, and using Kronecker product rules [10]. So $\overline{\Gamma \otimes \Phi}$ needs only to be calculated once, while the st and st^{-1} operations involve only the renumbering of computer memory locations. Furthermore, note that $A_i \in S^n$, thus $\|A_i\| = \rho(A_i)$. Then calculation of the norm is the same as calculation of the spectral radius, which is easy. Finally, it is remarked that often $\|A_{i+1}\| / \|A_i\|$ converges faster to $\bar{\rho}$ than $\|A_i\|^{1/i}$.

In view of detectability consider the system

$$x_{i+1} = \Phi_i x_i, \qquad i = 0, 1, \ldots, \tag{6a}$$

$$y_i = C_i x_i, \qquad i = 0, 1, \ldots, \tag{6b}$$

where $x_i \in R^n$ is the state, $y_i \in R^l$ the observation, and Φ_i, C_i are real matrices of appropriate dimensions. The processes $\{\Phi_i\}$ and $\{C_i\}$ are sequences of independent random matrices with constant statistics. The initial value is deterministic. System (6) is characterized by the pair (Φ_i, C_i).

Definition 3. (Φ_i, C_i) is called ms-detectable if $\overline{\|y_i\|^2} = 0$, $i = 0, 1, \ldots$, implies that $\overline{\|x_i\|^2} \to 0$ as $i \to \infty$.

Denote the $m \times n$ zero matrix by Θ and define $A_L^i X$ by $A_L(A_L^{i-1} X)$. Define the matrix $U \in S^n$ by

$$U = \sum_{i=0}^{p-1} A_{\Theta}^i \overline{C^T C}, \qquad p = \frac{1}{2}n(n+1). \tag{7}$$

Denote the null space of U by N(U).

Theorem 3. (Φ_i, C_i) is ms-detectable if and only if $x_0 \in N(U)$ implies that

$$x_0^T A_{\Theta}^i Ix_0 \to 0 \text{ as } i \to \infty.$$

Proof. See [7].

Algorithm 3. The ms-detectability of (Φ_i, C_i) may be checked as follows. Because $U \geq 0$ it has an orthonormal set of eigenvectors and non-negative eigenvalues. Suppose $e_1, ..., e_k$ are the orthonormal eigenvectors corresponding to the zero eigenvalues of U. Then $N(U) = \text{span}\{e_1, ..., e_k\}$. Choose $x_0 = e_1 + ... + e_k$. If $x_0^T A_{\Theta}^i Ix_0 \to 0$ as $i \to \infty$, then (Φ_i, C_i) is ms-detectable, otherwise it is not. Furthermore, note that $A_{\Theta}^i X = \text{st}^{-1}[\overline{(\Phi \otimes \Phi)}^{Ti} \text{st}(X)]$.

It can be shown [6, 7] that (Φ_i) is ms-stable implies that (Φ_i, Γ_i) is ms-stabilizable and (Φ_i, C_i) is ms-detectable. Furthermore, if Φ_i, Γ_i, and C_i are deterministic and constant, then ms-stability, ms-stabilizability, and ms-detectability are identical to, respectively, stability, stabilizability, and detectability in the usual sense.

III. OPTIMAL CONTROL

Consider the system

$$x_{i+1} = \Phi_i x_i + \Gamma_i u_i + v_i, \qquad i = 0, 1, ..., \tag{8}$$

where $x_i \in R^n$ is the state, $u_i \in R^m$ the control, $v_i \in R^n$ the system noise, and Φ_i, Γ_i are real matrices of appropriate dimensions. The processes $\{\Phi_i\}, \{\Gamma_i\}$ are sequences of independent random matrices and $\{v_i\}$ a sequence of independent stochastic vectors with constant statistics. The initial condition x_0 is independent of $\{\Phi_i, \Gamma_i, v_i\}$. Moreover, Φ_i and Γ_i are independent of v_j, $i \neq j$, and uncorrelated with v_i. The process $\{v_i\}$ is zero-mean with covariance V.

Furthermore, consider the criterion

$$\sigma_\infty(U_\infty) = \lim_{N \to \infty} \frac{1}{N} E\left(\sum_{i=0}^{N-1}\left(x_i^T Q x_i + 2x_i^T M u_i + u_i^T R u_i\right)\right),$$

where Q and R are real symmetric matrices of appropriate dimensions with $Q - MR^{-1}M^T \geq 0$ and $R > 0$, and u_i denotes the control sequence $\{u_0, ..., u_i\}$.

The control sequence U_∞ is called admissible if u_i is a function of x_i for $i = 0, 1, ...$ and $\overline{\|x_i\|^2}$ converges as $i \to \infty$ to the same constant value for all x_0.

Definition 4. The problem of finding the admissible control sequence $U_\infty^* = \{u_0^*, u_1^*, ...\}$ that minimizes $\sigma_\infty(U_\infty)$ and of finding the minimal value $\sigma_\infty^* = \sigma_\infty(U_\infty^*)$ is called the optimal control problem.

Define the recursive equation

$$S_{i+1} = \overline{\Phi^T S_i \Phi} - \overline{\left(\Phi^T S_i \Gamma + M\right)}\overline{\left(\Gamma^T S_i \Gamma + R\right)}^{-1} \times \overline{\left(\Gamma^T S_i \Phi + M^T\right)} + Q, \qquad S_0 = I. \tag{9}$$

Define also

$$\Phi_i^c = \Phi_i - \Gamma_i R^{-1} M^T, \tag{10a}$$

$$Q^c = Q - MR^{-1} M^T. \tag{10b}$$

Now we may formulate the solution of the optimal control problem.

Theorem 4. If (Φ_i^c, Γ_i) is ms-stabilizable and $(\Phi_i^c, Q^{c\ 1/2})$ is ms-detectable, then $S = \lim_{i \to \infty} S_i$ exists, and

$$U_\infty^* = \{-Lx_0, -Lx_1, ...\}, \tag{11a}$$

$$L = \overline{\left(\Gamma^T S \Gamma + R\right)}^{-1} \overline{\left(\Gamma^T S \Phi + M^T\right)}, \tag{11b}$$

and

$$\sigma_\infty^* = tr(VS). \tag{12}$$

Proof. See [1].

Algorithm 4. The stabilizability and detectability condition in Theorem 4 may easily be checked with Algorithms 2 and 3. Calculation of S, by iterating (9), and then L is easy by recognizing the terms like $(\overline{\Phi^T X\Gamma})$ and using the remarks in Algorithm 1.

IV. OPTIMAL ESTIMATION

Consider the system

$$x_{i+1} = \Phi_i x_i + v_i, \qquad i = 0, 1, \ldots, \tag{13}$$

$$y_i = C_i x_i + w_i, \qquad i = 0, 1, \ldots, \tag{14}$$

where $x_i \in R^n$ is the state, $y_i \in R^l$ the observation, $v_i \in R^n$ the system noise, $w_i \in R^l$ the observation noise, and Φ_i, C_i are real matrices of appropriate dimensions. The processes $\{\Phi_i\}$, $\{C_i\}$ are sequences of independent random matrices, and $\{v_i\}$, $\{w_i\}$ are sequences of independent stochastic vectors with constant statistics. The initial condition x_0 is independence of $\{\Phi_i, C_i, v_i, w_i\}$. Moreover, Φ_i and C_i are independent of v_j, w_j, $i \neq j$, and uncorrelated with v_i, w_i. The processes $\{v_i\}$ and $\{w_i\}$ are zero-mean with covariances V and W, with $V \geq 0$ and $W > 0$, and cross covariance D.

Let x_i^e denote an arbitrary estimator of x_i and Y_i the observation sequence $\{y_0, \ldots, y_i\}$. The estimator x_i^e is called admissible if it is an affine function of the observation sequence Y_{i-1}. The estimation error is $x_i - x_i^e$.

Definition 5. The problem of finding the admissible estimator $\hat{x}_i$ that minimizes the estimation error variance as $i \to \infty$ and of finding the covariance of $x_i - \hat{x}_i$ as $i \to \infty$ is called the optimal estimation problem.

Define the recursive equation

$$X_{i+1} = \overline{\Phi X_i \Phi^T} + V, \qquad X_0 = \Theta \tag{15}$$

Suppose $X = \lim_{i \to \infty} X_i$ exists. Define the decomposition of Φ_i and C_i

$$\Phi_i = \overline{\Phi} + \tilde{\Phi}_i, \tag{16a}$$

$$C_i = \overline{C} + \tilde{C}_i, \tag{16b}$$

and the matrices

$$V_s = V + \overline{\tilde{\Phi} X \tilde{\Phi}^T}, \tag{17a}$$

$$W_s = W + \overline{\tilde{C} X \tilde{C}^T}, \tag{17b}$$

$$D_s = D + \overline{\Phi X \bar{C}^T}.$$
(17c)

Furthermore, define the recursive equation

$$P_{i+1} = \bar{\Phi} P_i \bar{\Phi}^T - \left(\bar{\Phi} P_i \bar{C}^T + D_s\right)\left(\bar{C} P_i \bar{C}^T + W_s\right)^{-1}$$
$$\times \left(\bar{C} P_i \bar{\Phi}^T + D_s^T\right) + V_s, \quad P_0 = \Theta$$
(18)

Now we may formulate the solution of the optimal estimation problem.

Theorem 5. If (Φ_i) is ms-stable, then $X = \lim_{i\to\infty} X_i$ exists, $P = \lim_{i\to\infty} P_i$ exists,

$$\hat{x}_{i+1} = \bar{\Phi}\hat{x}_i + K\left(y_i - \bar{C}\hat{x}_i\right), \quad \hat{x}_0 = 0,$$
(19a)

$$K = \left(\bar{\Phi} P \bar{C}^T + D_s\right)\left(\bar{C} P \bar{C}^T + W_s\right)^{-1},$$
(19b)

P is the covariance of $x_i - \hat{x}_i$ as $i \to \infty$, and $(\overline{\Phi} - K\overline{C})$ is stable; i.e., estimator (19) is stable.

Proof. See [8].

Algorithm 5. The stability condition in Theorem 5 may easily be checked with Algorithm 2. The calculation of X by iterating (15), then V_s, W_s, and D_s, and then P, by iterating (19) and K is straightforward using the remarks in Algorithm 1. X may also be calculated directly as follows. If (Φ_i) is ms-stable, then $X \geq 0$ and X is the unique solution of the equation

$$X = \overline{\Phi X \Phi^T} + V.$$
(20)

Applying the stack operator, we have

$$st(X) = \overline{(\Phi \otimes \Phi)}\, st(X) + st(V).$$
(21)

Collecting terms with X and applying st^{-1} gives

$$X = st^{-1}\left[(I - \overline{(\Phi \otimes \Phi)})^{-1}\, st(V)\right]$$
(22)

V. OPTIMAL COMPENSATION

Consider the system

$$x_{i+1} = \Phi_i x_i + \Gamma_i u_i + v_i \qquad i = 0, 1, \ldots, \tag{23a}$$

$$y_i = C_i x_i + w_i, \qquad i = 0, 1, \ldots, \tag{23b}$$

where $x_i \in R^n$ is the state, $u_i \in R^m$ the control, $y_i \in R^l$ the observation, $v_i \in R^n$ the system noise, $w_i \in R^l$ the observation noise, and Φ_i, Γ_i, C_i are real matrices of appropriate dimensions. The processes $\{\Phi_i\}$, $\{\Gamma_i\}$, $\{C_i\}$ are sequences of independent random matrices, and $\{v_i\}$, $\{w_i\}$ are sequences of independent stochastic vectors with constant statistics. The initial condition x_0 is independent of $\{\Phi_i, \Gamma_i, C_i, v_i, w_i\}$. Moreover, $\Phi_i, \Gamma_i,$ and C_i are independent of v_j, w_j, $i \neq j$, and uncorrelated with v_i, w_i. The processes $\{v_i\}$ and $\{w_i\}$ are zero-mean with covariances V and W, with $V \geq 0$ and $W > 0$, and cross covariance D.

Furthermore, consider the criterion

$$\sigma_\infty(U_\infty) = \lim_{N \to \infty} \frac{1}{N} E\left(\sum_{i=0}^{N-1} \left(x_i^T Q x_i + 2 x_i^T M u_i + u_i^T R u_i \right) \right), \tag{24}$$

where Q and R are real symmetric matrices of appropriate dimensions with $Q - MR^{-1}M^T \geq 0$ and $R > 0$.

The control sequence U_∞ is called admissible if u_i is a function of Y_{i-1} for $i = 0, 1, \ldots$ and $\overline{\|x_i\|^2}$ and $\overline{\|u_i\|^2}$ converge as $i \to \infty$ to the same constant value for all x_0. Now because the system matrices are random, trying to find an admissible control sequence that minimizes $\sigma_\infty(U_\infty)$ does not lead to separate control and estimation problems; i.e., the separation principle does not hold [9]. Therefore, we choose as controller the linear dynamic compensator

$$\hat{x}_{i+1} = \hat{\Phi} \hat{x}_i + \hat{\Gamma} y_i, \qquad i = 0, 1, \ldots, \tag{25a}$$

$$u_i = \hat{C} \hat{x}_i, \qquad i = 0, 1, \ldots, \tag{25b}$$

where $\hat{x}_i \in R^n$ is the compensator state and $\hat{\Phi}, \hat{\Gamma}, \hat{C}$, are real matrices of appropriate dimensions. Compensator (25) is characterized by $(\hat{\Phi}, \hat{\Gamma}, \hat{C})$. The compensator matrices are free to choose instead of U_∞, so

$$\sigma_\infty(\hat{\Phi}, \hat{\Gamma}, \hat{C}) = \lim_{N \to \infty} \frac{1}{N} E\left(\sum_{i=0}^{N-1} \left(x_i^T Q x_i + 2 x_i^T M u_i + u_i^T R u_i \right) \right). \tag{26}$$

The closed loop system may be described by

$$
\begin{bmatrix} x_{i+1} \\ \hat{x}_{i+1} \end{bmatrix} = \begin{bmatrix} \Phi_i & \Gamma_i\hat{C} \\ \hat{\Gamma}C_i & \hat{\Phi} \end{bmatrix} \begin{bmatrix} x_i \\ \hat{x}_i \end{bmatrix} + \begin{bmatrix} v_i \\ \hat{\Gamma}w_i \end{bmatrix}
\tag{27}
$$

Define

$$
x_i' = \begin{bmatrix} x_i \\ \hat{x}_i \end{bmatrix}, \quad v_i' = \begin{bmatrix} v_i \\ \hat{\Gamma}w_i \end{bmatrix},
$$

$$
\Phi_i' = \begin{bmatrix} \Phi_i & \Gamma_i\hat{C} \\ \hat{\Gamma}C_i & \hat{\Phi} \end{bmatrix}, \quad V' = \begin{bmatrix} V & D\hat{\Gamma}^T \\ \hat{\Gamma}D^T & \hat{\Gamma}W\hat{\Gamma}^T \end{bmatrix}
$$

then (27) becomes

$$
v_{i+1}' = \Phi_i'x_i' + v_i', \qquad i = 0,1,\ldots,
\tag{28}
$$

where $\{\Phi_i'\}$ is a sequence of independent random matrices and $\{v_i'\}$ a sequence of independent stochastic vectors. The initial condition x_0' is independent of $\{\Phi_i', v_i'\}$. Moreover, Φ_i' is independent of v_j', $i \neq j$, and uncorrelated with v_i'. The process $\{v_i'\}$ is zero-mean with covariance V'.

The compensator $(\hat{\Phi}, \hat{\Gamma}, \hat{C})$ is called admissible if (Φ_i') is ms-stable. Note that ms-stability of (Φ_i') implies that $\overline{\|x_i\|^2}$ converges as $i \to \infty$ to the same constant value for all x_0. Note also that u_i is an affine function of Y_{i-1} for $i = 0, 1, \ldots$.

Definition 6. The problem of finding the admissible compensator $(\hat{\Phi}*, \hat{\Gamma}*, \hat{C}*)$, that minimizes $\sigma_\infty(\hat{\Phi}, \hat{\Gamma}, \hat{C})$ and of finding the minimal value $\sigma_\infty* = \sigma_\infty(\hat{\Phi}*, \hat{\Gamma}*, \hat{C}*)$ is called the optimal compensation problem.

Define the matrix

$$
Q' = \begin{pmatrix} Q & M\hat{C} \\ \hat{C}^T M^T & \hat{C}^T R\hat{C} \end{pmatrix},
$$

then using (25b), criterion (26) may be written as

$$\sigma_\infty\left(\hat{\Phi},\hat{\Gamma},\hat{C}\right) = \lim_{N\to\infty} \frac{1}{N} E\left(\sum_{i=0}^{N-1} x_i^T Q' x_i'\right) \tag{29}$$

Let P_i' denote $\overline{x_i' x_i^T}$, then from (28)

$$P_{i+1}' = \overline{\Phi' P_i' \Phi'^T} + V'. \tag{30}$$

Now (28) may be written as

$$\sigma_\infty\left(\hat{\Phi},\hat{\Gamma},\hat{C}\right) = \lim_{N\to\infty} \frac{1}{N} E\left(\sum_{i=0}^{N-1} \operatorname{tr}\left(Q' P_i'\right)\right) \tag{31}$$

Suppose $(\hat{\Phi}, \hat{\Gamma}, \hat{C})$ is admissible, i.e., (Φ_i') is ms-stable, then [8] $P' = \lim_{i\to\infty} P_i'$ exists, $P' \geq 0$, and P' is the unique solution of the equation

$$P' = \overline{\Phi' P' \Phi'^T} + V', \qquad P' \in S^n. \tag{32}$$

Furthermore (31) may be written as

$$\sigma_\infty\left(\hat{\Phi},\hat{\Gamma},\hat{C}\right) = \operatorname{tr}\left(Q' P'\right). \tag{33}$$

It follows that the optimal compensation problem is equivalent to the problem of finding the admissible compensator $(\hat{\Phi}^*, \hat{\Gamma}^*, \hat{C}^*)$ that minimizes (33) subject to (32).

Define the set of admissible compensators C_{adm} by

$$C_{adm} = \left\{\left(\hat{\Phi},\hat{\Gamma},\hat{C}\right) \mid (\Phi_i') \text{ is ms} - \text{stable}\right\}.$$

Since the eigenvalues of $\overline{\Phi' \otimes \Phi'}$ depend continuously on $(\hat{\Phi}, \hat{\Gamma}, \hat{C})$, it follows that C_{adm} is an open set. Define the Hamiltonian H by

$$H\left(\hat{\Phi},\hat{\Gamma},\hat{C},P',S'\right) = \operatorname{tr}\left[Q'P' + \left(\overline{\Phi'X'\Phi'^T} + V' - P'\right)S'\right], \tag{34}$$

where $S' \geq 0$ is the Lagrange multiplier. Then, because C_{adm} is an open set, the necessary optimality conditions are

$$\frac{\partial H}{\partial \hat{\Phi}} = \frac{\partial}{\partial \hat{\Phi}} \operatorname{tr}\left(\Phi' P' \Phi'^T S'\right) = 0, \tag{35a}$$

$$\frac{\partial H}{\partial \hat{\Gamma}} = \frac{\partial}{\partial \hat{\Gamma}} \; \mathrm{tr}\overline{\left(\Phi'P'\Phi^T S' + V'S'\right)} = 0, \tag{35b}$$

$$\frac{\partial H}{\partial \hat{C}} = \frac{\partial}{\partial \hat{C}} \; \mathrm{tr}\overline{\left(Q'P' + \Phi P'\Phi^{'T} S'\right)} = 0, \tag{35c}$$

$$\frac{\partial H}{\partial P'} = Q' + = \overline{{}^\iota\Phi^{'T}S'\Phi'} - S' = 0, \tag{35d}$$

$$\frac{\partial H}{\partial S'} = \overline{\Phi^{'T}P'\Phi^T} + V' - P' = 0. \tag{35e}$$

Algorithm 6. There are essentially two ways to solve numerically the optimal compensation problem. First, we may minimize (33) subject to (32). This approach has recently been surveyed in [12]. Only the deterministic parameter case is treated, but the discussed methods are easy to adopt to the stochastic parameter case. Using the remarks in Algorithm 1, calculation of the equations is easy. However, this approach will give us no further theoretical insight. Second, we may solve the set of linear equations (35). Partitioning of P' and S' as

$$P' = \begin{pmatrix} P_1 & P_{12} \\ P_{12}^T & P_2 \end{pmatrix}, \qquad S' = \begin{pmatrix} S_1 & S_{12} \\ S_{12}^T & S_2 \end{pmatrix},$$

according to the partitioning of Φ', and taking the partial derivatives in (35ac) leads to 9 linear equations in $\hat{\Phi}, \hat{\Gamma}, \hat{C}, P_1, P_2, P_{12}, S_1, S_2,$. and S_{12}. This set of equations is hard to solve in general. An interesting new method, however, has been introduced in [5]. The authors manage in the continuous-time case to convert the 9 equations into 3 equations explicit in $\hat{\Phi}, \hat{\Gamma}, \hat{C}$, and 2 modified Lyapunov equations and 2 modified Riccati equations that are coupled but independent of $\hat{\Phi}, \hat{\Gamma}, \hat{C}$. The number and the sort of equations are in a numerically tractable form. Furthermore, they give further theoretical insight.

VI.   CONCLUSIONS

In this article the problem of optimal control, estimation, and compensation has been considered in the case of linear discrete-time systems with stochastic parameters and quadratic criteria. Descriptive algorithms have been given for the calculation of the different results.

Representation of parameter uncertainties by stochastic parameters leads automatically to control systems that are inherently robust with respect to parameter variations. We hope this paper provides the basic insights to help develop the idea of robust control system design with the tool of stochastic parameters further.

REFERENCES

1. W. L. DE KONING, "Stationary Optimal Control of Stochastically Sampled Continuous-Time Systems," *Automatica* **24**, 77–79 (1988).
2. A. J. M. VAN WINGERDEN and W. L. DE KONING, "The Influence of Finite Word Length on Digital Optimal Control," IEEE Trans. Autom. Control **AC-29**, 385–391 (1984).
3. A. R. TIEDEMANN and W. L. DE KONING, "The Equivalent Discrete-Time Optimal Control Problem for Continuous-Time Systems with Stochastic Parameters," Int. J. Control **40**, 449–466 (1984).
4. J. C. DOYLE, "Guaranteed Margins for LQG Regulators," IEEE Trans. Autom. Control **AC-23**, 756–757 (1978).
5. D. S. BERNSTEIN and D. C. HYLAND, "Optimal Projection/ Maximum Entropy: Stochastic Modelling and Reduced-Order Design Methods," Proc. IFAC Workshop Model Error Concepts and Compensation, Boston, 1985.
6. W. L. DE KONING, "Infinite Horizon Optimal Control of Linear Discrete-Time Systems with Stochastic Parameters," Automatica **18**, 443–453 (1982).
7. W. L. DE KONING, "Detectability of Linear Discrete-Time Systems with Stochastic Parameters," Int. J. Control **38**, 1035–1046 (1983).
8. W. L. DE KONING, "Optimal Estimation of Linear Discrete-Time Systems with Stochastic Parameters," Automatica **20**, 113–115 (1984).
9. G. P. M. DE GROOT and W. L. DE KONING, "On Variance Neutrality of Systems Within General Random Parameters," IEEE Trans. Autom. Control **AC-28**, 101–103 (1983).
10. R. BELLMAN, "Introduction to Matrix Analysis," McGraw-Hill, New York, 1970.
11. S. BARNETT, "Matrices in Control Theory," Van Nostrand-Reinhold, London, 1971.
12. P. M. MÄKILÄ and H. T. TOIVONEN, "Computational Methods for Parametric LQ Problems – A Survey," IEEE Trans. Autom. Control **AC-32**, 658–671 (1987).

AN ALGORITHM FOR THE
APPROXIMATION OF
MULTIVARIABLE LINEAR SYSTEMS

YUJIRO INOUYE

Department of Control Engineering
Faculty of Engineering Science
Osaka University, Toyonaka
Osaka 560, Japan

I.   INTRODUCTION

The approximation of linear systems or model reduction arises in many important applications for simplifying system modeling and/or controller design. There are several cases, depending on what kinds of data are given for characterizing an original system: for example, the usual case for a deterministic system is that for which its data are either the state-space realization (A, B, C, D) or the impulse response sequence $\{H_k\}_0^\infty$. For a stochastic system, it is the autocorrelation sequence (or the output covariance sequence). Both the accuracy of the system modeling and its approximation scheme depend on a choice of the characterization of an original system.

A myriad of approximation techniques have been presented in the past two decades [1–32]. Most of them have been based on analysis of the system modes [1–3], on optimization of an error criterion [4–8], on continued fraction expansions [9–11], or on matching a finite portion of the impulse response sequence (or the Markov parameters) [12–14]. The approximation based on optimization of an error criterion generally leads to a set of nonlinear equations to be solved [4–8]. This nonlinearity of equations is a severe drawback of the approximation method. It is well known that the approximation based on continued fraction expansions, or on matching a finite portion of the impulse response sequence, is a special case of the Padé approximation. The Padé approximation method can in many cases lead to a more accurate approximation method than the modal analysis method but has a very serious disadvantage. It is possible for a Padé approximant to be unstable even if the original system is stable.

In order to overcome this disadvantage, several techniques have been proposed, for example, by Shamash [15–17], Shief and Wei [18], Hutton and Fried-

209

lant [19], and Ledwich and Moore [20]. They are restricted to the single-input–single-output (SISO) case, except in [17, 18].

Recently, two novel methods for model reduction have been proposed, which yield stable approximants for a stable system. One is presented by Moore [21], which is based on principal component analysis. It has been further developed by Pernebo and Silverman [22]. The other is proposed by Kung [23] and subsequently by Glover [24]. The former involves the computation of a singular value decomposition, while the latter involves that of solving a generalized eigenvalue problem. These computations are heavy tasks when the original system is of higher order and has multiple inputs and multiple outputs. Further, the methods employ finite data of the impulse response sequence. In order to produce reliable approximants, we need to acquire a data sequence long enough so as to accurately characterize the original system. They appear, however, to be very promising.

When the impulse response in the later (or tail) part has not died away significantly, a data sequence of the impulse response should be taken to be very long. Characterizing a system by finite data of the impulse response involves a fundamental defect: there is no information on the tail part of the impulse response sequence. It can be seen that the use of a finite portion of the autocorrelation sequence (or the output covariance sequence) in conjunction with that of the impulse response sequence can correct this defect. Along with this idea, Mullis and Roberts [25] proposed a novel approach, which yields stable approximants for a stable system, in connection with an approximation of digital filters. This approach was subsequently extended to the multi-input–multi-output (MIMO) case by Inouye [26]. More recently, this approach has been studied by Skelton et al. [27–29]. Several other reduction methods have been proposed by Desai et al. [30, 31] and Jonckheere and Helton [32] using only the autocorrelation sequence of a system.

In this article we shall consider the construction of approximants of a linear discrete-time MIMO system, using two sets of finite data of the impulse response and the autocorrelation sequences, along with the work in [26]. We shall show a fast recursive algorithm to construct a stable approximant of a stable MIMO system, which is closely related to the multivariate version of the Levinson algorithm [33]. This algorithm is easily programmable and requires less computation time and memory storage than existing ones [21–24]. A simulation example will be shown to illustrate the results of the proposed method.

The following notation will be used in this article. The symbol tr H denotes the trace of a matrix H which is square. For a matrix H, rank H, H^T, H^*, and H^+ denote, respectively, the rank, the transpose, the conjugate transpose, and the pseudoinverse (that is, the generalized inverse defined by Penrose). $\|H\|$ denotes the Euclidean or Schur norm given by $\|H\| = \sqrt{\text{tr } HH^*}$. For symmetric matrices K and L, $K \geq L$ means $K - L$ is positive-semidefinite, and $K > L$ means $K - L$ is positive-definite. For a positive-semidefinite matrix L, $\sqrt{L}$ denotes the symmetric square root of L. I and 0 denote, respectively, an identity matrix and a zero matrix of appropriate dimension.

II.   LEAST-SQUARES APPROXIMATION

Consider a linear discrete-time system with q inputs and r outputs represented by the impulse response real matrix sequence $\{H_k\}_0^\infty$ satisfying the following condition

$$\{H_0, H_1, H_2, \cdots\} \in l_2, \tag{1}$$

where l_2 is the square summable space defined as follows:

$$l_2 = \left\{ \{H_0, H_1, \cdots\} \middle| \sum_{k=0}^\infty \|H_k\|^2 < \infty \right\}$$

The z transfer function matrix is defined by

$$H(z) = \sum_{k=0}^\infty H_k z^{-k}, \tag{2}$$

which is square integrable on the unit circle $|z| = 1$. Let $\{u_t\}$ be an uncorrelated (wide-sense) stationary q-vector sequence (or a white random process) that is zero-mean and unit-variance, and let $\{y_t\}$ be the output r-vector sequence corresponding to the input $\{u_t\}$, that is,

$$y_t = \sum_{k=0}^\infty H_k u_{t-k}. \tag{3}$$

The autocorrelation sequence $\{R_k\}_{-\infty}^\infty$ for the impulse response sequence $\{H_k\}$ is defined as follows:

$$
\begin{aligned}
R_k &= E\left\{ y_{t+k} y_t^T \right\} = \sum_{i=0}^\infty H_{i+k} H_i^T \\
&= \frac{1}{2\pi j} \int_c H(z) H(z)^* z^{k-1}\, dz, \qquad -\infty < k < \infty,
\end{aligned}
\tag{4}
$$

where $E\{\cdot\}$ denotes expectation, c is the unit circle $|z| = 1$, and $H_k = 0$ for $k < 0$. It is clear from the definition (4) that $R_{-k} = R_k^T$. The conditions of $\{u_t\}$ and (3) produce

$$H_k = E\left\{ y_{t+k} u_t^T \right\}, \qquad -\infty < k < \infty, \tag{5}$$

which implies H_k is the cross correlation for time shift k between the output $\{y_t\}$ and the input $\{u_t\}$.

In the approximation of a linear system $\{H_k\}$, the Padé approximation technique commonly employs finite matrices $\{H_0, H_1, ..., H_m\}$ of the impulse response sequence $\{H_k\}_0^\infty$ as finite data. Throughout this article, we are given at the same time two kinds of data: the first are finite matrices $\{H_0, ..., H_m\}$ of the impulse response sequence $\{H_k\}_0^\infty$, and the second are finite matrices $\{R_0, ..., R_n\}$ of the autocorrelation sequence $\{R_k\}_{-\infty}^\infty$.

Assume an approximant $\hat{H}(z)$ of an original system $H(z)$ is represented by the following matrix fraction

$$\hat{H}(z) = \left\{ I + A_1 z^{-1} + ... + A_n z^{-n} \right\}^{-1} \left\{ Q_0 + Q_1 z^{-1} \right.$$

$$\left. + ... + Q_m z^{-m} \right\}. \tag{6}$$

If the approximant $\hat{H}(z)$ is identical to the original system $H(z)$, the input u_t and output y_t are then related by a difference equation

$$y_t = -A_1 y_{t-1} - A_2 y_{t-2} - ... - A_n y_{t-n}$$
$$+ Q_0 u_t + Q_1 u_{t-1} + ... + Q_m u_{t-m}.$$

On the other hand, if we made a particular guess for the A_i and Q_i, we can predict the value $\hat{y}_t$ of the present output y_t from the values $\{y_{t-1}, ..., y_{t-n}, u_t, ..., u_{t-m}\}$ based on the above relation as follows:

$$\hat{y}_t = -A_1 y_{t-1} - A_2 y_{t-2} - ... - A_n y_{t-n}$$
$$+ Q_0 u_t + Q_1 u_{t-1} + ... + Q_m u_{t-m}. \tag{7}$$

The least-squares approximation problem considered in the following is to find the coefficient matrices A_i and Q_i that minimize $E\{\|y_t - \hat{y}_t\|^2\}$. The substitution of these obtained values A_i and Q_i into (6) yields an *approximant* $\hat{H}(z)$.

Let $e_t = y_t - \hat{y}_t$. It is notationally convenient in the following to define $A_0 = I$ and $H_k = 0$ for $k < 0$. Using (3) and (7) gives

$$e_t = \sum_{k=0}^m \left(\sum_{j=0}^n A_j H_{k-j} - Q_k \right) u_{t-k}$$

$$+ \sum_{k=m+1}^\infty \left(\sum_{j=0}^n A_j H_{k-j} \right) u_{t-k}. \tag{8}$$

Therefore, the following is obtained:

$$E\left\{\|e_t\|^2\right\} = \mathrm{tr}\left[\sum_{k=0}^{m}\left(\sum_{j=0}^{n} A_j H_{k-j} - Q_k\right)\right.$$

$$\times \left.\left(\sum_{j=0}^{n} A_j H_{k-j} - Q_k\right)^T\right]$$

$$+ \mathrm{tr}\left[\sum_{k=m+1}^{\infty}\left(\sum_{j=0}^{n} A_j H_{k-j}\right)\left(\sum_{j=0}^{n} A_j H_{k-j}\right)^T\right] \tag{9}$$

Minimizing the above function (9) with respect to $\{Q_0, Q_1, \ldots, Q_m\}$ yields

$$Q_k = \sum_{j=0}^{n} A_j H_{k-j}, \qquad \text{for } 0 \le k \le m. \tag{10}$$

Definition. For the data $\{H_0, \ldots, H_m, R_0, \ldots, R_n\}$, define a symmetric $(n + 1) \times (n + 1)$ block matrix [that is, a $(n + 1)r \times (n + 1)r$ matrix] $K(m, n)$ with the (i, j)-th block element $[K(m, n)]_{i,j}$ as follows:

$$[K(m,n)]_{i,j} = R_{j-i} - \sum_{k=0}^{m-j} H_{k+j-1} H_k^T, \tag{11}$$

where $i, j = 0, 1, \ldots, n$.

When $\{R_k\}$ is the autocorrelation sequence for the impulse response sequence $\{H_k\}$, (11) is identical with

$$K(m,n) = \sum_{k > m+1} \begin{bmatrix} H_k \\ H_{k-1} \\ \vdots \\ H_{k-n} \end{bmatrix} \begin{bmatrix} H_k \\ H_{k-1} \\ \vdots \\ H_{k-n} \end{bmatrix}^T, \tag{12}$$

which implies that $K(m, n)$ is positive-semidefinite. By means of (12), the substitution of (10) into (9) becomes

$$E\left\{\|e_t\|^2\right\} = \mathrm{tr}\left[A_0, A_1, \ldots, A_n\right] K(m,n)$$

$$\times \left[A_0, A_1, \ldots, A_n\right]^T. \tag{13}$$

The minimization $E\{\|e_t\|^2\}$ with respect to $\{A_1, A_2, ..., A_n\}$ requires the following lemma.

Lemma 1. Let K be a symmetric positive-semidefinite n × n block (or nr × nr) matrix, and let φ^T be a 1 × n block (or r × nr) matrix. For the problem which is to minimize $\mathrm{tr}\{X^TKX\}$ subject to $\Phi^TX = I$, a solution $\hat{X}$ exists and satisfies

$$\hat{X}^TK = \Gamma\Phi^T$$

where Γ is an r × r symmetric matrix uniquely determined by K, and satisfies

$$\Gamma = \hat{X}^TK\hat{X}.$$

Furthermore, the solution $\hat{X}$ satisfies

$$X^TKX \geq \hat{X}^TK\hat{X}$$

for any X subject to $\Phi^TX = I$.

Proof. For the minimization problem, define the following Lagrangian

$$L(X, \Gamma) = \mathrm{tr}\{X^TKX + 2\Gamma(I - \Phi^TX)\}.$$

From the fact that the Lagrangian derivatives vanish at a solution $\hat{X}$, we obtain $\hat{X}^TK - \Gamma\Phi^T = 0$. Clearly, $\Gamma = \hat{X}^TK\hat{X}$. For any X subject to $\Phi^TX = I$, we obtain

$$\hat{X}^TK(X - \hat{X}) = \Gamma\Phi^TX - \Gamma\Phi^T\hat{X} = 0.$$

Therefore, it follows that

$$X^TKX = \{\hat{X} + (X - \hat{X})\}^TK\{\hat{X} + (X - \hat{X})\}$$

$$= \hat{X}^TK\hat{X} + (X - \hat{X})^TK(X - \hat{X}) \geq \hat{X}^TK\hat{X}.$$

Applying the above inequality twice to two solutions yields the uniqueness of Γ. Conversely, we shall show that there exists a solution $\hat{X}$ of the equations $\hat{X}^TK = \Gamma\Phi^T$ and $\Phi^T\hat{X} = I$, which implies, by the above inequality, that the minimization problem has a solution $\hat{X}$. Since $\Phi^T\hat{X} = I$, we can find an orthogonal transformation U such that $\Phi^TU = [I, 0, ..., 0]$. The forms of the equations and the positive-semidefiniteness of the matrix UKU^T corresponding to K are not changed by the orthogonal transformation U. Therefore, we can assume without loss of generality that Φ is given by $\Phi^T = [I, 0, ..., 0]$. We can also partition K and $\hat{X}$ as follows:

$$K = \left[\begin{array}{c|c} E & D^T \\ \hline D & F \end{array} \right], \qquad \hat{X}^T = \left[I, \hat{A} \right],$$

where F is an $(n - 1) \times (n - 1)$ block matrix, $\hat{A}$ is a $1 \times (n - 1)$ block matrix, E and D are block matrices of the proper size. Then the original equations are reduced to

$$\hat{A}F = -D^T, \qquad \Gamma = E + \hat{A}D.$$

It can be seen [see (87) in Appendix C] that the positive-semidefiniteness of K implies

$$\text{Im } D \subset \text{Im } F,$$

where Im D denotes the image of D. This means that there exists a solution $\hat{A}$ to the above first equation. Thus, a solution $\hat{X}$ is given by $\hat{X}^T = [I, \hat{A}]$. This completes the proof of Lemma 1.

Using the above arguments, we obtain the characterization of the least-squares approximation as follows.

Lemma 2. For the data $\{H_0, ..., H_m; R_0, ..., R_n\}$, let $K(m, n)$ be the matrix defined by (11).

(1) When the data $\{H_0, ..., H_m; R_0, ..., R_n\}$ are taken from an impulse response sequence and its autocorrelation sequence, $K(m, n)$ is positive-semidefinite.

(2) Minimizing (9) with respect to $\{Q_0, ..., Q_m\}$ satisfies

$$Q_k = \sum_{j=0}^{n} A_j H_{k-j}, \qquad \text{for } 0 \le k \le m. \tag{14a}$$

(3) If $K(m, n)$ is positive-semidefinite, then the minimization of (13) with respect to $\{A_1, ..., A_n\}$ satisfies

$$\left[I, A_1, ..., A_n \right] K(m, n) = \Gamma_{m,n} [I, 0, ..., 0], \tag{14b}$$

where $\Gamma_{m,n}$ is a symmetric $r \times r$ matrix uniquely determined by the data.

We shall call the problem of solving (14) the *least-squares approximation problem* for the data $\{H_0, ..., H_m; R_0, ..., R_n\}$ with positive-semidefiniteness of $K(m, n)$.

Some remarks will be given about (14). Equation (14b) corresponds to the Yule–Walker equation in autoregression [33]. All the properties derived in the following are based on (14). When the matrix $K(m, n)$ is nonsingular, the properties in the scalar case can be extended to the multivariable case without difficulty. The case for which $K(m, n)$ is singular is rare in the scalar case but often occurs in the multivariable case. Equation (14b) possesses a set of solutions in this case. Thus, the questions are whether one can construct a stable approximant $\hat{H}(z)$ that is uniquely determined from given data, and whether one can obtain a recursive algorithm for solving (14b) even when $K(m, n)$ is singular. These questions will be answered satisfactorily in the following. In the computation of (14b), however, the multiplications usually required are approximately proportional to n^3, and the storage requirements are approximately proportional to n^2. Therefore, these become very large with an increase in the size of n. Further reduction in computation time and storage is possible in solving (14b) because of the special form of $K(m, n)$. A recursive algorithm will be obtained in Section III, which is closely related to a multivariate version of the Levinson algorithm [33].

By substituting a solution $\{A_1, ..., A_n; Q_0, ..., Q_m\}$ of (14) into (6), we obtain an approximant $\hat{H}(z)$ of the original system $H(z)$. The z transfer function $\hat{H}(z)$ has an impulse response sequence $\{\hat{H}_k\}$ satisfying

$$\hat{H}_k = 0, \quad \text{for } k < 0$$

$$= Q_k - \sum_{j=1}^{n} A_j \hat{H}_{k-j}, \quad \text{for } k \geq 0, \tag{15}$$

where $Q_j = 0$ for $j > m$.

The approximant $\hat{H}(z)$ may be realized as a difference equation of order one in the following form:

$$\hat{x}_{t+1} = A\hat{x}_t + Bu_{t-(m-n)} \tag{16a}$$

$$\hat{y}_t = C\hat{x}_t + \sum_{k=0}^{m-n} \hat{H}_k u_{t-k}, \tag{16b}$$

where $\hat{x}_t$ is an n-block vector (or nr-vector) defined by

$$
\hat{x}_t = \begin{bmatrix} \hat{y}_{t+n-1} - \sum_{k=1}^{m} \hat{H}_{k-1} u_{t+n-k} \\ \vdots \\ \hat{y}_{t+n-i} - \sum_{k=i}^{m} \hat{H}_{k-i} u_{t+n-k} \\ \vdots \\ \hat{y}_t - \sum_{k=n}^{m} \hat{H}_{k-n} u_{t+n-k} \end{bmatrix},
\tag{16c}
$$

and the triplet $\{A, B, C\}$ is given by

$$
A = \begin{bmatrix} -A_1 & -A_2 & \cdots & -A_n \\ I & 0 & \cdots & 0 \\ 0 & I & \cdots & 0 \\ \vdots & & & \\ 0 & 0 & I & 0 \end{bmatrix}, \quad B = \begin{bmatrix} \hat{H}_m \\ \hat{H}_{m-1} \\ \vdots \\ \hat{H}_{m-n+1} \end{bmatrix}
$$

$$
C = [0 \quad \cdots \quad 0 \quad I].
\tag{16d}
$$

In the case $m \geq n$, the above realization (16) of $\hat{H}(z)$ does not contain in the state space those states of pure delays which are serially connected to the input. Another realization can be presented that possesses all these states in its state space, but the realization (16) simplifies the arguments in the following.

The stability of the approximant $\hat{H}(z)$ will be shown in Theorem 1. If the approximant $\hat{H}(z)$ is stable, then the state vector has a covariance matrix $\hat{K}$ satisfying

$$
\hat{K} = E\left\{ \hat{x}_t \hat{x}_t^T \right\} = \sum_{k=0}^{\infty} A^k B \left(A^k B \right)^T
\tag{17a}
$$

and the following Lyapunov equation:

$$
\hat{K} = A\hat{K}A^T + BB^T.
\tag{17b}
$$

Using the definition of the input sequence $\{u_k\}$, we can compute the impulse response and autocorrelation sequence from the realization (16) as follows.

$$
\hat{H}_k = \hat{H}_k, \qquad \text{for } k \leq m - n
$$

$$
= CA^{k-1-(m-n)}B, \qquad \text{for } k \geq m - n + 1,
\tag{18}
$$

$$\hat{R}_k = CA^k \hat{K} C^T + \sum_{i=0}^{m-n} \hat{H}_{i+k} \hat{H}_i^T. \tag{19}$$

Let $\hat{K}(m-1, n-1)$ be the matrix defined by (11) for the data $\{\hat{H}_0, \ldots, \hat{H}_{m-1};$ $\hat{R}_0, \ldots, \hat{R}_{n-1}\}$. Equation (16c) and the same relations as (5) for $\hat{H}(z)$, yielding the fact that $\hat{K}$ is identical to $\hat{K}(m-1, n-1)$.

The following lemma, which is concerned with a Lyapunov equation, will be required later.

Lemma 3. Let A and B be, respectively, $n \times n$ and $n \times r$ matrices, and let

$$H(z) = (zI - A)^{-1} B.$$

(1) $H(z)$ is stable[1] if and only if there exists a symmetric positive-semidefinite matrix K satisfying the Lyapunov equation

$$K = AKA^T + BB^T. \tag{20}$$

(2) If all the eigenvalues of A lie in the open unit disk, then there exists at most one solution of (20).

(3) Suppose $H(z)$ is stable. Let

$$\hat{K} = \sum_{k=0}^{\infty} A^k B \left(A^k B \right)^T. \tag{21}$$

The matrix $\hat{K}$ is then a solution of (20), which is symmetric and positive-semidefinite. Furthermore, every other solution K of (20) that is symmetric and positive-semidefinite is ordered by $K \geq \hat{K}$; namely, $\hat{K}$ is the minimal solution of (20) that is symmetric and positive-definite.

The proof of Lemma 3 is found in Appendix A. A few remarks are given here. Part (1) of Lemma 3 is an extension of the following widely known fact: If the pair $\{A, B\}$ is reachable (or controllable from origin) and there exists a symmetric positive-definite matrix K satisfying (20), then all eigenvalues of A are in the open unit disk. The connection between stability and Lyapunov equations are discussed by Barnett [34]. Part (1) of Lemma 3 is a slight extension of Theorem 4.2 in Barnett [34]. Part (2) of Lemma 3 is similar to Theorem 4.3 in Barnett [34].

In the remainder of this section, we shall see the properties of the least-squares approximation problem. The first important one is concerned with stability of the approximant $\hat{H}(z)$.

---

[1]$H(z)$ is said to be stable (or externally stable) if any bounded inputs to $H(z)$ produces a bounded output.

Theorem 1. Assume the matrix $K(m, n)$ defined by (11) is positive-semidefinite. Then the approximant $\hat{H}(z)$ obtained by (6) and (14) is stable.

Proof. Equation (14b) is equivalent to the following pair of equations:

$$K(m-1, n-1) = AK(m-1, n-1)A^T + BB^T + \check{B}\Gamma_{m,n}\check{B}^T \tag{22}$$

$$\sum_{k=0}^{n} A_k [K(m,n)]_{k,n} = 0, \tag{23}$$

where A and B are the matrices given by (16d), and $\tilde{B}$ is the $n \times 1$ block matrix given by

$$\check{B} = [I, 0, ..., 0]^T. \tag{24}$$

This statement can be derived as follows. Equation (23) follows directly from equating the last block elements on both sides of (14b). From (11) we obtain

$$[K(m-1, n-1)]_{i,j} = [K(m,n)]_{i+1,j+1},$$
for $i, j = 0, ..., n-1$.

This and the block companion form of A in (16d), together with (14b), yield

$$[AK(m-1, n-1)]_{i,j} = [K(m,n)]_{i,j+1},$$
for $i, j = 0, ..., n-1$,

$$\left[AK(m-1, n-1)A^T\right]_{i,j} = [K(m,n)_{0,0}] - \Gamma_{m,n},$$
for $(i, j) = (0, 0)$
$$= [K(m,n)]_{i,j}, \qquad \text{otherwise.}$$

Also from (11)

$$[K(m,n)]_{i,j} = [K(m-1, n-1)]_{i,j} - H_{m-1}H_{m-j}^T,$$
for $i, j = 0, ..., n-1$.

Then we obtain (22) from the last two equations. Conversely, it can be shown by an elementary calculation that (22) and (23) imply (14b).

By (22) and Part (1) of Lemma 3, the z transfer function $(zI - A)^{-1} \times [B_,, \widetilde{B\sqrt{\Gamma_{m,n}}}]$ is stable, which implies the stability of $\hat{H}(z)$ from the realization (16). This completes the proof of Theorem 1.

A few remarks are given here. Note that the realization (16) may have an unstable mode when it is not reachable (see the proof of Lemma 3 in Appendix A). This is not an issue in the scalar case, since the realization (16) is reachable if $\Gamma_{m,n} \neq 0$ or if $\Gamma_{m,n} = 0$ and $\Gamma_{m-1,n-1} \neq 0$ (see Mullis and Roberts [25]).

Theorem 2. Assume the matrix $K(m, n)$ is positive-semidefinite.

(1) The first m + 1 matrices of the impulse response sequence of the approximant $\hat{H}(z)$ are identical with those of the given data; that is,

$$\hat{H}_k = H_k, \qquad \text{for } k = 0, 1, \ldots, m. \tag{25}$$

(2) The double sequence $\{\Gamma_{m,n}\}$, whose element is uniquely determined by (14b) for (m, n), satisfies the following:

$$\Gamma_{m,0} = R_0 - \left(H_0 H_0^T + \ldots + H_m H_m^T \right) \tag{26a}$$

$$\Gamma_{m+1,n} \leq \Gamma_{m,n} \tag{26b}$$

$$\Gamma_{m,n+1} \leq \Gamma_{m,n} \tag{26c}$$

$$\text{rank } \Gamma_{m,n} = \text{rank } K(m,n) - \text{rank } K(m-1, n-1)$$
$$\text{for } m > 0, n > 0. \tag{26d}$$

(3) Assume the data $\{H_0, \ldots, H_m; R_0, \ldots, R_n\}$ are taken from the impulse response and autocorrelation sequences of an original system $H(z)$. Then the rank $\Gamma_{m,n}$ is equal to r-p if and only if p is the largest integer such that for a $p \times r$ matrix V of rank p and some matrices $A_1, \ldots, A_n, Q_0, \ldots, Q_m$, it holds that

$$V\{y_t + A_1 y_{t-1} + \ldots + A_n y_{t-n} - Q_0 u_t$$
$$- \ldots - Q_m u_{t-m}\} = 0, \qquad \text{a.e. for all } t. \tag{27}$$

As a special case, the approximant $\hat{H}(z)$ is identical with the original system $H(z)$ if and only if $\Gamma_{m,n} = 0$.

Proof. The relation (25) follows from (14a) and (15). Equation (26a) comes directly from the definition (11) of $K(m, n)$ and the fact that $\Gamma_{m,0} = K(m, 0)$. The relations (26b) and (26c) follow from Lemma 1, the definition (11) of $K(m, n)$, and the fact that the solution to the (m, n) problem satisfies the constraints for the (m + 1, n) and (m, n + 1) problems. Equation (26d) comes as follows: Let $\{A_1, A_2, ..., A_n; \Gamma_{m,n}\}$ be a solution of (14b). Let T be the $(n + 1) \times (n + 1)$ block matrix, whose diagonal elements are unity, defined by

$$T = \left[\begin{array}{c|c} I & A \; ... \; A_n \\ \hline 0 & I \end{array} \right] \begin{array}{l} \} \quad \text{1 block} \\ \} \quad \text{n blocks} \end{array} .$$

1 block   n blocks

Then from (14b) and the definition (11) of $K(m, n)$, we obtain

$$TK(m,n)T^T = \left[\begin{array}{c|c} \Gamma_{m,n} & 0 \\ \hline 0 & K(m-1,n-1) \end{array} \right].$$

Since T is nonsingular, the above equation implies (26d). From (8) and (10), we can obtain the following in an argument similar to the derivation of (13).

$$E\left\{e_t e_t^T\right\} = \left[A_0, ..., A_n\right] K(m,n) \left[A_0, ..., A_n\right]^T.$$

This and (14b) give

$$E\left\{e_t e_t^T\right\} = \Gamma_{m,n}.$$

On the other hand, (7) yields

$$e_t = y_t - \hat{y}_t = y_t + A_1 y_t + ... + A_n y_{t-n}$$
$$- Q_0 u_t - ... - Q_m u_{t-m}.$$

It is clear that rank $\Gamma_{m,n} \le r - p$ if and only if there exists a $p \times r$ matrix of rank p such that $V\Gamma_{m,n}V^T = 0$. Therefore, rank $\Gamma_{m,n} \le r - p$ if and only if $VE\{e_t e_t^T\} V^T = 0$, or equivalently $Ve_t = 0$ a.e. for all t, which implies (27). This completes the proof of Theorem 2.

    We note that there may exist two different solutions of (14b) when the matrix $K(m - 1, n - 1)$ is singular. The following theorem shows that these different solutions of (14b) produce the identical z transfer function $\hat{H}(z)$.

    Theorem 3. Presume the matrix $K(m, n)$ is positive-semidefinite. Then the z transfer function $\hat{H}(z)$ obtained by (6) and (14) is invariant with the solutions of (14); that is, $\hat{H}(z)$ is uniquely determined by the data $\{H_0, ..., H_m; R_0, ..., R_n\}$.

Proof. Let $\{A_1', \ldots, A_n'\}$ and $\{A_1'', \ldots, A_n''\}$ be two solutions of (14b). Let $D_i = A_i' - A_i''$, where $i = 1, 2, \ldots, n$. From the two equations obtained by substituting $\{A_1', \ldots, A_n'\}$ and $\{A_1'', \ldots, A_n''\}$ into $\{A_1, \ldots, A_n\}$ of (14b), respectively, we obtain

$$\begin{bmatrix} D_1, \ldots, D_n \end{bmatrix} K(m-1, n-1) = 0. \tag{28}$$

Let $\hat{H}'(z)$ and $\hat{H}''(z)$ be, respectively, the z transfer functions [obtained from (6) and (14)] corresponding to $\{A_1', \ldots, A_n'\}$ and $\{A_1'', \ldots, A_n''\}$; let $\{\hat{H}_k'\}$ and $\{\hat{H}_k''\}$ be, respectively, their impulse response sequences; and let $\hat{K}'(m-1, n-1)$ be the covariance matrix given by (17a) for the system $\hat{H}'(z)$. Part (1) of Theorem 2 gives

$$\hat{H}_k' = H_k = \hat{H}_k'', \qquad \text{for } k = 0, 1, \ldots, m. \tag{29}$$

From (22) we obtain

$$K(m-1, n-1) = A' K(m-1, n-1) A'^{T} + B' B'^{T}$$
$$+ B\Gamma_{m,n} B^{T}, \tag{30}$$

where A' and B' are the matrices given by (16d) for the system $\hat{H}'(z)$. Part (3) of Lemma 3 gives

$$K(m-1,n-1) \geq \sum_{k=0}^{\infty} A'^{k} \left(B' B'^{T} + B\Gamma_{m,n} B^{T} \right) \left(A'^{T} \right)^{k}$$
$$\geq \sum_{k=0}^{\infty} A'^{k} B' \left(A'^{k} B' \right)^{T} = \hat{K}'(m-1, n-1). \tag{31}$$

This and (28) yield

$$\begin{bmatrix} D_1, \ldots, D_n \end{bmatrix} \hat{K}'(m-1, n-1) \begin{bmatrix} D_1, \ldots, D_n \end{bmatrix}^{T} = 0. \tag{32}$$

On the other hand, we obtain from (16c) [or (12)]:

$$\hat{K}'(m-1,n-1)= \sum_{t\geq m+1} \begin{bmatrix} \hat{H}'_{t-1} \\ \vdots \\ \hat{H}'_{t-n} \end{bmatrix} \begin{bmatrix} \hat{H}'_{t-1} \\ \vdots \\ \hat{H}'_{t-n} \end{bmatrix}^T . \tag{33}$$

The above two equations give

$$[D_1,...,D_n] \begin{bmatrix} \hat{H}'_{t-1} \\ \vdots \\ \hat{H}'_{t-n} \end{bmatrix} \begin{bmatrix} \hat{H}'_{t-1} \\ \vdots \\ \hat{H}'_{t-n} \end{bmatrix}^T [D_1,...,D_n]^T$$

$$= 0, \quad \text{for } t \geq m + 1,$$

which implies

$$\sum_{j=1}^{n} D_j \hat{H}'_{t-j} = 0, \quad \text{for } t \geq m + 1. \tag{34}$$

Assume $\hat{H}_k' = \hat{H}_k''$ for $k = 0, 1, ..., t - 1$, where $t \geq m + 1$. Then from (15) and (34),

$$\hat{H}'_t - \hat{H}''_t = - \sum_{j=1}^{n} \left(A'_j \hat{H}'_{t-j} - A''_j \hat{H}''_{t-j} \right)$$

$$= - \sum_{j=1}^{n} D_j \hat{H}'_{t-j} = 0, \quad \text{for } t \geq m + 1. \tag{35}$$

This means the sequences $\{\hat{H}_k'\}$ and $\{\hat{H}_k''\}$ are identical, which completes the proof of Theorem 3.

It is examined how well the approximant $\hat{H}(z)$ matches the given data $\{H_0, ..., H_m; R_0, ..., R_n\}$. From Part (1) of Theorem 2, the first $m + 1$ data are matched exactly.

Some preparations will be made for the evaluation of differences between the data $\{R_0, ..., R_n\}$ and the first $n + 1$ matrices of the autocorrelation sequence of the approximant $\hat{H}(z)$. Let

$$\tilde{H}(z) = A(z)^{-1} z^{-m-1} \sqrt{\Gamma_{m,n}}, \tag{36a}$$

where

$$A(z) = I + A_1 z^{-1} + \ldots + A_n z^{-n}. \tag{36b}$$

We see from (22) and Part (1) of Lemma 3 that the system $\widetilde{H}(z)$ is stable. It will be said to be *residual* corresponding to the approximant $\hat{H}(z)$. Let $\{\widetilde{H}_k\}$ and $\{\widetilde{R}_k\}$ be, respectively, the impulse response and autocorrelation sequences of $\widetilde{H}(z)$. Note that $\widetilde{H}_k = 0$ for $k \leq m$ and $\widetilde{H}_{m+1} = \sqrt{\Gamma_{m,n}}$. Let $\widetilde{R}(n-1)$ be a symmetric $n \times n$ block matrix with the (i, j)-th block element being $\widetilde{R}_{j-i}$. Then $\widetilde{R}(n-1)$ is a block Toeplitz matrix whose first row block is $[\widetilde{R}_0, \widetilde{R}_1, \ldots, \widetilde{R}_{n-1}]$. It can be seen from the definitions that $\widetilde{R}(n-1)$ is identical to $K(m-1, n-1)$ defined by (11) for the data $\{0, \ldots, 0; \widetilde{R}_0, \ldots, \widetilde{R}_n\}$. By means of the realization of $\widetilde{H}(z)$ [defined by (16) for the system $\widetilde{H}(z)$] and Part (3) of Lemma 3, we obtain

$$\widetilde{R}(n-1) = K(m-1, n-1) = \sum_{k=0}^{\infty} A^k B \Gamma_{m,n} B^T \left(A^T\right)^k. \tag{37}$$

The following lemma is also required.

Lemma 4. Let $\{x_t\}$ be a purely nondeterministic (wide-sense) stationary n-vector random process, and let $K_0 = E\{x_t x_t^T\}$ and $K_1 = E\{x_{t+1} x_t^T\}$. If the covariance K_0 satisfies a Lyapunov equation

$$K_0 = A K_0 A^T + BB^T \tag{38}$$

and a condition

$$A K_0 = K_1, \tag{39}$$

then K_0 is the minimal solution of (38) that is symmetric and positive-semidefinite.

The proof of Lemma 4 is found in Appendix B.

By means of these preparations, the evaluation of differences mentioned above is shown as follows.

Theorem 4. Presume the matrix $K(m, n)$ is positive-semidefinite. Let $\hat{H}(z)$ be the approximant obtained by (6) and (14), $\widetilde{H}(z)$ the residual system defined by (36), and $\{\hat{R}_k\}$ and $\{\widetilde{R}_k\}$, respectively, their autocorrelation sequences.

(1) When the data $\{H_0, \ldots, H_m; R_0, \ldots, R_n\}$ are taken from the impulse response and autocorrelation sequences of an original system $H(z)$,

$$R_k - \hat{R}_k = \widetilde{R}_k, \qquad \text{for } k = 0, 1, \ldots, n. \tag{40}$$

(2) Let A be the companion matrix (16d) for a solution $\{A_1, \ldots, A_n\}$ of (14b). If the eigenvalues of A all lies on the open unit disk (this assumption is attained if $\Gamma_{m,n} > 0$), the above relations (40) also hold.

Proof. Let x_t be an n-block vector given by

$$
x_t = \begin{bmatrix}
y_{t+n-1} - \sum_{k=1}^{m} H_{k-1} u_{t+n-k} \\
\vdots \\
y_{t+n-i} - \sum_{k=i}^{m} H_{k-i} u_{t+n-k} \\
\vdots \\
y_t - \sum_{k=n}^{m} H_{k-n} u_{t+n-k}
\end{bmatrix}
\tag{41}
$$

Since the input sequence $\{u_t\}$ is stationary and purely nondeterministic, the output sequence $\{y_t\}$ and therefore the sequence $\{x_t\}$ defined by (41) become stationary and purely nondeterministic. Let $K_0 = E\{x_t x_t\}$ and $K_1 = E\{x_{t+1} x_t^T\}$. Then from an elementary calculation, (41) and (11) give

$$
K_0 = K(m-1, n-1),
\tag{42}
$$

$$
\left[K_1\right]_{i,j} = \left[K(m,n)\right]_{i,j+1},
\tag{43}
$$

$$
\text{for } i,j = 0, 1, \ldots, n-1.
$$

For the given data, we obtain (22) and (23), which are equivalent to (14b). These, together with (42) and (43), ensure the relations

$$
K_0 = AK_0 A^T + BB^T + \check{B}\Gamma_{m,n}\check{B}^T,
\tag{44}
$$

$$
AK_0 = K_1.
\tag{45}
$$

By Lemma 4, K_0 is the minimal solution of (44) that is symmetric and positive-semidefinite. This yields by Part (3) of Lemma 3

$$
K(m-1, n-1) = \sum_{k=0}^{\infty} A^k \left[B, \check{B}\sqrt{\Gamma_{m,n}}\right]\left[B, \check{B}\sqrt{\Gamma_{m,n}}\right]^T (A^T)^k
\tag{46}
$$

$$= \sum_{k=0}^{\infty} A^k BB^T \left(A^T\right)^k + \sum_{k=0}^{\infty} A^k \breve{B} \Gamma_{m,n} \breve{B}^T$$
$$\times \left(A^T\right)^k ,$$

which implies from (17a) and (37)

$$K(m-1,n-1) = \hat{K}(m-1,n-1) + \breve{K}(m-1,n-1) \tag{47}$$

From the definition (11), the first block rows of $K(m-1, n-1)$ and $\hat{K}(m-1, n-1)$ are, respectively, given by

$$\left[K(m-1,n-1)\right]_{0,j} = R_j - \sum_{k=0}^{m-1-j} H_{k+j} H_k^T, \tag{48a}$$

for $j = 0, 1, \dots, n-1$,

$$\left[\hat{K}(m-1,n-1)\right]_{0,j} = \hat{R}_j - \sum_{k=0}^{m-1-j} \hat{H}_{k+j} \hat{H}_k^T, \tag{48b}$$

for $j = 0, 1, \dots, n-1$.

Since $H_i = \hat{H}_i$ for $0 \leq i \leq m$, (47), (48), and (37) yield

$$R_j = \hat{R}_j + \breve{R}_j, \qquad \text{for } j = 0, 1, \dots, n-1. \tag{49}$$

Equation (23), which was derived from (14b), gives

$$\left[K(m,n)\right]_{0,n} = - \sum_{k=1}^{n} A_k \left[K(m,n)\right]_{k,n}. \tag{50a}$$

Similarly, we obtain

$$\left[\hat{K}(m,n)\right]_{0,n} = - \sum_{k=1}^{n} A_k \left[\hat{K}(m,n)\right]_{k,n} \tag{50b}$$

$$\breve{R}_n = - \sum_{k=1}^{n} A_k \breve{R}_{n-k}. \tag{50c}$$

From the definition (11), the last block columns of $K(m, n)$ and $\hat{K}(m, n)$ are, respectively, given by

$$\left[K(m,n) \right]_{i,n} = R_{n-i} - \sum_{k=0}^{m-n} H_{k+n-i} H_k^T,$$

(51a)

for $i = 0, \ldots, n$

$$\left[\hat{K}(m,n) \right]_{i,n} = \hat{R}_{n-i} - \sum_{k=0}^{m-n} \hat{H}_{k+n-i} \hat{H}_k,$$

(51b)

for $i = 0, \ldots, n$.

Since $H_i = \hat{H}_i$ for $0 \leq i \leq m$, (49), (50), and (51) yield

$$R_n = \hat{R}_n + \tilde{R}_n.$$

(52)

This implies Part (1).

If the eigenvalues of the companion matrix A all lie in the open unit disk, the relation (46) also follows from (22) and Part (2) of Lemma 3, which yields the relations (40) in the same argument as above. This completes the proof of Theorem 4.

III.   A RECURSIVE ALGORITHM

This section will provide a recursive algorithm for computing a solution $\{A, \ldots, A_n\}$ to (14b) for the case $m = n$. In the same way as the scalar case, the case $m \neq n$ of the problem of computing a solution to (14b) may be handled by deriving an equivalent problem for which $m' = n' = n$. This technique was provided by Mullis and Roberts [25] in the scalar case and can be presented as follows. Denote the sequence $\{H_0, H_1, H_2, \ldots\}$ by $\mathscr{H}$, and define the operators σ_L and σ_R by

$$\sigma_L \mathscr{H} = \{H_1, H_2, H_3, \ldots\},$$

$$\sigma_R \mathscr{H} = \{0, H_0, H_1, \ldots\}.$$

Let $\{R_k\}$ be the autocorrelation sequence for $\mathscr{H}$, which is given by (4). For any positive integer k, the autocorrelation sequence for $(\sigma_R)^k \mathscr{H}$ is the same as that of $\mathscr{H}$ itself. The autocorrelation for $(\sigma_L)^k \mathscr{H}$ is, however,

$$R'_i = R_i - \sum_{j=0}^{k-1} H_{j+i} H_j^T.$$

Lemma 5. For any $\mathcal{H}$, let $K(m, n)$ be defined by (11). Let

$$\mathcal{H}' = \sigma_L^{(m-n)}\mathcal{H}, \quad \text{if } m > n$$

$$= \mathcal{H}, \quad \text{if } m = n \tag{53}$$

$$= \sigma_R^{(n-m)}\mathcal{H}, \quad \text{if } m < n.$$

Define $K'(n, n)$ for the sequence $\mathcal{H}'$ by (11). Then $K'(n, n) = K(m, n)$.

The proof is made by an elementary calculation. We may compute a solution to the (m, n) problem by first deriving the data $\{H_0', ..., H_n'; R_0', ..., R_n'\}$ and then applying the algorithm in the case $m = n$ to get $\{A_1, A_2, ..., A_n\}$. $\{Q_0, Q_1, ..., Q_m\}$ is computed from (14a) by using the original data $\{H_0, ..., H_m\}$.

Now, a recursive algorithm for computing a solution to (14b) for the case $m = n$ is described. For notational simplicity, let $K(n) = K(n, n)$ and $\Gamma_n = \Gamma_{n,n}$.

Algorithm. The data $\{H_0, ..., H_M; R_0, ..., R_M\}$ are given. At the completion of step n, the quantities

$$A_k(n), B_k(n), C_k(n) : (0 \le k \le n), \Gamma_n, \Omega_n$$

have been calculated. To obtain step $n + 1$, the following calculations are carried out.

$$\Delta_n = \sum_{k=0}^{n} A_k(n)R_{n+1-k} \tag{54a}$$

$$\Lambda_n = -\sum_{k=0}^{n} A_k(n)H_{n+1-k} \tag{54b}$$

$$\Theta_n = \Delta_n B_0(n) + \Lambda_n C_0(n) \tag{54c}$$

$$\Phi_n = \Delta_n C_0(n)^T + \Lambda_n \Omega_n \tag{54d}$$

$$\Gamma_{n+1} = \Gamma_n - \Delta_n \Theta_n^T - \Lambda_n \Phi_n^T \tag{54e}$$

$$\Omega_{n+1} = \Omega_n + \Phi_n^T \Gamma_{n+1}^+ \Phi_n \tag{54f}$$

$$A_k(n+1) = A_k(n) - \Delta_n B_{n+1-k}(n) - \Lambda_n C_{n+1-k}(n)$$

$$B_k(n+1) = B_k(n) - \Theta_n^T \Gamma_{n+1}^+ A_{n+1-k}(n+1)$$

$$C_k(n+1) = C_k(n) - \Phi_n^T \Gamma_{n+1}^+ A_{n+1-k}(n+1),$$

$$(54g)$$

for $0 \leq k \leq n+1$, where $A_{n+1}(n) = B_{n+1}(n) = 0$ and $C_{n+1}(n) = 0$. As initial values for $n = 0$, we set

$$A_0(0) = I, \qquad \Gamma_0 = R_0 - H_0 H_0^T, \qquad B_0(0) = \Gamma_0^+,$$

$$C_0(0) = H_0^T \Gamma_0^+, \qquad \Omega_0 = I + H_0^T \Gamma_0^+ H_0.$$

As far as the matrices $\{\Gamma_0, \Gamma_1, \ldots, \Gamma_M\}$ are positive-semidefinite (see Theorem 5 below), this procedure is carried out until step M is obtained. When K(M) is positive-semidefinite, this provides a solution $\{A_1(M), \ldots, A_M(M)\}$ of (14b) for $m = n = M$, and the approximant $\hat{H}(z)$ is given by

$$\hat{H}(z) = \left(\sum_{k=0}^{M} A_k(M) z^{-k} \right)^{-1} \sum_{k-0}^{M} \left(\sum_{j=0}^{M} A_j(M) H_{k-j} \right) z^{-k}. \tag{55}$$

If $\Gamma_n = 0$ for some step n, the approximant $\hat{H}(z)$ for step n is identical with the original system. If Γ_n is not positive-semidefinite for step n, then K(n, n) is not positive-semidefinite (see Theorem 5 below), which implies there is no system which matches the data $\{H_0, \ldots, H_n; R_0, \ldots, R_n\}$; that is, the data are never identical with those taken from the impulse response and autocorrelation sequences for any system with its impulse response sequence in space l_2.

The proof of validity of the algorithm is found in Appendix C. If we set $H_i = 0$ for $0 \leq i \leq m$, then the algorithm becomes a multivariate version of the Levinson algorithm [33]. The computations in step n of the algorithm require about $3nr^3 + 2nqr^2$ multiplications. The algorithm hence requires $O(n^2)$ multiplications for a problem of size n. It also requires $O(n)$ storage locations, if we overwrite previous results by their new results derived from the recursion. The notation $O(n)$ indicates here that $O(n)/n$ is a constant.

In step n of the computation, the above algorithm requires one calculation of a pseudoinverse if Γ_n is singular. The singular value decomposition of a matrix provides the computational machinery for calculating the pseudoinverse [35, 36].

The matrices Δ_n and Λ_n are the errors in the predicted values of R_{n+1} and H_{n+1}, respectively, based on the n-th approximation. If these both vanish, then the (n + 1)-st approximation is equivalent to the n-th.

The Levinson algorithm was also extended to non-Toeplitz cases by Morf *et al.* [37] and by Friedlander *et al.* [38], where they used the displacement rank properties.

As shown below, the above algorithm can be used to examine whether the matrix K(m, n) for some data $\{H_0, ..., H_m; R_0, ..., R_n\}$ is positive-semidefinite or not.

Theorem 5. Let K(M) be the matrix defined by (11) for some data $\{H_0, ..., H_M; R_0, ..., R_M\}$, and $\{A_0(j), ..., A_j(j); \Gamma_j\}$ be the quantities generated from the above algorithm (54) at step j. Then, K(M) is positive-semidefinite if and only if $\Gamma_0, ..., \Gamma_M$ are all positive-semidefinite and $\{A_0(j), ..., A_j(j); \Gamma_j\}$ satisfies (14b) for m = n = j, where $0 \leq j \leq M$.

Proof. As far as K(M) is positive-semidefinite, $\{A_0(j), ..., A_j(j); \Gamma_j\}$ satisfies (14b) for m = n = j, where $0 \leq j \leq M$ (see Appendix C). Let T(M) be the upper triangular (M + 1) × (M + 1) block matrix defined by

$$[T(M)]_{i,j} = 0, \qquad \text{for } i > j$$
$$= A_{j-i}(M - j), \qquad \text{for } i \leq j, \tag{56}$$

where i, j = 0, 1, ..., M. Then, we obtain from (14b),

$$T(M)K(M)T(M)^T = \text{block diag}\{\Gamma_M, \Gamma_{M-1}, ..., \Gamma_0\}. \tag{57}$$

Since T(M) is nonsingular, the positive-semidefiniteness of K(M) implies that all $\Gamma_0, \Gamma_1, ..., \Gamma_M$ are positive-semidefinite.. Conversely, if $\{A_0(j), ..., A_j(j); \Gamma_j\}$ satisfies (14b) for m = n = j (where $0 \leq j \leq M$), then (57) holds. Therefore, if $\Gamma_0, \Gamma_1, ..., \Gamma_M$ are all positive-semidefinite, then K(M) is also positive-semidefinite. This completes the proof of Theorem 5.

IV.   A SIMULATION EXAMPLE

In order to illustrate the least-squares approximation, the above algorithm (54) has been implemented in a Fortran program. The computations are carried out for several examples by the ACOS-1000 computer. The following system is taken to be approximated. It is a 2-input, 2-output system described by the z transfer function

$$H(z) = \left(I + \sum_{i=1}^{5} A_i z^{-1}\right) - 1\left(I + \sum_{i=1}^{5} Q_i z^{-1}\right), \tag{58}$$

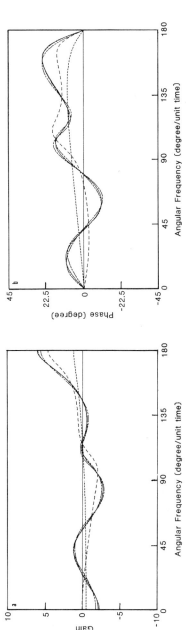

Fig. 1. (a) Gains of the (1, 1) element of the approximants of order n = 1, 2, 3, 4 and the original system. (b) Phases of the (1, 1) element of the approximants of order n = 1, 2, 3, 4 and the original system. (–), values for the original system (i.e., n = 5); ($\cdot \cdot$), values for n = 1; (– – –), values for n = 2; ($\cdot$ –), values for n = 3; ($\cdot$ –), for n = 4.

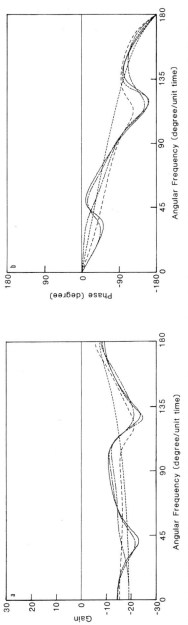

Fig. 2. (a) gains of the (1, 2) element of the approximants of order n = 1, 2, 3, 4 and the original system. (b) Phases of the (1, 2) element of the approximants of order n = 1, 2, 3, 4 and the original system.

TABLE I. COEFFICIENT MATRICES A_i AND Q_i
FOR THE ORIGINAL SYSTEM

i	A_i		Q_i	
1	0.12	−0.05	−0.03	0.12
	−0.04	0.10	0.09	0.10
2	−0.10	−0.03	0.07	−0.04
	0.05	0.01	−0.06	−0.03
3	0.13	−0.09	0.02	−0.11
	0.08	−0.10	−0.07	0.08
4	−0.05	0.07	−0.10	0.06
	−0.11	−0.03	0.02	−0.11
5	0.10	−0.05	−0.02	0.05
	−0.09	0.12	−0.03	0.12

TABLE II. IMPULSE RESPONSE AND AUTOCORRELATION SEQUENCES FOR THE ORIGINAL SYSTEM

k	H_k		R_k	
0	0.1000×10^1	0.0000×10^0	0.1172×10^1	-0.2578×10^{-1}
	0.0000×10^0	0.1000×10^1	-0.2578×10^{-1}	0.1150×10^1
1	-0.1500×10^0	0.1700×10^0	-0.2426×10^0	-0.6927×10^0
	0.1300×10^0	0.0000×10^0	0.8643×10^{-1}	-0.6223×10^{-1}
2	0.1945×10^0	-0.3040×10^{-1}	0.2603×10^0	0.9960×10^{-2}
	-0.1290×10^0	-0.1232×10^0	-0.5257×10^{-1}	-0.1702×10^0
3	-0.1509×10^0	-0.5512×10^{-2}	-0.2200×10^0	-0.8902×10^{-2}
	-0.1348×10^0	0.1826×10^0	-0.1777×10^0	0.2272×10^0
4	0.8146×10^{-2}	-0.2904×10^{-1}	0.8594×10^{-1}	-0.5548×10^{-1}
	0.1656×10^0	-0.9824×10^{-1}	0.1601×10^0	-0.9335×10^{-1}
5	-0.1853×10^0	0.1049×10^0	-0.2249×10^0	0.1142×10^0
	0.2373×10^{-1}	-0.5105×10^{-3}	0.4457×10^{-1}	-0.3649×10^{-1}

where A_i's and Q_i's are presented in Table I. The values of the A_i's are selected so that the system $H(z)$ is stable. Table II gives its impulse response matrices H_k's and autocorrelation matrices R_k's for $k = 0, 1, 2, ..., 5$. The results of the com-

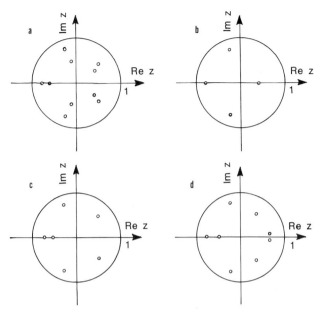

Fig. 3. (a) Poles of the original system. (b) Poles of the approximant of order 2. (c) Poles of the approximant of order 3. (d) Poles of the approximant of order 4.

TABLE III. COVARIANCE MATRICES Γ_n

	Γ_n	
0	0.1718×10^{0} -0.2578×10^{-1}	-0.2578×10^{-1} 0.1500×10^{0}
1	0.6903×10^{-1} -0.3646×10^{-1}	-0.3646×10^{-1} 0.8968×10^{-1}
2	0.3412×10^{-1} 0.2653×10^{-3}	0.2653×10^{-3} 0.2966×10^{-1}
3	0.6288×10^{-2} -0.2111×10^{-2}	-0.2111×10^{-2} 0.3479×10^{-2}
4	0.1224×10^{-2} -0.5319×10^{-3}	-0.5319×10^{-3} 0.5315×10^{-3}
5	-0.2070×10^{-15} 0.3069×10^{-16}	-0.1782×10^{-15} 0.4258×10^{-16}

TABLE IV. IMPULSE RESPONSE SEQUENCES OF THE APPROXIMANTS OF ORDER n = 2, 3, 4

k	$\hat{H}_{k,2}$		$\hat{H}_{k,3}$		$\hat{H}_{k,4}$	
0	$0.1000{\times}10^1$	$0.0000{\times}10^0$	$0.1000{\times}10^1$	$0.0000{\times}10^0$	$0.1000{\times}10^1$	$0.0000{\times}10^0$
	$0.0000{\times}10^0$	$0.1000{\times}10^1$	$0.0000{\times}10^0$	$0.1000{\times}10^1$	$0.0000{\times}10^0$	$0.1000{\times}10^1$
1	$-0.1500{\times}10^0$	$0.1700{\times}10^0$	$-0.1500{\times}10^0$	$0.1700{\times}10^0$	$-0.1500{\times}10^0$	$0.1700{\times}10^0$
	$0.1300{\times}10^0$	$0.0000{\times}10^0$	$0.1300{\times}10^0$	$0.0000{\times}10^0$	$0.1300{\times}10^0$	$0.0000{\times}10^0$
2	$0.1945{\times}10^0$	$-0.3040{\times}10^{-1}$	$0.1945{\times}10^0$	$-0.3040{\times}10^{-1}$	$0.1945{\times}10^0$	$-0.3040{\times}10^{-1}$
	$-0.1290{\times}10^0$	$-0.1232{\times}10^0$	$-0.1290{\times}10^0$	$-0.1232{\times}10^0$	$-0.1290{\times}10^0$	$-0.1232{\times}10^0$
3	$-0.5658{\times}10^{-1}$	$0.5471{\times}10^{-1}$	$-0.1509{\times}10^0$	$-0.5512{\times}10^{-2}$	$-0.1509{\times}10^0$	$-0.5512{\times}10^{-2}$
	$-0.6782{\times}10^{-1}$	$0.8752{\times}10^{-1}$	$-0.1348{\times}10^0$	$0.1826{\times}10^0$	$-0.1348{\times}10^0$	$0.1826{\times}10^0$
4	$0.2676{\times}10^{-1}$	$-0.5981{\times}10^{-1}$	$0.1516{\times}10^{-1}$	$-0.6353{\times}10^{-1}$	$0.8146{\times}10^{-2}$	$-0.2904{\times}10^{-1}$
	$0.1372{\times}10^0$	$-0.5384{\times}10^{-2}$	$0.1543{\times}10^0$	$-0.9124{\times}10^{-1}$	$0.1656{\times}10^0$	$-0.9824{\times}10^{-1}$
5	$-0.3894{\times}10^{-1}$	$0.6250{\times}10^{-1}$	$-0.1777{\times}10^0$	$0.6321{\times}10^{-1}$	$-0.1867{\times}10^0$	$0.9390{\times}10^{-1}$
	$-0.5773{\times}10^{-1}$	$-0.2476{\times}10^{-1}$	$0.1924{\times}10^{-1}$	$-0.1284{\times}10^{-1}$	$0.2445{\times}10^{-1}$	$0.2295{\times}10^{-2}$

TABLE V. IMPULSE RESPONSE SEQUENCES OF THE APPROXIMANTS OF ORDER n = 2, 3, 4

k	$\hat{R}_{k,2}$	$\hat{R}_{k,3}$	$\hat{R}_{k,4}$
0	$\begin{bmatrix} 0.1117\times10^{1} & -0.2831\times10^{1} \\ -0.2831\times10^{-1} & 0.1089\times10^{1} \end{bmatrix}$	$\begin{bmatrix} 0.1164\times10^{1} & -0.2225\times10^{-1} \\ -0.2225\times10^{-1} & 0.1143\times10^{1} \end{bmatrix}$	$\begin{bmatrix} 0.1170\times10^{1} & -0.2526\times10^{-1} \\ -0.2526\times10^{-1} & 0.1149\times10^{1} \end{bmatrix}$
1	$\begin{bmatrix} -0.2192\times10^{0} & 0.1803\times10^{0} \\ 0.1032\times10^{0} & -0.3722\times10^{-1} \end{bmatrix}$	$\begin{bmatrix} -0.2421\times10^{0} & 0.1699\times10^{0} \\ 0.8510\times10^{-1} & -0.5946\times10^{-1} \end{bmatrix}$	$\begin{bmatrix} -0.2431\times10^{0} & 0.1699\times10^{0} \\ 0.8616\times10^{-1} & -0.6208\times10^{-1} \end{bmatrix}$
2	$\begin{bmatrix} 0.2371\times10^{0} & -0.1312\times10^{-1} \\ -0.7013\times10^{-1} & -0.1549\times10^{0} \end{bmatrix}$	$\begin{bmatrix} 0.2587\times10^{0} & 0.8373\times10^{-2} \\ -0.5123\times10^{-1} & -0.1689\times10^{0} \end{bmatrix}$	$\begin{bmatrix} 0.2601\times10^{0} & 0.9936\times10^{-2} \\ -0.5228\times10^{-1} & -0.1700\times10^{0} \end{bmatrix}$
3	$\begin{bmatrix} -0.9443\times10^{-1} & 0.3869\times10^{-1} \\ -0.1054\times10^{0} & 0.1223\times10^{0} \end{bmatrix}$	$\begin{bmatrix} -0.2189\times10^{0} & -0.9026\times10^{-2} \\ -0.1764\times10^{0} & 0.2251\times10^{0} \end{bmatrix}$	$\begin{bmatrix} -0.2200\times10^{0} & -0.8942\times10^{-2} \\ -0.1774\times10^{0} & 0.2269\times10^{0} \end{bmatrix}$
4	$\begin{bmatrix} 0.6768\times10^{-1} & -0.5918\times10^{-1} \\ 0.1412\times10^{0} & -0.3148\times10^{-2} \end{bmatrix}$	$\begin{bmatrix} 0.7693\times10^{-1} & -0.8727\times10^{-1} \\ 0.1508\times10^{0} & -0.8714\times10^{-1} \end{bmatrix}$	$\begin{bmatrix} 0.8587\times10^{-1} & -0.5533\times10^{-1} \\ 0.1598\times10^{0} & -0.9342\times10^{-1} \end{bmatrix}$
5	$\begin{bmatrix} -0.7386\times10^{-1} & 0.6958\times10^{-1} \\ -0.5395\times10^{-1} & -0.4640\times10^{-1} \end{bmatrix}$	$\begin{bmatrix} -0.2146\times10^{0} & 0.7557\times10^{-1} \\ 0.3177\times10^{-1} & -0.4356\times10^{-1} \end{bmatrix}$	$\begin{bmatrix} -0.2225\times10^{0} & 0.9853\times10^{-1} \\ 0.4355\times10^{-1} & -0.2988\times10^{-1} \end{bmatrix}$

putation are shown in Tables III–V and in Figs. 1–3. Table III presents the co-variance matrices Γ_n's for n = 0, 1, 2, 3, 4, 5, which shows that Γ_n converges to zero at n = 5. Table IV presents the impulse response sequences of the approxi-mants of order n = 2, 3, 4, where $\{\hat{H}_{k,2}\}$, $\{\hat{H}_{k,3}\}$, and $\{\hat{H}_{k,4}\}$ are the impulse response sequences of the approximants of order 2, 3, and 4, respectively. This verifies the relations (25). Table V presents the autocorrelation sequences of the approximants of order n = 2, 3, 4, where $\{\hat{R}_{k,2}\}$, $\{\hat{R}_{k,3}\}$, and $\{\hat{R}_{k,4}\}$ are the au-tocorrelation sequences of the approximants of order 2, 3, and 4, respectively. This shows that Theorem 4 holds [see (40)]. The frequency responses of the ap-proximants are shown in Figs. 1 and 2. Figures 1a and b show, respectively, the gains and the phases of the (1, 1)-th elements of the approximants of order n = 1, 2, 3, 4 and the original system. Figures 2a and b show, respectively, the gains and the phases of the (1, 2)-th elements of the approximants of order n = 1, 2, 3, 4 and the original system. In Figs. 1 and 2 the dot–dashed line almost overlaps the solid line. This implies the approximant of order 4 is fitted well to the original system. This is confirmed by Table II, which shows all elements of Γ_4 are of the order of 10^{-2} or less. The graphs for the (2, 1)-th element and the (2, 2)-th element are omitted since the convergence aspects for these elements are similar to those of the (1, 1)-th element and the (1, 2)-th element. Figure 3 plots the poles of the original system and those of the approximants of order 2, 3, 4. It is seen that, for each n = 2, 3, 4, the poles of the n-th-order approximant approximate well 2n dominant poles of the original system.

V.   CONCLUSIONS

We have considered the construction of approximants of a linear discrete-time MIMO system, using two sets of finite data of the impulse response and the autocorrelation sequences. We formulated the least-squares approximation problem, which was reduced to that of solving a linear matrix-valued equation. This equation can be solved recursively by the algorithm, which is closely re-lated to the Levinson algorithm. This algorithm is easily programmable and re-quires less computation time and storage than existing ones. A simulation ex-ample was presented to illustrate the least-squares approximation.

VI.   APPENDIX A: PROOF OF LEMMA 3

Proof of (1). If H(z) is stable, then it is proved that there exists the limit $\Sigma_{k=0}^{\infty} A^k B (A^k B)^T$ as shown in (17a), which is denoted by

$$\hat{K} = \sum_{k=0}^{\infty} A^k B \left(A^k B \right)^T .$$
(59)

Then (59) becomes

$$\hat{K} = BB^T + A \left(\sum_{k=0}^{\infty} A^k B \left(A^k B \right)^T \right) A^T = A\hat{K}A^T + BB^T .$$
(60)

Conversely, assume that (20) holds. Let λ be an eigenvalue of A and let $v*$ be a left eigenvector associated with λ. Then

$$v* A = \lambda v* , \qquad v* \neq 0.$$
(61)

From (20) and (61), it follows

$$v* Kv = v* AKA^T v + v* BB^T v = |\lambda|^2 v* Kv + v* BB^T v ,$$
(62)

which means

$$\left(1 - |\lambda|^2 \right) v* Kv = \|v* B\|^2 \geq 0.$$
(63)

If λ is an unstable eigenvalue of A, that is, $|\lambda| \geq 1$, then (63) implies $v*B = 0$. Therefore,

$$v* [A - \lambda I, B] = 0,$$
(64)

which yields

$$\text{rank } [A - \lambda I, B] < n.$$
(65)

This fact means that λ is an input-decoupling zero; namely, the mode associated with λ is uncontrollable (see Rosenbrock [39]). Hence this unstable mode is absent in the output behavior of H(z).

   Proof of (2). The uniqueness of the solution of (20) comes from the fact that if all the eigenvalues of A lie in the open unit disk, then the matrix equation $K = AKA^T$ has the unique trivial solution $K = 0$.

   Proof of (3). The former part obviously follows from (59) and (60) above. The latter part comes as follows. Let

$$\Delta(n) = \sum_{k=n+1}^{\infty} A^k B \left(A^k B \right)^T . \tag{66}$$

Then from (66), (59) becomes

$$\hat{K} = \sum_{k=0}^{n} A^k B \left(A^k B \right)^T + \Delta(n). \tag{67}$$

Since the sequence $\{\Delta(n)\}$ is monotone decreasing and $\hat{K}$ exists, it follows that

$$\lim_{n \to \infty} \Delta(n) = 0. \tag{68}$$

From (20) we obtain

$$K = AKA^T + BB^T$$

$$AKA^T = A^2 K \left(A^2 \right)^T + AB(AB)^T$$

$$\vdots$$

$$A^n K \left(A^n \right)^T = A^{n+1} K \left(A^{n+1} \right)^T + A^n B \left(A^n B \right)^T . \tag{69}$$

Hence we get

$$K = A^{n+1} K \left(A^{n+1} \right)^T + \sum_{k=0}^{n} A^k B \left(A^k B \right)^T . \tag{70}$$

Combining (67) and (70) gives

$$K - \hat{K} = A^{n+1} K \left(A^{n+1} \right)^T - \Delta(n). \tag{71}$$

Since K is positive-semidefinite, (71) implies

$$K - \hat{K} \geq -\Delta(n). \tag{72}$$

Letting $n \to \infty$ in the above inequality together with (68) yields $K \geq \hat{K}$.

VIII.   APPENDIX B; PROOF OF LEMMA 4

All the properties mentioned in Lemma 4 are not changed by a coordinate transformation. We can assume without loss of generality that the pair $\{A, B\}$ is written in the following reachable canonical form

$$
A = \begin{bmatrix} A_1 & A_3 \\ 0 & A_2 \end{bmatrix}, \quad B = \begin{bmatrix} B_1 \\ 0 \end{bmatrix}, \tag{73}
$$

where the pair $\{A_1, B_1\}$ is reachable (or controllable from the origin). According to the above partition, let

$$
x_t = \begin{bmatrix} x_t^1 \\ x_t^2 \end{bmatrix}, \quad K_0 = \begin{bmatrix} K_0^{11} & K_0^{12} \\ K_0^{21} & K_0^{22} \end{bmatrix},
$$

$$
K_1 = \begin{bmatrix} K_1^{11} & K_1^{12} \\ K_1^{21} & K_1^{22} \end{bmatrix}. \tag{74}
$$

From (38), (39), (73), and (74), we obtain

$$
K_0^{22} = A_2 K_0^{22} A_2^T, \tag{75}
$$

$$
A_2 K_0^{22} = K_1^{22}. \tag{76}
$$

From (75) and (76), it follows

$$
K_0^{22} = A_2 \left(K_1^{22} \right)^T. \tag{77}
$$

Using (76) and (77) yields

$$
E \left\{ \left(x_{t+1}^2 - A_2 x_t^2 \right) \left(x_{t+1}^2 - A_2 x_t^2 \right)^T \right\}
$$

$$
= K_0^{22} - K_1^{22} A_2^T - A_2 \left(K_1^{22} \right)^T + A_2 K_0^{22} A_2^T = 0, \tag{78}
$$

which implies

$$x^2_{t+1} = A_2 x^2_t, \qquad \text{a.e.} \quad -\infty < t < \infty \tag{79}$$

Since $\{x_t\}$ is purely nondeterministic, this means $x_t^2 = 0$ a.e. for all t. Thus we get

$$K^{22}_0 = 0, \qquad K^{21}_0 = 0, \qquad K^{12}_0 = 0. \tag{80}$$

This yields, together with (38) and (74),

$$K^{11}_0 = A_1 K^{11}_0 A^T_1 + B_1 B^T_1. \tag{81}$$

Since the pair $\{A_1, B_1\}$ is reachable, by Parts (1) and (3) of Lemma 3, it follows

$$K^{11}_0 = \sum_{k=0}^{\infty} A^k_1 B_1 \left(A^k_1 B_1 \right)^T, \tag{82}$$

which means, together with (73), (74), and (80),

$$K_0 = \sum_{k=0}^{\infty} A^k B \left(A^k B \right)^T \tag{83}$$

By Part (3) of Lemma 3, this implies that K_0 is the minimal solution of the Lyapunov equation (38) that is symmetric and positive-semidefinite. This completes the proof of Lemma 4.

VIII.   APPENDIX C: PROOF OF VALIDITY
OF THE ALGORITHM (54)

The following notation will be used. For a matrix K, Im K and Ker K denote, in the same order, the image of K and the kernel of K. K^r denotes a reflexive generalized inverse of K, that is, a matrix that satisfies $KK^rK = K$ and $K^rKK^r = K^r$ (see Boullion and Odell [40]).

Using the definition (11) of $K(n)$, we can show that with the proper definitions of the matrices $E(n)$ and $D(n)$,

$$
K(n+1) =
\left[
\begin{array}{ccc|c}
 & & & R_{n+1} \\
 & & & \vdots \\
 & K(n) & & R_1 \\
\hline
R_{-n-1} & \cdots & R_{-1} & R_0
\end{array}
\right]
\left[
\begin{array}{c}
H_{n+1} \\
H_n \\
\vdots \\
H_0
\end{array}
\right]
$$

$$
\times \left[H_{n+1}^T, \ldots, H_0^T \right]
$$

$$
=
\left[
\begin{array}{c|c}
E(n) & D(n)^T \\
\hline
D(n) & K(n)
\end{array}
\right].
\tag{84}
$$

Let

$$
A(n) = \left[A_0(n), \ldots, A_n(n) \right]
\tag{85a}
$$

$$
B(n) = \left[B_n(n), \ldots, B_0(n) \right]
\tag{85b}
$$

$$
C(n) = \left[C_n(n), \ldots, C_0(n) \right],
\tag{85c}
$$

where A(n) satisfies (14b) for the case m= n, and

$$
B(n) = [0, \ldots, 0, I]K(n)^r
\tag{86a}
$$

$$
C(n) = \left[H_n^T, \ldots, H_0^T \right]K(n)^r.
\tag{86b}
$$

Here, $K(n)^r$ is a reflexive generalized inverse of $K(n)$ recursively given by Lemma C.2 below.

The following two lemmas are required

Lemma C.1. Suppose $K(n+1)$ is positive-semidefinite. Then

$$
\text{Im } D(n) \subset \text{Im } K(n),
\tag{87}
$$

$$
\text{Ker } \left\{ \left[0, \ldots, 0, \Delta_n \right] + \Lambda_n \left[H_n^T, \ldots, H_0^T \right] \right\} \supset \text{Ker } K(n)
\tag{88}
$$

where Δ_n and Λ_n are given by (54a) and (54b), respectively.

Proof. It is easy to show that (87) follows from (84) and the positive-semidefiniteness of $K(n + 1)$. From (87) and the symmetry of $K(n)$, it follows

$$\ker D(n)^T \supset \ker K(n).$$
(89)

On the other hand, it holds

$$[\Gamma_n, 0, \ldots, 0, \Delta_n] + \Lambda_n \left[H_{n+1}^T, \ldots, H_0^T \right] = [A(n), 0] K(n + 1)$$
(90)

$$= [A(n), 0] \begin{bmatrix} E(n) & | & D(n)^T \\ - & | & - \\ D(n) & | & K(n) \end{bmatrix}.$$

It is easily shown that (89) and (90) imply (88).

Lemma C.2. Suppose $A(n)$ and Γ_n satisfy (14b) for the case $m = n$, and $K(n)$ is positive-semidefinite. Then a reflexive generalized inverse of $K(n)$ that is symmetric is given by

$$K(n)^r = A(n)^T \Gamma_n^+ A(n) + \begin{bmatrix} 0 & | & 0 \\ - & | & - \\ 0 & | & K(n-1)^r \end{bmatrix}.$$
(91)

By the relation (87) for $n - 1$, it is easy to show that $K(n)^r$ given by (91) satisfies the definition of the reflexive generalized inverse.

From (84) and the above two lemmas, it is easy to derive the following:

$$A(n + 1) = [A(n), 0] - \Delta_n [0, B(n)] - \Lambda_n [0, C(n)]$$
(92a)

$$B(n + 1) = [0, B(n)] - \hat{\Theta}_n^T \Gamma_{n+1}^+ A(n + 1)$$
(92b)

$$C(n + 1) = [0, C(n)] - \hat{\Phi}_n^T \Gamma_{n+1}^+ A(n + 1)$$
(92c)

$$\Gamma_{n+1} = \Gamma_n - \Delta_n \hat{\Theta}_n^T - \Lambda_n \hat{\Phi}_n^T,$$
(92d)

where $\tilde{\Theta}_n$, $\tilde{\Phi}_n$, $\hat{\Theta}_n$ and $\hat{\Phi}_n$ are given as follows:

$$\tilde{\Theta}_n = D(n)^T B(n)^T \tag{93a}$$

$$\tilde{\Phi}_n = D(n)^T C(n)^T - H_{n+1} \tag{93b}$$

$$\hat{\Theta}_n = - A(n+1)[0,...,0,I]^T \tag{93c}$$

$$\hat{\Phi}_n = - A(n+1)\left[H_{n+1}^T,...,H_0^T \right]^T . \tag{93d}$$

Here we employed the following equation, which is derived from (86) and (88):

$$\left[0...0 \ \Delta_n \right] + \Lambda_n \left[H_n^T...H_0^T \right]$$

$$-\{ \Delta_n N(n) + \Lambda_n C(n) \} K(n) = \left\{ \left[0...0 \ \Delta_n \right] + \Lambda_n \left[H_n^T...H_0^T \right] \right\}$$

$$\times \left\{ I - K(n)^r K(n) \right\} = 0. \tag{94}$$

Define

$$\Omega_n = I + C(n)\left[H_n^T...H_0^T \right]^T . \tag{95}$$

Let

$$\left[F_n^T...F_0^T \right] = B(n)K(n), \tag{96a}$$

$$\left[G_n^T...G_0^T \right] = C(n)K(n) - \left[H_n^T...H_0^T \right]. \tag{96b}$$

From the definition of $D(n)$, it follows that

$$D(n)^T = \left[D(n-1)^T, R_{n+1} \right] - H_{n+1}\left[H_n^T...H_0^T \right] \tag{97}$$

Equations (14b) and (84) give

$$D(n-1)^T = -\left[A_1(n)...A_n(n)\right]K(n-1). \tag{98}$$

It follows from (96), (84), and (86) that

$$\left[F_n^T \ ... \ F_1^T\right] = B(n) \begin{bmatrix} K(n-1) \\ R_{-n} \ ... \ R_{-1} \end{bmatrix}$$

$$- B(n) \begin{bmatrix} H_n \\ \vdots \\ H_0 \end{bmatrix} \begin{bmatrix} H_n^T \ ... \ H_1^T \end{bmatrix}$$

$$= \left[B_n(n) \ ... \ B_1(n)\right]K(n-1)$$

$$+ B_0(n)\left[R_{-n} \ ... \ R_{-1}\right]$$

$$- C_0(n)^T\left[H_n^T \ ... \ H_1^T\right], \tag{99}$$

which implies

$$D(n-1)^T \begin{bmatrix} B_n(n)^T \\ \vdots \\ B_1(n)^T \end{bmatrix} = \left[A_1(n)...A_{(n)}\right] \begin{bmatrix} R_n \\ \vdots \\ R_1 \end{bmatrix} \begin{matrix} B_0(n)^T \\ \\ \\ \end{matrix}$$

$$- \begin{bmatrix} H_n \\ \vdots \\ H_1 \end{bmatrix} C_0(n) - \begin{bmatrix} F_n \\ \vdots \\ F_1 \end{bmatrix} \Bigg\}. \tag{100}$$

Equation (93a) therefore becomes, from (97), (100), (54a), (54b), and (54c),

$$\Theta_n = D(n)^T B(n)^T$$

$$= \Delta_n B_0(n) + \Lambda_n C_0(n) - \sum_{k=1}^{n} A_k(n)F_{n+1-k}$$

$$= \Theta_n - \sum_{k=1}^{n} A_k(n)F_{n+1-k}. \tag{101}$$

Here we made use of the fact that $B_0(n) = B_0(n)^T$. It follows from (96), (84), and (95) that

$$\left[G_n^T \cdots G_1^T \right] = \left[C_n(n) \cdots C_1(n) \right] K(n-1)$$
$$+ C_0(n \{ R_{-n} \cdots R_{-1}]$$
$$- \Omega_n \left[H_n^T \cdots H_1^T \right], \tag{102}$$

which means, together with (98),

$$D(n-1)^T \begin{bmatrix} C_n(n)^T \\ \vdots \\ C_1(n)^T \end{bmatrix} = \left[A_1(n) \cdots A_n(n) \right] \left\{ \begin{bmatrix} R_n \\ \vdots \\ R_1 \end{bmatrix} C_0(n)^T \right.$$

$$\left. - \begin{bmatrix} H_n \\ \vdots \\ H_1 \end{bmatrix} \Omega_n^T - \begin{bmatrix} G_n \\ \vdots \\ G_1 \end{bmatrix} \right\} \tag{103}$$

Equation (93b) therefore becomes, from (97), (103), (95), (54a), (54b), and (54d),

$$\Phi = D(n)^T C(n)^T - H_{n+1}$$
$$= \Delta_n C_0(n)^T + \Lambda_n \Omega_n - \sum_{k=1}^{n} A_k(n)G_{n+1-k}$$
$$= \Phi_n - \sum_{k=1}^{n} A_k(n)G_{n+1-k}. \tag{104}$$

Here, we made use of the fact $\Omega_n = \Omega_n^T$.
On the other hand, since

$$A(n+1)K(n+1) = \left[\Gamma_{n+1}, 0, \ldots, 0 \right], \tag{105}$$

it follows from (84), (92), (93a), and (93b) that

$$\left[\Gamma_{n+1},0,\ldots,0\right]$$
$$= \left[\Gamma_n,0,\ldots,0,\Delta_n\right] + \Lambda_n\left[0,H_n^T,\ldots,H_0^T\right]$$
$$- \left[\Delta_n\widetilde{\Theta}_n^T + \Lambda_n\Phi_n^T, \Delta_n B(n)K(n) + \Lambda_n C(n)K(n)\right], \tag{106}$$

which implies, together with (96),

$$\left[\Gamma_{n+1},0,\ldots,0\right] = \left[\Gamma_{n+1},0,\ldots,0,\Delta_n\right]$$
$$- \left[\Delta_n\widetilde{\Theta}_n^T + \Lambda_n\Phi_n^T, \Delta_n\left[F_n^T \ \cdots \ F_0^T\right]\right.$$
$$\left. + \Lambda_n\left[G_n^T \ \cdots \ G_0^T\right]\right]. \tag{107}$$

Therefore, it holds

$$\Delta_n\left[F_n^T \ \cdots \ F_1^T\right] + \Lambda_n\left[G_n^T \ \cdots \ G_1^T\right] = 0. \tag{108}$$

Using (101), (104), and (108), we obtain

$$\Delta_n\left(\widetilde{\Theta}_n^T - \Theta_n^T\right) + \Lambda_n\left(\widetilde{\Phi}_n^T - \Phi_n^T\right) = 0, \tag{109}$$

which yields, together with (92d),

$$\Gamma_{n+1} = \Gamma_n - \Delta_n\Theta_n^T - \Lambda_n\Phi_n^T. \tag{110}$$

It follows from (92a), (54b), (86a), (86b), and (94a) that

$$A(n+1)\left[H_{n+1}^T,\ldots,H_0^T\right]^T$$
$$= [A(n),0]\left[H_{n+1}^T,\ldots,H_0^T\right]^T$$
$$- \Delta_n[0,B(n)]\left[H_{n+1}^T,\ldots,H_0^T\right]^T$$

$$-\Lambda_n[0,C(n)]\left[H_{n+1}^T,\ldots,H_0^T\right]^T$$

$$=A(n)\left[H_{n+1}^T,\ldots,H_1^T\right]^T-\Delta_n B(n)\left[H_n^T,\ldots,H_0^T\right]^T$$

$$-\Lambda_n C(n)\left\{H_n^T,\ldots,H_0^T\right\}^T$$

$$-\Lambda_n-\Lambda_n[0\ldots0\ \ I]K(n)^T\left[H_n^T,\ldots,H_0^T\right]^T$$

$$-\Lambda_n C(n)\left\{H_n^T,\ldots,H_0^T\right\}^T$$

$$=-\Delta_n[0\ldots\ \ 0\ I]C(n)^T$$

$$-\Lambda_n\left\{I+C(n)\left[H_n^T,\ldots,H_0^T\right]^T\right\}$$

$$=-\Delta_n C_0(n)^T-\Lambda_n\Omega_n, \tag{111}$$

which, together with (93d) and (54d), implies $\hat{\Phi}=\Phi_n$. It follows from (92a), (93c), and (54c) that

$$\hat{\Theta}_n=-A(n+1)[0\ldots0\ I]^T$$

$$=\Delta_n[0,B(n)][0\ldots0\ I]^T$$

$$+\Lambda_n[0,C(n)][0\ldots0\ I]^T$$

$$=\Delta_n B_0(n)+\Lambda_n C_0(n)=\Theta_n. \tag{112}$$

Using (95), (92c), (93d), and the fact that $\hat{\Phi}_n=\Phi_n$, we obtain

$$\Omega_{n+1}-\Omega_n=\{C(n+1)-[0,C(n)]\}\left[H_{n+1}^T,\ldots,H_0^T\right]^T$$

$$=-\hat{\Phi}_n\Gamma_{n+1}^+A(n+1)\left[H_{n+1}^T,\ldots,H_0^T\right]^T$$

$$= \hat{\Phi}_n^T \Gamma_{n+1}^+ \hat{\Phi}_n = \Phi_n^T \Gamma_{n+1}^+ \Phi_n \tag{113}$$

which becomes (54f). This completes the derivation of the algorithm (54).

ACKNOWLEDGMENT

The author would like to thank Toshiyuki Kojima for his cooperation in the computer programming.

REFERENCES

1.   E. J. DAVISON, "A Method for Simplifying Linear Dynamical Systems," *IEEE Trans. Autom. Control* AC-11, 93–101 (1966).
2.   S. A. MARSHALL, "An Approximation Method for Reducing the Order of a Linear System," *Control* 10, 642–643 (1966).
3.   M. R. CHIDAMBARA, "On a Method for Simplifying Linear Constant Systems," *IEEE Trans. Autom. Control* AC-12, 119–121 (1967).
4.   L. MEIER, III and D. G. LUENBERGER, "Approximation of Linear Constant Systems," *IEEE Trans. Autom. Control* AC-12, 585–588 (1967).
5.   J. B. RIGGS and T. F. EDGAR, "Least Squares Reduction of Linear Systems Using Impulse Response," *Int. J. Control* 20, 213–223 (1974).
6.   D. A. WILSON, "Optimal Solution of Model-Reduction Problem," *Proc. Inst. Electr. Eng.* 117, 1161–1165 (1970).
7.   D. A. WILSON, "Model Reduction for Multivariable Systems," *Int. J. Control* 20, 57–64 (1974).
8.   J. D. APLEVICH, "Approximation of Discrete Linear Systems," *Int. J. Control* 17, 565–575 (1973).
9.   C. F. CHEN and L. S. SHIEF, "A Novel Approach to Linear Model Simplification," *Int. J. Control* 8, 561–570 (1968).
10. C. F. CHEN and L. S. SHIEF, "An Algebraic Method for Control System Design," *Int. J. Control* 11, 717–739 (1970).
11. C. F. CHEN, "Model Reduction of Multivariable Control Systems by Means of Matrix Continued Fractions," *Int. J. Control* 20, 225–238 (1974).
12. A. J. TETHER, "Construction of Minimal Linear Model from Finite Input-Output Data," *IEEE Trans. Autom. Control* AC-15 427–436 (1970).
13. J. RISSANEN, "Recursive Identification of Linear Systems," *SIAM J. Control* 9, 420–430 (1971).
14. D. J. AUDLEY, "A Method of Constructing Minimal Approximate Realization of Linear Input-Output Behavior, *Automatica* 13, 409–415 (1977).
15. Y. SHAMASH, "Stable Reduced-Order Model Using Padé-Type Approximations," *IEEE Trans. Autom. Control* AC-12, 615–616 (1974).
16. Y. SHAMASH, "Linear System Reduction Using Padé-Approximation to Allow Retention of Dominant Modes," *Int. J. Control* 21, 257–272 (1975).
17. Y. SHAMASH, "Multivariable System Reduction via Modal Methods and Padé Approximation," *IEEE Trans. Autom. Control* AC-20, 815–817 (1975).

18. L. S. SHIEF and Y. J. WEI, "A Mixed Method for Multivariable Reduction," *IEEE Trans. Autom. Control* **AC-20**, 429–432 (1975).

19. M. F. HUTTON and B. FRIEDLANT, "Routh Approximations for Reducing Order of Linear, Time-Invariant Systems," *IEEE Trans. Autom. Control* **AC-20**, 329–337 (1975).

20. G. LEDWICH and J. B. MOORE, "Minimal Stable Partial Realization," *Automatica* **12**, 497–506 (1976).

21. B. C. MOORE, "Principal Component Analysis in Linear Systems: Controlability, Observability and Model Reduction," *IEEE Trans. Autom. Control* **AC-26**, 17–32 (1981).

22. L. PERNEBO and L. M. SILVERMAN, "Model Reduction via Balanced State Space Representations," *IEEE Trans. Autom. Control* **AC-27**, 382–387 (1982).

23. S. KUNG, "Optimal Hankel-Norm Reduction: Scalar Systems," *Proc. 1980 J. Autom. Control Conf., San Francisco*, Paper FA8.D (1980).

24. K. GLOVER, "All Optimal Hankel-Norm Approximations of Linear Multivariable Systems and Their L^∞-Error Bounds," *Int. J. Control* **39**, 1115–1193 (1984).

25. C. T. MULLIS and R. A. ROBERTS, "The Use of Second-Order Information in the Approximation of Discrete-Time Linear Systems," *IEEE Trans. Acoust., Speech, Signal Process.* **ASSP-24**, 226–238 (1976).

26. Y. INOUYE, "Approximation of Multivariable Linear Systems with Impulse Response and Autocorrelation Sequences," *Automatica* **19**, 265–277 (1983).

27. A. YOUSUFF, D. A. WAGIE, and R. E. SKELTON, "Linear System Approximation via Covariance Equivalent Realization," *J. Math. Anal. Appl.* **106**, 91–115 (1985).

28. D. A. WAGIE and R. E. SKELTON, "A Projection Approach to Covariance Equivalent Realizations of Discrete Systems," *IEEE Trans. Autom. Control* **AC-31**, 1114–1120 (1986).

29. R. E. SKELTON and E. G. COLLINS, JR., "Set of q-Markov Covariance Equivalent Models of Discrete Systems," *Int. J. Control* **46**, 1–12 (1987).

30. U. B. DESAI and D. PAL, "A Transformation Approach to Stochastic Model Reduction," *IEEE Trans. Autom. Control* **AC-29**, 1097–1100 (1984).

31. U. B. DESAI, D. PAL, and R. KIRKPATRICK, "A Realization Approach to Stochastic Model Reduction," *Int. J. Control* **42**, 821–838 (1985).

32. E. A. JONCKHEERE and J. W. HELTON, "Power Spectrum Reduction by Optimal Hankel Norm Approximation of the Phase of the Outer Spectral Factor," *IEEE Trans. Autom. Control* **AC-30**, 1192–1201 (1985).

33. Y. INOUYE, "Modeling of Multichannel Time Series and Extrapolation of Matrix-Valued Autocorrelation Sequences," *IEEE Trans. Acoust., Speech, Signal Process.* **ASSP-31**, 45–55 (1983).

34. S. BARNETT, "Matrices in Control Theory," Van Nostrand Reinhold, New York 1971.

35. G. GOLUB and W. KAHAN, "Calculating the Singular Values and Pseudo-Inverse of a Matrix," *J. SIAM Numer. Anal.* **B-2**, 205–224 (1965).

36. J. J. DONGARRA, C. B. MOLER, J. R. BUNCH, and G. W. STEWART, "LINPAk Users' Guide," SIAM Press, Philadelphia , 1979.

37. M. MORF, B. DICKINSON, T. KAILATH, and A. VIEIRA, "Efficient Solution of Covariance Equations for Linear Prediction," *IEEE Trans. Acoust., Speech, Signal Process.* **ASSP-25**, 429–433 (1977).

38. B. FRIEDLANDER, M. MORF, T. KAILATH, and L. LJUNG, "New Inversion Formulas for Matrices Classified in Terms of their Distance from Toeplitz Matrices," *Linear Algebra Appl.* **27**, 31–60 (1979).

39. H. H. ROSENBROCK, "State-Space and Multivariable Theory," Nelson, London, 1970.

40. T. L. BOULLION and P. L. ODELL, "Generalized Inverse Matrices," Wiley, New York, 1971.

ALGORITHMS FOR DISCRETE-TIME ADAPTIVE CONTROL OF RAPIDLY TIME-VARYING SYSTEMS

R. J. EVANS, XIANYA XIE, C. ZHANG, and Y. C. SOH

Department of Electrical and Computer Engineering
The University of Newcastle
New South Wales 2308, Australia

I. INTRODUCTION

Adaptive control algorithms depend critically upon real-time knowledge of plant parameters; so it is important to consider techniques for estimating on-line the parameters of a time-varying system. This problem is of considerable practical interest in the areas of signal processing, estimation, system identification, and adaptive control. It is immediately clear that a key aspect of this problem is the conflict between the ability to rapidly respond to parameter changes versus the ability to improve the signal-to-noise ratio. In other words, accurate estimation of system parameters demands a low 'bandwidth' system, whereas the ability to follow rapid changes in parameters demands high 'bandwidth.' Consequently most of the successful algorithms for estimating time-varying systems can be thought of as variable-bandwidth filters where the bandwidth is either data dependent or varies according to some *a priori* model of the parameter time variations. Parameter estimators based on a stochastic linear parameter model and employing a Kalman filter [1] are of the latter type, whereas most of the variable forgetting factor schemes [2, 3] and covariance resetting schemes [4, 5] are of the former type. Below we consider these techniques and their properties in more detail.

In adaptive control of time-varying systems there are basically two lines of research. One is to study the performance of fairly simple adaptive controllers such as the self-tuning regulator [6] on time-varying plants [7–9, 30]. In this area the results of Anderson and Johnstone [9], Middleton and Goodwin [8], and Kreisselmeier [30] are of particular interest. These papers essentially show that for certain classes of slow, small parameter variations the standard adaptive controller structures will remain stable and achieve an output tracking error related to the size of the parameter variations. The two main types of parameter variation studied in these results are drift and jump. A drift parameter remains within an ϵ neighborhood of some nominal parameter value for a reasonably large number of time samples and ϵ grows at most linearly. Jump parameters, on the other hand, are assumed to make step changes at infrequent intervals.

The second line of research is to try to devise new algorithms that will perform well for plants with larger and more rapid time variations. These algorithms are the subject of this article and are typified by the techniques in [5, 10, 11, 28].

In Section II we consider several parameter estimation algorithms that may be suitable for rapidly time-varying systems. We then move on in Section III to consider the application of these techniques to adaptive control. Finally, in Section IV we examine theoretical convergence properties of one algorithm.

II.   RECURSIVE PARAMETER ESTIMATION FOR TIME-VARYING SYSTEMS

In this section we consider several schemes for recursive estimation of the parameters of a sampled linear time-varying plant whose output y(t) is given in the form

$$y(t+1) = \theta'(t)\phi(t),$$

where $\theta'(t) \triangleq [\theta_1(t), \theta_2(t), ..., \theta_l(t)]$ is an l-dimensional time-varying parameter and $\phi'(t) \triangleq [y(t), ..., y(t-n+1), u(t), ..., u(t-m+1]$ is an $l = (n + m)$-dimensional vector of past system inputs and outputs. The immediate problem is to compute estimates $\hat{\theta}(t)$ that remain in some sense "close to" $\theta(t)$ for all time, given only plant input/output data samples. Now if $\theta(t) = \theta$, a constant, then the least-squares method determines the estimate $\hat{\theta}$ that minimizes the convex cost

$$J(\theta) = \sum_{t=1}^{N} [y(t) - \theta'\phi(t-1)]^2$$

after N time samples. It is well known that $\hat{\theta}$ can be computed recursively by

$$\hat{\theta}(t+1) = \hat{\theta}(t) + K(t+1)[y(t+1) - \hat{\theta}'(t)\phi(t)]$$

where the gain matrix

$$K(t+1) = \frac{P(t)\phi(t)}{1 + \phi'(t)P(t)\phi(t)}$$

and

$$P(t+1) = P(t) - \frac{P(t)\phi(t)\phi'(t)P(t)}{[1 + \phi'(t)P(t)\phi(t)]}$$

It is not difficult to show that for $P(0)$ suitably chosen these recursions minimize $J(\theta)$ for every t. Furthermore, asymptotically the gain matrix $K(t)$ decreases so that the algorithm takes equal notice of all data, past and new, and the 'bandwidth' goes to 0 as $1/t$.

This situation is clearly unsatisfactory if θ is time-varying, and several straightforward modifications have been proposed to the basic recursive least-squares technique. One obvious method is to stop updating P after a certain number of iterations, or to set $K(t) = \alpha I$, $0 < \alpha < 2$, which is a gradient scheme. For these cases the gain no longer goes to 0, and, as shown in [8], drift and the jump parameter can be tolerated. Some other useful methods are:

(1) Sliding window filter [1, 12]. The idea here is to perform the least-squares fit to the last N data points only. Thus as a new data point arrives at time t, the data point at time $t - N$ is discarded and the current best estimate of $\theta(t)$ is based on the window of data from t back until time $t - N$. This has the effect of stopping $K(t)$ becoming too small and keeping the estimator 'bandwidth' finite. In [1] it is shown that this estimate is given recursively as

$$\hat{\theta}(t+1) = \hat{\theta}(t) + \bar{K}(t+1)\left[y(t+1) - \hat{\theta}'(t)\phi(t)\right]$$

$$\bar{K}(t+1) = \frac{\bar{P}(t)\phi(t)}{[1 + \phi'(t)\bar{P}(t)\phi(t)]}$$

$$\bar{P}(t+1) = \bar{P}(t) - \frac{\bar{P}(t)\phi(t)\phi'(t)\bar{P}(t)}{[1 + \phi'(t)\bar{P}(t)\phi(t)]}$$

$$\hat{\theta}(t+1) = \hat{\theta}(t+1) - K(t+1)[y(t+1-N)$$

$$- \hat{\theta}'(t+1)\phi(t-N)]$$

$$K(t+1) = \frac{P(t)\phi(t-N)}{[1 + \phi'(t-N)P(t)\phi(t-N)]}$$

$$P(t+1) = P(t) + \frac{P(t)\phi(t-N)\phi'(\bar{t}N)P(t)}{[1 + \phi'(t-N)P(t)\phi(t-N)]}.$$

Here $\hat{\theta}(t+1)$ is the estimate based on the last N + 1 data points given the new data at time t + 1, and $\hat{\theta}(t + 1)$ is the estimate after the data point at t + 1 − N is removed. The main disadvantages of this method are that the last N data points must be remembered, and the choice of N is dependent on the rate of time variation in θ. Thus if the bandwidth of $\theta(t)$ varies, then the window size N should vary. This filter gives equal weight to the past N data points and zero weight to all other data.

(2) Fading memory [1, 2, 12]. The idea in this case is to take more notice of recent data and place an exponentially decreasing weight on old data. This is accomplished by introducing a "forgetting factor" $0 < \alpha < 1$ as follows:

$$\hat{\theta}(t+1) = \hat{\theta}(t) + K(t+1)\left[y(t+1) - \hat{\theta}'(t)\phi(t)\right]$$

$$K(t+1) = \frac{P(t)\phi(t)}{[\alpha + \phi'(t)P(t)\phi(t)]}$$

$$P(t+1) = -\frac{1}{\alpha}\frac{P(t)\phi(t)\phi'(t)P(t)}{[\alpha + \phi'(t)P(t)\phi(t)]}$$

$$= \frac{1}{\alpha}[I - K(t+1)\phi'(t)]P(t).$$

It can be shown that in this case with θ constant, $\hat{\theta}$ minimizes the cost

$$\sum_{t=1}^{N} \alpha^{N-t}[y(t) - \theta'\phi(t-1)]^2.$$

when $\alpha = 1$ this algorithm becomes the ordinary least-squares algorithm above, and, as we have seen, this has decreasing 'bandwidth' or equivalently increasing memory and P(t) approaches 0 for large t. The memory of the algorithm above is approximately $2/(1 - \alpha)$. Thus an exponential forgetting estimator is a bit like a sliding memory estimator with window length $N = 2/(1 - \alpha)$. It also suffers from the estimator windup problem, where the P matrix will grow if the input data are not sufficiently rich, i.e., if $P(t)\phi(t)$ is zero or very small. This causes the gain vector K to grow, so that when a parameter changes the algorithm overacts and tends to oscillate for a period of time before it once again settles down. This problem makes the standard forgetting factor method unusable in practice.

Many techniques, such as variable forgetting factors, covariance matrix resetting, constant trace algorithms, and, more recently, directional forgetting have been introduced to solve this problem.

(3) Variable forgetting factor [2, 3]. The key idea is to observe that if the prediction error $[y(t + 1) - \hat{\theta}'(t)\phi(t)]$ is small, then things are going along satisfactorily and α should be near 1 to retain as much information as possible. If, however, the prediction error is large, then the memory should be reduced by reducing α, thus increasing the estimator bandwidth and allowing the estimator to quickly respond. In order to achieve this, an information measure $\Sigma(t)$ is introduced in [3] and this is used to determine $\alpha(t)$ as follows:

$$\hat{\theta}(t + 1) = \hat{\theta}(t) + K(t + 1)\left[y(t + 1) - \hat{\theta}'(t)\phi(t)\right]$$

$$K(t + 1) = \frac{P(t)\phi(t)}{[\alpha(t + 1) + \phi(t)P(t)\phi(t)]}$$

$$P(t + 1) = \frac{1}{\alpha(t + 1)}[1 - K(t + 1)\phi'(t)]P(t)$$

$$\alpha(t + 1) = 1 - \frac{1}{\Sigma(t)}[1 - \phi'(t)K(t + 1)]$$

$$\times \left[y(t + 1) - \hat{\theta}'(t)\phi(t)\right]^2$$

if $\alpha(t + 1) < \alpha_{min}$, then $\alpha(t + 1) = \alpha_{min}$.

The aim of this algorithm is to keep the information measure $\Sigma(t)$ constant at Σ_0, where

$$\Sigma(t) = \alpha(t)\Sigma(t - 1) + [1 - \phi'(t - 1)K(t)]e^2(t)$$

and

$$e^2(t) \triangleq \left[y(t) - \hat{\theta}'(t - 1)\phi(t - 1)\right]^2.$$

This produces an estimator with a variable memory

$$N(t) = \frac{\Sigma_0}{[1 - \phi'(t-1)K(t)]e^2(t)},$$

which ensures that P(t) remains bounded, thus preventing the estimator windup problem described above.

(4) Constant trace algorithms [13]. The aim of this approach is to control the growth of P by normalizing it with the trace of P, tr[P], at every step. The algorithm has been found to work well in practice for slowly time-varying systems

$$\hat{\theta}(t+1) = \hat{\theta}(t) + K(t+1)\left[y(t+1) - \hat{\theta}'(t)\phi(t)\right]$$

$$K(t+1) = \frac{P(t)\phi(t)}{[1 + \phi'(t)P(t)\phi(t)]}$$

$$\bar{P}(t+1) = P(t) - \frac{P(t)\phi(t)\phi'(t)P(t)}{1 + \phi'(t)P(t)\phi(t) + \bar{C}\phi'(t)\phi(t)}$$

$$P(t+1) = C_1 \frac{\bar{P}(t)}{tr[\bar{P}(t)]} + C_2 I,$$

where $C_1 > 0$, $C_2, \bar{C} > 0$ and with $C_1/C_2 \gg 1$ (typically 10^4), and further

$$C_1 \gg max\left[\frac{1}{\phi'(t)\phi(t)}\right]$$

and

$$\bar{C} \cong \frac{1}{\phi'(t)\phi(t)}$$

for typical values of $\phi(t)$.

(5) Directional forgetting [14]. The key idea of this recent approach is to forget information only in the directions where new information is gathered. Thus this estimator has a different memory length in different directions, and the size of these memories will vary depending on the amount of information arriv-

ing (just as in the variable forgetting factor algorithms). The directional forgetting estimate satisfies

$$\hat{\theta}(t+1) = \hat{\theta}(t) + K(t+1)\left[y(t+1) - \hat{\theta}'(t)\phi(t)\right]$$

$$K(t+1) = \frac{P(t)\phi(t)}{V(t+1) + \phi'(t)P(t)\phi(t)[1 - a(t+1)V(t+1)]}$$

$$P(t+1) = P(t) - \frac{P(t)\phi(t)\phi'(t)P(t)}{\left[\dfrac{1}{V(t+1)} - a(t+1)\right]^{-1} + \phi'(t)P(t)\phi(t)}$$

$$a(t+1) = 0, \qquad \text{for } a_d(t+1) < 0$$

$$= a_d(t+1), \qquad \text{for } 0 < a_d(t+1) < \frac{1}{\phi'(t)P(t)\phi(t)}$$

$$= \{\phi'(t)P(t)\phi(t)\}^{-1}, \text{ for } [\phi'P\phi]^{-1} < a_d \leq V^{-1}(t+1) + [\phi'P\phi]^{-1}$$

$$= 0, \qquad \text{for } a_d > V^{-1}(t+1) + [\phi'P\phi]^{-1}$$

$$\delta_d(t+1) = \frac{\left[\dfrac{\phi'(t)P(t)P(t)P(t)\phi(t)}{\phi'(t)P(t)P(t)\phi(t)} - a(t+1)\right]}{[\phi'(t)P(t)P(t)\phi(t)]}$$

$$a_d(t+1) = V^{-1}(t+1) \frac{\delta_d(t+1)}{\delta_d(t+1)\phi'(t)P(t)\phi(t) - 1},$$

where $V(t+1)$ is an estimate of the variance of the prediction error.

(6) Stochastic modeling. For this approach we assume that the time-varying parameters can be modeled by a stochastic difference equation of the form

$$\theta(t+1) = F(t)\theta(t) + \omega(t),$$

where $F(t)$ are known matrices and $\omega(t)$ is an independent identically distributed (i.i.d.) sequence with zero mean and covariance $Q(t)$. We also let the unknown linear plant satisfy the equation

$$y(t + 1) = \theta'(t)\phi(t) + \mu(t)$$

where $\mu(t)$ is i.i.d. with variance $\Omega(t)$.

Now the Kalman filter equations [15] are directly applicable and

$$\hat{\theta}(t + 1) = F(t)\hat{\theta}(t) + K(t + 1)\left[y(t + 1) - \hat{\theta}'(t)\phi(t)\right]$$

$$K(t + 1) = \frac{F(t)P(t)\phi(t)}{[\Omega(t) + \phi'(t)P(t)\phi(t)]}$$

$$P(t + 1) = F(t)P(t)F'(t) + Q(t)$$

$$- F(t)P(t)\frac{\phi(t)\phi'(t)}{[\Omega(t) + \phi'(t)P(t)\phi(t)]}P(t)F'(t).$$

It is interesting to note that for $Q(t) = 0$, $\Omega(t) = 1$ and $F(t) = I$ (i.e., the unknown parameters are assumed constant), then these equations are equivalent to the least-squares estimator, and for $Q(t) = (1/a - 1)$ $[I - K(t + 1)\phi'(t)]P(t)$, $\Omega(t) = a$, and $F(t) = I$ the equations become the least-squares system with exponential forgetting [1].

The Kalman filtering approach is applicable to rapidly time-varying systems, but only if the time-variation model is known. The other techniques described so far are generally applicable only to slowly varying systems, systems with drift parameters, and possibly systems with jump parameters. For rapidly varying systems a technique along the line of that developed in [5, 10, 11, 28] is required. We will now describe this method and then go on in Section III to consider its application to adaptive control.

(7) Covariance resetting and restricted complexity modeling. Assume that the plant can be described by the time-varying model

$$y(t + 1) = a_1(t)y(t) + \dots + a_n(t)y(t - n + 1)$$

$$+ b_1(t)u(t) + \dots + b_m(t)u(t - m + 1), \tag{1}$$

where y and u are the plant output and control variables, respectively. $a_i(t)$, $b_j(t)$ $(i = 1, \dots, n; j = 1, \dots, m)$ are the unknown time-varying parameters, with n and m assumed to be known. We now use the following restricted complexity time-varying model to approximate the real plant

$$y(t + 1) = \left(a_{10} + ta_{11}\right)y(t) + \dots + \left(a_{n0} + ta_{n1}\right)y(t - n + 1)$$

$$+ \left(b_{10} + tb_{11}\right)u(t) + \dots + \left(b_{m0} + tb_{m1}\right)u(t - m + 1). \tag{2}$$

Defining the $2(m + n) \times 1$ estimated vector

$$\hat{\theta}'(t) \overset{\Delta}{=} \left(\hat{\theta}'_1(t), \hat{\theta}'_2(t) \right), \tag{3}$$

where

$$\hat{\theta}'_1(t) \overset{\Delta}{=} \left(\hat{a}_{10}, \dots, \hat{a}_{n0}, \hat{b}_{10}, \dots, \hat{b}_{m0} \right)$$

$$\hat{\theta}'_2(t) \overset{\Delta}{=} \left(\hat{a}_{11}, \dots, \hat{a}_{n1}, \hat{b}_{11}, \dots, \hat{b}_{m1} \right).$$

and the $2(m + n) \times 1$ augmented measurable information vector

$$\phi'(t) \overset{\Delta}{=} \left(\theta'_1(t), t\phi'_1(t) \right) \tag{4}$$

and where

$$\theta'_1(t) \overset{\Delta}{=} (y(t), y(t - n + 1), u(t), \dots, u(t - m + 1)),$$

then the parameter estimation algorithm is given by

$$e(t) = y(t) - \hat{\theta}'(t - 1)\phi(t - 1)$$

$$\hat{\theta}(t + 1) = \hat{\theta}(t) + \frac{P(t - 1)\phi(t)e(t + 1)}{\alpha + \phi'(t)P(t - 1)\phi(t)}$$

$$P(t - 1) = \frac{1}{\alpha}\left(P(t - 1) - \frac{P(t - 1)\phi(t)\phi'(t)P(t - 1)}{\alpha + \phi'(t)P(t - 1)\phi(t)} \right) \tag{5}$$

where $\alpha \in (0, 1)$ is a forgetting factor.

At the start of the computation $t = t_1 = 1$, $P(-1) = K_0 I$, where I is the $2(m + n) \times 2(m + n)$ identity matrix and $K_0 > 0$.

As computation proceeds, we determine t_1 by $t_1 = t - kT$ when $kT < t < (k + 1)T$, $k = 0, 1, 2, \dots$, where T is defined as the resetting period. When $t = kT$, we first compute all the variables and then reset $\hat{\theta}(t)$, t_1, and $P(t - 1)$ as follows:

$$t_1 = 0$$

$$\hat{\theta}(kT) = \begin{bmatrix} I_1 & TI_1 \\ 0 & I_1 \end{bmatrix} \hat{\theta}(kT^-)$$

$$P(kT-1) = \begin{bmatrix} I_1 & TI_1 \\ 0 & I_1 \end{bmatrix} P(kT^- - 1) \begin{bmatrix} I_1 & 0 \\ TI_1 & I_1 \end{bmatrix},$$

(6)

where kT^- means the time just before resetting and I_1 and 0 are the $(m + n) \times (m + n)$ identity matrix and null matrix, respectively.

Remarks.

(1) If we know *a priori* that some parameters, say $a_2(t)$, $b_1(t)$ are constant or only slowly time varying, then we can use the simplified time-varying model

$$
\begin{aligned}
y(t+1) = & \left(a_{10} + ta_{11} \right) y(t) + a_2 y(t-1) \\
& + \left(a_{30} + ta_{31} \right) y(t-2) + \dots \\
& + b_1 u(t) + \left(b_{20} + tb_{21} \right) u(t-1) + \dots
\end{aligned}
$$

(7)

to approximate the real plant. In this case, the dimensions of $\hat{\theta}(t)$, $\phi(t)$, and $P(t)$ accordingly reduce, which results in a considerable reduction in computational effort.

(2) We can see that $P(kT - 1)$ can be determined uniquely from $P(kT^- - 1)$ and vice versa; so this resetting procedure retains all the information contained in the P matrix.

III.   ADAPTIVE CONTROL

Most of the adaptive control algorithms used in practice and studied in the literature are based on the idea of "certainty equivalence" [15]. Consider a controller design procedure such as pole placement or one step ahead [15], which achieves satisfactory performance on a plant with known parameters. The adaptive controller simply uses estimated parameters in place of the nominal known parameters in this design. Thus any of the estimators described above can be used for adaptive control.

Adaptive controllers are basically classified into two categories: direct adaptive controllers and indirect adaptive controllers, depending on how the parameters are used in the controller design. In a direct control algorithm the plant model is parametrized so that the parameters of the controller are estimated directly, whereas in an indirect control algorithm the plant is estimated and then a suitable controller design method is applied to the estimated plant to obtain the controller.

In this section we describe conventional direct and indirect adaptive controllers and also discuss some practical aspects of adaptive control system design.

A.   DIRECT ADAPTIVE CONTROL

Consider a plant in the form

$$A\left(q^{-1}\right)y(t) = B\left(q^{-1}\right)u(t), \tag{8}$$

where q^{-1} is a backward shifting operator. $A(q^{-1}) = 1 + a_1 q^{-1} + \ldots + a_n q^{-n}$, $B(q^{-1}) = b_1 q^{-1} + \ldots + b_m q^{-m}$ are polynomials in q^{-1}, and $b_1 \neq 0$. Given a specified stable reference model

$$A_m\left(q^{-1}\right)y_m(t) = B_m\left(q^{-1}\right)y*(t), \tag{9}$$

where $y*(t)$ is the system reference input, $y_m(t)$ is the reference model output to which the desired system output follows, and $A_m(q^{-1}) = 1 + a_{m1}q^{-1} + \ldots + a_{m\bar{n}}q^{-\bar{n}}$, $B_m(q^{-1}) = b_{m1}q^{-1} + \ldots + b_{m\bar{m}}q^{\bar{m}}$ are specified polynomials in q^{-1}, then there exist unique polynomials $F(q^{-1}) = 1 + f_1 q^{-1} + \ldots + f_{\bar{n}-n}q^{-\bar{n}+n}$ and $G(q^{-1}) = g_0 + g_1 q^{-1} + \ldots + g_{n-1}q^{-n+1}$ such that

$$A_m\left(q^{-1}\right) = F\left(q^{-1}\right)A\left(q^{-1}\right) + q^{-1}G\left(q^{-1}\right)$$

Let

$$\alpha\left(q^{-1}\right) = \alpha_0 + \alpha_1 q^{-1} + \ldots + \alpha_{n-1}q^{-n+1} = G\left(q^{-1}\right)$$

$$\beta\left(q^{-1}\right) = \beta_0 + \beta_1 q^{-1} + \ldots + \beta_{l-1}q^{-l+1} = qF\left(q^{-1}\right)B\left(q^{-1}\right)$$

$$\phi'(t-1) = \left[y(t-1) \ldots y(t-n)u(t-1) \ldots u(t-l)\right]$$

$$\theta' = \left[\alpha_0 \ldots \alpha_{n-1}, \beta_0 \ldots \beta_{l-1}\right]$$

and

$$\bar{y}(t) = A_m\left(q^{-1}\right)y\,(t).$$

Then the plant can be written as

$$A_m\left(q^{-1}\right)y\,(t) = \alpha\left(q^{-1}\right)y\,(t-1) + \beta\left(q^{-1}\right)u\,(t-1) \tag{10}$$

that is

$$\bar{y}(t) = \phi'(t-1)\theta.$$

Let the control law be implicitly determined by

$$\bar{y}^*\,(t) = \phi'(t-1)\theta, \tag{11}$$

where $\bar{y}^*(t) = B_m(q^{-1})y^*(t)$. Then the closed-loop system is

$$A_m\left(q^{-1}\right)y\,(t) = B_m\left(q^{-1}\right)y^*\,(t). \tag{12}$$

This is a model reference control system because the system is characterized by the specified reference model. A special case of model reference control is when $A_m(q^{-1}) = 1$ and $B_m(q^{-1}) = q^{-1}$, the system output y(t) follows y*(t) in one sampling interval and is called a one-step-ahead controller. Following the idea of "certainty equivalence," we obtain the model reference adaptive control in the form

$$\bar{y}^*\,(t+1) = \phi'(t)\hat{\theta}(t). \tag{13}$$

Now if the standard least-squares algorithm is used in estimating θ, this model reference adaptive control is stable [15] in the sense that {y(t)}, {u(t)} are bounded and $\lim_{t\to\infty}[\bar{y}(t) - \bar{y}^*(t-1)] = 0$, provided that the plant is stably invertible. Here the plant delay is considered to be 1, but the stability results are easily extended for arbitrary known plant delay.

The direct adaptive control described above is derived by minimizing the cost functional

$$J = \left[\hat{y}(t) - \bar{y}^*\,(t-1)\right]^2, \tag{14}$$

where $\overset{\approx}{y}(t) = \phi'(t - 1)\hat{\theta}$. A more general adaptive control can be obtained by introducing a control weighting polynomial, $Q(q^{-1})$, into the cost functional such that

$$J = \left[\hat{y}(t) - \bar{y}*(t-1)\right]^2 + \left[Q\left(q^{-1}\right)u(t-1)\right]^2. \tag{15}$$

The resultant control law is now applicable to certain nonminimum phase systems.

B.   INDIRECT ADAPTIVE CONTROL

The indirect adaptive control described here is based on a pole-placement approach, where the closed-loop system poles are assigned to certain desired positions. Given the plant $A(q^{-1})y(t) = B(q^{-1})u(t)$ as described above and the specified polynomials $M(q^{-1})$ and $A*(q^{-1})$, where $A*(q^{-1}) = 1 + a_1*q^{-1} + \ldots + a_{2n-1}*q^{-2n+1}$, the polynomials

$$L\left(q^{-1}\right) = 1 + l_1 q^{-1} + \ldots + l_{n-1}q^{-n+1}$$

$$P\left(q^{-1}\right) = p_0 + p_1 q^{-1} + \ldots + p_{n-1}q^{-n+1}$$

can be uniquely determined by the Diophantine equation

$$A\left(q^{-1}\right)L\left(q^{-1}\right) + B\left(q^{-1}\right)P\left(q^{-1}\right) = A*\left(q^{-1}\right) \tag{16}$$

provided $A(q^{-1})$ and $B(q^{-1})$ are relative prime.
Then the pole-placement control law is given by

$$L\left(q^{-1}\right)u(t) = M\left(q^{-1}\right)y*(t) - P\left(q^{-1}\right)y(t). \tag{17}$$

The closed-loop system becomes

$$y(t) = \frac{M\left(q^{-1}\right)B\left(q^{-1}\right)}{A\left(q^{-1}\right)L\left(q^{-1}\right) + B\left(q^{-1}\right)P + B\left(q^{-1}\right)} y*(t)$$

$$= \frac{M\left(q^{-1}\right)B\left(q^{-1}\right)}{A*\left(q^{-1}\right)} y*(t) \tag{18}$$

and it can be seen that the closed-loop poles are specified by the characteristic polynomial $A*(q^{-1})$.

Given $\hat{A}(t, q^{-1})$, $\hat{B}(t, q^{-1})$, the estimates of $A(q^{-1})$, $B(q^{-1})$, respectively, the polynomials $\hat{L}(t, q^{-1})$, $\hat{P}(t, q^{-1})$ can be solved from the Diophantine equation

$$\hat{A}(t,q^{-1})\hat{L}(t,q^{-1}) + \hat{B}(t,q^{-1})\hat{P}(t,q^{-1}) = A*(q^{-1}),$$

where the values of coefficients $\hat{A}(t, q^{-1})$, $\hat{B}(t, q^{-1})$ are constrained in the estimation algorithm [15] such that $\hat{A}(t, q^{-1})$ and $\hat{B}(t, q^{-1})$ are relative prime to ensure the equation is solvable. The pole-placement adaptive control law is then given by

$$\hat{L}(t,q^{-1})u(t) = M(q^{-1})y*(t) - \hat{P}(t,q^{-1})y(t). \tag{19}$$

This control law combined with a least-squares estimation algorithm gives a stable closed-loop system in the sense that $\{y(t)\}$, $\{u(t)\}$ are bounded and

$$\lim_{t \to \infty} \left[A*(q^{-1})y(t) - M(q^{-1})\hat{B}(t,q^{-1})y*(t) \right] = 0. \tag{20}$$

C.   SOME PRACTICAL ISSUES
      OF ADAPTIVE CONTROL

The stability results for the adaptive control systems described above are based on idealized conditions, i.e., the plant is linear, time-invariant, the degree of $A(q^{-1})$, $B(q^{-1})$ and the plant time delay are known exactly and the plant is free from external disturbances. It is obvious that these conditions can hardly be satisfied in practical situations. It has been shown that even slight perturbations from the assumptions can result in the system becoming unstable [16].

Some practical issues of adaptive control systems are addressed in [15, 17, 18]. Here we briefly introduce some recent results.

1.   Robust Estimation

The robustness of estimation algorithms can be enhanced by introducing a fixed dead zone [15, 19, 20] into the estimator. The idea is to update the estimator only when the estimation error exceeds a certain threshold. This is to ensure that the influence of disturbances is rejected. More recently, a relative dead zone has been introduced [21, 22] to deal with unmodeled dynamics whose boundedness cannot be guaranteed *a priori* . In this case, the dead zone operation is based on a normalized relative estimator error.

2.   Robust Control Design

It is well known [15] that the pole-placement equation (16) can be stated as

$$Mx = d, \tag{21}$$

where M is the Sylvester form matrix of plant parameters, x is the controller vector, and d is the desired pole vector. In applying the "certainty equivalence" principle, we get $x = \hat{M}^{-1}d$ without considering the uncertainties in $\hat{M}$, where $\hat{M}$ is the matrix formed from the estimated parameters.

A different line of approach is to choose an x by directly considering the uncertainties in the parameters. Let v be the plant vector and X be the Sylvester form matrix of controller parameters. Then (21) can be rewritten [23] as

$$Xv = d. \tag{22}$$

First, we shall let the desired pole vectors be specified as a region $\{d : d \in S_d\}$. Now suppose that the plant vectors are known to lie in a region $\{v : v \in S_v\}$, then we want to choose an x in the set

$$S_x = \left\{ x : Xv \in S_d, \forall v \in S_v \right\}. \tag{23}$$

The above formulation can be reformulated into a convex set for various cases of S_v and S_d [23], in which case we can apply optimization procedures to choose an x. Clearly the above approach may not be suitable for on-line application. But for off-line or for cases where infrequent update can be applied, it has the advantage that the controller is able to stabilize a given set of parameter uncertainties and may therefore be applicable to time-varying systems.

3.   Saturation Nonlinearities

It is known that saturation nonlinearities exist in almost every physical system. In [24–26], saturation-constrained adaptive control systems, both direct and indirect, are studied. It is shown that for a certain class of plants the conventional adaptive control algorithms when symmetrically constrained by a saturation nonlinearity can still maintain system stability in the sense that the system output is bounded and the adaptive control approaches that of the corresponding nonadaptive control with known plant parameters. Furthermore, the saturation-constrained adaptive control algorithms combined with a fixed dead zone in the estimator can stabilize a system in the presence of disturbances and unmodeled dynamics.

4.   Filtering

All practical adaptive controllers have filters for disturbance rejection, antialiasing, and attenuation of noise and high-frequency dynamics. A discussion on the role of these filters may be found in [27], while an analysis of their role in robust adaptive control is given in [8].

For further discussion on the status of adaptive control algorithms in practice the reader is directed to the excellent review paper by Astram [31].

IV.   CONVERGENCE CONSIDERATIONs

In this section we consider theoretical convergence properties of adaptive controllers based on estimation algorithm (7) together with a model reference type control law. The results, however, are also applicable to a pole placement control law.

Lemma 1. Selection of the resetting period T does not affect the results of algorithm (5), (6) in Section II(7). In fact, algorithm (5) with resetting procedure (6) is equivalent to algorithm (5) without any resetting except that the latter will result in computation overflow [because in this case $t_1 \to \infty$ as $t \to \infty$ and thus $\phi(t) \to \infty$] and thus cannot be used in practice.

Proof. For convenience we call algorithm (5) without any resetting algorithm A and algorithm (5) with resetting procedure (6) algorithm B. We can show that under the same initial conditions, for $kT < t \le (k + 1)T^-$

$$\hat{\theta}_B(t) = \begin{bmatrix} I_1 & kTI_1 \\ 0 & I_1 \end{bmatrix} \hat{\theta}_A(t)$$

$$P_B(t-1) = \begin{bmatrix} I_1 & kTI_1 \\ 0 & I_1 \end{bmatrix} P_A(t-1) \begin{bmatrix} I_1 & 0 \\ kTI_1 & I_1 \end{bmatrix}$$

$$u_B(t) = u_A(t), \qquad y_B(t) = y_A(t) \qquad e_B(t) = e_A(t)$$

$$\phi_B(t) = \begin{bmatrix} I_1 & 0 \\ -kTI_1 & I_1 \end{bmatrix} \phi_A(t).$$

(24)

Thus algorithm A and B are equivalent to each other in the sense that they have the same control results and the resetting period T will not affect the control performance.

When $0 \le t \le T^-$ (note that T^- means the time $t = T$ just before resetting), it is clear that the results of A and B are the same, i.e., when $0 \le t \le T^-$

$$\hat{\theta}_A(t) = \hat{\theta}_B(t)$$
$$P_A(t-1) = P_B(t-1)$$
$$u_A(t) = u_B(t)$$
$$y_A(t) = y_B(t) \tag{25}$$
$$\phi_A(t) = \phi_B(t).$$

Thus (24) is true when $k = 0$.

Now we show that if (24) is true when $kT \le t \le (k+1)T^-$, then (24) is also true in $(k+1)T \le t < (k+2)T^-$. If (24) is true in $kT \le t \le (k+1)T^-$, then at time $t = (k+1)T^-$, just before B resetting, from (24) we have

$$\hat{\theta}_B[(k+1)T^-] = \begin{bmatrix} I_1 & kTI_1 \\ 0 & I_1 \end{bmatrix} \hat{\theta}[(k+1)T^-]$$

$$P_B[(k+1)T^- - 1] = \begin{bmatrix} I_1 & kTI_1 \\ 0 & I_1 \end{bmatrix} P_B[(k+1)T^- - 1] \begin{bmatrix} I_1 & 0 \\ kTI_1 & I_1 \end{bmatrix}$$

$$y_B[(k+1)T^-] = y_A[(k+1)T^-]$$

$$e_B[(k+1)T^-] = e_A[(k+1)T^-] \tag{26}$$

$$u_B[(k+1)T^-] = u_A[(k+1)T^-]$$

$$\phi_{1B}[(k+1)T^-] = \phi_{1A}[(k+1)T^-]$$

$$\phi_B[(k+1)T^-] = \begin{bmatrix} I_1 & 0 \\ -kTI_1 & I_1 \end{bmatrix} \phi_A[(k+1)T^-].$$

Thus after B resetting as (6),

$$\hat{\theta}[(k+1)T] = \begin{bmatrix} I_1 & TI_1 \\ 0 & I_1 \end{bmatrix} \hat{\theta}_B[(k+1)T^-]$$

$$= \begin{bmatrix} I_1 & TI_1 \\ 0 & I_1 \end{bmatrix} \begin{bmatrix} I_1 & kTI_1 \\ 0 & I_1 \end{bmatrix} \hat{\theta}_B[(k+1)T^-]$$

$$= \begin{bmatrix} I_1 & (k+1)TI_1 \\ 0 & I_1 \end{bmatrix} \hat{\theta}_A[(k+1)T^-] \qquad (27)$$

$$P_B[(k+1)T-1] = \begin{bmatrix} I_1 & TI_1 \\ 0 & I_1 \end{bmatrix} P_B[(k+1)T^- - 1] \begin{bmatrix} I_1 & 0 \\ TI_1 & I_1 \end{bmatrix}$$

$$= \begin{bmatrix} I_1 & TI_1 \\ 0 & I_1 \end{bmatrix} \begin{bmatrix} I_1 & kTI_1 \\ 0 & I_1 \end{bmatrix}$$

$$\times P_A[(k+1)T^- - 1] \begin{bmatrix} I_1 & 0 \\ kTI_1 & I_1 \end{bmatrix} \begin{bmatrix} I_1 & 0 \\ TI_1 & I_1 \end{bmatrix} \qquad (28)$$

$$= \begin{bmatrix} I_1 & (k+1)TI_1 \\ 0 & I_1 \end{bmatrix}$$

$$\times P_A[(k+1)T^- - 1] \begin{bmatrix} I_1 & 0 \\ (k+1)TI_1 & I_1 \end{bmatrix}$$

and noting (4), (6), and (26)

$$\phi_B[(k+1)T] = \left(\phi'_{1B}[(k+1)T], OT \right)'$$

$$= \left(\phi'_{1B}[(k+1)T^-], (T-T)\phi'_{1B}[(k+1)T^-] \right)'$$

$$= \begin{bmatrix} I_1 & 0 \\ -TI_1 & I_1 \end{bmatrix} \left(\phi'_{1B}[(k+1)T^-], T\phi'_{1B}[(k+1)T^-] \right)'$$

$$= \begin{bmatrix} I_1 & 0 \\ -TI_1 & I_1 \end{bmatrix} \phi_B[(k+1)T^-]$$

$$= \begin{bmatrix} I_1 & 0 \\ -TI_1 & I_1 \end{bmatrix} \begin{bmatrix} I_1 & 0 \\ -kTI_1 & I_1 \end{bmatrix} \phi_A[(k+1)T]$$

$$= \begin{bmatrix} I_1 & 0 \\ -(k+1)TI_1 & I_1 \end{bmatrix} \phi_A[(k+1)T].$$
(29)

Thus, from (28), (29)

$$P_B[(k+1)T-1] \phi_B[(k+1)T]$$

$$= \begin{bmatrix} I_1 & (k+1)TI_1 \\ 0 & I_1 \end{bmatrix} P_A[(k+1)T-1] \phi_A[(k+1)T]$$
(30)

and

$$\phi'_B[(k+1)T] P_B[(k+1)T-1] \phi_B[(k+1)T]$$
$$= \phi'_A[(k+1)T] P_A[(k+1)T-1] \phi_A[(k+1)T]$$
(31)

since

$$u_B[(k+1)T] = u_B[(k+1)T^-]$$
$$= u_A[(k+1)T^-] = u_A[(k+1)T]$$

hence

$$y_A[(k+1)T+1] = y_B[(k+1)T+1]$$
(32)

and

$$e_A[(k+1)T+1] = e_B[(k+1)T+1]$$
(33)

Now considering (27), (30), and (31), from (5) we have

$$\hat{\theta}[(k+1)T+1] = \hat{\theta}_B[(k+1)T]$$

$$+ \frac{P_B[(k+1)T-1] \phi_B[(k+1)T] e_B[(k+1)T+1]}{\alpha + \phi'_B[(k+1)T] P_B[(k+1)T-1] \phi_B[(k+1)T]}$$

$$= \begin{bmatrix} I_1 & (k+1)TI_1 \\ 0 & I_1 \end{bmatrix} \hat{\theta}_A[(k+1)T+1] \tag{34}$$

$$P_B[(k+1)T] = \frac{1}{\alpha}\Big(P_B[(k+1)T-1]$$

$$- \frac{P_B[(k+1)T-1]\phi_B[(k+1)T]\phi'_B[(k+1)T]P_B[(k+1)T-1]}{\alpha + \phi'_B[(k+1)T]P_B[(k+1)T-1]\phi_B[(k+1)T]}\Big)$$

$$= \begin{bmatrix} I_1 & (k+1)TI_1 \\ 0 & I_1 \end{bmatrix} P_A[(k+1)T] \begin{bmatrix} I_1 & 0 \\ (k+1)TI_1 & I_1 \end{bmatrix}. \tag{35}$$

Also, from (5), for the same desired output at $t = (k+1)T + 2$, $y^*[(k+1)T+2]$, the control variables $u_A[(k+1)T+1]$ and $u_B[(k+1)T+1]$ should be determined so that

$$y^*[(k+1)T+2] = \hat{\theta}'_A[(k+1)T+1]\phi_A[(k+1)T+1]$$

$$= \hat{\theta}'_B[(k+1)T+1]\phi_B[(k+1)T+1] \tag{36}$$

Noting (4), and considering now for algorithm B, $t_1 - 1 = t - 1(k+1)T = 1$:

$$\theta_A[(k+1))T+1] \tag{37}$$

$$\Big(\phi'_{1A}[(k+1)T+1],[(k+1)T+1]\phi'_{1A}[(k+1)T+1]\Big)$$

and

$$\phi_B[(k+1)T+1] = \Big(\phi'_{1B}[(k+1)T+1],\phi'_{1B}[(k+1)T+1]\Big)'. \tag{38}$$

where

$$\phi'_{1A}[(k+1)T+1] = \Big(y_A[(k+1)T+1],\dots,y_A[(k+1)T+2-n],$$

$$u_A[(k+1)T+1],\dots,u_A[(k+1)T+2-m]\Big) \tag{39}$$

$$\phi'_{1B}[(k+1)T+1] = \left(y_B[(k+1)T+1],...,y_B[(k+1)T+2-n],\right.$$
$$\left. u_A[(k+1)T+1],...,u_B[(k+1)T+2-m]\right). \tag{40}$$

We already have that

$$y_A(t) = y_B(t), \qquad \text{for } 0 \le t \le (k+1)T+1$$
$$u_B(t) = u_B(t), \qquad \text{for } 0 \le t \le (k+1)T \tag{41}$$

and

$$\hat{\theta}_B[(k+1)T+1] = \begin{bmatrix} I_1 & (k+1)\Pi_1 \\ 0 & I_1 \end{bmatrix} \hat{\theta}_A[(k+1)T+1]. \tag{42}$$

Thus

$$\hat{\theta}'_B[(k+1)T+1]\phi_B[(k+1)T+1]$$
$$= \hat{\theta}_A[(k+1)T+1] \begin{bmatrix} I_1 & 0 \\ (k+1)\Pi_1 & I_1 \end{bmatrix} \begin{bmatrix} \phi_{1B}[(k+1)T+1] \\ \phi_{1B}[(k+1)T+1] \end{bmatrix}$$
$$\hat{\theta}'_A[(k+1)T+1] \begin{bmatrix} \phi_{1B}[(k+1)T+1] \\ [(k+1)T+1]\phi_{1B}[(k+1)T+1] \end{bmatrix}. \tag{43}$$

Finally, considering (36)(43), we can see

$$u_A[(k+1)T+1] = u_B[(k+1)T+1],$$

which results in

$$y_A[(k+1)T+2] = y_B[(k+1)T+2]$$

and

$$e_A[(k+1)T+2] = e_B[(k+1)T+2].$$

We can also prove step by step that (24) is true when $(k + 1)T \le t \le (k + 2)T^-$ by using (34)–(38) and (5).

Thus by induction Lemma 1 has been proved.

Remark. In the course of proving Lemma 1, it is clear that the result is true even if the real parameters are not linearly time varying. In view of this we can choose T as large as possible so long as no computation overflow occurs, which results in considerable reduction in computational effort.

Corollary. Under the assumption of all real parameters being linearly time varying, for algorithm B, the Lyapunov function $V(t) \triangleq \tilde{\theta}'(t)P(t-1)^{-1}\tilde{\theta}(t)$ is invariant at the resetting time, i.e., for all k

$$\hat{\theta}'_B(kT)P_B(kT-1)^{-1}\tilde{\theta}_B(kT)$$

$$(44)$$

$$= \tilde{\theta}'_B(kT^-)P_B(kT^- -1)^{-1}\tilde{\theta}_B(kT^-),$$

where $\tilde{\theta}(t)$ is the estimate error vector. Furthermore, for algorithms A and B,

$$V_A(t) = V_B(t), \qquad \text{for all t.} \tag{45}$$

Proof. See Appendix A.

As stated in Lemma 1 algorithm A has numerical problems because $\phi_A(t-1) \to \infty$ as $t_1 \to \infty$ (i.e., $t \to \infty$). While for algorithm B, t_1 is bounded by T. However, because of resetting, $P_B(kT-1)$ is no longer nonincreasing even if $\alpha = 1$; thus there is a potential danger that $P_B(t-1)$ could become unbounded. In order to avoid this problem, it appears that the persistent excitation condition is crucial.

Lemma 2. For $P_B(kT-1)$ to be bounded in the sense that $\lambda_{\max}\{P_B[(k+1)T-1]\} < \eta I$, $0 < \eta < \infty$ for all k, it is sufficient that there exists a ρ such that

$$\sum_{j=kT+1}^{(k+1)T^-} \phi_B(j-1)\phi'_B(j-1) \ge \rho I \tag{46}$$

and

$$\rho \ge \alpha^{1-T}\eta^{-1}(m+n)\left(T^2+2\right), \tag{47}$$

where $2(m+n)$ is the dimension of $\Phi_B(t-1)$.

Proof. According to the matrix inversion lemma for $kT < t \le (k+1)T^-$, from (5) we have

$$P_B(t-1)^{-1} = \alpha P_B(t-2)^{-1} + \phi_B(t-1)\phi'_B(t-1).\tag{48}$$

Thus

$$P_B[(K+1)T^- - 1]^{-1} = \alpha^T P_B(kT-1)^{-1}$$

$$+ \sum_{j=kT+1}^{(k+1)T^-} \alpha^{(k+1)T^- - j}\phi_B(j-1)\phi'_B(j-1)$$

$$> \sum_{j=kT+1}^{(k+1)T^1}\alpha^{(k+1)T^- - j}\phi_B(j-1)\phi'_B(j-1)$$

$$\ge \alpha^{T-1}\sum_{j=kT+1}^{(k+1)T^-}\phi_B(j-1)\phi'_B(j-1).\tag{49}$$

After resetting

$$P_B[(k+1)T-1]^{-1} = \begin{bmatrix} I_1 & 0 \\ -TI_1 & I_1 \end{bmatrix} P_B[(k+1)T^- -1]^{-1}$$

$$\times \begin{bmatrix} I_1 & -TI_1 \\ 0 & I_1 \end{bmatrix}$$

$$\ge \alpha^{T-1}\begin{bmatrix} I_1 & 0 \\ -TI_1 & I_1 \end{bmatrix}$$

$$\times \left\{ \sum_{j=kT+1}^{(k+1)T^-}\phi_B(j-1)\phi'_B(j-1)\right\}\begin{bmatrix} I_1 & -TI_1 \\ 0 & I_1 \end{bmatrix}\tag{50}$$

so in order to guarantee that

$$\lambda_{max}\{P_B[(k+1)T-1]\} \le \eta,$$

it is sufficient that

$$\alpha^{T-1} \begin{bmatrix} I_1 & 0 \\ -TI_1 & I_1 \end{bmatrix} \left\{ \sum_{j=kT+1}^{(k+1)T^-} \phi_B(j-1)\phi_B(j-1) \right\}$$

$$\begin{bmatrix} I_1 & -TI_1 \\ 0 & I_1 \end{bmatrix} \geq \eta^{-1} I. \tag{51}$$

Thus we need

$$\sum_{j=kT+1}^{(k+1)T^-} \phi_B(j-1)\phi'_B(j-1)$$

$$\geq \alpha^{1-T}\eta^{-1} \begin{bmatrix} I_1 & 0 \\ TI_1 & I_1 \end{bmatrix} \begin{bmatrix} I_1 & TI_1 \\ 0 & I_1 \end{bmatrix}$$

$$= \alpha^{1-T}\eta^{-1} \begin{bmatrix} I_1 & TI_1 \\ TI_1 & (T^2+1)I_1 \end{bmatrix}. \tag{52}$$

For (52) to be satisfied, it is sufficient that

$$\sum_{j=kT+1}^{(k+1)T^-} \phi_B(j-1)\phi'_B(j-1)^T$$

$$\geq \alpha^{1-T}\eta^{-1} \operatorname{tr} \left\{ \begin{bmatrix} I_1 & TI_1 \\ TI_1 & (T^2+1)I_1 \end{bmatrix} \right\} I$$

$$= \alpha^{1-T}\eta^{-1}(m+n)(T^2+2) I.$$

Thus (46) and (47) have been proved.
Theorem 1. Given the plant

$$y(t+1) = a_1(t)y(t) + a_2(t)y(t-1) + \ldots$$
$$+ \alpha_n(t)y(t-n+1) + b_1(t)u(t) + \ldots$$

$$+ b_m(t)u(t - m + 1). \tag{53}$$

Let the adaptive control law be

$$y^*(t + 1) = \hat{\theta}'(t)\phi(t).$$

If the algorithm (4), (6) is applied to plant (53), then with bounded $\{y(t)\}$, $\{u(t)\}$, and $\{\phi(t)\}$,

$$\lim_{t \to \infty} [y(t) - y^*(t)] = 0, \tag{54}$$

provided that the following assumptions are satisfied.
      (1) $a_i(t)$, $b_j(t)$ are linearly time varying;
      (2) $a_i(t)$, $b_j(t)$ are unknown but n, m are known;
      (3) The plant is stably invertible and with $|y^*(t)| \le m_1 < \infty$ the control objective $\lim_{t \to \infty} [y(t) - y^*(t)] = 0$ can be achieved with a bounded sequence $\{u(t)\}$ if the plant parameters are known;
      (4) The persistent excitation condition (46), (47) is satisfied.
      Proof. Along the lines developed in [10], for algorithm A we obtain

$$\lim_{t \to \infty} \frac{\alpha^{-(t-1)}\phi'_A(t - 1)\tilde{\theta}_A(t - 1)}{\alpha + \phi'_A(t - 1)P_A(t - 2)\phi_A(t - 1)} = 0$$

or

$$\lim_{t \to \infty} \frac{\alpha^{-(t-1)}e'_A(t)}{\alpha + \phi'_A(t - 1)P_A(t - 2)\phi_A(t - 1)} = 0.$$

In the light of Lemma 1, we also have

$$\lim_{t \to \infty} \frac{\alpha^{-(t-1)}e_B^2(t)}{\alpha + \phi'_B(t - 1)P_B(t - 2)\phi_B(t - 1)} = 0. \tag{55}$$

Now from (48) for $kT < t \le (k + 1)T^-$

$$P_B(t-1)^{-1} = \alpha P_B(t-2)^{-1} + \phi_B(t-1)\phi_B(t-1)$$

$$\geq \alpha^{t-kT} P_B(kT-1)^{-1}.$$

In view of Lemma 2 and under assumption (4)

$$P_B(kT-1) \leq \eta I, \qquad \text{for all } k.$$

Thus

$$P_B(t-1) \leq \alpha^{-(t-kT)}\eta I, \qquad \text{for } kT < t \leq (k+1)T^-$$

$$\leq \alpha^{-T}\eta I. \tag{56}$$

From (4),

$$\left\| \phi_B(t-1) \right\|^2 = \left\| \phi_{1B}(t-1) \right\|^2 \left(1 + t_1^2\right)$$

$$\leq \left\| \phi_{1B}(t-1) \right\|^2 \left(1 + T^2\right)$$

$$= \left[y(t-1)^2 + \ldots + y(t-n)^2 + u(t-1)^2 + \ldots \right.$$

$$\left. + u(t-m)^2 \right]\left(1 + T^2\right). \tag{57}$$

Under assumption (3) there exist $0 \leq C_1 < \infty$, $0 < C_2 < \infty$ such that

$$\left\| \phi_B(t-1) \right\| \leq C_1 + C_2 \max\left|e_B(t)\right|$$

$$\leq C_1 + C_2 \max\left|\lambda^{(1-t)/2} e_B(t)\right|, \qquad t > 3 \tag{58}$$

substituting (56) into (55)

$$\lim_{t \to \infty} \frac{\alpha^{-(t-1)} e_B^2(t)}{\alpha + \alpha^{-T}\eta\left\| \phi_B(t-1) \right\|^2} = 0. \tag{59}$$

$$\lim_{t \to \infty} \alpha^{(1-T)/2} e_B(t) = 0$$

or

$$\lim_{t \to \infty} \alpha^{(1-t)/2} [y(t) - y*(t)] = 0, \tag{60}$$

which implies output convergence ($\alpha = 1$), or output exponential convergence ($\alpha < 1$).

Furthermore, we can prove the exponential parameter convergence when $\alpha < 1$. Also along the lines in [29], we have, for algorithm A

$$V_A(t) \le \alpha V_A(t-1), \tag{61}$$

where $V_A(t)$ is Lyapunov function as defined before. Thus when $0 < \alpha < 1$, $V_A(t) \to \infty$. In view of the corollary following Lemma 1, we also have

$$\lim_{t \to \infty} V_B(t) = 0 \tag{62}$$

exponentially when $\alpha < 1$.

Under assumption (4), in the light of Lemma (2), $P_B(t-1)^{-1}$ is bounded away from zero. Thus from (62) we can conclude that when $\alpha < 1$ exponentially

$$\lim_{t \to \infty} \left\| \hat{\theta}_B(t) \right\| = 0. \tag{63}$$

V.   CONCLUSION

We have carried out simulation studies on many of the recursive estimation algorithms presented in this article and believe that the technique presented in Section II(7) using offset ramp modeling, forgetting factors, and covariance resetting is a viable approach for rapidly time-varying systems. The situation is still not clearly resolved, and the best approach in any individual case depends on a number of factors including the nature of the time variations and the control technique used. However, it does seem that estimates of the rate of change of parameters is an extremely valuable piece of information and should be used if at all possible.

On a more philosophical note, we believe that the term *estimation* as used in adaptive controllers is misleading. It would be more appropriate to consider the estimation algorithm as a data modeling algorithm. Thus rather than "estimating" time-varying system parameters, we are simply trying to build a time-varying model to "approximate" the observed input/output data. While this distinction may seem trivial or pedantic, we believe it is often forgotten. The real issue in adaptive control is to approximate the input/output data with a restricted complexity model and then show that a controller based on this model will also satisfactorily control the real system.

APPENDIX A

First note that in order to make $\tilde{\theta}(t)$ meaningful, we have to assume that the real parameters are linearly time varying (which includes the time-invariant parameters as a special case). In this case, the parameters in (1) can be described by

$$a_i(t) = a_{i0}(kT) + (t - kT)a_{i1}$$
$$b_j(t) = b_{j0}(kT) + (t - kT)b_{j1}, \tag{64}$$

where $a_{i0}(kT)$, $b_{j0}(kT)$ are the values of $a_i(t)$ and $b_j(t)$ at time $t = kT$, respectively. a_{i1} and b_{j1} are the derivatives of $a_i(t)$ and $b_j(t)$, respectively. $i = 1, ...,$ n, $j = 1, ..., m$. a_{i1} and b_{j1} are constant. For algorithm A, we define the parameter vector

$$\theta_A \overset{\Delta}{=} \left(\theta'^T_{1A}, \theta'_{2A} \right)'$$
$$\theta_{1A} \overset{\Delta}{=} \left(a_{10}(0), ..., b_{m0}(0) \right)' \tag{65}$$
$$\theta_{2A} \overset{\Delta}{=} \left(a_{11}, ..., b_{m1} \right)'$$

and the estimate error vector

$$\theta_A \overset{\Delta}{=} \left(\bar{\theta}'_{1A}, \bar{\theta}'_{2A}(t) \right)$$
$$\bar{\theta}_{1A} \overset{\Delta}{=} \theta_{1A} - \hat{\theta}_{1A}(t) \tag{66}$$
$$\bar{\theta}_{2A}(t) \overset{\Delta}{=} \theta_{2A} - \hat{\theta}_{2A}(t).$$

$\hat{\theta}(t), \hat{\theta}_1(t), \hat{\theta}_2(t)$ have been defined in (3).

As for algorithm B, when $kT \le t \le (k + 1)T^-$, the algorithm estimates $a_{i0}(kT)$, b_{j0}, a_{i1}, b_{j1} ($i = 1, ..., n$; $j = 1, ..., m$). When $t = (k + 1)T$, resetting with (5) implies starting the recursive least-squares estimation of $a_{i0}[(k + 1)T]$, $b_{j0}[(k + 1)]$, a_{i1}, b_{j1}. Thus for the algorithm we have implicitly defined for $kT \le t \le (k + 1)T^-$

$$\theta_B(kT) \stackrel{\Delta}{=} \left(\theta'_{1B}(kT), \theta'_{2B}(kT) \right)', \tag{67a}$$

where

$$\theta_{1B}(kT) \stackrel{\Delta}{=} \left(a_{10}(kT), ..., b_{m0}(kT) \right)' \tag{67b}$$

$$\theta_{2B}(kT) \stackrel{\Delta}{=} \left(a_{11}, ..., b_{m1} \right)'. \tag{67c}$$

For algorithm B, the estimate error vector should be defined as, for $kT \le t \le (k + 1)T^-$,

$$\tilde{\theta}_B(t) \stackrel{\Delta}{=} \theta_B(kT) - \hat{\theta}_B(t), \tag{68a}$$

where

$$\hat{\theta}_B(t) = \left(\hat{\theta}'_{1B}(t), \hat{\theta}'_{2B}(t) \right) \tag{68b}$$

$$\hat{\theta}_{1B}(t) = \left(\hat{a}_{10}, ..., \hat{b}_{m0} \right)' \tag{68c}$$

$$\hat{\theta}_{2B}(t) = \left(\hat{a}_{11}, ..., \hat{b}_{m1} \right)' \tag{68d}$$

and where the $\hat{a}_{i0}$, $\hat{b}_{j0}$, $\hat{a}_{i1}$, $\hat{b}_{j1}$, and $\hat{\theta}_B(t)$ are the estimates of $a_{i0}(kT)$, $b_{j0}(kT)$, a_{i1}, b_{j1}, and $\theta(kT)$, respectively. But these estimates are obtained at time t.

Hence for algorithm B, if at time $t = (k + 1)T^-$ just before resetting the estimate error is

$$\tilde{\theta}_B[(k + 1)T^-] = \theta_B(kT) - \tilde{\theta}_B[(k + 1)T^-], \tag{69}$$

then, after resetting

$$\tilde{\theta}_B[(k+1)T] = \theta_B[(k+1)T] - \hat{\theta}_B[(k+1)T] \tag{70}$$

and

$$
\begin{aligned}
\theta_B[(k+1)T] &= \left(\theta'_{1B}[(k+1)T], \theta'_{2B}\right)' \\
&= \left(\theta'_{1B}(kT) + T\theta'_{2B}, \theta'_{2B}\right)' \\
&= \begin{bmatrix} I_1 & TI_1 \\ 0 & I_1 \end{bmatrix} \theta_B(kT).
\end{aligned} \tag{71}
$$

Considering the resetting procedure for $\hat{\theta}(t)$ in (6)

$$\hat{\theta}_B[(k+1)T] = \begin{bmatrix} I_1 & TI_1 \\ 0 & I_1 \end{bmatrix} \hat{\theta}_B[(k+1)T^-] \tag{72}$$

substituting (71), (72) into (70) and using (69), we have

$$\tilde{\theta}_B[(k+1)T] = \begin{bmatrix} I_1 & TI_1 \\ 0 & I_1 \end{bmatrix} \tilde{\theta}_B[(k+1)T^-]. \tag{73}$$

In fact it was because of (73) that we proposed the covariance matrix resetting procedure in (6).

Now in view of (6) and (73), (44) can be proved. Also from (26) we have, for $kT \le t \le (k+1)T^-$

$$\hat{\theta}_B(t) = \begin{bmatrix} I_1 & kTI_1 \\ 0 & I_1 \end{bmatrix} \hat{\theta}_A(t). \tag{74}$$

From (65), (67)

$$\theta_B(kt) = \begin{bmatrix} I_1 & kTI_1 \\ 0 & I_1 \end{bmatrix} \theta_A(t) \tag{75}$$

so

$$\tilde{\theta}_B(t) = \begin{bmatrix} I_1 & kTI_1 \\ 0 & I_1 \end{bmatrix} \tilde{\theta}_A(t). \tag{76}$$

and using (24) we get

$$V_A(t) = V_B(t). \tag{77}$$

REFERENCES

1. G. C. GOODWIN and R. L. PAYNE, "Dynamic System Identification: Experiment Design and Analysis," Academic Press, New York, 1977.
2. A. CORDERO and D. Q. MAYNE, "Deterministic Convergence of a Self-tuning Regulator with Variable Forgetting Factor," *Inst. Electr. Eng., Proc. Part D* **128**, No. 1, 19–23, January 1981.
3. T. R. FORTESCUE, L. S. KERSHENBAUM, and B. E. YDSTIE, "Implementation of Self-tuning Regulators with Variable Forgetting Factors," *Automatica* **17**, No. 6,831–835 (1981).
4. G. C. GOODWIN, D. J. HILL, and M. PALANISWAMI, "A Perspective on Convergence of Adaptive Control Algorithms," *Automatica* **20**, No. 3, 519–531 (1984).
5. X. XIE and R. J. EVANS, "Discrete-time Adaptive Control for Deterministic Time-varying Systems," *Automatica* **20**, No. 3, 309–319 (1984).
6. K. J. ASTROM, "Theory and Applications of Adaptive Control – A Survey," *Automatica* **19**, No. 5, 471–486 (1983).
7. R. J. EVANS and R. E. BETZ, "Adaptive Control of Time-varying Systems – Some Technical Results," Department of Electrical and Computer Engineering, Tech. Rep. EE8415, University of Newcastle, Australia, January 1984.
8. R. H. MIDDLETON and G. C. GOODWIN, "Adaptive Control of Time-varying Linear Systems," Department of Electrical and Computer Engineering, Tech. Rep. EE8623, University of Newcastle, Australia, January 1987.
9. B. D. ANDERSON and R. M. JOHNSTONE, "Adaptive Systems and Time-varying Plants," *Int. J. Control* **37**, 367–376 (1983).
10. X. XIE and R. J. EVANS, "Discrete-time Stochastic Adaptive Control for Time-Varying Systems," *IEEE Trans. Autom. Control* **AC-29**, No. 7, 638–641, July 1984.
11. L. ZHANG, "Stochastic Adaptive Control for Time-varying Systems Via an Auxiliary Variable," *IEEE Conf. Decis. Control, Los Angeles*, December 1987.
12. N. MORRISON, "Introduction to Sequential Smoothing and Prediction," McGraw-Hill, New York, 1969.
13. E. IRVING, "New Developments in Improving Power Network Stability with Adaptive Control," *Yale Workshop Appl. Adapt. Control, Yale*, 1979.
14. T. HAGGLUND, "Recursive Estimation of Slowly Time-varying Parameters," *IFAC Symp. Identif., York, England*, July 1985.

15.   G. C. GOODWIN and K. S. SIN, "Adaptive Filtering Prediction and Control," Prentice-Hall, Englewood Cliffs, New Jersey, 1984.
16.   C. ROHRS, L. VALAVANI, M. ATHANS, and G. STEIN, "Robustness of Adaptive Control Algorithms in the Presence of Unmodelled Dynamics," *IEEE Trans. Autom. Control* AC-30(9), 881–889 (1985).
17.   P. J. GAWTHROP and K. W. LIM, "Robustness of Self-tuning Controllers," *Proc. Inst. Electr. Eng.* 129, 21–29.
18.   B. WITTENMARK and K. J. ASTROM, "Practical Issues in the Implementation of Self-tuning Control," *Automatica* 20, No. 5, 595–605 (1985).
19.   C. SAMSON, "Stability Analysis of Adaptive Control Systems Subject to Bounded Disturbances, *Automatica* 19, No. 1, 81–86 (1983).
20.   B. B. PETERSON and K. S. NARENDRA, "Bounded Error Adaptive Control," *IEEE Trans. Autom. Control* AC-27, No. 6, 1161–1168 , December 1982.
21.   G. KREISSELMEIER and B. D. O. ANDERSON, "Robust Model Reference Adaptive Control, *IEEE Trans. Autom. Control* AC-31, 127–133 (1986).
22.   G. KREISSELMEIER, "A Robust Indirect Adaptive Control Approach," *Int. J. Control* 43(1), 161–175 (1986).
23.   Y. C. SOH, R. J. EVANS, I. R. PETERSEN, and R. E. BETZ, "Robust Pole Placement," *Automatica* September 1987.
24.   C. ZHANG and R. J. EVANS, "Amplitude Constrained Adaptive Control," *Int. J. Control* 46, (1), 53–64 (1987).
25.   C. ZHANG and R. J. EVANS, "Amplitude Constrained Pole-placement Adaptive Control," *Int. J. Control* 46(4), 1391–1398 (1987).
26.   C. ZHANG and R. J. EVANS, "Amplitude Constrained Direct Self-tuning Control," *IFAC Symp. Identification Syst. Param. Est.* Beijing, China (1988).
27.   B. WITTENMARK, "On the Role of Filters in Adaptive Control," Department of Electrical and Computer Engineering, Tech. Rep. EE8662, University of Newcastle, Australia, December 1986.
28.   X. XIE and R. J. EVANS, "Deterministic Convergence Properties of an Adaptive Control Algorithm for Time-varying Systems," Department of Electrical and Computer Engineering, Tech. Rep. EE8332, University of Newcastle, Australia, July
29.   R. M. JOHNSTONE and B. D. ANDERSON, "Exponential Convergence of Recursive Least Squares with Exponential Forgetting Factor-adaptive Control," *Syst. Control Lett.* 2, No. 2, 69–76 (1982).
30.   G. KREISSELMEIER, "Adaptive Control of a Class of Slowly Time-varying Plants," *Syst. Control Lett.* 8, 97–103 (1986).
31.   K. J. ASTROM, "Adaptive Feedback Control," *Proc.* IEEE 75(2), 185–217 (1987).

ALGORITHMS FOR DECENTRALIZED HIERARCHICAL SYSTEMS WITH APPLICATION TO STREAM WATER QUALITY

MAGDI S. MAHMOUD

Electronics and Communication Engineering Department
Cairo University
Giza, Egypt

I. INTRODUCTION

A major difficulty in the implementation of feedback controls for interconnected systems arises from the fact that such systems are often rather widely distributed in space. Feedback control requires exchanges of state information. To provide this information exchange capability, one can incur significant cost in control implementation. It seems therefore desirable to seek methods that aim at some savings in cost. In this article we examine techniques of eliminating (or reducing to a minimum) such state information exchange during on-line operation. We restrict our attention to the case of linear dynamical systems, with particular emphasis on water quality systems.

In the literature, the foregoing problem is termed a "decentralized control problem," for which several approaches have been developed [1–4]. The approach adopted here follows closely [1, 4], in which we separate the off-line design phase from the on-line implementation phase. In the design phase we experiment with algorithms to produce the "best" block-diagonal gain matrix that takes into account the fact that each subsystem interacts with the other subsystems. Then the implementation phase follows, in which each independent block of the global gain matrix provides local decentralized control for a subsystem, and consequently no state information is transferred between subsystem controllers on line.

In this article, we introduce the decentralized control problem in Section 2 and then develop three different hierarchical algorithms in Section III. The first algorithm has a three-level structure by constraining the nonlocal feedback gain matrix to be diagonal. The second algorithm has a two-level structure by converting the problem into a matrix optimization problem. Then we move to the construction of an iterative block diagonalization to yield the desired decentralized gains. Application to water-quality control problems illustrates the feasibility of the algorithms and the potential of their use in practical situations.

II.   THE DECENTRALIZED OPTIMAL CONTROL PROBLEM

The linear-quadratic optimal control problem of interconnected systems is formulated as follows:

Fine $u^0(t) = -Gx^0(t)$ that minimizes the performance index

$$\min J = 1/2 \int_0^\infty \left[x^t(t) Qx(t) \right.$$

$$\left. + u^t(t)Ru(t) \right] \quad dt \tag{1}$$

subject to the dynamic equality constraint:

$$\dot{x}(t) = Ax(t) + Bu(t), \qquad x(0) = x_0, \tag{2}$$

where $x(t) \in R^n$ is the state vector; $u(t) \in R^m$ is the control vector; $A \in R^{n \times n}$ is the system matrix; $B \in R^{n \times m}$ is the input matrix; $Q \in R^{n \times n}$ is a positive-definite state weighting matrix; and $R \in R^{m \times n}$ is a positive-definite control weighting matrix.

It is well known that optimal control $u^*(t)$ exists provided the pairs (A, B), $(A, Q^{1/2})$ are completely controllable and observable, respectively [5]. In this case,

$$G = - R^{-1}B^t P, \tag{3}$$

where $P \in R^{n \times n}$ is the positive-definite solution of the algebraic Riccati equation (ARE):

$$PA + A^t P - PBR^{-1}B^t P + Q = 0, \tag{4}$$

where the superscript t denotes matrix transposition.

To lessen the off-line computational load, it is found beneficial to reflect the interconnection pattern in manipulating (3) and (4). This amounts to basing the control design on the subsystem level [6]. Accordingly, the integrated system (2) is viewed to be formed explicitly by N subsystems; that is:

$$A = \begin{bmatrix} A_{11} & \cdots & A_{1N} \\ A_{N1} & \cdots & A_{NN} \end{bmatrix} \tag{5}$$

$$B = \text{block diag} \begin{bmatrix} B_j \end{bmatrix}; \qquad Q = \text{block diag} \begin{bmatrix} Q_j \end{bmatrix}; \qquad R = \text{block diag} \begin{bmatrix} R_j \end{bmatrix}. \tag{6}$$

We emphasize that (5), (6) imply that the couplings among subsystems are "internal" and that each subsystem (well-defined part of the system) is individually controlled by an "external" control signal. To facilitate further development, we let

$$n = \sum_{j=1}^{N} n_j, \qquad m = \sum_{j=1}^{N} m_j \tag{7}$$

$$G^* = \text{block diag} \begin{bmatrix} G_j^* \end{bmatrix}, \qquad G_j^* \in R^{m_j \times n_j}. \tag{8}$$

Condition (8) characterizes a decentralized control constraint. Our aim now is to present methods to compute the decentralized gains.

III.   HIERARCHICAL ALGORITHMS

The basis of a class of hierarchical algorithms [1, 4, 7–9] arises from the fact that the minimizing solution of (1) subject to (2) with (5) and (6) can be cast into the form:

$$u(t) = -G_0 x(t) - Tx(t), \tag{9}$$

where G_0 is the block-diagonal gain matrix obtained by solving the ARE independently for each subsystem and T is a full matrix reflecting the coupling effects. We take note that G in (3) is equivalent to $(G_0 + T)$, with the apparent difference that G has a global nature, whereas G_0 has a local nature which is of interest to our analysis. To produce the decentralized gain G^* in (8), it is proposed [4, 6–8, 10–12] that T should be constrained to be a diagonal matrix T_0. The use of (9), with $T = T_0$, in (1) yields

$$\min J_0 = 1/2 \int_0^\infty \left(\|x\|_Q^? + \|\bar{G}_0 x + T_0 x\|_R^2 \right) \quad dt$$

$$= 1/2 \int_0^\infty \left(\|x\|_{Q+W}^2 \right) \quad dt, \tag{10}$$

where $\|a\|_S^2 = a^t S a$ and

$$W = G_0^t R G_0 + G_0^t R T_0 + T_0^t R G_0 + T_0^t R T_0 \tag{11}$$

The problem at hand is that of minimizing (10), (11) subject to

$$\dot{x} = (A - B G_0)x - B T_0 x. \tag{12}$$

Introducing the matrix decomposition:

$$G_0 = G_{00} + G_{0n}, \qquad F_0 = G_{00} + T_0$$

$$B = B_0 + B_n, \qquad Q = Q_0 + Q_n \tag{13}$$

$$A_0 = \mathrm{diag}\left(A - B G_0 \right), \qquad A = A_0 + A_n,$$

where in (13) the first component denotes the diagonal part and the second component stands for the nondiagonal part; that is, G_{00} is the diagonal part of G_0, Q_n is the nondiagonal part of Q, and so on. Using (13), we rewrite (10)–(12 as

$$\min J_0 = 1/2 \int_0^\infty \left[\|x\|_{Q_0}^2 + x^t F_0^t R F_0 x \right.$$

$$\left. + h\left(x, F_0, G_{0,n} \right) \right] \quad dt \tag{14a}$$

$$h(\,\cdot\,,\cdot\,,\cdot\,) = \|x\|_{Q_n}^2 + x^t F_0^t R G_{0n} x$$

$$+ x^t G_{0n}^t R F_0 x + x^t G_{0n}^t F_0 G_{0n} x \tag{14b}$$

$$W = \left(F_0^t + G_{0n}^t \right) R \left(F_0 + G_{0n} \right) \tag{15}$$

$$\dot{x} = A_0 x - B_0 T_0 x + g\left(x, T_0 \right) \tag{16a}$$

$$g\left(x, T_0 \right) = A_n x - B_n T_0 x. \tag{16b}$$

A.   A THREE-LEVEL ALGORITHM

Additional equality constraints of the form

$$x^* = x; \qquad T_0^* = T_0 \tag{17}$$

are added into our problem so that it becomes

$$\min J_0 = 1/2 \int_0^\infty \left[\| x \|_{Q_0}^2 + x^{*t} F_0^t R F_0 x^* \right.$$

$$\left. h\left(x^*, F_0, G_{0n} \right) \right] \, dt, \tag{18}$$

where

$$h(\cdot, \cdot, \cdot) = \| x^* \|_{Q_n}^2 + x^{*t} F_0^{*t} R G_{0n} x^*$$

$$+ x^{*t} G_{0n}^t R G_{0n} x^* + x^{*t} G_{0n}^t R F_0^* x^* \tag{19}$$

$$\dot{x} = A_0 x - B_0 T_0 x^* + g\left(x^*, T_0^* \right) \tag{20}$$

$$g(\cdot, \cdot) = A_n x^* - B_n T_0 x^* \tag{21}$$

together with (17). From the Hamiltonian

$$H = 1/2 \|x\|^2_{Q_0} + 1/2 x^{*t} F_0^t R F_0 x^*$$

$$+ 1/2 h\left(x^* F_0, G_{0n} \right) + \beta^t [x - x^*]$$

$$+ \sum_{j=1}^{n} \alpha_j \left[T_{0j} - T_j^* \right] + \lambda \left[A_0 x - B_0 T_0 x^* + g\left(x^*, T_0^* \right) \right], \tag{22}$$

where β *and* α_j $(j = 1, ..., n)$ are Lagrange multipliers and λ is the costate vector, one obtains the optimality conditions:

$$T_{0j}^* = T_{0j}; \qquad x^* = x \tag{23}$$

$$\beta = \left[F_0^t R F_0 + Q_n + F_0^{*t} R G_{0n} + G_{0n}^t R G_{0n} \right.$$

$$\left. + G_{0n}^t R F^* \right] x^* + \left[A_n - T_0^{*t} B_n - T_0^{*t} B_0^t \right] \lambda \tag{24}$$

$$\alpha = \text{diag} \left[\left(R G_{0n} x^* - B_n^t \lambda \right) x^{*t} \right] \tag{25}$$

$$T_{0j} = G_{00j} - \frac{1}{\left[R_j x_j^{*2} \right]} \left(\alpha_j - B_{0j} \lambda_j x_j^* \right),$$

$$j = 1, ... n \tag{26}$$

$$\dot{x}_j = A_{0j} x_j + B_{0j} \left[G_{00j} + \frac{\left(\alpha_j - B_{0j} \lambda_j x_j^* \right)}{\left[R_j x_j^{*2} \right]} \right] x_j^*$$

$$+ g_j\left(x^*, T_0^* \right), \qquad j = 1, ..., n \tag{27}$$

$$\dot{\lambda}_j = - Q_{0j} x_j - A_{0j} x_j - \beta_j, \qquad j = 1, ..., n. \tag{28}$$

Solution of (27), (28) is attained by using $\lambda_j = P_j x_j + \eta_j$ to yield after some algebraic manipulations:

$$\dot{P}_j = 0$$

$$= -2A_{0j}P_j + B_{0j}^2 P_j^2 / R_j - Q_j \tag{29}$$

$$\dot{\eta}_j = 0$$

$$= \left(-A_{0j} + P_j B_{0j}^2 / R_j \right) \eta_j - \beta_j$$

$$- P_j \left(B_{0j} G_{00j} x_j^* + B_0 \alpha_j / R_j x_j^* + g_j \right) \tag{30}$$

The three-level algorithm is:

(1) At level 3 we start with an initial guess for the trajectories x*, T* and set the iteration index k = 1.

(2) We guess, at level 2, initially the trajectories β, α and we set the iteration index m = 1.

(3) Using the trajectories from levels 2, 3 we compute at level 1:
    (i) P_j and η_j using (29) and (30);
    (ii) x_j using (27);
    (iii) λ_j using $P_j x_j + \eta_j = \lambda_j$;
    (iv) T_{0j} using (26);
and convey this information to levels 2, 3.

(4) Using (24), (25) and the values of x_j, λ_j from level 1, we calculate at level 2 the new trajectories β, α at the iteration cycle (m + 1). If

$$\int_0^{T_s} \left\| \beta^{m+1} - \beta^m \right\| \, dt \le \varepsilon_1$$

$$\int_0^{T_s} \left\| \alpha^{m+1} - \alpha^m \right\| \, dt \le \varepsilon_2,$$

go to level 3, otherwise go to step 3, level 1. ϵ_1, ϵ_2 are prechosen tolerances, and T_s is the simulation period.

(5) Using (23) and the information from levels 1, 2, we compute at level 3 the new trajectories x*, T_0^*. If

$$\int_0^{T_s} \left\| x^{*k+1} - x^{*k} \right\| \, dt \le \varepsilon_3$$

$$\int_0^{T_s} \left\| T^{*k+1} - T^{*k} \right\| \, dt \le \varepsilon_4,$$

stop and record T_0^{*k+1} as the decentralized gain matrix. Otherwise, go to step 2, level 2, with T^{*k+1}, x^{*k+1} as the new predictions.

Remarks.

(1) This algorithm is of the prediction type, and it is possible to develop a convergence condition for it using similar arguments to those of [13].

(2) The decentralized gain matrix computation is done off-line.

(3). The algorithm is very simple since at levels 2 and 3 simple substitution is required, while at level 1 only single-variable integrations are performed.

(4) Although the decentralized gains T_0 are initial state dependent, computational experience shows that in fact gains are insensitive to small variations in the initial states (see Section IV).

(5) In terms of (8), we have

$$G^* \cong G_0 + T_0^*$$

as a suboptimal decentralized gain.

A bound on suboptimality is given by [8, 14]:

$$J_0 \le (1 + \varepsilon_s) J$$

$$0 \le \varepsilon_s \le \mu_M(\mathscr{S}) \mu_m^{-1}(Q_0 + W),$$

where J is the optimal value in (1), J_0 is the suboptimal value in (10), and

$$\Phi^t = (A - BG_0 - BT_0) \Phi^t(t, \tau)$$

$$\Psi(t, 0) = \int_0^{t_f} \left[\Phi(t, \tau) B (T - T_0) \Phi^t(t, \tau) \right] \, d\tau \quad \Phi(0, t)$$

$$\Gamma(t,0) = I + \Psi(t,0)$$

$$\begin{aligned}
\mathscr{F} = &\; [\Gamma(t,0) - I]^t \left(Q_0 + W \right) [\Gamma(t,0) - I] \\
&+ [\Gamma(t,0) - I]^t \left(Q_0 + W \right) \\
&+ \Gamma^t(t,0)\left(T - T_0 \right)^t R\left(T - T_0 \right)\Gamma(t,0) \\
&- 2\Gamma^t(t,0)\left(T - T_0 \right)^t R\left(G_0 - T \right)\Gamma(t,0)
\end{aligned}$$

$\mu_M(\cdot), \mu_m(\cdot)$ are the respective maximum and minimum eigenvalues.

B.   A TWO-LEVEL ALGORITHM

A different route to derive G* would be to convert the problem under consideration into constraint optimization by substituting $u(t) = -G^*x(t)$ into (1), (2) along with (5), (6) to obtain

$$\dot{x}(t) = (A - BG^*)x(t), \qquad x(0) = x_0 \tag{31}$$

$$J = 1/2 \int_0^\infty \left\{ x^t(t)\left[Q + G^{*t}RG^* \right]x(t) \right\} \, dt. \tag{32}$$

To eliminate the dependence of J on the initial condition x_0, we assume that x_0 is a random vector uniformly distributed over the surface of a hypersphere [5]. Since the solution of (31) is

$$\begin{aligned}
x(t) &= \Phi(t,0)x(0) \\
&= \exp[(A - BG^*)t]\, x(0), \tag{33}
\end{aligned}$$

then (32) can be written using (33) as

$$j = 1/2 x_0^t \left[\int_0^\infty \left\{ \Phi^t(t,0)\left(Q + G^{*t}RG^* \right)\Phi(t,0) \right\} \, dt \right] x_0. \tag{34}$$

On taking the expectation of (34) and manipulating using the cyclic properties of the trace operator [5], we arrive at

$$\hat{J} = \text{Tr}\left[\left(Q + G^{*t}RG^*\right)P\right] \tag{35}$$

$$P = 1/2 \int_0^\infty \left[\Phi(t,0)E\left(x_0 x_0^t\right)\Phi^t(t,0)\right] \, dt, \tag{36}$$

where $E(\cdot)$, $\text{Tr}(\cdot)$ denote the expected value and trace operator, respectively. It is well known that if the matrix $(A - BG^*)$ is stable (has its eigenvalues in the left half-plane), then P satisfies

$$P(A - BG^*)^t + (A - BG^*)P + X = 0 \tag{37}$$

$$X = E\left(x_0 x_0^t\right), \tag{38}$$

We are now in a position to state the decentralized control problem:

$$\min_{G^* \in \mathscr{F}} \text{Tr}\left[\left(A + G^{*t}RG^*\right)P\right]$$

subject to (37) and (38), where

$\mathscr{F} = \{G^* : G^*$ satisfies (2.8) and
$(A - BG^*)$ is asymptotically stable$\}$.

In terms of (5) we let $A_d = \text{diag}\{A_{jj}\}$, $A_u = A - A_d$, and use it to partition (37) to:

$$P\left(A_d - BG^*\right)^t + \left(A_d - BG^*\right)P + X + Z = 0 \tag{39a}$$

$$Z = A_u P + PA_u. \tag{39b}$$

We take note that (6) implies that B is block-diagonal; however, the term $(A_d - BG^*)$ will always be diagonal in view of (8). Proceeding to derive the necessary conditions for solution, we append (39a, b) to (35) using suitable multipliers to form the Lagrangian:

$$\mathscr{L} = \mathrm{Tr}\Big[\Big(Q + G^{*t}RG^*\Big)P\Big] + \mathrm{Tr}\Big[V\Big(A_uP + PA_u^t - Z\Big)\Big]$$

$$+ \mathrm{Tr}\Big[W\Big\{P\Big(A_d - BG^*\Big)^t + \Big(A_d - BG^*\Big)P + X + Z\Big\}\Big]. \tag{40}$$

On setting the first partial derivatives to zero, we arrive at

$\partial\mathscr{L}/\partial V = 0$ gives

$$Z = A_uP + PA_u^t; \tag{41}$$

$\partial\mathscr{L}/\partial Z = 0$ gives

$$V = W; \tag{42}$$

$\partial\mathscr{L}/\partial W = 0$ gives

$$\Big(A_d - BG^*\Big)P + P\Big(A_d - BG^*\Big)^t + X + Z = 0; \tag{43}$$

$\partial\mathscr{L}/\partial P = 0$ gives

$$\Big(A_d - BG^*\Big)^t V + V\Big(A_d - BG^*\Big) + Q + G^{*t}RG^*$$

$$A_u^t W + WA_u = 0; \tag{44}$$

$\partial\mathscr{L}/\partial G^* = 0$ gives

$$G^* = R^{-1}B^t M_d P_d^{-1} \tag{45}$$

$$M_d = \mathrm{diag}\,[VP], \qquad P_d = \mathrm{diag}\,[P]. \tag{46}$$

We have the following two-level algorithm:

    (1) We start by guessing an initial value of the decentralized gain matrix G^*.

    (2) Compute $\mu(A_d - BG^*)$. If all the eigenvalues have negative real parts, go to step 3. Otherwise upgrade G^* using a suitable routine [11, 15].

(3) Start the two-level algorithm by guessing initial values of Z and W. Send these values plus G* to level 1. Set iteration index m = 1.

(4) Solve (43), (44) using an appropriate routine. The matrices P and V are conveyed to level 2.

(5) New predictions of the matrices Z, W, G* are computed by

$$Z^{m+1} = A_u P^m + P^m A_u^t$$

$$W^{m+1} = V^m$$

$$G^{*m+1} = R^{-1} B^t M_d^m \left(P_d^m \right)^{-1}.$$

If

$$\sqrt{\left\| \left\| Z^{m+1} \right\| - \left\| Z^m \right\| \right\|} \le \varepsilon_Z$$

$$\sqrt{\left\| \left\| W^{m+1} \right\| - \left\| W^m \right\| \right\|} \le \varepsilon_W$$

$$\sqrt{\left\| \left\| G^{*m+1} \right\| - \left\| G^{*m} \right\| \right\|} \le \varepsilon_G$$

are satisfies, regard G^{*m+1} as the desired gain and stop. Otherwise update the matrices Z, W, G* using the rules:

$$Z^{m+1} = c_1 Z^{m+1} + d_1 Z^m$$

$$W^{m+1} = c_2 W^{m+1} + d_2 W^m$$

$$G^{*m+1} = c_3 G^{*m+1} + d_3 G^{*m},$$

where $c_j + d_j = 1$; $j = 1, 2, 3$. $\varepsilon_Z, \varepsilon_W, \varepsilon_G$ are small tolerances. Go back to step 2.

Remarks.

(1) The iterative procedure of step 2 is required to detect the fixed modes [1].

(2) The two-level algorithm is of the predictive–corrective type. Experience has indicated its usefulness and feasibility [11, 14].

C.   ITERATIVE BLOCK DIAGONALIZATION

Following an alternative way of formulating the decentralized control problem, it is shown [10] that minimizing (1) subject to (2) along with (5), (6) with u = –G*x is equivalent to

$$\min_{G^* \in \mathscr{F}} \; \mathrm{Tr}[V], \tag{47}$$

where $V = V^t > 0$ satisfying

$$[A - BG^*]^t V + V[A - BG^*] + G^* RG + Q$$

$$\equiv r(G^*, V) = 0 \tag{48}$$

and Re $\mu[A - BG^*] < 0$ and x_0 is a uniformly distributed random vector over a unit hypersurface. Recalling the matrix minimum principle [16], the optimality conditions are (48) plus:

$$[A - BG^*]^t S + S[A - BG^*] + I_n = 0 \tag{49}$$

$$2RG^* - B^t VS = 0. \tag{50}$$

The matrix difference in (50) is taken as a preferred direction in the search of the optimal solution. Since $G^* = R^{-1}B^t V$, the iterative block-diagonalization algorithm is:

(1) Solve (48) in the form

$$A^t V + VA - VBR^{-1}B^t V + Q = 0$$

to get V and then compute $G^* = R^{-1}B^t V$ as the overall gain matrix.

(2) Set iteration index $j = 1$ and write

$$G^{*j} = \begin{bmatrix} G_{11} & G_{12} & \cdots & G_{1N} \\ G_{21} & G_{22} & \cdots & G_{2N} \\ \vdots & & & \vdots \\ G_{N1} & & \cdots & G_{NN} \end{bmatrix}, \qquad j = 1.$$

Discard one block from G^{*j}, say G_{1N}, leaving G^{*i} as

$$
G^{*m} = \begin{bmatrix} G_{11} & G_{12} & \cdots & G_{1N} \\ G_{21} & G_{22} & \cdots & G_{2N} \\ \vdots & & & \vdots \\ G_{N1} & & \cdots & G_{NN} \end{bmatrix}, \qquad m = j+1,
$$

check if $\mu[A - BG^{*m}] < 0$, go to step 3. Otherwise upgrade G^{*m} using a suitable routine.

(3) Solve (48), (49), and obtain J_0.

(4) Discard another block from G^{*m} such as G_{N1}, yielding

$$
G^{*m+1} = \begin{bmatrix} G_{11} & G_{12} & \cdots & 0.0 \\ G_{21} & G_{22} & \cdots & G_{2N} \\ \vdots & & & \vdots \\ 0.0 & & \cdots & G_{NN} \end{bmatrix}
$$

and then go to step 2 with $m \leftarrow m+1$. Continue until a block-diagonal form of G^* is obtained.

Remarks.

(1) The maximum number of steps is $N(N-1)$. There is no restriction on the sequence followed in eliminating off-diagonal blocks, which is an apparent merit of the procedure.

(2) The overall computation is simple and utilizes standard routines [17, 18].

D.   OTHER APPROACHES

We take note that there are approaches different from the one cited before. One approach [19] relies on the use of the exponential stabilization concept to yield a set of sufficient decentralized controllers. With reference to problem (1)–(8), it is shown [19] that the set of controllers

$$
u_j = -R_j^{-1} B_j^t P_j x_j, \qquad j = 1,\ldots,N \tag{51}
$$

yield an asymptotically stable closed-loop matrix, where P_j is the solution of

$$P_j\left(A_j + \beta I\right) + \left(A_j + \beta I\right)^t P_j + Q_j$$

$$- P_j B_j R_j^{-1} B_j^t P_j = 0. \tag{52}$$

$\beta > 0$ is the desired exponential rate.

Focusing on the notion of decentralized synthesis, effort was directed to solving the robust servomechanism problem using various techniques [20–22]. The main features were:

(1) Closed-loop system under decentralized control produces satisfactory dynamic behavior;

(2) Certain outputs asymptotically track given reference inputs;

(3) Controllers are to be connected to the system one at a time (in a sequential way).

Despite the detailed mathematical treatment, the resulting controllers are either PID or output feedback type [20–22]. It must be stressed that the approaches [19–22] do not have hierarchical structures.

IV.   APPLICATIONS TO STREAM WATER QUALITY

In this section we examine the use of hierarchical decentralized algorithms in problems of stream water quality. Mathematical models of such problems are numerous and, in general, nonlinear, expressing variations in the concentration of water-quality constituents along the stream. A brief discussion of some of these models is presented in [13]. With focus on the physicochemical changes occurring in river systems [23], the fundamental one-dimensional transport (mass balance) equation

$$\left(A_x \quad dx\right)\frac{\partial c}{\partial t} = \left(A_x D_c \frac{\partial c}{\partial x}\right) \quad dx - \frac{\partial}{\partial x}[A_x u_m c] \quad dx$$

$$\left(A_x \quad dx\right)\frac{dc}{dt} \pm S \tag{53}$$

represents an approach for partial maxing of fluid mixing in a stream, which varies in time and space. Thus, it describes the temporal and spatial change in the concentration of the constituents within the river. In (53) c is the concentration (M/L^3); x is the distance (L); t is the time (T); A_x is the cross-sectional area at distance x (L^2); D_c is the dispersion coefficient (L^2/T); u_m is the mean stream velocity (L/T); and S is the source or sink (M/T). It should be noted that the first term on the right-hand side of (53) represents the transport of material by turbulence effects, and the second term represents the advection of the constituents by the flowing water. The third term describes the individual constituents' changes due to biochemical transformation, whereas the fourth term designates external output sources.

The dynamic model QUAL II [24] simulates the in-stream interaction in steady flow rivers. It has been pointed out [13] that the application of the QUAL II model in some streams revealed some limitations that have been rectified in [25]. The revised QUAL II model is based on (53) under the following assumptions:

(1) It traces a drop of water along the basin from the uppermost stream part to the downmost stream part.

(2) It applies steady-state conditions; that is, $\partial c/\partial t = 0$.

(3) It considers the flow in-stream as turbulence free; that is, $(\partial/\partial x)[A_x D_c \partial c/\partial x] = 0$.

(4) It includes effects of input junctions, water load points, and output canals.

To develop a control model of the type (2), the mass balance (53) was manipulated based on assumptions (1)–(4) above and expressed in terms of variations of the concentrations the water-quality constituents [23] (algae, ammonia nitrogen, nitrite nitrogen, nitrate nitrogen, phosphate phosphorus, BOD, and DO) with

$$A = \begin{bmatrix} -0.8925 & 0.0 & 0.0 & 0.00298 & 0.02587 & 0.0 & 0.0 \\ 0.005 & -1.0457 & 0.0 & 0.0 & 0.0 & 0.0 & 0.0 \\ 0.0 & 0.3 & -1.2457 & 0.0 & 0.0 & 0.0 & 0.0 \\ -0.0031 & 0.0 & 0.5 & -0.746 & -0.00259 & 0.0 & 0.0 \\ -0.00019 & 0.0 & 0.0 & -0.0003 & -0.74596 & 0.0 & 0.0 \\ 0.0 & 0.0 & 0.0 & 0.0 & 0.0 & -0.9757 & 0.0 \\ -0.00681 & -0.966 & -0.56 & 0.00387 & 0.03363 & -0.23 & -1.2457 \end{bmatrix}$$

$$B = \begin{bmatrix} 0.05 & 0.0 & 0.0 & 0.0 & 0.0 & 0.0 & 0.0 \\ 0.0 & 0.4 & 0.0 & 0.4 & 0.4 & 0.4 & 0.0 \end{bmatrix}$$

We emphasize that the structure of A reflects the biological reactions in fresh water streams [23, 26–28], which is the case of the Nile River. In applying the decentralized algorithms, we set $Q = I_7$ and $R = \alpha I_2$, where α is a relative weighting factor. We have considered the water-quality model to be composed of two submodels: one of first order representing dynamics of algae and another of order six representing the remaining constituents.

Several simulation studies were conducted, and the results showed that a period of four days can be taken to correspond to the integral limits in (1). For $\alpha = 1$, the three-level structure (Section III,A) gave

$$G_0 = \begin{bmatrix} 0.02781 & 0.0 & 0.0 & 0.0 & 0.0 & 0.0 & 0.0 \\ 0.0 & 0.24188 & 0.10121 & 0.22615 & 0.21466 & 0.18636 & -0.07326 \end{bmatrix}$$

$$T_0 = \begin{bmatrix} -0.000875 & 0.0 & 0.0 & 0.0 & 0.0 & 0.0 & 0.0 \\ 0.0 & 0.03013 & 0.0 & 0.05575 & -0.07598 & -0.03184 & 0.0 \end{bmatrix}$$

This took 31 second-level and 3 third-level cycles with a tolerance value 10^{-5}, executed in 290 sec of CPU time on a UNIVAC 1100.

On simulating the two-level algorithm (Section III,B) for an accuracy of 10^{-5}, convergence was attained after 29 iterations executed in 68.989 sec of CPU time to yield the decentralized gain matrix

$$G^* = \begin{bmatrix} 0.02782 & 0.0 & 0.0 & 0.0 & 0.0 & 0.0 & 0.0 \\ 0.0 & 0.24188 & 0.10121 & 0.22615 & 0.2148 & 0.18635 & -0.07325 \end{bmatrix}$$

with an optimal value of the performance index of 0.37108.

By varying the relative weighting factor α over a wide range (0.01–100), it was found that the optimal value of the performance index J_0 increases monotonically with α at a slow rate of 0.083%. In Table I a summary of computational efforts is given, from which it is evident that by increasing α (or by heavily penalizing the sewage work) the required overall cost increased, but the computing time decreased.

The gain matrix G^* was found to decrease almost linearly with increasing α; see Fig. 1. This result can be immediately explained in the light of (39a) and (44), since P is independent of α and V is nearly linear with α. We take note of the slight difference between the decentralized gains.

In a different set of simulation experiments, the input matrix was changed to

$$B = \begin{bmatrix} 0.01 & 0.0 & 0.0 & 0.0 & 0.0 \\ 0.0 & 0.1 & 0.0 & 0.0 & 0.0 \\ 0.0 & 0.0 & 0.0 & 0.0 & 0.0 \\ 0.0 & 0.0 & 0.1 & 0.0 & 0.0 \\ 0.0 & 0.0 & 0.0 & 0.1 & 0.0 \\ 0.0 & 0.0 & 0.0 & 0.0 & 0.1 \\ 0.0 & 0.0 & 0.0 & 0.0 & 0.0 \end{bmatrix}$$

and all other information remained intact. The two-level algorithm took 29 iterations executed in 64.139 sec of CPU time to converge to

$$G = \begin{bmatrix} 0.00557 & 0.0 & 0.0 & 0.0 & 0.0 & 0.0 & 0.0 \\ 0.0 & 0.06867 & 0.01539 & 0.00269 & -0.00076 & 0.00430 & -0.01804 \\ 0.0 & 0.00269 & 0.01665 & 0.06673 & -0.00011 & -0.00002 & 0.00008 \\ 0.0 & -0.00076 & -0.00039 & -0.00011 & 0.0668 & -0.00017 & 0.00068 \\ 0.0 & 0.00430 & 0.00196 & -0.00002 & -0.00017 & 0.05208 & -0.00414 \end{bmatrix}$$

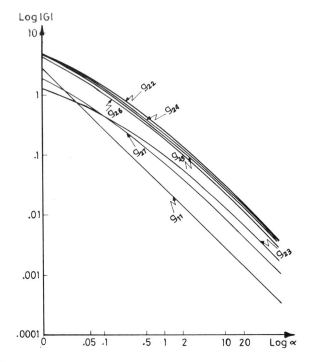

Fig. 1. Log-log plot of gain elements vs. relative weighting factor.

TABLE I. SUMMARY OF COMPUTATIONAL EFFORTS OF THE TWO-LEVEL ALGORITHM

Relative weighting factor α	Number of iterations	CPU time (sec)	J_0
0.01	37	82.480	0.35495
0.05	33	76.970	0.35972
0.1	31	71.438	0.36221
0.5	29	70.282	0.36866
1	29	69.989	0.37108
2	29	69.233	0.37291
10	29	70.212	0.37498
20	30	70.372	0.43765
100	32	72.453	0.43778

for an accuracy of 10^{-5}. The optimal value of the performance index was 0.43764. This case of equal weighting matrices ($\alpha = 1$) was examined for different operating conditions. It was found that the computational effort and the decentralized gain do not change significantly. On the average, the decentralized algorithms required about 0.6 day (almost 14 h) to reach the steady-state level.

On studying the effect of the element a_{11}, since it consists of some factors of the environmental conditions such as the photo period (amount of daily radiation), by increasing a_{11} to 10 or 100 times its nominal value, we found that:

(1) The matrix block G_2 (associated with the second subsystem) remained intact;

(2) The gain element g_1 (associated with the first subsystem) increased in direct proportion;

(3) Only one eigenvalue (-0.8985) of the open-loop eigenvalues (-0.7458, -0.74619, -0.8985, -0.9757, -1.0454, -1.2467, -1.24576) moved to positions of value that are proportional to changes in a_{11}. For example, when a_{11} changed to $10a_{11}$, this eigenvalue became -8.985, and so on.

By examining the eigenstructure of the system, it was observed that this eigenvalue is associated with the algae subsystem. Hence, the result is quite obvious. The physical basis for this feature is that extending the photo period or by exposing the algae to more radiation, the photosynthesis process increased, which allows rapid production of green algae. However, by the same reasoning the rate of algae deaths increases to the extent that makes the algae dynamics all but effective only during very short periods. This is the reason for the gain G_{22} being constant under various operational factors. We must emphasize that the decentralized scheme developed requires the measurement of all state variables. This can in general be carried out at the polluter stations by extensive analyses.

V. CONCLUSIONS

We have developed techniques for the decentralized control algorithms of hierarchically structured systems. Detailed treatment of each algorithm is given and the main steps are summarized for ease in programming. The algorithms are applied to the stream water-quality problem of the Nile River and the obtained results are found feasible and encouraging.

REFERENCES

1.   M. G. SINGH, "Decentralized Control," North-Holland, Amsterdam, 1981.
2.   J. P. CORFMAT and A. S. MORSE, "Decentralized Control of Linear Multivariable Systems," *Automatica* 12, 479–485 (1976).
3.   J. BERNUSSOU and A. TITLI, "Interconnected Dynamical Systems: Stability, Decomposition, and Decentralization," North-Holland, Amsterdam, 1982.

4.   M. G. SINGH and M. F. HASSAN, "Synthesis of Robust Decentralized Controllers for
      Large-Scale Systems," in "Large Scale Systems Engineering Applications" (M. G.
      Singh and A. Titli, eds.), pp. 129–144, North-Holland, Amsterdam, 1979.
5.   W. S. LEVINE and M. ATHANS, "On the Determination of the Optimal Constant Out-
      put Feedback Gains for Linear Multivariable Systems," IEEE Trans. Autom. Control
      AC-15, 44–49 (1970).
6.   M. S. MAHMOUD and M. G. SINGH, "Large Scale Systems Modelling," Pergamon
      Press, Oxford, 1981.
7.   M. F. HASSAN and M. G. SINGH, "A Robust Decentralized Controller for Linear In-
      terconnected Dynamical Systems," Proc. Inst. Electr. Eng. 125, 429–433 (1978).
8.   M. F. HASSAN and M. G. SINGH, "A Hierarchical Computational Structure for Com-
      puting Near-Optimal Decentralized Control," IEEE Trans. Syst., Man, Cybernet.
      SMC-8, 575–578 (1978).
9.   M. F. HASSAN and M. G. SINGH, "A Decentralized Controller with Trajectory Im-
      provement," Proc. Inst. Electr. Eng. 127, 142–146 (1980).
10.   Y. CHEN, M. S. MAHMOUD, and M. G. SINGH, "An Iterative Block-Diagonalization
      Procedure for Decentralized Optimal Control," Int. J. Syst. Sci. 15, 563–573 (1984).
11.   T. C. XINOGALAS and M. S. MAHMOUD, "Hierarchical Computation of Decentralized
      Gains for Interconnected Systems," Automatica 18, 473–478 (1982).
12.   J. C. GEROMEL and J. BERNUSSOU, "An Algorithm for Optimal Decentralized Reg-
      ulation of Linear Quadratic Interconnected Systems," Automatica 15, 489–493
13.   M. S. MAHMOUD, M. F. HASSAN, and M. G. DARWISH, "Large Scale Control Sys-
      tems," Dekker, New York, 1985.
14.   M. S. MAHMOUD, "Multilevel Systems: Information Flow in Large Linear Control
      Problems," in "Handbook of Large Scale Systems Engineering Applications" (M. G.
      Singh and A. Titli, eds.), pp. 96–109, North-Holland, Amsterdam, 1979.
15.   D. E. McBRINN and R. J. RAY, "Stabilization of Linear Multivariable Systems by
      Output Feedback," IEEE Trans. Autom. Control AC-17, 243–246 (1972).
16.   M. ATHANS, "The Matrix Minimum Principle," Inf. Control 11, 592–602 (1968).
17.   Y. BAR-NESS, "Solution of Discrete Infinite-Time, Time Invariant Regulator by the
      Euler Equation," Int. J. Control 22, 49–56 (1975).
18.   T. PAPPAS, A. J. LAUB, and N. R. SANDELL, "On the Numerical Solution of the
      Discrete-Time Algebraic Riccati Equation," IEEE Trans. Autom. Control 25, 631–641
      (1980).
19.   H. M. SOLIMAN, M. DARWISH, and J. FANTIN, "Decentralized and Hierarchical Sta-
      bilization Techniques for Interconnected Power Systems," Large Scale Syst 2, 113–
      122 (1981).
20.   E. J. DAVISON and W. GESING, "Sequential Stability and Optimization of Large
      Scale Decentralized Systems," Automatica 15, 307–324 (1979).
21.   E. J. DAVISON, "The Robust Decentralized Control of a General Servomechanism
      Problem," IEEE Trans. Autom. Control AC-21, 16–24 (1976).
22.   S. H. WANG and E. J. DAVISON, "On the Stabilization of Decentralized Control
      Systems," IEEE Trans. Autom. Control AC-18, 473–478 (1978).
23.   M. S. MAHMOUD and M. F. HASSAN, "A Decentralized Water-Quality Control
      Scheme," IEEE Trans. Syst., Man, Cybernet. SMC-16, 694–702 (1986).
24.   Environmental Protection Agency, "Computer Program Documentation for the Stream
      Quality Model QUAL II," Systems Development Branch, Washington, D.C., 1972.
25.   M. F. HASSAN, M. I. YOUNIS, and K. H. MANCY, "A Developed Stream Water
      Quality Model: A Case Study on the River Nile," Proc. IFAC Syst. Approach Dev.,
26.   M. S. MAHMOUD, M. F. HASSAN, and S. J. SALEH, "Decentralized Structures for
      Stream Water Quality Control Problems," Optim. Control Appl. Methods 6, 167–186
      (1985).
27.   M. S. MAHMOUD and S. J. SALEH, "Regulation of Water Quality Standards in
      Streams by Decentralized Control," Int. J. Control 41, 525–540 (1985).
28.   M. S. MAHMOUD and A. M. NASSAR, "Hybrid Technique for Decentralized Water-
      Quality Control," Int. J. Syst. Sci. 18, 513–516 (1987).

INDEX